Risky Shores

Risky Shores

SAVAGERY AND COLONIALISM
IN THE WESTERN PACIFIC

George K. Behlmer

STANFORD UNIVERSITY PRESS
STANFORD, CALIFORNIA

Stanford University Press
Stanford, California

Printed in the United States of America on acid-free, archival-quality paper

Library of Congress Cataloging-in-Publication Data

Names: Behlmer, George K., author.
Title: Risky shores : savagery and colonialism in the western Pacific / George K. Behlmer.
Description: Stanford, California : Stanford University Press, 2018. | Includes
    bibliographical references and index.
Identifiers: LCCN 2018004274 (print) | LCCN 2018005314 (ebook) |
    ISBN 9781503605954 (e-book) | ISBN 9781503604926 | ISBN 9781503604926
    (cloth : alk. paper) | ISBN 9781503605947 (pbk. : alk. paper)
Subjects: LCSH: Melanesia—Social life and customs. | Melanesia—Foreign public opinion,
    British. | Great Britain—Colonies—Oceania—History. | Primitive societies—Melanesia.
Classification: LCC DU490 (ebook) | LCC DU490 .B44 2018 (print) | DDC 995—dc23
LC record available at https://lccn.loc.gov/2018004274

Cover design: Cadence Design Studio | Preston Thomas
Cover art: *Massacre of the Rev. John Williams,* Possibly a George Baxter print commissioned by the London Missionary Society. British Museum.

Typeset by Newgen in 11/14 Adobe Garamond

For Jane,
Loving critic

Contents

List of Illustrations

List of Maps

Acknowledgments

The "risky shores" of this book's title refer to islands occupying the western Pacific Ocean. The encounters thereon between Europeans and indigenous peoples sometimes proved hazardous for all concerned. How white strangers and dark "savages" understood the risks they were taking by consorting with one another is the question at the core of this study.

Librarians and archivists on three continents have been gracious collaborators in my work. Two relentlessly helpful librarians deserve special thanks. Andy Carr, senior librarian at the State Library of New South Wales, Sydney, knew where to launch every investigation, however obscure the issue. And among research specialists at the University of Washington's Suzzallo Library, Theresa Mudrock personified calm competence.

In Britain, I benefited from guidance at these London-based institutions: the British Library; the British Museum; the National Archives of the United Kingdom; Lambeth Palace Library; the Royal Geographical Society; and the School of Oriental and African Studies. The Bodleian Library and Rhodes House Library, venerable Oxford research centers both, could not have been more helpful. Selwyn College Archives, Cambridge, accommodated this scholar-on-the-fly.

Pacific archives supplied much of my evidence. Staff at the state libraries of New South Wales and Queensland were models of patience and good humor. In New Zealand, the Special Collections unit of Auckland University Library saw to it that I never waited for a file. In Suva, staff at the Fijian National Archives and the Fiji Museum Library unearthed materials that I would never have found unaided.

Several American records collections must be acknowledged as well: the Bancroft Library, University of California, Berkeley; the Library of the Marine Corps, Quantico, Virginia; the National Library of Medicine, Bethesda,

Maryland; the Martin and Osa Johnson Safari Museum, Chanute, Kansas; the Phillips Library, Peabody Essex Museum, Salem, Massachusetts; and the Special Collections Department, Suzzallo-Allen Library, University of Washington, Seattle.

Numerous colleagues commented on parts of the manuscript. Philippa Levine, Theresa Mudrock, Frank Prochaska, Satadru Sen, and Susan Thorne vetted individual chapters. Jordanna Bailkin, Peter Hoffenberg, Rebecca Hughes, and David Smith plowed through most of a long study. Jane Cater, Jane Samson, and Pat Thane tackled the entire draft, as did two anonymous readers. Without these extra eyes, *Risky Shores* would have been much the poorer. Formulaic as it may be to say, I alone am responsible for all errors of fact and interpretation. Fortunately, I am not at all responsible for the photography and cartography on display in this volume. I thank Patricia Mc-Giffert of University of Washington (U.W.) Health Sciences for the former, and Bill Nelson for the latter. Margo Irvin, history acquisitions editor at Stanford University Press, offered wise advice at key points in the publishing process.

Authors based at universities seldom manage to self-fund their research. That is certainly true in this case. A Christiansen Fellowship from St. Catherine's College, Oxford, enabled me to spend three months reading widely on matters Pacific. It was during this Michaelmas Term 2000 that I decided to pursue the notion of "savagery" as applied to Pacific peoples. Thereafter, material support from University of Washington sources has been vital. The university's Royalty Research Fund made possible an extended visit to Oceanic archives. A teaching-release grant from the Walter Chapin Simpson Center for the Humanities carved out uninterrupted time to write. Finally, the U.W. History Department has done much through its Keller Endowed Fund and Lenore Hanauer Faculty Research Fund to keep this project afloat.

My greatest debt, however, is to my wife, Jane Cater. I dedicate this book, as I did the last, to her.

G.K.B.

Risky Shores

The Protean Savage

On 2 April 1782, the *Northumberland*, a British ship engaged in the East India trade, left Sumatra bound for the Spice Islands and beyond. What cut short its voyage was a catastrophic encounter between the crew and "savadges" (as the only surviving eyewitness called them) living along the western shore of New Guinea. That eyewitness, an unnamed carpenter's mate, would later present his journal to a gentleman in Calcutta. Although modern readers should not discount the possibility that the journal's narrative was largely an exercise in fantasy, its tale added to the gradually emerging portrait of the western Pacific islands as citadels of barbarism.[1]

Several months into its voyage, the *Northumberland* had become a death trap. Seven or eight sailors were perishing daily from "want of greens . . . to Nourish them, for they were very bad with scurvy." In addition to fetching wood and water, therefore, the ship's supply boat was ordered to find vegetables, and quickly. When the boat's crew rowed within a quarter mile of the beach, the first mate could distinguish people carrying bamboo containers toward an apparent fresh water source; presumably the *Northumberland*'s empty casks could be replenished there as well. "But we were very much mistaken," explained the carpenter's mate. Four low-ranking members of the resupply party—three "Lascars" and a "Portugue"—struggled ashore with the casks. Dark bodies rushed them from the jungle, hauling away these unfortunates to a nearby village. Simultaneously, arrows arced toward the waiting boat. The resupply party carried a few muskets with which they now returned fire. They did not possess sufficient weaponry to support a direct attack on the "savadges," however, so a tense standoff followed. Taking a calculated risk, the first mate finally led fourteen men onto the beach. Mayhem ensued: "They came down upon us like unto a half moon, men, women and children, such as could take a bow and arrow into

1

there hand." Once every occupant of the boat had been dragged ashore, the Islanders sliced open the stomach of a twelve-year-old midshipman and "threw his bowels into the air out of braverdo." The remains of Mr. Sayce, the first mate, were "broil[ed]" and, inexplicably, offered to the author. As if to crown their victory, the local people "came around me . . . hollowing and hooting." Some unspecified time later, the traumatized carpenter's mate made his escape during a battle between these Islanders and a trading ship belonging to the sultan of Ceram.[2]

Whether an accurate rendering of events or a flight of fancy, this author's text was rich in the signs of savagery. The New Guineans depicted here were treacherous because they refused to fight in a civilized manner—that is, using weapons and tactics familiar to Europeans. These Islanders were also impulsive, creatures of sudden passion. Savages were, moreover, capricious. (Why did these people spare one life and not another?) Most seemed cruel. From a European perspective at least, offering the carpenter's mate broiled bits of his superior constituted malicious self-gratification: cruelty. Connecting these characteristics and imposing a degree of coherence on an otherwise unwieldy set of images was the notion that savage acts derive from "unnatural" feelings. Such acts involved a short-circuiting of instinct, a displacement of the normal by the grotesque. Thus, only an unnatural mother could kill her own infant. Similarly, the wish of a wife to be burned on her husband's pyre, or to be strangled before he went into the ground, struck Europeans as examples of perverted fidelity. And unless imminent starvation served to justify the unthinkable, South Seas cannibalism mocked the supposed dignity of man.

This book charts the twisting course of an idea that has long sustained inequality among human groups. The defamatory idea examined here is "savagery," together with its agent, "the savage." *Risky Shores* will argue that Britain's early visitors to the Pacific—mainly cartographers and missionaries—manipulated the notion of savagery to justify their own interests. But savage talk did more than merely denigrate. It would serve as well to emphasize the fragility of indigenous cultures. The so-called "doomed native" thesis gained plausibility through its focus on the Pacific's least known Islanders. Indeed, as this book will show, the reputed strongholds of Oceanic savagery were also believed to harbor the most endangered tribes on earth.

Precisely what marks a savage has always been difficult to say. Toward the end of his meditation on the destruction of indigenous culture in the Marquesas Islands, Greg Dening admits, "What made *Enata* (the Marquesans) savage was a mystery." They were no more violent than so-called civilized people. *Enata* had their moral failings to be sure, but so did *Aoe* (outsiders). That the Islanders possessed "primitive" technologies did not alone render them objects of pity, or of disgust, in white eyes. Dening speculates that perhaps the root defect of *Enata*, according to *Aoe*, was their emotional superficiality, their carelessness: "Their carelessness showed in their indolence and their indolence showed their satisfaction with the present and their unconcern for the future." "They were savage," then, "because of their sense of time."[3] Stepping back from individual cases, we will find that the persistence of the "savage" trope derives from its imprecision; until quite recently, one could invoke it to insult, to objectify, to marginalize, even to romanticize without fear of serious contradiction. "Savage," Andrew Sinclair has observed, is "a hydra of a word."[4] It is both a noun that gestures toward early anthropology, where it signified a preliterate culture, and a condemnatory adjective meaning bestial. As Bernard Smith first noted a generation ago, pictorial treatments of the Pacific savage during the late eighteenth and early nineteenth centuries varied enormously depending upon the aims of European intruders.[5]

Risky Shores takes as its geographic focus the islands of the western Pacific. Its temporal frame is the period between Captain James Cook's death on a Hawai'ian beach in 1779 and the end of World War II in 1945. If the savage is by definition a creature often imagined out of time and space, why choose these boundaries? The answer is that the western Pacific offers opportunities to study savagery in its most exotic form. Although the ethnographic prejudices of Alexander von Humboldt (1769–1859) may not have been universally shared during a brilliant career, his views were widely echoed. In the wakes of Captains Cook, Bougainville, and d'Entrecasteaux arrived news of odd people inhabiting islands bathed in warmth and lush with tropical verdure. Humboldt, after Napoleon "the most famous man in Europe,"[6] had spent several years exploring both North and South America. Curiously, he had never seen any part of the South Pacific when he declared around 1810 that "The savages of America, who have been the objects of so many systematic reveries . . . inspire less interest since celebrated navigators have made known to us the inhabitants of South Sea islands, in whose character we find a striking mixture of perversity and meekness. The state of half-civilization existing among those islanders gives a peculiar charm to the description of their manners."[7]

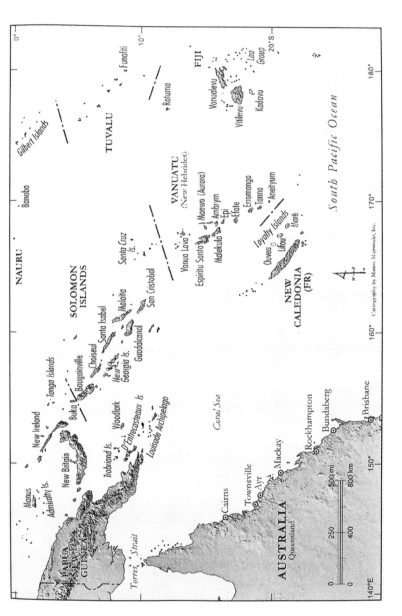

Map I.1 The Southwest Pacific and Queensland.

SOURCE: Cartography by Manoa Mapworks, Inc. Reprinted with the permission of the University of Hawai'i Press, from *Violence and Colonial Dialogue* by T. Banivanua-Mar (2007).

Tahitians and Tongans (and the paradisiacal settings in which they lived) had surpassed North America's Iroquois in exotic allure. New Zealand was not tropical,[8] but its people, the elaborately tattooed Maori, possessed a "charm" all their own. The Tahitians, Tongans, and Maori appeared to share enough cultural characteristics to warrant inclusion in the same racial family. By the 1840s, European philologists had categorized them as "Polynesians." When Humboldt wrote about Pacific Islanders in the early years of the nineteenth century, he either did not know, or perhaps did not care, about another South Seas "race." The typically darker peoples who dominated such western Pacific island groups as Fiji, the New Hebrides (now Vanuatu), the Solomons, New Caledonia, and New Guinea would soon acquire their own racial classification: "Melanesian." (See Map I.1.) A contested designation today, Melanesia subsumed most of the Islanders examined in this book.

The etymology of the word "savage" provides some sense of its unstable usage. From the early fourteenth century if not before, "savage" tended to be associated with rugged or uncultivated landscapes. The root word here is *silva*, Latin for forest or wood. Over time the notion of forest acquired the additional sense of boundary or frontier—a demarcation between civilization and its opposite, for example. One of the most controversial arguments in American historiography, the so-called "frontier thesis" of Frederick Jackson Turner, understood the westward-moving boundary of the United States as the "hither edge of free land." Beyond this edge, Turner reckoned, American settlement gave way to "savagery."[9] Because frontiers connote difference beyond, we should not be surprised that that difference has been imagined since late medieval times as wild or fierce. These distinctly unflattering connotations gained reinforcement from the early French *sauvage*, a word that added to its Latin root the qualities of "gloomy" and "horrible." The first reference in English to a savage person as one given to cruelty or brutality dates from 1522. "Savagery" and "savagism" entered English usage in the seventeenth century.[10]

Among the many satellite meanings of "savagery," three merit closer attention. First and most straightforward in the Pacific context, the alleged ferocity of certain island peoples struck both European voyagers and their reading publics as a defining essence. New Zealand's Maori appeared to prove the point. No less proud than any white aristocrat, their pride allegedly compelled the Maori to avenge all insults with fearsome single-mindedness.[11]

Similarly, Solomon Island headhunters knew no pity when collecting their trophies. The New Hebridean bent on battle reportedly viewed women and children as legitimate targets. And Fijian chiefs would stop at nothing to obtain slaves. For without slaves to bury alive beside the foundation posts of a new temple, the local community faced an uncertain future. Sir John Lubbock, Victorian Britain's influential popularizer of archaeology, condensed a widely shared view that savages "unite the character of childhood with the passions and strengths of men."[12] When "childish" Melanesian preoccupations were set in motion, great damage could result.

Perhaps less obvious was the important association of savagery with frontiers. Sometimes, of course, a frontier needs no imagining: physical barriers could temporarily separate the savage and the civilized. As H.M. Stanley made clear to his late Victorian readers, equatorial Africa's immensity hid all manner of savage folk.[13] Island frontiers, too, could wall off the "primitive" from the modern. New Guinea, the world's second largest island, guarded its own impenetrable forests with vast mud banks. Surveying its southern coast during the 1840s, HMS *Fly* pierced this alluvial bulwark just far enough to heighten curiosity:

> New Guinea! the very mention of . . . the interior of New Guinea sounds like being allowed to visit some of the enchanted regions of the "Arabian Nights," so dim an atmosphere of obscurity rests at present on the wonders it probably conceals.[14]

If mud banks and jungle did not discourage exploration of the western Pacific, other hazards might. In an age of sail, contrary trade winds and rogue currents narrowed opportunities for visiting "new" islands. More terrifying still was the threat of hull-shredding reefs in poorly charted seas. Prior to the 1830s, for instance, the Torres Strait, which separates New Guinea from Australia, served as a nautical graveyard. Finally, rumors of indigenous hostility could persuade cautious Europeans to steer clear of certain islands—as was the case with Captain Cook and the Fijian archipelago.[15]

The notion of "savages" as those who dwelt beyond a frontier would have made sense to British society in the nineteenth century. Domestic frontiers, after all, preoccupied moral reformers at home. Indeed "home," often hailed as the locus of family privacy, could serve to mask misery as well as provide a haven in a heartless world.[16] The 1841 Stockport poisoning case confirmed this disturbing fact. At the Chester Assizes that summer, evidence emerged that an impoverished Irish couple, cellar-dwellers and doormat-makers, had used arsenic to kill their two young daughters, each of whom carried funeral insurance policies worth over £3. Although white, Mr. and Mrs. Sandys qualified as "brutal savages."[17] A generation later, the perils of privacy returned as a more lasting public concern. In 1886, Cardinal Manning, leader of Britain's Catholic community, joined forces with Benjamin Waugh, a Congregational minister, to publish "The Child of the English Savage." They were blunt. The abusive parent too often escaped punishment because his most "fiendish" deeds occurred inside the brute's own "castle."[18] Thus, tales of diabolical cruelty in the South Seas reached a British public already grappling with home-grown monsters. The behavioral kinship of British and Pacific savages received explicit comment in a *Times* report of 1872. A succession of vicious street assaults tried at the Northern Assizes had "presented a picture of drunken brutality such as might be more fitly expected in some savage island in the far Pacifics."[19]

Among anthropologists and historians, it is obligatory to note that early European accounts of Pacific Islanders often maligned them. While unarguably true, this observation would profit from a closer reading of context. As the preceding discussion of domestic frontiers should suggest, Pacific savagery emerged from a broader calumny against the poor, the ethnically different, and the assertively female. It would be reductionist to treat anti-Irish and anti-Fijian rhetorics as equivalent distortions. Yet if we entertained such comparisons more often, the framing of new, cross-cultural questions would likely result. By keeping both Pacific island and home island experiences in focus, then, this book will broaden the field within which misrepresentations of the Pacific Other were produced.

The third affiliated meaning of "savage" in its Oceanic setting emphasized wildness. Most of the British explorers, traders, and missionaries from whose writings a composite "South Seas savage" took shape wasted little effort on categorical precision. We can do better. The Melanesian Islander certainly qualified as "wild," but not as "natural"—*Homo sapiens ferus.* The celebrated case of "Wild Peter" had early on undermined belief in a "state of nature." Captured amid thick forest near Hamelen, Germany, during the summer of 1724, age judged to be between eleven and fifteen, Peter had apparently subsisted on berries, acorns, and tree bark. He could not speak at first, and seemed to possess very limited intelligence. Fifteen months after his capture, this living specimen was shipped to London, where the

Hanoverian king, George I, saw to it that Peter's innate ideas—if any he had—would be scientifically probed. He lived into his seventies, eventually managed to pronounce his own name, and learned to like beer but not women (a disappointment for those who hoped to find in Peter evidence of "wild" virility).[20] The savages of Melanesia struck Western visitors as occupying a higher plane of consciousness. They were "ignorant" to be sure, but hardly slow-witted. More than anything else, their customs defined them as Other. The armchair explorer James Greenwood assured his Victorian readership that the prototypical savage—"forest-haunting, clothes-eschewing, arrow-poisoning, [and] man-devouring"—remained "vigorous."[21]

Although wild in the sense of untamed, western Pacific peoples did not make ideal primitives. Charles Darwin met what he took to be the quintessential primitive when the *Beagle* visited Tierra del Fuego in 1833 and 1834. The Fuegians repulsed Darwin:

> These were the most abject and miserable creatures I any where beheld. . . . These poor wretches were stunted in their growth, their hideous faces bedaubed with white paint, their skins filthy and greasy, their hair tangled, their voices discordant, their gestures violent and without dignity. Viewing such men, one can hardly make oneself believe they are fellow-creatures, and inhabitants of the same world.[22]

Save perhaps for the denizens of Malekula in the northern New Hebrides, or some of the Aboriginal bands of eastern Australia, the Fuegians would continue to impress Europeans as the most aesthetically "low" people on earth. Employed differently as a designation for technological backwardness, "primitive" Islanders occupied both temperate Tasmania and the tropical Andaman archipelago. The Andamanese were reputedly treacherous, the Tasmanians rather shy. But these island cultures appeared to share a preference for "Stone-Age" ways. As Satadru Sen has explained, Western fascination with the idea of "the primitive" involved "an affected rejection of modernity." That is, the attraction of the nonmodern was itself quite modern; and the denigration of Western civilization was initially a prerogative of whiteness.[23] The material creations of Melanesian peoples, however, often mocked the "primitive" label. Hence the brilliantly designed *tomako* (war canoe) of the Solomon Islanders challenged imputations of crude craftsmanship, as did the handsome hardwood clubs and fine *tapa* cloth mats of the Fijians.

Further complicating their location within ethnological hierarchies, the people of the western Pacific often figured as "monstrous" in the behavioral sense but not in the meaning of abnormal physiology. As early as 1710, well before Cook's oceanic exploits captivated British readers, the 3rd Earl of Shaftesbury blamed "a new race of authors" for perverting public tastes: "monstrous accounts of monstrous men and manners" were crowding out the uplifting literature on Christian miracles.[24] A generation later, the eminent surgeon John Hunter began building his collection of anatomical curiosities. Although the word "teratology"—meaning the study of "monstrosities" in animals and humans—did not enter British medical literature until the 1830s, the investigation and display of anomalous bodies had a longer history. So did the commercialized exhibition of human oddities, later to be known as "freaks."[25] The South Sea "savages" who paraded around Europe and North America in the nineteenth century were often prized specimens in ethnographic zoos. But except for their understandable aversion to cold, these people were neither freaks nor anatomical monsters.

Ultimately, it may be impossible to unpack a portmanteau word like "savage." British writers obviously did not have Melanesia in mind whenever they deployed it. By 1890, when *The Picture of Dorian Gray* appeared, Wilde could unself-consciously use "savage" to convey three distinct conditions: uncultured, self-denying, and animalistic.[26] From the late eighteenth century well into the twentieth, the presumed essence of the "savage state" varied widely among European commentators. One held that ignorance about private property was the root problem, while another blamed the savage's want of self-reflection. A satisfaction with the "mere necessaries of life" rendered industry meaningless, declared a political economist, whereas the absence of altruism struck an anthropologist as a grave defect in savage psychology.[27] Victorian ethnologists, obsessed with moral evolution, hoped to establish the "original condition" of savage tribes. Were they the residue of "degradation" from a "higher level," or had they been simply left behind by the progress of more adaptable peoples?[28] Uncertainty prevailed.

Yet an underlying coherence can be identified within the explanatory tangle of savage talk. Consider the "romance" of empire. During the middle third of the nineteenth century, the critics of British imperial expansion wielded considerable power both within and without Parliament. But among less ideologically committed citizens, what seemed remarkable about the nation's territorial landmass abroad was its capaciousness. The variety of peoples living in British colonies (or in areas likely soon to become colonies) impressed even many critics of formal colonization. In the words of one paean to empire published in 1909, Britain's guidance of "quaint" and "curious" people around the globe should bring a "glow of satisfaction":

> It need not be the satisfaction which comes from acquisition and conquest . . . but the knowledge that whatever mistakes have been made, however many blots there may be on the page of our national history, the extension of the Empire really counts for good in the story of the world.[29]

J.F. Fraser's *Quaint Subjects of the King* sought to familiarize its readers with the "strange and little-known races" who inhabited "out-of-the-way corners" of the Edwardian empire.[30]

Actually, dozens of such triumphalist accounts had earlier appeared during Victoria's reign (1837–1901). Nineteenth-century museums also helped to reify the racially peculiar. Although never built, a proposed "Aboriginal Museum and Library" in central London had aimed to blend "public amusement" with "public instruction": rich and poor alike needed to appreciate how difficult it was to pacify "barbarians and savages" without destroying them.[31] Ethnological display, Patrick Wolfe has observed, necessarily involved a racial ranking. The same can be said about the music hall songs, broadside ballads, novels, and maps that embroidered exotic lives.[32] The Queen herself never set foot on a Pacific island, much less remonstrated with man-eaters. But at least notionally, her subject population contained the fierce as well as the meek. We might term Victoria's connection to Melanesian savages "ornamental possession"; she was the apex of an empire whose heterogeneity distinguished it from all others. Readers will find that cannibal designations simultaneously referenced a specific form of savagery and a more diffuse sense of wildness. It was quite common in nineteenth- and early twentieth-century travel literature for the "cannibal" name to be uncoupled from the act.

More must be said about the affiliations of exoticism, primitivism, conceptions of savagery, and the writing of Pacific history. Some specialists in the Oceanic past, for example, have expressed puzzlement over the way that Edward Said's *Orientalism* (1978) acquired an almost fetishistic status among scholars of the postcolonial condition. For *Orientalism* was by no means the first work to focus attention on representations of "otherness" and their uses in the project of imperial domination. Both Philip Curtin's *The Image of*

Africa (1964) and Bernard Smith's *European Vision and the South Pacific* (1960) grappled with precisely these concerns—and, some would say, in a more nuanced fashion.[33] Smith in particular broke new ground by leavening his accounts of scientific practice with an art historian's attention to pictorial technique. The resulting cross-fertilization produced a less abstract Other than would appear in *Orientalism*.[34]

Yet even Bernard Smith found the meanings of Pacific savagery so fractured that he, like many more commentators before and after him, took refuge in broad categorical distinctions. Some eager categorizers insisted on distinguishing between "savagery" and "barbarism." (In a "savage state," humans subsisted on what they could forage, neither tilling the soil nor domesticating animals. Humans entered a "barbaric state" when they became agriculturalists.)[35] But far more often invoked has been the binary opposition between "noble" and "ignoble" savages. There persists today a mistaken belief that the noble savage concept was an outgrowth of eighteenth-century sentimentalism. Rousseau's essays are often identified as the source of this now iconic phrase. Ter Ellingson has shown that in fact Rousseau never mentioned a "noble savage."[36] Rousseau *did* suggest that uncivilized humans were "rather wild than wicked." And *Émile* certainly attacked the corrupting influence of traditional (civilized) education.[37] But the idealizing of savage life, a process applied to the North American Indian well before the South Sea Islander, was less coherent than we have been led to believe. A curious mixture of admiration and condemnation more often characterized British reports of Pacific peoples. Thus, J.R. Forster, the naturalist on Cook's second voyage, found the Maori an impressive race except for one "odious and cruel" custom—eating their slain enemies.[38] Even sophisticated analysts such as Bernard Smith have tried to explain change-over-time as a representational shift from noble to ignoble Islanders. More recently, another otherwise careful analyst of Western image-creation, Patrick Brantlinger, has emphasized a new addition to the old binary: the "self-exterminating" savage.[39]

Coexisting with the notion of savage nobility was a parallel discourse that traduced Pacific peoples. John Hawkesworth's 1773 *Account of the Voyages Undertaken . . . for Making Discoveries in the Southern Hemisphere*, a compilation of captains' journals, sold well and shocked many. For Hawkesworth's portrait of unbridled sexuality, especially among the Tahitians, impressed evangelical readers as proof of the need for Christian intervention in the

South Seas.[40] Missionaries representing several Protestant denominations would answer this call. But "saving" the Islanders, it turned out, often involved more than coaxing the heathen to pray and cover up. There was also the work of rescuing infants and widows from strangulation; the elderly from live burial; and slaves from becoming meals. Nor need one have been a churchgoer to find the Pacific Islander unsympathetic. Dickens's infamous rant against savages everywhere (1853) was thoroughly secular:

> I beg to say that I have not the least belief in the Noble Savage. I consider him a prodigious nuisance, and an enormous superstition. . . . I call a savage a something highly desirable to be civilized off the face of the earth. I think a mere gent (which I take to be the lowest form of civilization) better than a howling, whistling, clucking, stomping, jumping, tearing savage. It is all one to me whether he sticks a fish-bone through his visage, or bits of trees through the lobes of his ears or birds' feathers in his head. . . . Yielding to whichsoever of these agreeable eccentricities, he is a savage—cruel, false, thievish, murderous; addicted more or less to grease, entrails, and beastly customs; a wild animal with the questionable gift of boasting; a conceited, tiresome, bloodthirsty, monotonous humbug.[41]

Treating such an odious creature as a "pet," much "whimper[ed] over" by humanitarians, struck self-styled realists as utter stupidity.[42]

Pushing beyond the noble/ignoble binary in constructions of Pacific peoples, more recent scholarship has emphasized Islander agency. Dramatic tales of the ruin of Pacific island societies not surprisingly emphasized cursed imports; epidemic disease, alcohol, firearms, and convicts topped this list. Alan Moorehead's *The Fatal Impact: An Account of the Invasion of the South Pacific, 1767–1840* (1966) was probably the most compelling of these laments. Yet because the ravages of Western civilization commanded center stage in such historical work, the Islanders themselves generally figured as victims: passive, helpless, invisible except as casualties.[43] Ultimately, Eurocentrism produced its own antidote. Inspired in large part by J.W. Davidson, founder of the Department of Pacific History at the Australian National University in Canberra, a younger generation of scholars sought to create an interdisciplinary, island-oriented history of the Pacific.[44] Plainly, an insular perspective required active, sentient Islanders.

Finding an Islander voice demands caution as well as imagination, however. The search for indigenous agency must avoid replacing one monolithic category ("British interests," for example) with another ("the Islanders' side of the story").[45] Given widespread illiteracy among Pacific island populations before the mid-nineteenth century, written evidence of "native" intentions is often scarce. Oral traditions can be vital supplements to a patchy written record. But because oral traditions, unlike physical documents, are not fixed at a point in time, the vagaries of group memory may obscure more than they explain.[46]

Agency can also be inferred through the location and distribution of material objects. As Nicholas Thomas has observed, Oceanic items housed in museums today can sometimes reveal differences in Islanders' reception of European strangers. It is noteworthy, for instance, that ethnographic collections of eastern Pacific artifacts tend to contain a wide range of both everyday and sacred objects—suggesting that early European visitors were accorded "degrees of inclusion appropriate to guests." Artifacts from the western Pacific, by contrast, are more often limited to weapons. Although we know that a tradition of large-scale sculpture flourished in the pre-contact New Hebrides archipelago, Cook's crew on his second voyage obtained mostly clubs, spears, and arrows. It would appear that the men of Tanna, Erromango, and Malekula wished Cook and crew to see only these Islanders' martial side.[47] Similarly, Bronwen Douglas reminds us that certain European texts and illustrations are imbued with the "countersigns" and "oblique stamps" of Islander agency. Through a theatrical display of cannibalism, for example, the Kanaks of New Caledonia sought to intimidate the first French visitors. If so, the Kanaks prevailed.[48]

Where the evidence—written, spoken, or inferred—permits, this book will probe Islander logics. Thus, the ferocity of "highlanders" on Viti Levu, Fiji's largest island, aimed to intimidate white planters. Or examine the recruitment of indentured labor from New Hebridean isles. Those who agreed to cut sugarcane in Queensland had often made a complex cost/benefit calculation about working for Europeans abroad. But because a main aim of this study is to assess British "pacification" efforts in Melanesia, its principal emphasis will be the wide variety of British perceptions. Manichean distinctions between white oppressors and hapless Pacific Islanders easily slide into caricature.

The British, it will be shown, worried nearly as much about white savagery as about the menace of dark tribes. The alleged depredations of European "beachcombers," according to British evangelists, caused "incalculable mischief."[49] Beachcombers included three overlapping groups of men:

escaped convicts; deserters from visiting whaling and trading vessels; and castaways, the human flotsam of shipwrecks. Missionaries often collapsed these groups into undifferentiated "gangs" bent on fomenting disorder among Islanders and corrupting converts.[50] H.E. Maude has offered a less alarmist profile. What distinguished beachcombers from other outsiders, Maude contends, was their integration into, and reliance for their survival upon, indigenous island communities. Where he flaunted local customs, however, the beachcomber risked severe punishment.[51] By the 1830s, these storied wanderers between civilization and savagery could be found in most Pacific island groups. That they appeared less commonly in Melanesia, whose islands lay closest to Australia, impressed contemporaries as further proof of the western Pacific's unwelcoming people.

Although escaped convicts formed part of the minute beachcomber population of the South Seas, the prospect of a mass convict "invasion" of Australia or the New Hebrides long concerned European residents Down Under. Two penal settlements, one British the other French, shared island space with aboriginal populations during the latter half of the nineteenth century. The Andaman archipelago, located 800 miles off the eastern coast of India, eventually absorbed over 10,000 convicts, convict-settlers, and administrators. The clearing of jungle for this penal experiment virtually guaranteed a hostile response from the Andamanese—"oceanic negroes" whose reputation for mutilating runaways served to discourage escape attempts.[52] But even if the Andamanese had been sweet-tempered, there were relatively few commercial ships on which convicts might have tried to hide.

The French penal settlement on New Caledonia, however, posed a direct threat to the nearby Australian colonies, or so some colonists claimed. New Caledonia's convicts appeared ideologically suspect, especially after about 4,500 "Communards" began arriving in 1872. To French (and British) conservatives, the ten-week Commune of Paris in 1871 had shown that its supporters, godless "destroyers of all civilization," must either be exterminated or re-civilized.[53] The Communard *déportés* to New Caledonia had been judged worthy of regeneration. A few of them nevertheless decided to forgo that honor. In 1874, six *déportés* managed to escape from the Ducos peninsula, make contact with a sympathetic ship's captain, and eventually reach Sydney.[54] The European Left applauded them. The propertied classes of Australia and New Zealand did not. Improbable scenarios involving escaped French "communists" joined Australians' lengthy list of complaints about

British imperial docility. Since "scores" of these "highly dangerous men" had supposedly sneaked ashore, the nucleus of a "fair military force" already existed. Once armed, they would "kill, plunder, ravish, [and] destroy." The social debris of France, opined Sydney's *Daily Telegraph*, was already busy building a "dung-heap" in eastern Australia.[55] Nor was this alarmism confined to newspapers and pamphlets. The early 1880s saw agents for Queensland, New South Wales, and New Zealand beg Britain's Colonial Office to halt the flow of hardened criminals from New Caledonia to the New Hebrides—then an archipelago without colonial governance. What has been called Australian "sub-imperialism"[56] grew strident where territorial ambitions met caution at the imperial core.

Still, in both British and British colonial imaginations, color irrevocably split the savage ranks. An individual white predator might perish through accident or avarice, but his racial identity did not consign him to a doomed group. The "dusky savages" of the western Pacific, on the other hand, gradually emerged as targets of a "dying races" rhetoric. Nearly a generation before *The Origin of Species* appeared, one of Darwin's mentors, Charles Lyell, referred to the "extirpation of savage tribes" whose domains had the misfortune to attract colonial interest.[57] Sometimes depicted as essential for social progress, sometimes dressed in the language of regret, the "vanishing native" trope remained a key ethnographic theme well into the 1940s. *Risky Shores* will explore this idea in a western Pacific context. Public concern over endangered human groups was itself part of a broader British preoccupation with decay brought on by carelessness and greed. The "noble" animals of Britain's East African territories, for instance, stood on the brink of extinction thanks to reckless big-game hunting. A "grand national possession," these creatures, like the wild Islanders of Melanesia, cried out for the protection that only "reserves" promised to provide.[58] Yet Britain's leading anthropologist of the early twentieth century, W.H.R. Rivers, found that a Melanesian Islander's will to live might hinge on the savage customs for which he had been reviled. Suppress headhunting and demoralize the headhunter; move him to a reserve and watch him die.[59] How civilized people might act to preserve the "zest" of the savage would vex the Islander's allies.

We should also understand that "dying races" was more than a literary contrivance. Although they still numbered slightly over 2,000 individuals at the close of the nineteenth century, the Andamanese seemed bound for oblivion.[60] The Tasmanians had by then actually vanished from the earth—

if one refuses to count the "halfcast" progeny of aboriginal and non-aboriginal unions. "Truganini," thought to be the last full-blooded Tasmanian woman, concluded a racial autopsy. These people, unlike some other Pacific Islanders, had rarely practiced infanticide. They did not eat one another. Unprovoked attacks by white "bushrangers" had taken their toll, as had cheap gin. One peculiar theory held that Tasmanian women turned sterile following intercourse with white men. Far simpler was one indigenous woman's explanation for her childlessness: "What good hab him piccaninny?"[61] This ethnographic profile could be taken to exemplify the "fatal impact" thesis. Rich in pathological particulars although vague about weighting them, it effectively blamed the Tasmanians for failing to embrace modernity. But we should not discount the obverse. Perhaps the Tasmanian woman's reluctance to bear children constituted a radical expression of Islander agency?

The prospect of Islander extinctions heightened popular interest in their material cultures. Always of interest to metropolitan audiences, the strange weaponry of these people gained greater notoriety as island populations shrank and fierce tribes grudgingly came to terms with British colonial violence. The instigators of this violence often justified it by reference to the supposed fanaticism of "wild" warriors. At the 1899 armaments limitation talks held in The Hague, only the representatives of Britain and the United States objected to banning the use of expanding bullets, colloquially known as "dumdum" rounds. Major General Sir John Ardagh, Britain's chief military delegate, sought to save the dumdum by vilifying the savage. "The civilized soldier when shot recognizes that he is wounded," Ardagh reasoned. "He lies down on his stretcher and is taken off the field to his ambulance, where he is dressed or bandaged." The savage behaved differently: "Your fanatical barbarian, similarly wounded, continues to rush on, spear or sword in hand; and before you have had time to represent to him that his conduct is [irrational] . . . he may have cut off your head."[62] Variously located among the "fanatical" and the "cowardly," western Pacific warriors wielded weapons that could do great damage in close quarters. Fiji's hardwood clubs crushed skulls. Lighter axes, originally fashioned from stone but later incorporating steel blades brought by European traders, served the Islanders well. Equally adept at husking coconuts and slicing body parts, these axes continued to be identified in British travel literature as "tomahawks." An Amerindian word perhaps derived from the Algonquian verb *tomahuk* (to knock down), "tomahawk" rhetorically conflated savagery in northeastern America and the southwestern Pacific.[63]

Melanesia stood alone, however, as the imagined epicenter of deadly "poison" arrows. Cane shafts tipped with slivers of human bone and smeared with unknown matter acquired a mythic status in tales of Islander perfidy. As early as 1792, one of the sailors aboard d'Entrecasteaux's ship received a small scratch from such an arrow near Santa Cruz island. The wound healed nicely. But seventeen days after being nicked, the sailor died—a death that "left no doubt" in the minds of shipboard doctors "as to the arrow being poisoned."[64] Upon his arrival in Fiji around 1879, A.B. Brewster was relieved to find that the Fijians at least did not "steep" their arrows in "putrid corpses."[65] Deemed to be a weapon of the weak, these "treacherous" missiles earned unusually wide notice when the senior naval officer in Australia, Commodore J.G. Goodenough (1830–1875), succumbed to arrow wounds received on the already infamous island of Santa Cruz. Goodenough's matter-of-fact response to these wounds underscored their danger. Five days after the attack at Carlisle Bay, he wrote to the Lords Commissioners of the Admiralty reminding them that if the arrows had been poisoned, his case could "terminate fatally." Three days later, it did.[66]

By the time of Commodore Goodenough's death in 1875, most British contributors to the debate over Islander arrows recognized that the immediate cause of death was usually tetanus. The rapid course of the disease, its fearsome mortality, and the hideous convulsions ("tonic spasms") that wracked sufferers during their last days made diagnosis straightforward. But mystery remained. Did the Melanesians possess a poison that induced tetanic symptoms? Could the "pernicious dread" of lockjaw somehow lower one's resistance to it? How should this disease be treated?[67] British physicians offered a confusing array of palliatives: absolute quiet and bed rest; opium smoking; amputation of a limb above its wound site. But it was an Australian who probably spoke for most of his professional colleagues when he averred, "I can confidently say that I . . . never saw a case benefitted by treatment."[68] Victorian medicine's uncertainty over the nature of tetanus created an explanatory void within which it was possible to continue blaming the Islanders. Robert Codrington, an Anglican missionary and pioneering ethnographer of the western Pacific, put the issue succinctly: "The belief in the deadly virulence of the poison used . . . is too firmly fixed to readily give way."[69] Much the same thing could be said about British representations of the Melanesian in general.

There are of course analytical risks attached to concentrating on one part of a vast and borderless ocean. Treating the "western Pacific" as a bounded expanse of land and sea may seem arbitrary, perhaps even perverse.[70] It is also true, from a Eurocentric perspective, that New Guinea, the Solomons, Fiji, and the New Hebrides were understood as geographically and culturally remote from the centers of imperial power: London, to be sure, but also Sydney, Melbourne, Auckland, and Wellington. *Risky Shores* will show how this very remoteness beckoned white outsiders; the obscurity of these island groups constituted their appeal, as Victorian and Edwardian writers often noted. Some postcolonial theorists may insist that however attentive to Islander thought this book may be, it remains an artifact of European dominance and metropolitan hubris.[71] It is worth remembering, however, that the noun "dominance" and the adjective "metropolitan" themselves distort lived experience by homogenizing the powerful and the urban.

What ought a study of British encounters with western Pacific peoples call the place where these encounters occurred? Place names often encode cultural assumptions and thus invite controversy. It was a French navigator, Jules-Sébastien Dumont d'Urville, who in 1832 published an essay and an accompanying map that divided the Pacific into three regions: *Polynésie* ("many islands"); *Micronésie* ("tiny islands"); and *Mélanésie* ("black islands"). The so-called Polynesian "triangle" covered Hawai'i, New Zealand, and much of the central Pacific. Micronesia subsumed Kiribati (then known as the Gilbert Islands), the Marshalls, the Marianas, and smaller groups westward toward, but not including, the Philippines. Melanesia, as we have seen, encompassed New Guinea, the Solomons, Vanuatu (then the New Hebrides), New Caledonia, and Fiji. Today, Aboriginal Australians and Torres Strait Islanders are sometimes also regarded as Melanesian.[72] Tellingly, "Melanesian" is the only one of these three ethnic classifications that specifies a racial characteristic. Some scholars have proposed that the Pacific's "black islands" be renamed on this account.[73]

Then too, revisionists within academic anthropology today reject the ascription of different leadership styles to different parts of the Pacific. In 1963, Marshall Sahlins published a widely influential paper, "Poor Man, Rich Man, Big-Man, Chief," that sought to distinguish Polynesia's "elaborate forms of rank and chieftanship" from Melanesia's more "rudimentary" and egalitarian political structures. These distinctions, Nicholas Thomas and others have since argued, rest on a "discredited evolutionism," a typology that distorts rather than clarifies.[74] Why, then, should we not dispense altogether with the flawed geocultural construct "Melanesian"?

The answer is practicality. No reasonable alternative exists. Collapsing "Melanesia" into an undifferentiated "Oceania" would merely trade one imprecise label for another. What has been termed an "Oceanic approach to Pacific history," wherein "cross-talk" among many constituencies is encouraged,[75] can coexist with older designations. Besides, Clive Moore reminds us, as Melanesian territories evolved from colonies into independent states, their people consciously identified themselves as Melanesians, thereby "indigenizing the concept and divorcing it from any element of inferiority."[76] Largely as a matter of convenience, therefore, "Melanesia" and "Melanesians" will be retained in this book.

Other terminologies bear mention. If the word "native" meant simply "belonging to a place by birth," it would raise few eyebrows. But because it can also imply archaic or uncouth, "native" will appear here only to indicate a direct quotation or the clear sense of a text. The less loaded noun "Islander" will be preferred in the pages to follow. In some circles, for example among historians of Africa, the words "tribe" and "tribal" are notable for their absence. Insofar as they tend to promote a myth of primitive African timelessness, obscuring the forces of change, these words are justifiably suspect.[77] Since similar objections have not clouded these words in the Pacific cultural sphere, however, they will appear occasionally. For all its flaws, William Rivers's 1924 definition of "tribe" remains useful: "a social group of a simple kind, the members of which speak a common dialect, have a single government, and act together for such common purposes as warfare."[78] Finally, the phenomenon we call "colonialism" requires brief consideration. Brian Stanley has captured the essence of this often-undefined term. Colonialism, Stanley suggests, is "that form of imperialism in which the imperial power imposes governmental control on a territory without resort to large-scale human settlement."[79] So long as we recognize that "governmental control" nearly always involved racial exclusions, Stanley's definition will suffice. The imposition of such control often owed as much to the early interventions of traders, missionaries, and explorers as to subsequent "state" actions.[80] Put another way, British colonial hegemony in the western Pacific was never hegemonic.

Melanesia did not matter to the British Empire on the basis of population. As of 1914, the entire British Pacific, Australia and New Zealand included, accounted for a minuscule 1.5 percent of the entire imperial population.[81] Rather, the Pacific mattered to Britons because, along with Africa, it sustained the romance of space. This romance expressed itself on the material level with visions of escape from the crowded home islands. On the psychic level, the romance to which Captain Cook gave shape regarded the South Seas as a realm within which the ego could assert itself undiminished by humble birth or scant learning. The Victorian years above all found Britons' collective identity—as a humane yet enterprising race—tested on Pacific islands.[82] These tests would prove especially stiff in Melanesia.

The savage practices so closely connected in British minds with the western Pacific will be examined over the course of five chapters. In the first of these, cannibalism functions as the unifying trope for a highly diverse set of "barbaric" customs. Whether eaten or merely murdered, the three missionaries discussed in Chapter 2 made more urgent the task of pacifying Melanesia. Complicating these pacification efforts, Chapter 3 explains, were the white savages whose recruitment of plantation labor struck humanitarians as slavery by another name. Largely because their strongholds were so remote, some Solomon Islanders and coastal Papuans continued headhunting after the arrival of British administrators. As Chapter 4 reveals, the eventual suppression of this custom had unintended consequences. The prospect of savage extinctions fueled both awkward laments and a fascination with "doomed" people. Out of these mixed emotions, Chapter 5 notes, arose several attempts to locate the remnants of "Stone-Age" humanity. A brief conclusion examines the fate of savage constructions during and shortly after world war in the western Pacific. The story based upon these constructions will emphasize the stubborn endurance of stereotypes.

An early advocate of island-centered histories noted that the Pacific's vast expanse of sea and land offered a "happy hunting ground" for social scientists, a "regional laboratory" for the study of peoples who had come late to the modern world.[83] *Risky Shores* views the islands of Melanesia not as laboratories for the observation of sweeping social change but rather as sites for the production of mutual misunderstanding. That said, European images of the Pacific Islander involved more than a catalog of inhuman behaviors. Many British visitors to the South Seas recognized that their *own* humanity would be constantly questioned. In prescriptive terms, then, accounts of "treacherous" Pacific Islanders and fully "civilized" Britons are imbricated, overlapping in often surprising ways. This book seeks to enrich our sense of the colonial era by reconsidering the conduct of Islanders and the English-speaking strangers who encountered them. Among the historical forces that together created a unifying sense of Britishness during the nineteenth and early twentieth centuries were the frequently sensationalized depictions of Melanesian "savages." These exotic people inhabited the edges of empire. And precisely because they did, Britons who never had and never would leave the home islands could imagine, in vivid if spurious detail, their nation's imperial reach.

ONE

Island Stories of the Cannibal Kind

"Cannibal" is a metonym for "savage," a proxy word for that which appears culturally incomprehensible, disgusting, or dangerous. The strangeness of cannibalism—its assault on what modern societies regard as civilized behavior—continues to shock us. As if the horrors of World War Two had not already been documented in minute detail, recent additions to this grim literature have emphasized cannibal particulars. The consumption of corpses (and less often, murder for human meat) during the siege of Leningrad drives home as perhaps no other revelations could how harrowing these 872 days truly were. Similarly, the news that eating both prisoners of war and indigenous peoples was a "systematic and organized military strategy" of Japanese soldiers in the Asian-Pacific theater lends weight to the argument that this global conflict constituted the greatest human-made disaster in history.[1] Archaeologists continue to unearth disturbing evidence of cannibalism in earlier eras. It now seems likely, for example, that some English settlers at Jamestown, in Virginia, survived the harsh winter of 1609–10 by preying upon their weaker neighbors. Desperation drove such savagery.[2] But what could be said in defense of Armin Meiwes, the German computer expert who in early 2001 honored the wish of an internet acquaintance to be slaughtered and swallowed? Less certain if no less troubling have been the periodic reports of rebel troops in northeastern Congo consuming the hearts, livers, and lungs of rival ethnic groups.[3]

Why does cannibalism still transfix modern readers and viewers? The late-Victorian reflections of Alfred St. Johnston may provide a clue. A genteel English wanderer who toured Melanesia in the 1880s, St. Johnston associated man-eating with bygone times when constant vigilance was the price of survival. Traditional Fijian life, St. Johnston supposed, had been invigorating mainly because it was so precarious:

This subject of cannibalism has a terrible sort of fascination for me, and I have been making the skipper to-night tell me all the awful things he has seen or heard of the "old" Fijians . . . ; and although he has made me shudder with some of his ghastly tales, . . . yet—queer is it not?—I have enjoyed them thoroughly . . . *I should have gloried in the rush and struggle of old Fijian times—with my hand against everybody, and everybody against me*—and the fierce madness of unchecked passion and rage with which they went to battle, and the clubbing of my foes, and *I am sure I should have enjoyed the eating of them afterwards.*

At once Hobbesian and Darwinian, this nostalgic yearning for an imagined Pacific past "when every restraint was laid aside" thrilled St. Johnston.[4]

A postcolonial reading of his fantasy would pounce on the admission that the "ghastly tales" of a veteran skipper constituted the evidence for Fijian man-eating. Anthropologist Gananath Obeyesekere, among others, has dismissed much of what Europeans claimed to know about Pacific cannibalism as phony "sailors' yarns."[5] We will shortly return to the epistemological fog surrounding cannibal allegations. For now, though, it is enough to note that the modern scholarly impulse to deconstruct—and thereby to discredit—such stories derives in large part from a tendency to view cannibalism not as a behavior so much as a metaphor for racial difference; accusations of man-eating, some scholars hold, serve mainly to distance the civilized from the savage. Yet at the same time that it reifies difference, the rhetoric of cannibalism literally dissolves difference. For just as the cannibal act dramatically juxtaposes the eater and the eaten, so it must also suggest the incorporation of two into one.[6]

Whatever may explain cannibalism's capacity to shock, it is clear that the figure of the man-eater has long provided a screen on which to project the shifting fears of dominant cultures. The process whereby the word "cannibal" emerged as the signifier of unrestrained appetite illustrates the utility of libel. Prior to the late fifteenth century, he who ate human flesh earned the label "anthropophagite," a relatively neutral (if clumsy) melding of the Greek words "anthropos" (man) and "phagein" (to eat). Columbus's voyages of the 1490s produced not only sightings of a new world but also the far more accusatory word we use today. On his first voyage, Columbus visited islands inhabited by an indigenous people called the Arawak. Hospitable to their European visitors, the Arawak had only vile tales to tell about a murderous folk located in the south, the Caribs. Although neither the great navigator nor his surgeon on the second voyage, Diego Alvarez Chanca, ever witnessed the alleged man-eating and blood-drinking of the Caribs, this missing proof did not stop Dr. Chanca from writing a report for the municipality of Seville that treated wild rumor as fact.

Such wholesale invention, we may reasonably infer, helped justify the taking of Caribbean peoples as slaves—just in case the anticipated gold and spices failed to materialize. Through faulty translations, the tribal designation "Carib" eventually emerged as "caniba." And as Peter Hulme has explained, by a haphazard "augmentative process" European commentators viewed the Caribs' resistance to Spanish authority as presumptive evidence of human depravity in its most grotesque form.[7] Etymologically speaking, then, the word "cannibal" is a colonial creation.

Especially pernicious has been the rhetorical use of man-eating to affix racial boundaries. From the late eighteenth century down to the present, cannibalism and blackness have been mutually reinforcing. After living in the West Indies for twelve years, the historian Edward Long regarded himself as an authority on "African" physiology and culture. Besides their dark skin, thick lips, and hair "like bestial fleece," Africans, Long declared in 1774, were keen "devourers of human flesh, and quaffers of human blood."[8] Hegel agreed. Africans supposedly lacked the instinctive dread of cannibalism normally found in white people. Hence, "to the sensual Negro, human flesh is but an object of sense—mere flesh."[9] Five generations later, the protagonist in George Orwell's *Coming Up for Air* (1939) needs only to glimpse a newspaper headline—"King Zog's Wedding Postponed"—to descend into racial reverie: "King Zog! What a name! It's next door to impossible to believe a chap with a name like that isn't a jet-black cannibal."[10]

Yet when this dark creature entered the literature of Pacific exploration, a taxonomic problem arose. Although Pacific cannibals were fully Other, not all of them were black. The amateur anthropologists of Victorian times sought to draw a cannibal map of Oceania, a racial cartography that strained to explain why man-eating flourished on some islands and not on others. Skin color offered the most obvious marker of difference. Thus, the "clear olive" complexion of Polynesians was "comely," declared one supporter of missionary work in 1840, even when deepened through exposure to sun and wind.[11] Toward the end of the nineteenth century, another champion of British missions abroad observed that "light-skinned" Polynesians belonged to "a mild easy-tempered race." Fond of stealing perhaps and no doubt "terribly impure," Polynesians were still far superior to Melanesians, "a dark, treacherous, murderous people, great cannibals and skull hunters."[12] It behooved missionaries and their well-wishers to dwell on Melanesian wildness: wilder savages opened fatter purses. But many Victorians outside the evangelical ranks also accepted these racial profiles. The "Negro races of the Pacific" were an "undeniably . . . brutish and unintellectual people," thought John Crawfurd, the blinkered president of London's Ethnological Society. Small wonder that these Melanesians embraced cannibalism "in the fulness of its atrocity." R.L. Stevenson put it more succinctly: "All Melanesia appears tainted," declared the novelist.[13] Where black bodies mingled with brown, as for instance in Tonga and along the southeastern coast of New Guinea, cannibal lust allegedly survived only among the former. In what most Europeans regarded as the epicenter of Pacific cannibalism, Fiji, its people struck one white settler as "dark in every sense of the word."[14]

Given this equation of blackness with man-eating, it is worth recalling that Europe's first exposure to Pacific anthropophagy involved a "copper-colored" Polynesian race, the Maori. In November of 1773, during Captain Cook's second voyage, the *Resolution* anchored off Totara-Nui, a long beach located at the northern tip of New Zealand's South Island. Quite by accident several crewmembers discovered while ashore that local Maori men were used to consuming parts of the enemies they had recently killed in battle. Cook soon came to accept that this was a common practice:

> That the New Zealanders are Canibals can now no longer be doubted, the account I gave of it in my former Voyage was partly founded on circumstances and was, as I afterwards found, discredited by many people . . . [T]he New Zealanders are certainly in a state of civilization, their behaviour to us has been Manly and Mild, shewing always a readiness to oblige us; . . . they are far less addicted to thieving than the other Islanders and are I believe strictly honist among them-selves. This custom of eating their enemies slain in battle . . . has undoubtedly been handed down to them from the earliest times and we know that it is not an easy matter to break a nation of its ancient customs let them be ever so inhuman and savage.[15]

Not all members of Cook's second voyage shared their captain's detached view of man-eating among the Maori. James Burney, a young second lieutenant aboard the companion vessel, *Adventure*, was aghast to discover at Grass Cove the roasted remains of ten sailors from his own ship. So traumatic did Burney find these "most horrid proofs" of cannibalism that thereafter he "always spoke of it in a whisper, as if it was treason."[16]

Most of Britain's early visitors to New Zealand, however, managed to excuse, or at least contextualize, man-eating. In 1778, Johann Reinhold Forster, one of the *Resolution's* "botanical gentlemen," called the Maoris' cannibal habit an unsurprising product of primitive social development made worse by a meager diet: people who possess "no other animal food, than a few stupid dogs and fish, will soon reconcile themselves to human flesh."[17] Later commentators cited a thirst for revenge as another mitigating drive. Whatever had predisposed the aboriginal Maori to eat one another, British chroniclers praised the speed with which these "superior" brown people gave up their wild ways and embraced Christian civilization.[18]

That the imaginary locus of Pacific cannibalism shifted after about 1830 from New Zealand to other parts of Oceania is evident. One modern anthropologist has pointed out that with the coming of European settlers to New Zealand, the *pakeha* (whites) and the Maori often found themselves living in close proximity. Since "it is not pleasant to have cannibals as neighbors and members of the same state," there was, he reasons, an incentive to crown a new man-eating capital.[19] Neighborly considerations aside, a far simpler explanation for the relocation of cannibalism's heart of darkness involves pervasive racial stereotypes. The so-called "Cannibal Islands" of Victorian lore were nearly all Melanesian. Their dark inhabitants and sparse European settlement made them better palimpsests on which to inscribe and re-inscribe the faces of savagery. Because Fiji, the New Hebrides, and the satellite islands of New Guinea were so seldom visited during the early nineteenth century, they could better support a gothic "language of panic." In Howard Malchow's persuasive account, this gothic sensibility sought out the secret and the taboo, emphasizing that which repulsed or terrified.[20] And acting to unify these images was the dusky cannibal.

FOOD FOR THOUGHT

Recent scholarship, mostly in anthropology, links the subject of cannibalism to a broader debate over the meanings of non-Western cultural practices. Indeed, "cannibal studies" has sometimes been treated as a distinct field within this debate.[21] Like much postcolonial theory, the historicizing of cannibalism seeks to reveal the unequal power relations that sustain a "de-famatory" discourse about subject peoples. Eighteenth- and nineteenth-century discussions of man-eating, by contrast, rarely aimed to expose social injustice. Yet both these older discussions and modern, postcolonial criticism have recognized in the cannibal trope a useful starting point for probing the nature of violence. Just as Robert Darnton's French peasants of the Old Regime found folktales "good to think with,"[22] so cannibal stories have served to illuminate a wide range of campaigns. From missionary work among the heathen to the adoption of a flesh-free diet, from rationalizing the use of force against "savages" to detecting an indigenous voice in the past, cannibalism continues to provide rich food for thought.

Anthropologists in particular have sought to understand this practice as a behavior with highly diverse ritual meanings. As early as 1896, the German ethnologist Rudolf Steinmetz distinguished between the eating of relatives (*endokannibalismus*), an effort to bind the living to the dead, and the eating of strangers (*exokannibalismus*), usually a gesture of contempt for enemies. Steinmetz's dichotomy won over both French and British ethnologists and, with minor modifications, remains accepted today.[23] Otherwise, though, contention has ruled among theorists of cannibalism. Psychoanalytic readings seek to explain man-eating as a response to primal needs. Building on Freud's suggestion that "oral incorporation" is the most basic reaction to anger and frustration, one scholar has suggested that cannibalism met the psychosexual needs of primitive social groups.[24] More often asserted—because its logic so neatly meshes with a "rational choice" view of decision-making—is the materialist model of cannibalism. Simply put, this model holds that humans do what they must to survive; when necessary, they will adapt to severe calorie deficits by eating one another. Marvin Harris's *Cannibals and Kings* (1978) applied a version of this logic to the case of Aztec cannibalism. What Harris termed the Aztec "torture-sacrifice-cannibalism complex" allegedly derived not from blood lust but from protein hunger. Hundreds, sometimes thousands, of prisoners were annually butchered atop Aztec pyramids, their still-beating hearts held aloft by priests. Bodies then rolled back down the steep pyramids did not go to waste, however. For according to Harris, all edible parts of these corpses "were used in a manner strictly comparable to the consumption of the flesh of domesticated animals." True, the protein obtained through sacrifice could not have transformed the diets of a million Aztecs then living in the Valley of Mexico. But such "cannibal redistributions" *would* have been sufficient, Harris argued, to prevent "political collapse" if the release of this meat had been "synchronized to compensate for [periodic] deficits in the agricultural cycle."[25] So construed, Mesoamerican man-eating was reduced to a political cost/benefit calculation on the part of Aztec rulers.[26]

Scholars who could not otherwise agree among themselves about the ritual significance of cannibalism came together in condemning Harris's reductionist thinking. To ignore complex cultural traditions in favor of crude functionalism, Marshall Sahlins complained, was to trade thoughtful assessment of non-Western customs for a "Western business mentality." Such thinking undermined the very foundations of anthropology, Sahlins charged.[27] But beyond forming a united front against Harris's "vulgar" assertions, anthropologists have been less than kind to one another where cannibalism is concerned.

Highly controversial, for example, was Walter Arens's accusation that racial and cultural prejudices have shaped most discussions of cannibalism. Too many anthropologists and historians, Arens announced, have "felt the need to create and recreate savagery in its most gruesome form by calling into existence man-eaters at the fringes of our time and space." These scholars have an "investment" in preserving cannibalism as a cultural category: no more potent libel of non-Western societies exists.[28] Published in 1979, Arens's *The Man-Eating Myth* went further, declaring that the historical evidence for nearly all cannibal acts is, and must remain, suspect. If Arens aimed to provoke, he succeeded. One of his targets, fellow anthropologist Marshall Sahlins, lashed out at the ad hominem style of Arens's case. No less irresponsible was Arens's fixation with the idea that anthropology itself had exoticized and therefore marginalized cultures believed to be cannibalistic.[29]

Academic jousting over man-eating might have faded from public view had Arens's argument not received postcolonial reinforcement. It was above all Gananath Obeyesekere, a Sri Lankan by birth, who resumed the assault on those "naïve" scholars who trusted eyewitness accounts of cannibalism.[30] Obeyesekere did not categorically reject all historical evidence of man-eating. But the vehemence of his attack on most cannibal texts invited counterattack. Especially acerbic have been the words of Sahlins. The exchange between these two anthropologists has been all the more heated because of their previous quarrel over the meaning of Captain Cook's death on a Hawaiʻian beach in 1779. How did indigenous peoples regard Cook? What were they thinking when they first honored and later killed him? And how can we, strangers to this Pacific culture, know what "natives" thought? Others have dissected this epistemological feud.[31] Clearly though, both the earlier dispute over Cook's status in Hawai'ian eyes and the more recent clash over depictions of cannibalism have hinged on the question of authority. That is, who may speak for whom? Obeyesekere, raised in a nation still grappling with its colonial past, assumed that he possessed a special sensitivity to the disruptions created when alien cultures collide.[32] Sahlins denounced what he saw as special pleading based on racial identity. As for his opponent's suggestion that European accounts of Pacific cannibalism must insult the dignity of Islander peoples today, Sahlins had nothing but scorn.[33]

Fortunately, the rancor of the Sahlins-Obeyesekere exchange has since faded from prominence. Although unwavering in his commitment to the "genealogical exhumation" of cannibal texts, Obeyesekere has confessed that some such texts are "simply *impossible* to interpret."[34] Sahlins, confident that the attempt by "post-modernist types" to drown evidence of cannibalism in an "epistemic murk" had failed, reminds us simply that man-eating in the western Pacific was "always 'symbolic,' even when it [was] 'real.'"[35] Some of the most promising recent work on Oceanic cannibalism belongs to Tracey Banivanua-Mar. From her vantage point as a Fijian scholar at an Australian university, she has reconsidered the colonial context within which some of her ancestors may have consumed human flesh. Insofar as tales of Fijian cannibalism enabled colonial action, she reminds us, literary production and the application of military force became "irrevocably entwined." Thus, the "alterity" of man-eating—its profound strangeness—served to demonize indigenous Fijian resistance to British rule.[36]

Unlike modern anthropologists and historians disputing the purpose of "cannibal talk," British citizens of the eighteenth and early nineteenth centuries had no professional turf to defend. The generations that immediately preceded and followed Cook's voyages nonetheless carried on their own debates over man-eating. The changing depictions of anthropophagy in early editions of the *Encyclopaedia Britannica* help chart these debates. In its first edition (1768–1771), the *Britannica* offered enlightened skepticism: "It is greatly to be doubted if ever such a custom existed" on a widespread scale, readers learned. The underlying authority here was not Cook (whose first voyage only commenced in 1768) but rather William Dampier, whose *New Voyage Round the World* had appeared in 1688. At that time,

Dampier assured his public that he "did never meet with any such [cannibal] People."[37] By 1778, the *Britannica*'s second edition, which appeared well after the return of Cook's second voyage, had accepted the existence of cannibalism. Yet it was a relativistic acceptance, one that viewed man-eating as a common characteristic among societies at an early stage of their development.[38] Not until the third edition (1788–1797), however, did cannibalism acquire the meaning of a social danger, a class-based vice that threatened to destroy "the chief security of human life," namely respect for the person.[39] The *Britannica*'s third edition paid particular attention to evidence of distant cannibal practices among the Maori of New Zealand and the Battas of Sumatra. But it seems likely that dangerous folk much closer to home had heightened anxieties about the poor. Largely unrestrained, the Parisian mob of 1789 struck Burke as "reeking with . . . blood"—precisely the sort of murderous rage that was said to possess many South Sea man-eaters.[40]

Victorian editions of the *Britannica* not surprisingly played down the anarchic nature of cannibalism and played up its material basis. In the encyclopedia's ninth edition (1878), for example, ethnologist E.B. Tylor offered an evolutionary account of this custom. Since humans are by nature carnivorous, Tylor reasoned, what demanded explanation was not why people occasionally ate one another but instead why this behavior was not more common. Britain's leading armchair ethnologist identified six pressures that, singly or in combination, could induce humans to overcome the horror with which most societies regarded cannibalism. Chief among these pressures were famine, the "fury of hatred" against enemy tribes, and a "morbid kindness" reserved for dead kin.[41] The act had not lost its power to shock, certainly, but it was now being viewed as one of several savage customs destined to disappear before the advance of civilization.

A revived moral relativism accompanied this thinking. Herman Melville put the exculpatory case with memorable directness. In *Moby-Dick* (1851), he challenged his readers:

> Go to the meat-market of a Saturday night and see the crowds of live bipeds staring up at the long rows of dead quadrupeds. Does not that sight take a tooth out of the cannibal's jaw? Cannibals? [W]ho is not a cannibal? I tell you it will be more tolerable for the Fejee that salted down a lean missionary in his cellar against a coming famine; it will be more tolerable for the provident Fejee, I say, in the day of judgment, than for thee, civilized and enlight-

ened gourmand, who nailest geese to the ground and feastest on their bloated livers in thy paté-de-foie-gras.[42]

Melville was by no means alone in chiding those who would demonize the man-eater. R.L. Stevenson recognized that "nothing more strongly arouses our disgust than cannibalism." Yet:

> We consume the carcases of creatures of like appetites, passions, and organs with ourselves; we feed on babies, though not our own; and the slaughter-house resounds daily with screams of pain and fear. We distinguish, indeed, but the unwillingness of many nations to eat the dog . . . shows how precariously the distinction is grounded.[43]

The Scot Stevenson, like the American Melville, cautioned against condemnation based on a narrow acquaintance with the world. Such normalizing of humanity's most spectacular depravity could assume strange forms. Thus, one British colonial officer stationed in the western Pacific maintained that some cannibal tribes did not even qualify as savage. For he knew "inveterate" man-eaters who had proved "friendly and useful people to the whites."[44]

The pronouncements of colonial servants aside, how ordinary British citizens thought of cannibalism must be inferred from scattered shards of evidence. The immense popularity of Defoe's *Life and Strange Surprizing Adventures of Robinson Crusoe* must have focused public attention on the phenomenon of man-eating. Well over a century after its publication in 1719, even readers on the fringes of literacy continued to delight in the allegorical richness of this tale about epic individualism, the dignity of labor, and the weight of solitude. Over the course of two centuries, *Robinson Crusoe* went through literally hundreds of editions and abridgments.[45] Many contemporaries apparently knew that Defoe's novel built on accounts of real-life maroonings, notably that of a Scottish sailor named Alexander Selkirk, who had been stranded on a remote island in the eastern Pacific between 1704 and 1709.[46] But what seems to have captivated virtually all readers was the book's treatment of man-eating. As Dickens would later confess, when he thought of *Robinson Crusoe* he always thought of cannibals: cannibals chasing Friday across the creek, cannibals grounding their canoes on the beach.[47]

Readers searching for moral relativism in Defoe's story could find it. During one of his many mental debates, for example, Crusoe realizes that the cannibals who had shattered his illusions of safety ought not to be judged by civilized standards, since "They do not know it [man-eating] to be an Offence."[48] Yet it was this castaway's visceral fear that surely haunted most readers. After fifteen years alone on the island, Crusoe's discovery of a single footprint (wider than his own) in the sand terrified him "to the last degree." Later, finding a stretch of beach "spread with Skulls, Hands, Feet, and other Bones of humane Bodies" triggers an ineffable "Horror of . . . Mind," as well as violent vomiting. Crusoe may defer to God on moral judgments, but he quickly assumes the role of executioner when invading "monsters" prepare to kill and consume several of their prisoners, among them a European. Defoe spoke to a wide eighteenth-century audience when he explained that "Fear of Danger is ten thousand Times more terrifying than Danger itself."[49]

Robinson Crusoe has been aptly described as a colonial romance. After all, it recounts how a confirmed cannibal becomes a trusty servant to his white master; social progress occurs under the benign eye of a civilizing agent.[50] But the novel also invites a reading less supportive of colonial ambitions. Consider Friday. Reliable enough to bear firearms, this once-wild, now-docile creature nevertheless retains "the Relish of a Cannibal's Stomach." Crusoe manages, eventually, to wean Friday from his savage taste by substituting goat flesh for human. Friday's full rehabilitation is nevertheless slow and uncertain. A similar experience, this one purportedly "real," involved the American whaler Samuel Patterson, shipwrecked on a Fijian coast in 1808. Patterson reported that the "greediness" of the local Islanders for human meat was "astonishingly great." "[P]erhaps," he ventured, "there is no evil habit so hard to be eradicated as this inhuman one."[51] Patterson may or may not have read *Robinson Crusoe*. Indeed, he may not even have witnessed the cannibal greed he deplored. At the very least, though, Patterson had learned to view "native" behavior through the lens of appetite. The western Pacific in particular seemed to teem with people whose pacification by civilized authority would prove difficult.

British representations of cannibalism in the eighteenth century were not limited to novels. The imagery in William Hogarth's *The Four Stages of Cruelty* (1751) left little to the imagination. Plate four, "The Reward of Cruelty," depicts a murderer being dissected alive while at his feet a cauldron boils human skulls and bones into a ghastly broth. Georgian street literature—ballads, broadsides, chapbooks, and cartoons—lured plebeian readers with tales of legendary fiends. Of these, the career of one Sawney Beane held lasting interest. Supposedly a contemporary of Shakespeare, this Scottish brute found early on that he preferred robbing the unwary to toiling in the fields. What distinguished Beane from other highwaymen was the fate of his victims: all were killed, taken to his cave on the Galloway coast, and pickled for future enjoyment. Aided by a huge, incestuous progeny, he and his "cursed tribe" allegedly defied the law for a quarter century. It took King James himself and four hundred soldiers to end Beane's cannibalistic reign of terror.[52]

Thus, well before Britain's print industry began celebrating the discoveries of Captain Cook, a homegrown demand for news about man-eating had already been created. From the late eighteenth century onward, the two questions most often asked of Britons stationed in "primitive" lands were "Does cannibalism prevail?"; and if so, "Are any reasons assigned for it?"[53] This morbid curiosity about all things anthropophagous increasingly assumed a Pacific form. Melanesia appeared to contain a disproportionate share of the world's cannibals. There was also a geographic irony to be savored: Britain, a proud and self-consciously insular nation, soon found itself entangled with other Islanders whose savage pride appeared to be their ruin. "The King of the Cannibal Islands," a ballad at once comic and deeply racist, reflected the British public's desire to know the Pacific Other, but only within the confines of stereotype.

KING OF THE CANNIBAL ISLANDS

The rediscovery of Britain's "island-ness" was an eighteenth-century development closely linked to Cook's three voyages. That said, one needs only a passing familiarity with Shakespeare to know that the supposed relationship between insularity and national character long predated Cook's voyages. "[T]his sceptred isle," we know from *Richard II*, had been specially blessed because it was "set in the silver sea, Which serves it in the office of a wall, Or as a moat defensive to a house, against the envy of less happier lands."[54] Extending the metaphor, Britain's "wooden walls"—its navy—completed the defense that Providence had set in place.

Islands, of course, are never entirely insular. That is, islands exist in relation to other physical bodies such as seas, continents, and neighboring islands; they serve as the synapses in oceanic networks, making both trade and cultural exchange possible.[55] Despite the rapid spread of British commerce during the eighteenth century, however, an increasingly outward-looking people welcomed the fictions of insularity to explain their favored place among nations. As John Gillis has noted, the word "insularity" entered common usage around 1755, and at first carried none of the pejorative meaning that would later adhere to it. On the contrary, this word helped to anchor a renewed geographical determinism. William Falconer, a prosperous physician and prolific author, declared in 1781 that "The inhabitants of islands . . . have a higher relish for liberty than those of the continent; and therefore are, in general, free."[56] Borrowing from Montesquieu's reflections on terrain and law, Falconer explained why island living nurtured freedom: since tyranny often balked at crossing the sea, Islanders "preserve their laws more easily" than continental folk. Because islands tended to be cooler than continents, moreover, Falconer reckoned that denizens of the former were typically "less timid, indolent, and servile."[57]

It was presumably the confluence of an invigorating climate and a long seafaring tradition that yielded Captain Cook's practical "genius" for exploration. Georgian Britain's paragon of the island race, Cook offered an intriguing contrast between style and substance. His biographer reminds us that this matter-of-fact man—precise, even severe, in his approach to navigation—methodically "changed the face of the world."[58] That Cook's fame rested in part on charting South Sea islands whose savage inhabitants enjoyed none of the supposed benefits of insularity was an irony that escaped those who wished to canonize him. Perhaps the strangest homage was a play, actually a pantomime, entitled *Omai, or a Trip Round the World*, first performed at Covent Garden in December 1785. By then, the British reading public knew of Cook's fate in Hawai'i. This stage tribute reviewed the sainted captain's exploratory career—even though the title character, Omai, a Raiatean who reached London aboard HMS *Adventure* in mid-1774, had been the product of Cook's second voyage. As a specimen of the Pacific primitive, Omai had disappointed. For despite the exotic blackness of his "velvet skin," this South Sea visitor seemed so thoroughly "well bred" that no vestige of savagery clung to him. Still, an actor playing this now-familiar Polynesian joined a large and whimsical cast of characters who enlivened scene changes during the pantomime romance of Harlequin and his lover

Columbine. *Omai* provided a visual feast for audiences with its elaborate costumes, Tahitian landscapes, and wondrous flying balloon.[59] Through calculated contrast, then, the extravagance of this production would have reminded viewers of Cook's defining modesty.

The apotheosis of Captain Cook was serious business, even when it amused audiences. Less serious but likewise reflective of an emerging racial inventory of Pacific cultures was a ballad (and later a theatrical production) called *The King of the Cannibal Islands*. Published in 1830 by A.W. Humphreys, a London composer of topical parodies, it quickly became the key text in an accretion of popular images about cannibalism and the Pacific peoples allegedly addicted to it. Over time, the stereotypical cannibal would acquire specific physical features. In 1872, for example, *All the Year Round* imagined the classic man-eater as a "wild South Sea Islander, with face painted vermilion, a brass ring through his hideous nose, and the thigh-bone of a man stuck horizontally through his matted hair."[60] As of 1830, however, Humphreys had not yet embraced this stereotype. Nor did he write for the comfortable classes. He aimed instead to entertain the sort of common folk who bought cheap broadsides in the streets or frequented "saloon" theaters, concert-rooms, and lesser pantomime houses. The well-to-do people of Victorian times often sniffed at the "inanity" of these compositions. But broadside ballads, whether chanted by street performers called "patterers" or set to music indoors, remained very popular during the first half of the nineteenth century.[61]

Humphreys's ballads often did more than amuse. *The King of the Cannibal Islands* dressed mass murder in comic rhyme. Set to a tune known previously as "Vulcan's Cave," the ballad recounted the barbarism of a six-foot, six-inch Pacific island ruler named "Poonoowingkeewang Flibeedee-buskeebang." To feed one and all at a grand feast, this monstrous monarch ordered half his hundred wives to be roasted as the main course. The other fifty wives fared no better. Having dared to flee their husband's grotesque banquet, they lost their heads. A catchy chorus offered some relief from the gore:

Hookee pokee wongkee fum,
Puttee po pee kaibula cum,
Tongaree, wongaree, ching ree wum,
The King of the Cannibal Islands.[62]

Dirty, crude and vengeful, Humphreys's Pacific tyrant had nothing in common with the urbane Omai of Cook's day, save his blackness.

"Hookee pokee wongkee fum" would soon become a trigger line, a widely recognized code for rank savagery in a benighted sea of islands. Within a generation this ballad would penetrate popular culture throughout the English-speaking world. When in 1840 the Fijian chief Tanoa stepped aboard the flagship of American Lieutenant Charles Wilkes, a naval band struck up "King of the Cannibal Islands." (The insult presumably escaped Tanoa.) Dickens, on the other hand, aimed merely to amuse when he urged a friend to consult this Oceanic "Majesty."[63] Remnants of the ballad found their way into Melville's *Typee*, Thoreau's *Walden*, Joyce's *Ulysses*, and a best-selling crime novel; invaded pantomime productions of *Robinson Crusoe*; enriched a "travesty burlesque" of *Hamlet*; somehow seeped into the musical repertoire of a remote Mexican convent; and inspired a famous nursery rhyme.[64] The 1832 broadside catalog of James Catnach, then London's most prolific publisher of street ephemera, lists Humphreys's ballad as just one of some 720 "songs." Yet the imaginative hold it gained over citizens set it apart. Parodies of this parody appeared with remarkable speed. Among them, the "Queen of the Cannibal Islands" (1832) acknowledged the original's almost instant success:

> Oh, have you heard,—I'm sure you must,
> A song which on your ear has burst,
> . . . The King of the Cannibal Islands . . .
> Rich and poor, and old and young,
> It has taken root to every tongue.
> It told you of sad doings done,
> Of savage men and uncouth fun,
> But I'll tell you of another one,
> . . . The Queen of the Cannibal Islands.[65]

What might account for the original ballad's remarkable popularity?

Victorian commentators were themselves unsure about the inspiration for Humphreys's comic defamation of Pacific cultures. King George I of Tonga, who embraced Christianity and took an English name, struck one analyst as a likely model. But King George's conversion and his Anglicized name postdated the ballad's publication. Another authority observed that rumors emanating from any one of several Pacific island groups—Tonga, the Marquesas, the "Soo-loos," or the "Feejees"—could have caught the balladeer's notice.[66] A mix of distant sensations and local alarms would have encouraged the attribution of cannibal tendencies to these and other Islanders. Basil Thomson, a magistrate in Edwardian Fiji, proclaimed the miraculous escape of Peter Dillon from the clutches of Fiji's "Vilear people" as "the most dramatic passage in Polynesian literature."[67] Dillon was an experienced sea captain and trader who in 1812 joined an expedition to solve the mystery of La Pérouse's disappearance in the Pacific twenty-four years earlier. Dillon would eventually conclude that the French explorer and his ships had been wrecked on reefs in the Solomon Islands. What probably left a deeper impression on readers of Dillon's narrative, however, was his harrowing account of holding out against a horde of crazed man-eaters (Figure 1.1). Their ammunition exhausted and the prospect of torture imminent,

MASSACRE AT THE FEJEE ISLANDS IN SEPTR 1823.
Dreadful Situation of Capt Dillon and the two other Survivors

Figure 1.1   Peter Dillon and two white companions witness the cannibal rites of Fiji's "Vilear people" in 1823.

SOURCE: Dillon, *Narrative . . . of a Voyage in the South Seas* (1829). Courtesy, University of Washington Libraries, Special Collections.

Dillon and his two European friends considered suicide. But before all hope vanished, their capture of a cannibal "priest" allowed them to bargain for freedom. The besieging Islanders of Vilear Bay embodied savagery in its most brutal form. Dillon knew this to be true because he claimed to have watched from his hillside redoubt the baking and eating of several prisoners. Being taken alive terrified Dillon above all else, for the "cannibal monsters" surrounding him allegedly enjoyed skinning the soles of their victims' feet and slicing away their eyelids before turning them to face the tropical sun.[68]

It may well be true, as one modern skeptic has insisted, that Dillon's tale served as a form of self-invention rather than qualifying as credible ethnography.[69] What matters most for our purposes, though, is the timing of Dillon's revelations. Not published until 1829, his lurid narrative would have been newly available to the balladeer Humphreys just as he was conjuring *The King of the Cannibal Islands.*

Coincidentally, that same year saw a widely reported panic seize the inmates of one East London workhouse. A recently admitted pauper had smuggled into the facility details of the first Anatomy Bill in Parliament—details that suggested to his apprehensive audience that they might soon be legally compelled to satisfy the hunger of predatory anatomists. This rumormongering pauper also denounced his workhouse lunch: the broth, he believed, contained human remains along with bits of kitten and donkey.[70] As hysterical as these fears over "Natomy Soup" may seem today, they reflected a pervasive fear among the poor that doctors in particular and the rich more generally had unleashed a new weapon in an unfolding class war. The residents of the workhouse at St. Paul's, Shadwell, worried that they had been tricked into cannibalism by cruel Poor Law functionaries. We cannot know whether A.W. Humphreys learned of the paupers' fears through the *Morning Chronicle*'s reportage. We may reasonably speculate, however, that like Peter Dillon's narrow escape from Fijian man-eaters, the 1829 "Natomy Soup" panic would have invited translation into broadsides and ballads.

Indeed, the idea of cannibalism, freighted as it was with such dangerous states as desperation, vengeance, and total loss of restraint, found many applications in Victorian culture. Thomas Carlyle, for instance, chose cannibal imagery to dramatize the hazards of a meager peasant diet. Carlyle hinted that if scarcity continued to stalk English laborers, they might one day resort—as the "squalid" Irish poor had supposedly done before—to eating one another.[71] The New Poor Law, still more than the Old, found itself condemned through anthropophagous association. Thus, at the center of the 1845 Andover workhouse scandal lurked the specter of man-eating. Chronic semi-starvation had reportedly driven its inmates to gnaw the rancid animal bones that had been supplied to them for grinding into fertilizer. Worse, these bone shipments "occasionally" contained churchyard remains. Such desperation served to invert the Malthusian model of causation, for at Andover it appeared that heartless Poor Law officials, not feckless paupers, had caused this sorry state of affairs.[72]

Whereas "accidental cannibalism" (as these incidents were often labeled) involved unwitting victims, newspaper reports of "cannibal" violence in public emphasized the ungovernable fury of the rougher classes. Anticipating by forty years William Booth's "Darkest England" exposé, *The Times* in 1850 noted that "Wilder and more uncultivated savages do not exist in any part of Africa than are to be found within a few miles of our own homes." Entitled simply "Cannibalism," this short notice recounted a beer-house brawl near Halifax in which the aggressor had chewed a four-inch hole in his victim's cheek and then bit off his nose.[73] Body parts need not have been chewed and swallowed for the "cannibal" designation to adhere. Severe finger- and breast-biting allegedly predominated among women, whereas men favored noses, cheeks, and ears. More often than not alcohol fueled these assaults, which would explain why restraint vanished during them. Impulsiveness therefore linked the "real" man-eaters of hot climates with their less lethal if no less "vicious" cousins among the home island's poor.[74] Such rhetorical affiliation created what might be termed a savage feedback loop wherein monsters local and distant constantly referenced one another. They were, in this sense, mutually constituent.

The circulation of cannibal images between temperate core and tropical periphery might at first glance appear to have involved mainly marginal actors. Dietary reformers, for example, made frequent use of cannibal tropes. As early as the 1730s, the nerve doctor George Cheyne had urged his patients to purge their diets of flesh; meat-eaters, Cheyne believed, were all potential cannibals.[75] A generation later, the militant vegetarian Joseph Ritson left even less room for doubt: "those accustom'd to eat the brute, should not abstain from the man," especially "when toasted or broil'd."[76] (One wonders how Ritson knew.) While British vegetarians continued to warn of the slippery slope separating meat-eating from man-eating, other iconoclasts turned the forbidden act into a bohemian badge of honor. London's "Cannibal

Club," founded in 1863, brought together such cultural contrarians as the explorer and orientalist Richard Burton, the atheist Charles Bradlaugh, and the "decadent" poet Algernon Swinburne to drink heavily and subvert Victorian convention. Discussions of pornography, anthropology, and Christian doctrine enlivened meetings—whose chairman kept order by banging on the floor a mace decorated with the figure of an African gnawing a human thighbone.[77] By the close of the nineteenth century, it was even possible to depict cannibalism as an engine of evolutionary progress. For in the struggle to survive, killers of their own kind must have possessed special "ferocity and brutality," attributes essential to the emergence of a "dominant race."[78]

Yet cannibal imagery suffused not only these cultural back channels but also the British mainstream. And it was the ocean, an island's captor as well as its shield, that most often abetted the man-eater. Shipwrecks provided the classic cannibal setting. On some remote shores, as in some boats set adrift, desperate white men could be forced to butcher and consume their weakest members. "Survival cannibalism" had comic potential. Thackeray's "Little Billee," his 1845 parody of a traditional French song ("La Courte Paille"— "the Short Straw"), featured three English sailors who, on reaching the equator, find they have nothing left to eat but a single split pea. The youngest of this desperate trio, Little Billee, having drawn the short straw, spies a rescue ship moments before becoming nourishment for "fat Jack" and "guzzling Jimmy."[79] Victorian Britain's most famous case of survival cannibalism, however, drew few smiles. In 1884, the yacht *Mignonette* foundered in an Atlantic gale somewhere south of the line. Its small crew barely had time to cast off in a dinghy. When their pitiful food supply—two pounds of tinned turnips plus the meat of a turtle—gave out, three grown men reluctantly killed and ate the cabin boy, who appeared to be at death's door in any case. Because this terrible act had clearly been the consequence of extreme want, the British public tended to sympathize with the survivors during their subsequent trial. Hastening another's death, that trial determined, meant murder all the same. The defendants ultimately received pardons from Queen Victoria, but not before the moral boundaries of what one journal oxymoronically termed "civilized cannibalism" had been closely reviewed.[80]

Shipwrecks in the nineteenth century, as Brian Simpson reminds us, warranted close press coverage because, like airplane crashes today, they could destroy large numbers of people at one time: "Disasters at Sea" was not by chance a regular news category in *The Times*.[81] But shipwrecks that featured nonwhite man-eaters evoked a very different set of assumptions. And such racialized predation did much to harden stereotypes of Pacific Islanders as the world's most savage people. Granted, not all reports of flesh-craving Islanders withstood scrutiny. For instance, the wreck of the brig *Sterling Castle* in 1836, off what is today Queensland's southeastern coast, gave rise to a tale of female pluck that proved too good to be true. Eliza Fraser, the pregnant English wife of the ship's Scottish captain, was reportedly beaten, burned, and used as target practice for indigenous boomerangs. Unlike a few of her fellow "captives," however, Mrs. Fraser was not roasted over an Aboriginal fire. Rescued after a six-week ordeal, she returned to Sydney, whose kind citizens presented her with the substantial sum of £400. Upon reaching Britain, Eliza's now-thoroughly rehearsed tale of woe fetched a further subscription of £553—charity that the Lord Mayor soon wished he had not encouraged.[82] Increasingly, the Aboriginal peoples of coastal Queensland looked to be the aggrieved party.

In the majority of cases, however, the grim fates that reportedly befell those shipwrecked on Pacific shores aroused less skepticism. Thus, the only survivors of the *Charles Eaton*, a merchant vessel that in 1836 ran aground on a Torres Strait reef, were two English "lads." The rest of the crew, they claimed, had been beheaded, their skulls used to decorate a heathen idol.[83] James Oliver, a sailor aboard the Salem trader *Glide*, published in 1848 a detailed account of Fijian cannibal lust. His ship having been blown over in a storm off the island of Vanua Levu, Oliver found unwelcome free time to observe such "horrible" rites as the spinning of the "sacred cocoa-nut" to determine which strangers would be eaten. Gananath Obeyesekere has specified several grounds upon which to doubt the accuracy of Oliver's narrative. Published in London as well as New York, *The Wreck of the Glide* nevertheless would have confirmed popular assumptions about Islander appetites.[84]

For sheer scale of horror, though, priority must go to the loss of the *St. Paul* at Rossel Island in late September 1858. There, 140 miles off the southeastern tip of New Guinea, 326 Chinese "coolies" being carried from Hong Kong to Sydney struggled ashore as their ship sank. The captain and eight of his crew set out promptly to get help, which they eventually received from French officials on New Caledonia. But when the French steamer *Styx* reached Rossel Island four months after the *St. Paul*'s sinking, just one man remained to describe the methodical slaughter of his countrymen and women: carefully guarded by night, the "coolies" dreaded morning, when a few at a time would be clubbed, gutted, roasted, and eaten. From Sydney, news of this catastrophe spread to London, to Britain's provincial cities, and finally to Paris.[85] This "wholesale butchery" had been so thorough that several decades after the reported slaughter, British colonial administrators would feel compelled to visit the island and interrogate its people. Sir William MacGregor preferred to believe what some "natives" told him in 1888: that most of the marooned Chinese had built rafts that they launched in a northerly direction (the only direction possible at that season). Twenty years later, Hubert Murray found few grounds for MacGregor's optimism. "The whole incident is a depressing one," Murray allowed, "and I should like to think it was untrue, but I am afraid I cannot. Every one comes out of [the incident] so badly"—even the lone eyewitness who would later be arrested for selling liquor without a license.[86] Given these contradictory findings, it is unsurprising that as late as 1934 a chronicler of British rule in the Pacific could still brand Rossel "The World's Worst Cannibal Island."[87]

Some Enlightenment intellectuals, Diderot chief among them, saw islands blessed with tropical abundance as "natural" sites for cannibalism. After all, abundance bred overpopulation, and overpopulation summoned into existence various natural "checks" to reproduction such as infanticide and man-eating. Whether cannibalism was "insular in origin," as Diderot supposed,[88] remained a matter for conjecture. Much less theoretical was the nineteenth-century European tendency to juxtapose Pacific island beauty with the supposed habits of the Islanders themselves. For R.L. Stevenson, the "flamboyant" flora of the Marquesas could never quite expunge the "ominous" realization that man-eating had once flourished there.[89] And the western Pacific isles were deemed to be addicted still to this wretchedness. By the 1860s, *The King of the Cannibal Islands* called to mind a geographical realm far more distinct than had the ballad of 1830.

CANNIBAL LATITUDES

In the generation after Cook's death, Britons came to associate cannibalism with heat, primitive social organization, and southern latitudes. There were of course noteworthy exceptions. Man-eating had not always been a tropical phenomenon, for example. One prominent ethnologist believed that cannibalism was a "Stone-Age" custom, and that the ancient Scots, whose land had never seen a coconut palm, were probably keen consumers of human meat.[90] Nor did it always follow that the earth's most "primitive" peoples ate one another. The indigenous Tasmanians, reportedly too backward to survive in a modern world, nonetheless expressed "great horror" at the mention of cannibalism.[91] When calculating "grades of atrocity," moreover, most Britons would have agreed with Hume Nisbet that cannibal acts paled beside the villainies of Jack the Ripper.[92]

These exceptions noted, the Victorian mappers of human depravity spent a good deal of time and energy locating earth's anthropophagous center. That center was indeed tropical, but it did not lie in Africa, as Europe's preoccupation with the savage nature of black-skinned people might suggest. African cannibalism in the nineteenth century was entwined with the continent's seemingly endless expanse of jungle. It served William Booth's purpose to dwell on the unrelieved gloom of Africa's rain forests. This vast darkness, in H.M. Stanley's account, bore no resemblance to the pleasant shade of an English oak on a warm summer's day. "General" Booth was quick to connect Africa's deadly umbrage with the unenlightened conduct of its people:

> In all that spirited narrative . . . nothing has so much impressed the imagination, as [Stanley's] description of the immense forest, which offered an almost impenetrable barrier to his advance. The intrepid explorer, in his own phrase, "marched, tore, ploughed, and cut his way for one hundred and sixty days through this inner womb of the true tropical forest." The mind of man with difficulty endeavours to realize this immensity of wooded wilderness, covering a territory half as large again as the whole of France, where the rays of sun never penetrate, where in the dark, dank air, filled with the steam of the heated morass, human beings dwarfed into pygmies and brutalised into cannibals lurk and live and die.[93]

Booth, cofounder of the Salvation Army, went on to depict the brutalized denizens of "Darkest England." Stanley himself shared little of Booth's evangelical zeal; the explorer instead focused on advertising his transcontinental slog. Intriguingly, he reported stumbling upon preparations for a "cannibal dinner" near the Ituri River, a tributary of the Congo. He was generally eager to emphasize the "devilish malice" of the jungle folk whom his party encountered.[94]

Both before and after Stanley's epic treks became famous, the presumed existence of cannibalism in Africa fascinated armchair ethnologists. The French-American zoologist Paul Du Chaillu spent much of the late 1850s hacking his way through the "gloomy solitude" of West African jungles in what is today Gabon. Roughly 50 miles from the coast Du Chaillu made contact with a people then nearly unknown to Europeans, the Fan. Tall, strong, and intelligent, the Fan warriors characteristically filed their teeth, giving them "a ghastly and ferocious look." Although Du Chaillu claimed to respect these forest dwellers, he seasoned his widely read narrative with the news that Fan men were "regular ghouls" who ate corpses.[95] This zoologist never actually witnessed the custom he condemned. Nor, much to his regret, did Richard Burton, who explained that this curious form of cannibalism occurred "secretly." The mere rumor of corpse eating was enough, however, to confirm Burton's racial presumption—that there was in the "African brain" an impulse to destroy.[96]

By century's end, the list of African man-eaters had lengthened as European commercial interests pushed inland. Officials of the Royal Niger Company treated the discovery of human remains near Akassa in 1895 as proof that a "cannibal feast" had been celebrated there. Better publicized was the Congo basin, whose remote interior featured "the wildest cannibal country to be found anywhere." In late 1898, news reached Belgium that four agents of the Antwerp Trading Company had been killed and eaten on the Upper Ubangi River. Judging by the absence of further comment on this "massacre," neither Belgian nor British officials found it surprising. For as the British Association had learned three years earlier from Captain G.L. Hinde ("a traveller of the bold fighting type"), the Congo's black tribes carried on a brisk traffic in human flesh.[97] Reformers such as missionaries John and Alice Harris compiled a damning photographic record of King Leopold II's Congo Free State, a colony whose police and private "rubber sentries" were beginning to earn international infamy. What the humanitarians' photos could not capture, though, was the psychic impact of colonial terror. Thus, as news of Belgian atrocities spread among the Congolese, a myth gained credence that the tins of corned beef seen in European homes actually contained chopped-up hands.[98]

Still, the volume of references to African cannibalism paled beside that of the Pacific. Both locales attracted European explorers, missionaries, and voyeurs. Writing in the early 1860s, W.W. Reade could have been referring to New Guinea rather than equatorial Africa when he described his leisurely aims: "to *flaner* in the virgin forest; to flirt with pretty savages; and to smoke [a] cigar among cannibals."[99] But Old World toffs such as Reade followed in the wake of explorers and missionaries. And these earlier agents of European culture turned their attention to the indigenous people of Oceania first. Completing the ethnographic map that Captain Cook had painstakingly drawn in outline became an enterprise at once patriotic and salvific.

Some of the widely scattered islands of Polynesia, where Cook began his ethnographic survey, certainly harbored cannibals. Why some Polynesian cultures practiced man-eating while others did not was a question that perplexed nineteenth-century students of race theory. The boldest answer involved New Zealand. The Maori, as their language and physical appearance made plain, were racially Polynesian. Their anthropophagous ways, however, could not easily be attributed to ancestral custom alone, since in the eastern Pacific hub of Polynesian culture, cannibalism was far from universal. Instead, vast distance appeared to be the explanatory key for New Zealand. Enormously long voyages through open ocean must often have exhausted food supplies. It seemed to follow, therefore, that "absolute necessity" had driven the first Maori voyagers to cannibalism at sea. Necessity begat habit.[100]

Why Polynesian island groups far to the east did, or did not, countenance man-eating received less imaginative speculation. Tahiti and the Society Islands greeted the first European ships with nearly naked "maidens" but no trace of the fiendish hunger. By contrast, the Marquesas group, located some 850 miles northeast of Tahiti, clung to its cannibal traditions until repeated French naval bombardments in the 1860s and 70s discouraged the custom.[101] Sailing southwest from Tahiti, nineteenth-century ships often replenished food and water at Raratonga, largest of the Cook Islands group. Here, too, cannibalism persisted until the late 1840s, during which decade intense missionary pressure successfully demonized it.[102] Still further west, where Polynesian and Melanesian peoples began to mix, both Samoa and Tonga stood accused of owning cannibal pasts.[103]

A ship sailing east across the Indian Ocean toward the South Pacific would have passed by more man-eating lands en route to Sydney. Australia did not at first strike Europeans as cannibal country. Kay Schaffer notes in her study of the Eliza Fraser captivity stories that, prior to the late 1820s, "It is difficult to find even one reference to native cannibalism in the local

Australian press." But as white settlement expanded west, beyond the Blue Mountains, the *Sydney Gazette* began to publish letters from settlers who "confirmed" indigenous cannibalism. Such reports helped to justify "colonial practices of extermination."[104] George Angas, a self-styled "disinterested observer" of ethnographic curiosities, embellished these accounts. Angas assured his readers in 1847 that the interior of New South Wales contained savages who routinely devoured the bodies of their dead friends and relatives. A generation later, his outback ghouls would serve to support J.G. Frazer's landmark analysis of totemism.[105] So comfortably did the idea of Australian man-eating sit with late-Victorian readers that Carl Lumholtz's fictive study of North Queensland Aborigines, *Among Cannibals* (1889), could dazzle both *The Spectator* and the *Edinburgh Review*.[106]

Separated from the northern tip of Queensland by the reef-strewn Torres Strait, New Guinea hid man-eaters who posed a greater threat to unwary sailors. Some never made it past the beach. Given such welcomes, early European navigators approached the New Guinea mainland with great caution. Protestant missionaries, who later established spiritual beachheads along this huge island's southeastern shore, portrayed the threat of attack as proof of New Guinea's heathen depravity. But the good news, these godly pioneers assured their backers, was that even cannibals could be won for Christ.[107] A similar blend of moral condemnation and evangelical optimism flavored the missionary accounts of New Ireland and New Britain, two long, jungle-clad islands lying off New Guinea's northeastern shore. British and Australian Methodists wrote often about the cannibal atrocities of these remote peoples.[108]

Once a ship had cleared the Torres Strait and entered the Coral Sea, more savagery awaited. To the northeast stretched the Solomon archipelago, better known in Europe for its headhunters than for its cannibals.[109] Alternatively, a course bearing east by southeast might have brought three notorious island groups into view: New Caledonia, the New Hebrides, and Fiji. It is noteworthy that the Pacific's man-eating centers, New Zealand excepted, lay in a narrow band between the equator and the Tropic of Capricorn (the southernmost location where the sun can shine directly overhead). What could be termed the cannibal latitudes thus suggested an imaginary geographic and cultural coherence within Oceania. Having long since embraced the homogenizing term "South Seas," most Britons were disposed to regard Pacific cannibalism as a lamentable triumph of race over place. A newspaper review of John Coulter's Pacific *Adventures* (1847) noted the morbid enthusiasm for man-eating in an earthly "paradise":

> The prevalence of cannibalism in the islands of the Pacific, especially those lying between the tropics, is fearfully . . . proved by this book. . . . The fruits of the earth abound in these islands, the domestic animals have multiplied *ad infinitum,* among these people; the sea teams with fish of which the natives are expert snarers; . . . and yet these savages still banquet on the bodies of their fellow men. . . .[110]

In reality, prior to the 1770s, most of these Islanders would never have seen a land mammal larger than a rat or a fruit bat.

The cannibal latitudes contained nearly all of what Europe's racial classifiers had been calling "Melanesia" since the 1830s. While recognizing the cultural diversity within this classification, Victorian ethnographers—and the travel writers who raided ethnography for sensational details—persisted in its use. As late as 1911 the *Encyclopaedia Britannica* could assert that "certain common characteristics" set Melanesians apart from other Pacific peoples:

> Their civilization is lower. The Melanesians are mostly "negroid," nearly black, with crisp, curly hair elaborately dressed; their women hold a much lower position than among the Polynesians; their initiations, social, political and religious, are simpler their manners ruder; they have few or no traditions; cannibalism, in different degrees, is almost universal; but their artistic skill and taste . . . are remarkable, and they are amenable to discipline and fair treatment.[111]

This unflattering profile would endure across very different forms of colonial government in Melanesia.

New Caledonia, which served as a French penal colony between 1863 and 1896, had to contend with a serious uprising of "Kanak" clans in 1878. The need to kill over a thousand of these rebels did not cause French officials to rethink their heavy-handed dose of "civilization"; the inveterate savagery (and presumed cannibalism) of the *indigènes* was to blame. Tales of enthusiastic man-eating, Bronwen Douglas notes, had an "explosive" impact on the early French visitors to New Caledonia. Most of the 4,500 Communards exiled following the ill-fated Paris Commune of 1871 found the Islanders no more *sympathique.*[112]

A similar preoccupation with the "terrible hunger" was evident in nineteenth-century accounts of the New Hebrides island group. As will be discussed in the next chapter, the 1839 slaughter of British missionary John Williams on an Erromango beach did much to vilify the entire archipelago. Williams's martyrdom was of course far from the first proof of New Hebridean "treachery." As British evangelizing societies never tired of reminding their patrons, ever since Captain Cook encountered the hostile folk of Erromango and Tanna in 1774, "a fatality ha[d] attached" to these and their neighboring islands.[113] "Barbarous," "depraved," "disgusting," "horrid," and "execrable": such were the adjectives routinely used to describe the people of the New Hebrides.[114] There were mitigating circumstances, to be sure. "Humanitarians," as they anointed themselves, insisted that white sandalwood hunters and sea slug collectors had shot their way to profits, leaving these Islanders thirsting for revenge. Such considerations could not erase the cannibal stain, however. What saved the New Hebrides from coming first on the league table of savagery was Fiji.

Located at the eastern edge of Melanesia, the Fijian archipelago impressed most Europeans as the citadel of man-eating. Its distance from Britain helped harden rumor into fact. That is, the interval between the alleged commission of a cannibal act and its exposure in a British newspaper (or government office) rendered a careful examination of the original allegation nearly impossible. Until 1872, there was no telegraphic communication between Britain and Australia. Prior to that date, and to the opening of the Suez Canal in late 1869, it took between sixty and eighty days for a letter posted in London to reach Sydney. Depending on the sailing schedules of the small ships that called at Fijian ports, another month could easily be added to this journey. Thus occupying the "back of beyond," as a former colonial servant put it, Fiji was a place where knowledge was the sum of temporal disruption, self-replicating gossip, and outright fantasy. These elements of "truth" acquired what Edward Said has termed a "sheer knitted-together strength" when circulated simultaneously.[115]

Some basic features of Fiji's pre-colonial past remain unclear. For example, we cannot be certain about this island group's population on the eve of European settlement, although an estimate of 150,000 seems plausible. We are further still from knowing the extent and frequency of cannibal acts. Where internecine war led to the sacking of large towns, such as when Bau warriors overran Rewa in December 1845, hundreds might die—yielding more bodies (*bakola*) than could be eaten at one time. "Lust" and "addiction" were the most common characterizations of Fiji's defining habit. Yet even allowing for hyperbole, a few of these Islanders do appear to have been formidable eaters. The infamous chief of Rakiraki, Ratu Udreudre, alone consumed 872 people, or so the Methodist missionary Richard Lyth claimed.[116]

It is not the case, as modern skeptics have implied, that nineteenth-century reports of Fijian cannibalism were invariably expressions of cultural loathing. On the contrary, a good deal of this literature sought to exculpate, or at least relativize, Fiji's man-eating tradition. Before consigning these Islanders to "perpetual barbarism," argued Captain John Erskine in 1853, Britain's reading public ought to recall the fearful deeds of Alexander Pearce. A petty criminal from the North of Ireland, Pearce had been transported to Van Dieman's Land, where, during the early 1820s, he escaped into the bush four times. Lacking food (except, on one occasion, for his kangaroo skin coat, which he ate), this fiend "banqueted" on six fellow escapees, three of whom Pearce hacked into meal-size portions. His widely reported confession and execution at Hobart Town in November 1823 had shown that a taste for human flesh was not limited to certain dark races.[117] The Fijians, other defenders observed, were "manly," intelligent, and, for the most part, "kind." Their political system, "hallowed by age and tradition," derived its legitimacy from a "gentry" class; despots (as in Humphreys's comic ballad) violated indigenous ideals of good government.[118] Indeed, cannibalism itself may have been an alien practice. One British colonial administrator with long experience in the archipelago suggested that ancient strangers from Tonga had introduced both cannibalism and the art of war to Fiji.[119]

It is nevertheless true that the European critics of Fijian customs made more noise. Their denunciations held that these Islanders were not mere man-eaters but "inveterate" man-eaters. Fijian parents supposedly took care to ensure that a taste for *bakola* was acquired early on in life: these "unnatural" mothers and fathers rubbed "human flesh over the lips of their little children" and placed juicy bits in their mouths.[120] Fijian cannibalism tended to be fixed within a matrix of savage customs, among them infanticide, widow-strangling, live burial, and the ceremonial mutilation of fingers and ears. The "curious" conceits of these people served to heighten their moral perversity. Thus, the care lavished on chiefly hairstyles only underscored these leaders' callous disregard for the bodies of others. Similarly, the ceremonial subtleties associated with the exchange of whales' teeth (*tabua*) stood in revealing contrast to a wild enthusiasm for battle.[121] Beautifully carved war clubs owned "high-sounding" names (e.g., *Kadiga ni damuni*: "Damaged beyond hope") for their low purpose. So-called "cannibal forks" (*iculunibakola*) fascinated the Victorian public, linking as they seemingly did artifact with wretched practice.[122]

The manner in which these Islanders were maligned had consequences. Consider the British missionary agenda. The Methodist pioneers stipulated that the Fijians' "moral malady" was "deplorable" but "not incurable."[123] Such calibration of defect was essential. For if portrayed as either too degraded or not degraded enough, this mission field stood to lose vital public support. As Patrick Brantlinger rightly notes, there is no evidence that British missionaries in the Pacific "suffered from some sort of collective delusion about cannibalism." Yet it is also true that Victorian evangelists, whether toiling in Melanesia or slumming in London, tended to regard truth as that which led sinners to God's saving grace, rather than as the sum of secular evidence.[124] A thin line also separated courtesy from aggression in the conduct of ships visiting Fiji. After spending nearly two peaceful months cruising among these islands in 1840, the American Exploring Expedition received a sudden shock. On 3 July, responding to a request for proof of man-eating, canoes from the Naloa Bay village of Fokasinga came alongside the USS *Peacock*. The villagers had brought the freshly roasted arms and legs of an enemy, his limbs arranged on a bed of plantain leaves. It was no coincidence that soon thereafter a quarrel over ownership of a wrecked American cutter escalated into the burning of villages, the payback murder of Commander Wilkes's own nephew, and ultimately, the slaughter of over a hundred Malolo people. Wilkes had taught the cannibals what he termed a "salutary lesson." That lesson, in turn, convinced Britain's naval establishment to issue sailing instructions urging the "greatest circumspection" when dealing with Pacific Islanders.[125]

Fijian cannibalism therefore emerged early on as a political as well as a moral question for Islanders and white visitors alike. After Fiji became a British crown colony in 1874, indigenous resistance to that colonial government assumed the form that white men had done so much to decry. The rebels, as we will see, both embraced, and were demonized by, the "cannibal" name.

MEASLES, MOUNTAINEERS, AND COLONIAL DISCIPLINE

It is strange yet true to say that Fijian cannibalism was "known" to Europe before Europeans knew these islands. In 1643, the Dutch navigator Abel Tasman sighted, but dared not explore, a part of the archipelago: foul weather and lethal reefs had made Tasman wary. Over 140 years would pass before the next European arrivals, Cook and the crew of the *Resolution*, learned anything about "Fidgee." In early July 1774, Cook's flagship anchored off a coral speck in the Lau group, naming it Turtle Island (Vatoa). Several Islanders clutching clubs and spears could be seen ashore. A few crewmembers landed on the islet, staying only long enough to leave a knife and some nails. Cook sailed away the next day, having recorded in his journal that these Islanders seemed "a Docile people."[126]

The captain did not then realize that he had brushed the southeastern fringe of Fiji. If Cook *had* understood where he was, it is unlikely that he would have sent sailors ashore to greet armed savages. After all, the people of Tonga—which island cluster the *Resolution* would visit on several occasions, the first in October 1773—had warned him that the Fijians were inveterate cannibals. Cook actually met several of these formidable people in Tonga. They looked "a full shade darker than any of the other islanders," and did not deny their man-eating custom. Cook wondered, "[W]hat it is that induceth them to keep it [cannibalism] up in the midst of plenty?" One fact at least was certain: the Tongans to whom Cook spoke dreaded their martial neighbors.[127] William Bligh, the *Resolution*'s sailing master on Cook's third voyage, also took these warnings to heart. Therefore, in 1789, when Bligh and the nonmutinous remnant of his crew were set adrift in an open boat, the prospect of becoming a meal ranked high among his fears. Wherever he could, Bligh steered clear of large islands. (In fact, the wide passage between Fiji's two largest islands is still known as "Bligh Water.") And when local "sailing cannoes" began chasing him on 7 May, Bligh gave the "out oars" command "to get from them."[128] Fiji's grim reputation reached a far broader audience when Cook's journals became best sellers back home.

Captain Cook's secondhand observations of Fijian man-eating launched a publishing competition among supposed witnesses to this horror. The ships of sandalwood hunters, whalers, and *bêche-de-mer* collectors brought men eager to malign the Islanders. Right behind the first trading vessels came the missionaries, most of them British and nearly all Methodist. These godly men and women proved particularly skilled at defamation. The Reverend Walter Lawry, supervisor of Methodist missions in New Zealand, spoke for many of his agents when he branded Fiji's people "the most barbarous and hateful of human beings."[129] White visitors to Fiji could not agree on what motivated man-eating there. A hunger for revenge appeared to be one powerful inducement, although that hunger was not the "patient" hatred that allegedly expressed itself as scalp taking among North America's "Red Indians."[130] Then again, perhaps barbarism was the inevitable product of a society that had endured the "double yoke" of chiefs and priests. The pioneering sociologist Herbert Spencer thought so, citing Fiji as the "extremist" form of despotic rule. Where slaves were buried alive in postholes to consecrate a chief's new dwelling, or where their living bodies served as "rollers" over which heavy war canoes were dragged up the beach, could cannibalism fail to follow?[131]

Such reasoning, or rather imagining, united missionaries, traders, and drawing room ethnologists. The island stories reaching Britain did not agree about how bodies for eating were served, or which morsels went to those of high rank. Sahlins sums up what little can be generalized about Fijian man-eating: people of all ages and both genders were consumed; chopped-up body parts were typically cooked overnight in underground ovens; and a "priest" presided over these preparations.[132] Nor did European reports settle on the number of victims sent to the ovens each year. Writing at midcentury, Rev. Thomas Williams, for thirteen years a keen observer of Fijian customs, estimated that the total loss of life from fighting of all sorts ranged between 1,500 and 2,000 persons per year. These figures, Williams added, did not include the widows who were strangled upon the passing of their chiefly husbands. What percentage of these war dead ended up being baked, Williams does not say. But he does reckon, counterintuitively, that the introduction of firearms to Fiji during the first decade of the nineteenth century "tended to diminish" fighting: because bullets are promiscuous, striking chiefs as well as commoners, the former began to pick their fights more carefully.[133]

Other observers, though, emphasized the ease with which ceremonial requirements could trigger deadly disputes. On the basis of Rev. David Cargill's account of the Bau-Verata war of 1839, Fergus Clunie notes that the hunt for human sacrifices needed to celebrate the erection of a single spirit-house quickly escalated into a regional conflict that killed around 350 Islanders. Bullet-averse chiefs notwithstanding, the 1850s found Fiji highly unstable, Tongan rulers threatening invasion from without while local chiefs skirmished within. The state of Fijian society was "frightful," remarked an English ship's captain in 1853: "No man moves . . . for any cause whatever without his club."[134]

It would be wrong nonetheless to imply that such self-destruction finally convinced Britain to annex Fiji in 1874. British government officials took care to characterize this act as a "cession"—a reluctant yielding to Fijian pleas for intervention—rather than as adventurism. The anti-colonial mood still palpable in Britain encouraged such distinctions. But a complex amalgam of guilt, pressure from white settlers, and wishful thinking undergirded the Cession. Britain's humanitarian activists frequently reminded their fellow citizens that white "beachcombers" had done much to roil Fijian society. Beginning about 1804, it was said, escaped convicts from New South Wales, some carrying muskets, had sold their services to rival Fijian rulers. These mercenaries, according to one missionary, were "regarded as monsters even by the ferocious cannibals with whom they associated."[135] Fiji's most demonic beachcomber was a shipwrecked sailor who bore the all-too-appropriate surname of Savage. How much he contributed to the rise of Bau as a regional power remains in dispute. Still, British humanitarians insisted that Charles Savage and his ilk left Fiji more "vindictive and cruel" than they had found it.[136] Residual guilt over their nation's role in the degradation of these isles thus drove some Britons to urge annexation as a form of penance.

But more numerous were the white settlers in Australia and New Zealand who worried about geopolitics. Imperial inaction, they feared, would encourage foreign meddling in the archipelago. At the center of uncertainty stood the enigmatic Thakombau. Named "Seru" at his birth in 1817, this son of Tanoa, chief of Bau, mastered the art of revenge at an early age. Violence surrounded him. A chiefdom whose capital was a tiny, twenty-acre islet located a mile off the southeastern coast of Viti Levu, Bau had long skirmished against such neighboring states as Rewa and Verata. Seru was about fifteen when rebels forced his father into exile and murdered most of his family. Deemed too young to pose a threat, the boy began plotting against the rebels. Five years later he not only restored Tanoa to power but also devised

THAKOMBAU, KING OF FIJI.

Figure 1.2   Sketch of Thakombau, the so-called "King of Fiji."
SOURCE: *Illustrated Melbourne Post* (23 December 1865).

gruesome lessons in loyalty. A widely circulated story, for example, told of a rebel prisoner whose tongue Seru ordered cut out and then ate raw "while joking the unhappy wretch." Some Europeans saw Tanoa's heir—now called Thakombau, meaning "Evil to Bau"—as the "Napoleon of Fiji" (Figure 1.2). Others regarded him as the Pacific cannibal incarnate.[137]

Thakombau eventually did *lotu* (embrace Christianity) and proclaim the end of cannibalism. But he fell into a costly war with the Tongans and deeply into debt with the American government. Harassed on several sides, Thakombau in 1859 offered Fiji's sovereignty to Britain provided that his debts be paid and his grandiloquent title, *Tui Viti* (King of Fiji), be retained. Britain's government initially balked at acquiring another distant dependency. The suggestion that Fiji was a cotton-growing heaven begging for settlers left Colonial Office leaders cold. Besides, gauging the "well ascertained and deliberate wish" of these Islanders for annexation seemed an impossible task.[138] Yet the influx of European speculators—small merchants as well as cotton planters—continued. Painfully aware that both lawful commerce and racial harmony demanded far more attention than one British Consul could provide, the government in London unhappily recognized the need to fill a political vacuum.[139] These remote policymakers wished to believe that Thakombau commanded loyalty throughout the Fijian group. With the blessings of the *Tui Viti* and a council of chiefs, therefore, what had once been a cannibal hell might soon become a model of interracial harmony under benign British administration.

This cautious optimism flowed in large part from flawed assumptions about the structure of traditional authority. It has often been remarked that British depictions of Thakombau as the "King of Fiji" functioned to legitimate the subsequent transfer of sovereignty from this semi-savage ruler to a white governor and his minders back in Britain. The trappings of Thakombau's "kingship" had to be created. By the eve of Cession in 1874, he had acquired a royal flag, a tinsel crown, and a dysfunctional Legislative Assembly. To signal his allegiance to the new colonial order, Thakombau shipped his war club to Queen Victoria.[140]

In reality, however, the *Tui Viti* had never commanded archipelago-wide obedience, nor did all of his putative subjects welcome British rule. According to the version of Fiji's pre-colonial past favored by most of its leaders since independence in 1973, the people of these islands had once lived in several hierarchically arranged tribal groups. Each tribal group had its traditional chief who presided over a system of communal land ownership.[141] Social scientists have since called this model into question. These revisionists have argued that prior to sustained contact with Europeans, the Fijian people had lived in many small groups scattered across the larger islands. These communities differed in their customs, thereby rendering it "unlikely that any one system of government and social legislation would have been acceptable as a 'Fijian' institution in all areas."[142] Nowhere did this heterogeneity show itself more dramatically than in the "stubborn" resistance to colonial rule of certain highland tribes. Enter the "mountaineers."

As they took up their new colonial posts, British administrators assumed that the system of indigenous government common to some eastern parts of Fiji had gradually been adopted throughout. Yet compelling evidence to the contrary lay close at hand. Fiji's *Kai Tholo* (literally, people "from the mountains") looked and acted unlike coast-dwellers. The *Kai Tholo* often refused to shear off their "fuzzy-wuzzy mops of hair," or to trade their scanty bark and grass coverings for the decorous *sulu*.[143] Many of them remained heathen. True to their name, these people occupied the steep terrain found at the center of islands such as Ovalau, Vanua Levu, and especially Viti Levu. By nearly all accounts, cannibalism flourished among them. And tellingly, Fiji's mountaineers were conspicuous by the absence of their marks on the Deed of Cession. As Deryck Scarr reminds us, nobody signed for the upland valleys of Viti Levu, for the villages at the head of the rushing Sigatoka River, or for the fortress of Matanavatu, "where for generations people had defied successive coastal intrusions at the top of a sheer rock wall."[144]

The mountaineers' organized resistance to encroachments on their lands began well before the Deed of Cession was drafted. These people had never been integrated into the coastal alliances that dominated pre-colonial Fiji; they saw themselves as the stewards of tradition, not rebels. But it is surely true that the colonial encounter metaphorically "produced" Fijian cannibalism.[145] Put differently, the collision of indigenous customs with foreign cultural imperatives sustained the demonizing of a practice that was already in decline. We might push this point further. From the mountaineers' defiant embrace of man-eating rituals, we could infer that they sought to supplement their literal control of the high ground with psychological intimidation. That is, once these folk realized the white man's dread of cannibalism, they began exaggerating their own fondness for *bakola*. So viewed, the *Kai Tholo* become active agents in a war of gestures as well as clubs and muskets.

This varied weaponry went on display as early as 1871, when the so-called "Lovoni cannibals" attacked a rival tribe in the highlands of Ovalau. A relatively small island that contained "rum-soaked" Levuka, center of European influence in the archipelago, Ovalau now embarrassed Thakombau, to whom both of the warring tribes owed allegiance. But the Lovoni nursed old grudges against Bau and its ruler.[146] When the chief of highland Yarovudi was intercepted, therefore, he was immediately clubbed, butchered, and baked. No gesture of defiance could have been more potent than eating this vassal of Bau. That Thakombau understood the depth of the insult is suggested by the terrible vengeance he wreaked on the Lovoni. Indigenous memory and European reports agree: most of the tribe, wasted from hunger, was marched down to Levuka and auctioned off to white planters. Having also confiscated all Lovoni land, Thakombau used the combined profits to fund his new government. Four vanquished men suffered what may have been the ultimate humiliation. Sold to an American circus company, they were exhibited in traveling sideshows as cannibal freaks.[147]

If the Lovoni disruption of 1871 proved brief, Viti Levu's mountaineers worried both planters and coastal tribes for a decade prior to the start of colonial rule. Easily the most celebrated victim of highlander violence during these years was Thomas Baker. A headstrong Methodist missionary who underestimated the threat of the *Kai Tholo*, Rev. Baker and most of his party managed to get axed and eaten in July of 1867.[148] To Viti Levu's cotton planters, however, the more troubling "outrages" involved cannibals descending on their farms. The year 1873 confirmed white fears. February saw the Burns family annihilated on their property twelve miles from the mouth of the River Ba. If the slaughter of husband and wife seemed brutal, bashing the two Burns children against the wooden supports of their bungalow appeared wholly evil.[149] In July, two more planters from the Ba region fell to highlander clubs. A literal tug-of-war for the limbs of Mr. Gresham reportedly occurred, the cannibals failing to wrest their prize from the slain man's friends.[150] In February 1871, the *Fiji Times* backed the formation of a "Volunteer Corps" to deal with the "semi-barbarous natives who surround us." A year later, the British Subjects' Mutual Protection Society vowed to pursue this end—and to resist the collection of taxes by a "native" government.[151] Plainly, one of the first tasks of Britain's new colonial regime would be the building of a peacekeeping force.

Before a colonial police could be organized, however, British officials found themselves facing the worst demographic crisis in Fijian history. By European standards the Cession appeared well intended, perhaps even altruistic. Commodore J.G. Goodenough, one of two commissioners sent from London in 1873 to assess Fiji's need for Imperial guidance, never doubted Britain's moral obligation: annexing this remote island group would enable his nation to save "a very amiable aboriginal race who cannot protect themselves against the inroads of white planters."[152] The new crown colony's first governor, A.H. Gordon, struck some planters as a pawn of the "Exeter Hall party," a mawkish evangelical. The aristocratic Gordon was neither. He did, though, distance himself from those European and American settlers who wished above all else to "clear out the 'damn niggers.'"[153] Governor Gordon reached Fiji toward the end of June 1875. The archipelago he had been appointed to rule greeted him with waterlogged crops and, far worse, a measles epidemic that had already destroyed between a quarter and a third of Fiji's aboriginal population. As the new governor soon discovered, this medical catastrophe would compel some of its survivors to resume man-eating.

In some British possessions, most notably India, it is possible to speak of doctors attempting to "colonize" indigenous bodies. The professional surveillance of medical men, it has been argued, often entailed the deployment of a disciplinary regimen designed to civilize as well as heal.[154] But such theorizing cannot take us very far where the Fijian measles epidemic is concerned. First, as of early 1875 there existed no "medical service" in the archipelago—unless one counts the palliative care dispensed at some missionary outposts. Second, the speed with which this acutely infectious virus tore through an immunologically defenseless community spread over 300 islands left no time to devise treatment strategies. Small wonder the Fijians saw this swift killer as the work of a curse. For measles can spread as if by magic—not only through direct physical contact, but also through airborne droplets.[155]

The tale of transmission still makes one shudder. Sir Hercules Robinson, governor of New South Wales, had negotiated the Deed of Cession. Shortly after its signing in late 1874, Robinson invited "King" Thakombau to visit him in Sydney. HMS *Dido* was duly sent to collect the one-time cannibal chief, his two sons, and a retinue of uncertain size. While in Sydney, Thakombau contracted measles. By the time the twenty-two-day return voyage left him in Levuka, Thakombau, the *Fiji Times* observed, looked "anything but well." He had ceased to be contagious, however. His sons, regrettably, had not. In epidemiological terms, they and other infected passengers remained "disease vectors" (Figure 1.3). Although the illness had been reported to the *Dido*'s surgeon en route, no yellow flag (signaling quarantine) flew atop its mast, nor was there any attempt to prevent the mixing of passengers with a large welcoming crowd. High-ranking chiefs among this crowd soon returned to their island homes, carrying the virus with them. And on 22 January 1875, sixty-nine dignitaries from the mountain villages of Viti Levu gathered at Navuso on the Rewa River to learn what "cession" meant. So began the devastation of highland society.[156]

In 1876, one of the colony's new medical officers noted that the case mortality rate for measles in England hovered around five percent. Because the Fijians conducted their funeral rites in private, and given the absence of systematic census data, measles mortality among these Islanders could not be calculated. But the death toll of 1875, he ventured, may have been "greater than any epidemic on record." What might explain such losses, apart from

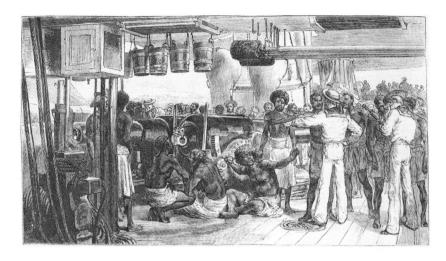

Figure 1.3   Despite knowing that measles had already appeared aboard HMS *Dido* in mid-1875, the ship's surgeon allowed healthy visitors to mix with the sick. A viral catastrophe ensued.

SOURCE: *The Graphic* (17 July 1875).

the virus's "fresh . . . field for its ravages"?[157] All too often European planters, merchants, and visitors blamed the victims. The Fijians in general and the mountaineers in particular had allegedly reverted to their superstitious traditions, refusing medicine and hospitalization. They rejected food even as starvation loomed. They threw themselves into creeks and rivers, "desperate to cool their burning fever[s]," and thereby contaminated their only source of potable water. Overwhelmed with corpses, these Islanders supposedly buried the dying as well as the dead. Proponents of the "vanishing races" theory found here terrible proof of their assumptions.[158]

Beyond this crude social Darwinist script a still more perverse narrative was emerging. The *Fiji Times* helped shape it. Beginning in late February 1875, letters to this newspaper lashed out at "the authorities" for their "absolutely culpable apathy" in responding to the epidemic. "Very strange" had been the failure of a British Navy captain to quarantine a ship he knew to contain a deadly illness. The editorial of 24 February did more than hint at conspiracy. John Bates Thurston, an Englishman long committed to guarding Islander interests against European commercial greed, was all but charged with "the careful fostering of measles."[159] Under normal circumstances this absurdity would never have been entertained beyond the saloons of Levuka. But with Fiji turning into "a vast charnel house," rumors about white sorcery suddenly gained credence among some indigenous communities. Ignoring Western medical advice represented one form of Islander resistance. Renewed highlander attacks on both European farms and Christianized Fijian villages represented another.[160] Especially in the western hills of Viti Levu, the *Kai Tholo* who launched these raids also sought bodies to eat. The "old spirit" of cannibalism had awakened. When Sir Arthur Gordon began his colonial governorship in June of 1875, therefore, he faced an outbreak of man-eating as well as measles.[161]

Earning the trust of a people whom Gordon placed somewhere between "cultivated" and "savage" on the evolutionary continuum would prove difficult but not impossible, he believed. As he assured the chiefs gathered at Bau on 10 September, their lands were secure. For Gordon himself would block foreign speculators from "eat[ing] the soil," and chiefs from recklessly selling it. "My eyes shall always be upon you," he promised. These words suggested more than fatherly solicitude, of course; they also invoked the unrelenting gaze that would see all "great crimes." The sale of wives, ritual infanticide, and cannibalism must cease immediately, Gordon stressed.[162] That Fiji's new colonial ruler felt obliged to issue this veiled threat surely puzzled some British readers. After all, in mid-July, London's *Graphic* magazine had proclaimed "Cannibalism Abandoned in Fiji" and had offered sketches of the pacified.[163] When toward the end of 1875 some of Viti Levu's mountaineers resumed raiding lowland targets, Gordon chose to enforce colonial discipline by overawing the rebellious. He understood that the mountaineers had cause to feel aggrieved. They "not unnaturally supposed the pestilence to have been purposely introduced by the new rulers to weaken their strength." "Tribal jealousies" and the "injudicious meddling" in highland life of "unauthorized agents" had also helped to convulse the interior.[164] Gordon saw this ferment as a direct challenge to Britain's colonial presence. Cannibalism, in his view, was an illegality, an instrument of defiance but not its driving force. Most of his white contemporaries, however, wished to locate man-eating at the center of the insurrection; the highlanders' "cruel" bamboo mantraps and tough wickerwork stockades constituted the martial face of cannibalism.[165]

Arthur Gordon's dismissively named "Little War" of 1876 brought down a colonial hammer on the mountaineers. In some white eyes, the alleged man-eating mania of these remote tribes *did* de-politicize indigenous resistance to British rule.[166] Whether Sir Arthur deserves credit for restraint in suppressing the *tevoro* ("devil people") of the hills will long stir debate. It is unlikely that the fifteen highlanders hanged or shot at Sigatoka on 30 June 1876 would have praised the governor. Before they died, these men learned through an interpreter that they must feel the "terror of the law." They had defied Britain's government. They had "murdered and eaten peaceable . . . people." And so they had "forfeited" their lives.[167] The conclusion of Gordon's Little War marked the end of cannibalism as an anti-colonial weapon in Fiji. It marked the start of colonial nostalgia for an imaginary time when appetite had ruled Oceania.

CANNIBAL SHOWS

Except in New Guinea, European efforts to suppress man-eating among the Islanders of Melanesia had generally succeeded by 1880. To white settlers, this accomplishment seemed an unqualified victory for civilization over savagery. But for Europeans who came to inspect "tamed" cannibals, the victory appeared somehow hollow. Had the domestication of these once fierce predators emasculated them? Could their sense of self-worth survive the cultural shock of peace? Lest the cannibals vanish forever before they could be studied, curious whites had two options. They could visit the pacified man-eaters *in situ* or else attend exhibitions of these wild people in the metropole. Both options involved projecting Western fears and fantasies onto dark bodies.

What aroused those who sought out the cannibals in their Pacific lairs was a whiff of danger, a blend of hope and worry that the savages might succumb to their old "lust" in the right ceremonial setting. James Edge Partington, a confessed English "globe-trotter," was much taken with the Fijian dances he observed near Levuka in 1879. The distinction between dancing and killing soon blurred for Partington.

> No description that could be written would give any adequate idea whatever of this wild savage *entertainment*. Weird and terrible did it look, the dusky forms of the savages decorated with huge head-dresses made out of tapa. . . . The first performance was to be a war dance, so they were all armed with clubs, and their faces in full war-paint, being daubed over with red and black stuff . . . which gave them a most diabolical look. So weird was it, that one

could almost see back some ten years, when in the midst would have been the body of a slaughtered foe, roasting over a huge fire. . . . One thing which struck me most forcibly was, that here we were, only six whites, three of whom were ladies, in the midst of over 100 wild savages, who as late as 1876 were cannibals, and really at heart are still so, as in talking with them they smack their lips at the mere mention of human flesh.[168]

Partington's eerie experience on Ovalau presupposed that cannibalism was a racial sickness, not easily cured.

Other Western fantasies allowed that this sickness could be masked if not eradicated. Published in 1888, "The Confessions of a Reformed Cannibal" acquainted an American readership with one Andrew Keller, the tall and "very dark" Scot who owned a successful meat-canning business. Although dignified, Keller had a "kind of weirdness" about him, a "sullen, savage impatience" with the world. He eventually admits to owning no Scottish blood. The offspring of a shipwrecked English father and a South Seas mother, Keller had been raised a man-eater. No surprise, then, that every spring Keller endures a longing for the "old savagery," a "maniacal desire" to discard civilized ways.[169] Melville, of course, held that the wildness propelling cannibalism transcended race. As Ishmael reasons before slipping into Queequeg's bed, "Better sleep with a sober cannibal than a drunken Christian."[170]

But Pacific Islanders made better exhibits. Between 1831 and 1892, several supposed cannibals impressed paying audiences in the United States and Britain. American showmen were especially keen to display their wares. In the autumn of 1831, New York City's *Morning Courier and Enquirer* announced the arrival of Pacific man-eaters at Tammany Hall. These Islanders clutched the expected clubs and spears. Quite unexpected, however, was "one of the seamen who [had been] wounded by these people." For an admission fee of twenty-five cents (children half price), curious citizens could learn about the cannibals' "habits and character" from the white man they had nearly killed.[171] One year later, another pair of alleged man-eaters dubbed "Sunday" and "Monday" toured the American Northeast. Their story required considerable suspension of disbelief. An enterprising ship's captain, Benjamin Morrell, had supposedly discovered them on two Pacific island groups whose location he refused to disclose. Morrell explained that he had brought these men to New York so that they might learn English and later help him form a joint stock company. He eventually lured some investors although not before Monday, constantly cold and terrified that he would be eaten, died of tuberculosis.[172]

More heralded still were the arrivals on American soil of the Fijian captive "Vendovi" in 1842 and the extended tour of P.T. Barnum's "four wild Fiji Cannibals" in the early 1870s. Vendovi reached New York City on 10 June 1842, living proof that the United States Exploring Expedition had begun the task of imposing American morality on the Cannibal Islands. As Tony Adler has argued, Vendovi's capture signaled America's emergence as a nation with Pacific aspirations. This alleged outlaw died of pneumonia mere hours after glimpsing New York.[173] P.T. Barnum's prized Fijian "man-eaters" survived longer, if no more comfortably. How America's impresario of the bizarre came to obtain these attractions remains unclear. We know that the opportunistic W.C. Gardenhire, late of Texas, happened to be scouting Fiji for savage souvenirs when the 1871 Lovoni revolt roiled the highlands of Ovalau. Gardenhire capitalized on the misery of the soon vanquished Lovoni, buying four of them from Thakombau.[174] Within a year, these Fijians had become fixtures in Barnum's American Museum and Travelling Show. At a moment in Anglo-American history when the illustration of human taxonomies excited popular interest, Barnum's cannibal tableau was a showman's dream.[175]

Beyond the epidemiological dangers and cultural traumas that faced such performers, the question of coercion bulked large. When Sara Baartman—a Khoikhoi woman displayed in London between 1810 and 1811 as "the Hottentot Venus"—intrigued metropolitan audiences, had she given informed consent to such treatment?[176] Roslyn Poignant has observed that aboriginal peoples whose cultures had collapsed under the weight of colonialism may sometimes have agreed to join traveling shows as the least bad choice. Britain abolished slavery throughout its empire in 1833. Yet fifty years on, the North Queensland "Boomerang Throwers," whose cruel fate Poignant has revealed, were in every meaningful respect "abducted."[177] P.T. Barnum had a hand in this as in many other ethnographic displays. For it was one of Barnum's agents, Robert A. Cunningham, who removed these Aborigines in 1883 and 1892, featured them in his employer's "Ethnological Congress of Strange Savage Tribes," and later presented them at anthropological meetings in London, Paris, Brussels, and Berlin. At least one of Cunningham's pamphlets promised British audiences a peek at "Ranting Man Eaters."[178]

Save perhaps for displays of Fijian males, the cannibal label served mostly to enhance the strangeness on offer. Topical issues often took precedence over anthropophagy. Advanced billing for "The Most Extraordinary Exhibition of Aborigines ever seen in Europe!" greeted the citizens of Birmingham in April 1847. Building on the 1842 publication of Robert Moffat's celebrated *Missionary Labours and Scenes in South Africa*, this show harped on the near extinction of the "Bushmen," five of whom awaited public inspection.[179] A generation later, another African people, the Zulus, aroused interest on different grounds. Having wiped out a British garrison of 1,600 at Isandhlwana in January 1879, the Zulus commanded attention. Thus, the showman G.A. Farini imported a few members of this martial tribe for visual consumption; displays featuring "Genuine Zulus," "Friendly Zulus," "Umgame, the Baby Zulu," and "Cetewayo's Daughters," among others, beckoned to the curious. Soon there were not enough Zulus to go around. By the close of the nineteenth century, so many fake Africans worked Britain's fairground circuit that the name "Zulu" had grown to signify artifice and disguise.[180]

Fakery also suffused the exhibition of "cannibals." But if there was one man-eating ritual that begged for illustration, one ceremony above all others that showmen and ethnographers longed to authenticate, it was the so-called "cannibal feast." One can speculate about the roots of this obsession. Perhaps the pairing of a pleasant custom, namely eating in social groups, with the most antisocial of acts must disturb? If so, the disturbed fail to recognize that sharing human meat is no less commensal than gathering to eat a Christmas goose. We need not speculate about other charges brought against feasting cannibals. Their eagerness to eat could go beyond lip-smacking to "limb tearing." But even when "quietly and skillfully" served, this flesh triggered "double savage" behavior in some diners.[181] Western observers of these "hideous banquets" also risked getting caught up in a "frenzy resembling intoxication." For the cannibal feast was simultaneously a "fearful and a wonderful thing."[182] Traders with a literary bent embellished such reports. William Wawn, the captain of a labor-recruiting vessel, wrote about witnessing "the assimilation of an unfortunate bushman" on Duke of York island, a slice of rain forest wedged between New Britain and New Ireland. The presiding chief revealed his people's meat preference: "Man o'-bush good; Man-Sydney no good . . . too much salt."[183] Thomas Andrew, a New Zealand-born photographer of Pacific exotica, applied modern technology to an old trope. Around 1894, Andrew shot a staged scene of seven ostensibly Fijian warriors dragging their lifeless prey toward an unseen oven. Entitled "The Vanquished," this image recalled an earlier age when cannibals carried murderous clubs, covered their loins in bark cloth, and had yet to meet a missionary.[184]

To modern eyes, Andrew's man-eaters look thoroughly unconvincing. Lacking facial detail, they appear to be what they are—mere props for one Westerner's idea of savages at their most bestial. For sheer absurdity, though, Andrew's scene must defer to Edward Reeves's image of cannibals dismembering their victims. Declaring himself bored by the "stiffly posed, unnatural groupings" of Islanders in Western drawings, Reeves sought truth through his camera. It is therefore peculiar that "A Cannibal Feast in Fiji, 1869" should appear so contrived as to be comic. Occupying page three of his travel narrative, *Brown Men and Women, or the South Sea Islands in 1895 and 1896* (1898), Reeves's scene features three very pale bodies being poked and pulled by six very dark warriors. The atmosphere is hazy; the warriors seem unsure about the next step in their ritual (Figure 1.4).[185] One can almost hear Reeves imploring his actors to behave authentically.

A CANNIBAL FEAST IN FIJI, 1869.
The meat, the fire, and the cooks.

Figure 1.4   "A Cannibal Feast in Fiji, 1869." The photographer of this staged slaughter, Edward Reeves, imagined pre-colonial Fiji as overrun with man-eaters.
SOURCE: Reeves, *Brown Men and Women* (1898).

Such clumsiness does not mar a remarkable oil painting by Charles Gordon Frazer (1863–1899).[186] Born and trained in London, Frazer gained recognition as a competent minor artist who specialized in portraits of civic leaders and "Colonial School" landscapes. Easily his best known work, then and now, is "Cannibal Feast on the Island of Tanna, New Hebrides" (Figure 1.5).[187] Sketched on this famously volatile island during 1890, "Cannibal Feast" contains nearly a hundred figures and, as one enthusiastic reviewer phrased it, "all the horrible details are reproduced with startling fidelity." The same "strange somber light" about which Henry Morton Stanley had written found its painter in Frazer. Two victims, slung on poles, occupy the oil's visual center. One body is clearly dead. The other has entered a "stupour approaching death" as suggested by its muscular relaxation.[188] At seven feet wide, this evocation of the abject Islander is hard to ignore.

Nineteen months after leaving Melbourne for Melanesia, Frazer returned to Victoria's capital. Entirely by chance, the first showing of "Cannibal

Figure 1.5 Charles Gordon Frazer's oil painting "Cannibal Feast on the Island of Tanna, New Hebrides" (1891) fascinated gallery-goers in Melbourne and Liverpool.

SOURCE: Courtesy, Bonhams.

Feast" coincided with H.M. Stanley's lecture tour in Melbourne. The explorer drew "enormous" crowds to several venues. Fittingly, his last lecture on 24 November 1891 discussed "Cannibals and Pigmies." By then, "Stanley Africanus" had already pronounced himself "greatly impressed" with Frazer's oil, then hanging in the National Gallery of Victoria.[189] The painter and the explorer, it appears, recognized in one another an impulse to naturalize the grotesque. Frazer probably admired Stanley's gift for treating risk as high-mindedness. Not coincidentally, just two days after Stanley left Melbourne, Frazer published an account of his trials on Tanna. Witnessing the nocturnal glow of an active volcano, tramping through jungle "where sunlight never penetrated," "treacherously" watched by "stalwart blackfellows": Frazer sought to depict "Cannibal Feast" as the product of physical danger as well as technical skill. His most audacious claim, however, was that he had sketched a real cannibal "*fête*" while peering through thick foliage.[190] Even Stanley could not top this tale.

In the spring of 1893, Frazer packed up the "barbaric treasures" of his studio and left Melbourne for London.[191] Although "Cannibal Feast" was not displayed in the Metropolis, Liverpool's Walker Art Gallery did show it during that institution's Autumn Exhibition of 1895. By the early 1890s, this major provincial gallery was attracting some 600,000 visits per year.[192] On Merseyside, as in distant Melbourne, visitors must have been drawn to Frazer's oil, which dominated the gallery's "Final Soiree" on 23 November. The artist's brief lecture described cannibalism as a dying custom and his painting as a form of ethnographic preservation:

> I would like just to say that in choosing this subject, it was not from any desire for sensation, nor from any sense of morbidness but from the fact of having by accident witnessed a scene of superstition so ancient, a custom that must soon become extinct all over the world before the great march of civilization, that I considered it my duty to illustrate this dark and terrible phase in the history of man. . . . I have endeavoured to treat the subject in a way that will create as little repulsion as possible. It is chosen at a time when the bodies of the enemy are carried on poles into the clearance while the warriors around sit down, occasionally joining in the strange chant [that] those of the procession are droning.[193]

After recounting the sights, sounds, and smells that reached him behind his jungle curtain, Frazer concluded with "a few kind words" for the maligned cannibal. Properly disgusted by the man-eating he had supposedly watched, yet able to perceive a "subtle charm" in the savages of Tanna, Frazer mesmerized his audience.[194]

Instead of trading on this success, however, the artist soon returned to his pursuit of the exotic. After further wanderings in Melanesia and South America, Frazer found himself in Siam painting portraits of the Siamese royal family. And it was there that he died of blackwater fever in 1899, at the age of thirty-six.[195]

Did Charles Gordon Frazer witness anything even vaguely resembling cannibalism on the island of Tanna? As with most Western accounts of a "cannibal feast," untangling truth from fiction is a task bound to confound. So is the attempt to trace the derivation of most cannibal jokes. How, for example, did the farcical image of the missionary in a cannibal pot originate? The pot, at least, is explicable. The early nineteenth-century ships built to hunt sperm whales extracted the coveted oil at sea, rendering the whale's blubber in huge iron "try-pots." Melville notes that each of an American whaler's two try-pots could easily hide a sailor looking for a private place to nap. The observant Berthold Seemann proposed an equally plausible cooking vessel: the great iron cauldrons in which the sea slugs prized in China were boiled. Some of these receptacles could hold "two men entire."[196] Explaining how missionaries came to occupy them requires more imagination. Perhaps the juxtaposition of self-righteous clergymen keen to save souls with hungry Islanders eager to enjoy the body without the Book was too striking to ignore? Recall the doggerel attributed to Bishop Samuel Wilberforce (1805–1873):

> If I were a cassowary
>   On the plains of Timbuctoo,
> I would eat a missionary,
>   Cassock, band, and hymn-book too.[197]

With apologies to Freud, one might say that where earnest was, there mocking must be.[198]

Beyond question is the fact that Pacific cannibalism has had a long afterlife. "Progress," "civilization," and "modernity" would become the watchwords for Fijian exhibits at various inter-colonial exhibitions mounted during the late-Victorian years. Despite efforts to sell Fiji as a paradise for the cultivation of cotton, sugarcane, and coffee, however, visitors to these exhibits apparently brought with them the old man-eating associations; the *idea* of Fiji remained rooted in a bygone era.[199] Curiously, the passing of this era fueled a fixation with its remnants. Beginning in the late 1870s and extending into our century, Western reports about assorted "last" cannibals continued to surface. Thus, in 1901, America's "last cannibal tribe," the Tonkawas of south-central Texas, had reportedly shrunk to an unsustainable fifty members. Three decades later, Fiji's oldest known inhabitant, Chief Takalaigau, was said to regard his cannibal youth with "wistful fondness."[200] During the 1960s and 1970s, Papua New Guinea's remote highlands yielded the disturbing news that members of the Fore tribe routinely ate the brains of their departed relatives. This practice, most anthropologists agreed, stemmed from the Fore belief that a loved one's spirit could literally be consumed. The medical consequences looked dire. Epidemiologists identified "kuru," a Fore word meaning trembling or fear, as a virus closely related to Creutzfeldt-Jakob disease. Tribe members with kuru progressed from an initial shivering tremor to complete motor incapacity and death within a year of infection. Although William Arens would subsequently admonish his fellow anthropologists for their uncritical acceptance of Fore testimony, the equation of this terrible illness with cannibalism has helped to assure Western audiences that man-eating remains a fact among earth's hidden peoples.[201]

Since the late twentieth century, cannibalism itself has been commodified. Cannibal treks—"niche tourism" for the well-heeled or the well-sponsored—hold out the promise of encounters with the authentically primitive. In Dennis O'Rourke's documentary *Cannibal Tours* (1987), wealthy Westerners, dripping with cameras and swaddled in safari garb, cruise up New Guinea's Sepik River in search of man-eating vestiges. Capitalism, it would seem, is delighted to market that which derives its value from being beyond markets.[202] Some leisured Victorians, as we have seen, were no less determined to observe "real savages." These connoisseurs of wildness longed to meet Pacific Islanders who had so far evaded the missionaries and their preaching. Yet Britain's Protestant missionaries were often the first Europeans to settle on Melanesian islands. The work they undertook forever changed both the Islanders' and Britain's sense of itself.

Missionary Martyrs of Melanesia

If the South Seas cannibal epitomized human savagery for many Victorians, the murders of missionaries on remote Pacific islands served to ennoble Britain's most potent export. This is not to say that British Protestantism found receptive audiences throughout the Pacific. Nor is it the case that missionary sacrifices abroad silenced domestic ridicule of this work. At the start of the nineteenth century, the Reverend Sydney Smith's dismissal of Baptist missionaries in Bengal as "little detachments of maniacs"[1] echoed a broader skepticism about the allocation of spiritual resources. Due to their labors among the "cannibal isles," South Seas missionaries drew more than their fair share of such gibes. It was again the irreverent Reverend Smith who in 1841 advised George Selwyn, missionary bishop of New Zealand, to placate man-eaters with this gustatory disclaimer: "I deeply regret, sirs, to have nothing on my own table suited to your tastes, but you will find plenty of cold curate and roasted clergyman on the side-board."[2] Toward the end of the century, the equally acerbic Oscar Wilde assured his dinner guests that "missionaries are the divinely provided food for destitute and underfed cannibals."[3] The missionary in the cannibal pot, as we have seen, was likely a comic assault on evangelical earnestness.

Beneath these caricatures of the missionary enterprise, however, lie serious questions about nineteenth-century religious organization, its role in extending Britain's imperial reach, and the reception of Christianity in Pacific island communities. Prior to the 1990s, the tendency within mainstream British imperial history was to marginalize missionary activity—and indeed the place of religion—in the grand narrative of Western expansion.[4] Intriguingly, Bernard Porter, whose widely read text *The Lion's Share* treats religion as an analytical afterthought, has more recently insisted that "imperial ideas, values, assumptions [and] prejudices" left few marks on metropolitan culture, and "scarcely touched" its working-class majority.[5] Porter's claim is a monument to selective research. For it conveniently ignores the essential parts that chapels, churches, and missionary societies played in linking the preoccupations of core and periphery.[6]

Where missionaries *have* been taken seriously, they tend to be seen either as the first wave of colonial exploiters or as blessed toilers in the vineyards of the lord. Both views are reductionist. When John Comaroff called nineteenth-century British missionaries in South Africa "the vanguards of empire and its most active ideological agents," he wisely recognized temperamental differences among these agents.[7] A "proto-Marxian" variation on this theme holds that missionaries introduced indigenous peoples to Western notions of work-discipline by dangling material goods in front of them: to buy these goods, natives would need money, and money could be earned only through regular ("civilized") labor.[8] The inescapable fact, however, is that many British missionaries did not fit the description of "colonizers." Missionary motives often differed from those of colonial administrators, soldiers, and explorers. Missionaries sometimes harbored theological doubts about colonial authority. And even when spiritual belief meshed with colonial aims, the saving of souls demanded close contact with indigenous peoples. Missionary and "native" worked side by side in the same schools, chapels, gardens, and villages—or, so often throughout Oceania, sat crammed together in the same battered whaleboats. As Susan Thorne has observed, "This degree of intimacy was a clear violation of the segregationist proclivities of those within the colonial community, for whom racial difference reconciled Britain's liberal pretensions and imperial interests."[9] The empire of Britain and the empire of Christ often diverged.

Britain's missionary thrust outwards to, and beyond, the edges of empire has also been framed as a chapter in the triumph of global Christianity. This interpretive pole likewise reduces cultural complexity and distorts lived experience. Victorian tales of missionary "heroes," a staple of popular publishing, typically blended hagiography with exotic particulars of savage lands. As reliable historical sources they are dubious, erasing signs of ambition and exalting acts of self-sacrifice. Indeed, so pervasive was the evangelical preoccupation with atonement for personal sin that these missionary paeans often seem nearly interchangeable.[10] They flatten personalities and homogenize courage. Yet they should not be dismissed as mere propaganda, although religious (and often imperial) propaganda they surely were.[11] What ought to give historians pause is the reality that some British missionaries, crowned "heroes" in the nineteenth century, are still revered in non-Western Christian communities. Twenty-first-century Indians accept the Baptist William Carey as a driving force behind the Bengali cultural renaissance; Jamaicans continue to honor William Knibb and other Baptist missionaries who denounced slavery at great personal risk.[12]

When personal risk led to death, missionary "heroes" often became "martyrs." At least in the western Pacific, these paragons of Christian commitment often command great respect today. This writer was struck by the affection with which worshipers in Fiji's largest Anglican church regard J.C. Patteson, the first missionary bishop of Melanesia, butchered at the hands of revenge-minded Islanders in 1871. On 17 September 2006, the clergy of Suva's Holy Trinity Cathedral led their congregation in an opening prayer:

> God of the southern isles and seas, we remember with thanksgiving your servant John Patteson, whose life was taken by those for whom he would freely have given it.[13]

The killings of three British missionaries who sought to evangelize the "southern isles and seas" were widely noted in their own day. For white audiences, their murders confirmed the benighted state of Melanesian peoples. The missionary societies that had sponsored these men capitalized on their deaths to plead for greater public support. Some evangelically disposed individuals, black and brown as well as white, were inspired by such self-sacrifice to enter the mission field themselves. But most noteworthy, the violent fates of John Williams, Thomas Baker, and J.C. Patteson encouraged even some of the unchurched to reflect on the frontier conditions that had, to a considerable extent, ordained their deaths.

HERO, MARTYR, FANATIC

The label "martyr" was applied almost as loosely in nineteenth-century British society as it is in the *jihad*-stained present. Etymological precision, for example, never stopped the Victorian foes of "medical despotism" from lauding their "martyrs of conscience"—namely, all those parents who endured repeated fines or jail for refusing to let their young be vaccinated against smallpox.[14] Similarly, when street gangs rewarded Salvation Army speakers with insults, kicks, and black eyes, the latter often welcomed such abuse as tests of their faith.[15] Christ, the original martyr, had been "faithful unto death."[16] And Christ's own words appeared to consecrate suffering: "Blessed are ye when men shall revile you, and persecute you, and shall say all manner of evil against you falsely for my sake. Rejoice and be exceedingly glad: for great shall be your reward in heaven" (Matthew 5:11–12).

Meanings migrate, of course, and charting their migrations can be revealing. Although the *Encyclopaedia Britannica* cannot be taken to represent the full range of literate opinion, its understanding of "martyr" is suggestive all the same. We read in the seventh edition (1842) that a martyr is "one who lays down his life . . . for the sake of his religion." The root word, we learn, is Greek and "properly signifies *a witness.*" So in its early Victorian sense, "martyr" denotes one who "suffered in witness of the truth of the gospel," and connotes a "singular constancy and fortitude under the most cruel torments."[17] For the comfortable classes of mid-Victorian Britain, more economically secure but probably also more skeptical of mass enthusiasm in any form, martyrdom possessed a darker side: "From this high estimation of the martyrs, [early] Christians were sometimes led to deliver themselves up voluntarily to the public authorities—thus justifying the charge of fanaticism brought against them by the heathen."[18] Self-sacrifice was not suicide, a distinction that Christ himself made: "When they persecute you in one town, flee to the next" (Matthew 10:23). In the eleventh edition of the *Britannica* (1910–1911), the cautionary note sounds more clearly still: "While the honour paid to martyrdom was a great support to early champions of the faith, it was attended by serious evils. . . . Fanatics sought death by insulting the magistrates or by breaking idols, and in their enthusiasm for martyrdom became self-centered and forgetful of their normal duty."[19] Then locked in a naval arms race with Germany and therefore acutely aware of the damage that rash action could cause, Edwardian Britain would have found such qualification only prudent.

Never stable, the political and cultural values bound up with the notion of martyrdom nonetheless constituted a core feature of British, and especially English, national identity. A.G. Dickens once pronounced the "Smithfield Fires"—the burning of Protestant heretics during the brief reign of Mary I (1553–1558)—as "the least English episode in our history."[20] Whether those martyrs who went to the stake were, in fact, "earnest and good and rather stupid fanatics" may be debated.[21] But no doubt surrounds two features of the Marian burnings: first, that the sufferings of the condemned were recounted in gruesome detail; and second, that this record of spiritual integrity would become a defining element of English Protestantism for the next 350 years. When John Foxe's *Acts and Monuments of these latter and perilous days,* popularly known as the *Book of Martyrs,* appeared in 1563, its stories of Protestant constancy in the face of Catholic torture served to support the fragile religious settlement of a young Queen Elizabeth. Constant himself, the Reverend Foxe guided three more editions (1570, 1576, and 1583) through to publication, each more imposing than the last. Foxe's death scenes would soon be seared into the English Protestant mind.[22] They emphasized sublime courage, not miraculous intervention; in the images that accompany some editions of the *Acts and Monuments,* Foxe's human candles stare out at the reader rather than toward heaven. Climate compounded the horror. For any reader (or listener) born under English skies would have understood that the odds of being burned with damp kindling were excellent.

The moral of these stories—that Providence had smiled on England because her people had remained steadfastly Protestant—did not elude nineteenth-century audiences. Foxe's threnody was reissued four times between 1837 and 1877.[23] Victorian evangelicals thus possessed not only Christ's example of steadfastness but also that of their Tudor forebears. As late as 1868, a magazine for young evangelicals warned its readers about the modern designs of a Catholicism that had, three centuries earlier, burned, chopped, hanged, and buried alive faithful Protestants.[24]

The gradual secularization of self-sacrifice was reflected in a tendency to conflate heroism and martyrdom. Samuel Smiles, described by his editor as "the authorized chronicler of the men who founded the industrial greatness of England,"[25] encouraged this conflation. "Real heroism," according to Smiles, involved suffering, "patiently and enduringly borne." Delayed gratification, in both the material and the spiritual realms, was thus the sweetest success. "Courage," Smiles maintained, should be a badge reserved for sustained grace under pressure. Finally, a "martyr" designated a special sort of courageous person, one whose influence is "magnetic," one who "creates an epidemic of nobleness." In the medieval past, William Wallace had been a martyr for Scottish freedom, Jeanne d'Arc for the preservation of France.[26]

In the Victorian present, the towering hero-martyr was the missionary-turned-explorer David Livingstone. Livingstone's life epitomized Smilesian virtue. From his humble childhood working in a cotton mill, Livingstone

(1813–1873) made his way, care of the London Missionary Society, to Africa, where for thirty years he won lasting fame as Britain's greatest "missionary pioneer." Livingstone was both less and more than he appeared: certainly less humble about his exploratory feats than an adoring public wished to believe; probably more concerned about promoting lawful commerce in East Africa to undercut the Arab slave trade.[27] The good doctor did not die a true martyr's death in the sense of suffering fatal violence for the sake of his faith. He was discovered in his tent kneeling by the side of the bed, head buried in his hands: Livingstone "died in prayer," or so his acolytes would declare.[28] But if the death was peaceful, the life had been heroically hard. The first European to cross Africa from coast to coast, Livingstone nearly lost an arm in a lion's jaws, suffered repeated attacks of dysentery, and, most disturbing for a man of tender conscience, endured the spectacle of Africans being dragged off to the slave markets of Zanzibar. Livingstone knew the qualities that a "missionary leader" must possess. "He ought to have physical and moral courage of the highest order, and a considerable amount of cultivation and energy, balanced by patient determination; and above all there [is] necessary a calm Christian zeal."[29] In the idiom of Samuel Smiles, "calm Christian zeal" became, simply, "uprightness." Since "rational progress" was deemed to be the sum of individual uprightness,[30] it followed that David Livingstone was a martyr of British commerce as well as British Christianity.

Perseverance in the face of overwhelming odds connected the otherwise very different paths of Livingstone and the Victorian Pacific's missionary heroes. Unlike the Livingstone legend, the narratives emanating from the South Seas featured spectacular physical violence.[31] Charges of cannibal desecration in two of the three cases studied here added a whiff of the grotesque to Oceanic martyrdom that no other mission field could match, although agents of the Lord were murdered around the globe. (Actually, the most lethal posting for British missionaries was Patagonia, where a large proportion of the few agents sent there succumbed to violence.[32]) The superior piety attributed to missionary martyrs could be linked to a fatalism that seemed to teeter between selflessness and monomania. In St. John Rivers, Charlotte Brontë gave literary voice to the doubts about such a calling. The Reverend Rivers is "[z]ealous in his ministerial labours, blameless in his life and habits . . . yet did not appear to enjoy that mental serenity, that inward content, which should be the reward of every sincere Christian and practical philanthropist." When the brooding Rivers fixes on a missionary future in

India, his moral unease dissolves into calm certainty. As Jane Eyre realizes, this is an unnatural calm, "inexorable as death," since the young clergyman seemed to know that his name was "already written in the Lamb's book of life."[33] So the death wish imputed to some missionaries tainted their sacrifice.

But the South Sea martyrs of Victorian times were more often praised than faulted for the risks they took. Their collective story was a "romance," an account redolent of "the adventurous and chivalrous."[34] This missionary romance masked three underlying truths, however. First and most significant, the typical Pacific "martyr for Christ" died without ever having glimpsed Britain. Indigenous preachers, recruited mainly from the Polynesian islands, were the everyday evangelists throughout Melanesia. Methodist Tongans carried the gospel to Fiji; Samoans, "themselves just rescued from the darkness of idolatry," formed an advance guard in the turbulent New Hebrides; and Raratongans led the way for the London Missionary Society in New Guinea.[35] These brown mediators between the white missionaries and the black heathens of the western isles occupied an intermediate status within the Pacific's hierarchy of otherness.[36] And "native teachers" in the Pacific (the title "missionary" being reserved for Europeans) endured terrible hardships for their faith. An English explorer sniffed in 1885 that the LMS's Raratongan teachers stationed at South Cape on the Gulf of Papua seemed to move as "little kings" among the people they had come to convert.[37] The price of authority was nonetheless high. Of the 250 LMS teachers deposited along the fever coast of southeastern New Guinea during the last three decades of the nineteenth century, at least 130 died, some violently. The mortality of their kin will never be known. Arguably the most poignant example of Polynesian devotion to the missionary cause in New Guinea was that of Ruatoka, a Cook Islander. Shortly after Reverend James Chalmers was murdered in 1901, this elder wrote to his white supervisor begging to be reassigned: "In that place where they kill men, Jesus Christ's Name and His Word would I teach."[38]

Two further facts qualify the Pacific missionary romance: not all martyrs were male, and some were not even Protestant. Melanesia could boast no equivalent of Mary Slessor (1848–1915), the Scottish shoemaker's daughter who, inspired by Livingstone's example, spent the last four decades of her life as an iron-willed Presbyterian agent (the "Queen of Okoyong") in up-country Nigeria. The Society for Promoting Female Education in China, India and the East dared not send its single women into the Pacific.[39] But the wife of a Presbyterian pastor on Erromango Island in the New Hebrides, Mrs. Gordon, suffered the same "fiendish" mutilation by tomahawks as her husband.[40] More commonly, missionary wives in Melanesia faced the prospect of pathetically short lives, both for themselves and their children. Margaret Cargill was comparatively fortunate. Becoming "a new creature in Christ" at age twenty, she went out with her Methodist husband to Fiji and was dead at thirty, four of six children surviving to mourn her. Mary Williams outlived her murdered husband John, although not before enduring six failed pregnancies and contracting *feefee*, a parasitic precursor to elephantiasis.[41] If the evangelization of Melanesia was built upon the graves of Polynesian pioneers, missionary wives sustained it.[42]

Although Catholic efforts to save souls in the western Pacific started later and remained far more geographically limited than the Protestant competition, they produced their own corps of martyrs. Had these Catholic campaigns been British, they would have generated anxiety enough. But much worse, they were French. In Britain, therefore, scant sympathy greeted the news that a Marist priest, Father Peter Chanel, had been axed to death on Futuna, an isolated speck of land located northeast of Fiji, in 1841.[43] Four years later, Bishop John-Baptist Epalle, the grandly designated Vicar Apostolic of Micronesia and Melanesia, dealt unwisely with the denizens of Santa Ysabel, in the Solomon Islands group. Leaving aboard ship the green tassels on his hat "so as not to excite the greed of the natives," but failing to stop them from cleverly dousing his muskets with seawater, Bishop Epalle also earned an axe to the head.[44] Halting though they were, these Catholic steps into the western isles struck some British Protestants as a grave challenge. The Methodists, for example, held that only aggressive proselytizing on unvisited islands could halt this "Romanist" advance.

Easily the most aggressive of the Pacific's Methodist agents—and a useful reminder that some British missionaries refused to water Melanesia with their own blood—was George Brown (1835–1917). Like Charles Frederick Mackenzie, the Anglican missionary bishop of Central Africa, Rev. Brown did not hesitate to kill those who threatened his converts. However, unlike Bishop Mackenzie, who could at least justify his guns as the only practical defense against "slave-hunters,"[45] George Brown's most controversial act reeked of revenge. Based for fourteen years in Samoa, Brown dreamt of extending the Wesleyan creed to the remote island of New Britain, just east of New Guinea. The dream became a reality in 1877 when, accompanied by

Fijian teachers, Brown and his wife settled on New Britain's Gazelle Peninsula. Unfortunately, a local big-man resented this new presence. Concerned about his monopoly over the supply of European trade goods to the island's interior, "Taleli" ordered four of the Fijian teachers to be dispatched and consumed in what one Wesleyan journal called "horrible cannibal repasts."[46] Rather than wait for a man-of-war to shell the offending district, Rev. Brown led a raid that torched Taleli's hamlets, wrecked his food stores, and shot "several" (perhaps as many as eighty) of his subjects. This was, to say the least, a "novel pastime for a missionary entrusted with the dissemination of Christian religion."[47] Exeter Hall, epicenter of British evangelical philanthropy, denounced the raid. Australian Methodists, who had funded the push into New Britain, wrung their hands. But Brown stood unrepentant. Insisting at his subsequent trial for manslaughter that he had done no more than was "absolutely necessary" to protect his flock, he escaped punishment.[48]

It would be foolish to suggest that the sins of maverick missionaries such as George Brown, or for that matter the exemplary acts of evangelizing "martyrs," impressed British citizens at home as deeply as they did indigenous peoples abroad. Yet it would be no less foolish to dismiss the possibility that dramatic accounts from the mission field did much to familiarize ordinary Britons with colonial issues.[49] Granted, to show that large expenditures were made on behalf of a cause is not necessarily to show society-wide support for that cause. The radical writer Harriet Martineau, no friend of Exeter Hall, noted that in 1855 alone, foreign and colonial missions had consumed nearly half a million pounds, not including the cost of translating the scriptures.[50] Perhaps this enormous sum signaled no more than the religious commitment of a middle-class minority? It may also be true that during much of the nineteenth century Britain's churches demonstrated "heroic insensitivity" toward both subject peoples far off and the poor under their noses. Many among the British working classes were, in fact, geographically illiterate and downright hostile to the pieties of religious visitors.[51] Did praise for missionary martyrs therefore fall on deaf ears?

The answer depends on where one looks for evidence of evangelical influence. Religious literature was unavoidable in nineteenth-century Britain. Tracts were flung from carriage windows, passed out at railway stations, delivered to jails and hospitals, dispensed in army barracks. Henry Mayhew's "wandering tribes"—the costermongers, navvies, and sailors—no doubt turned few of these pages.[52] But many among the self-described "respectable" working classes probably did.[53] Their children, moreover, often attended Sunday schools and joined juvenile missionary societies. The parent organizations had early on recognized the effectiveness of poor children as fundraisers. Tellingly, when in 1824 the London Missionary Society moved its popular Missionary Museum to Austin Friars in the City of London, it aimed to impress boys and girls with the degraded state of heathen lands: chief among the "singularly interesting objects" on display were the "*horrible* IDOLS" that South Sea islanders had relinquished (Figure 2.1). The Museum literally brought home the exotica of empire, helping to instantiate Pacific savagery for a metropolitan audience.[54] Two generations later, a London boy's most vivid childhood memory was that of a missionary collection box "with a picture of a nicely dressed missionary standing under a coconut palm surrounded by a crowd of very respectable brown people."[55] These collection boxes were ubiquitous. The small sums they attracted individually yielded tens of thousands of pounds for evangelical causes. The

THE MUSEUM OF THE LONDON MISSIONARY SOCIETY.—SEE SUPPLEMENT, PAGE 610.

Figure 2.1   Museum of the London Missionary Society, circa 1859. Its collection of "horrible idols" from the South Pacific proved especially popular with evangelical patrons. Source: *Illustrated London News* (25 June 1859).

SOURCE: Courtesy, University of Washington Libraries, Special Collections.

young thereby gained a proprietary interest in the conversion of "savages," a process made all the more compelling when children were told, for example, that the first native preacher from Raratonga had at one time baked his enemies.[56] Methodists in Bradford understood that the salvation of heathendom meant a long war; new troops would need to be constantly recruited. Hence the "main feature" of their Juvenile Missionary Society involved "training the young, almost from their very birth, to a love of Missions, Missionaries, and Missionary efforts."[57] Central to this indoctrination was the spellbinding tale of the missionary martyr.

JOHN WILLIAMS: AN ENTERPRISING DEATH

The London Missionary Society, first among Britain's evangelizing groups to reach the Pacific, needed a hero whose exploits could restore public confidence in its work. John Williams (1796–1839), a second-generation LMS agent, became that hero. By 1816, the year that Williams and his wife left London for the South Seas, his sponsor had already suffered several embarrassing failures there. Like the Baptists before them (1792) and the Anglicans after them (1799), the Congregationalists who dominated the officially nondenominational LMS (1795) were products of the great eighteenth-century evangelical revival. British evangelicals, whether "dissenting" Protestants—Baptists, Congregationalists, Methodists, and Presbyterians—or members of the "established" (Anglican) Church of England, shared common spiritual values: an insistence on the fact of personal sin; a belief in the individual's capacity to be born again through divine grace; and a recognition of the need for continuous self-examination lest the soul be waylaid on its path to salvation. For most evangelicals, the "good news" that salvation could be attained despite innate human corruption imposed a sense of joyful obligation, a powerful impulse to spread that news. Theological differences, as for example over the proximity of the millennium, did exist.[58] But such differences paled in importance beside the overwhelming enthusiasm with which nearly all evangelicals tackled the job of conversion.

Unfortunately, in their haste to save the "perishing heathen" of the South Seas, agents of the London Missionary Society left Britain thoroughly unprepared for the conditions that awaited them half a world away. These agents, mostly pious working-class men who were expected to "civilize" the benighted Islanders as well as evangelize them, had been taught to expect success. On 24 September 1795, Rev. Thomas Haweis, one of the founders of the LMS, had addressed three hundred ministers and "an immense concourse of people" in Surrey Chapel, clothing "marvelous facts in the dazzling embellishments of an impassioned eloquence." His marvelous facts demanded action. After all, South Pacific skies were "always serene." Heathen governments would be easy to deal with since they "seldom" resorted to violence. Because "religious prejudices" were weak in Oceania, and because "[e]very guilty creature feels the necessity of atonement, in some shape or form," conversion would be swift. The languages of the South Seas were, moreover, "simple" to learn.[59] Apparently neither Rev. Haweis nor any other LMS worthy pondered the possibility that some of their agents might be slaughtered while proclaiming God's word. Thus, the thirty missionaries and their families who cast off down the Thames on 10 August 1796 sailed with confidence. They had a godly captain in James Wilson, a sturdy ship in the *Duff*, and a shared sense that their mission would be an evangelical version of Cook's triumph.[60]

Six and a half months after leaving London, the *Duff* sighted Tahiti. Providential promise soon vanished in a public relations nightmare. Captain Wilson landed seventeen of the missionaries, including all the married couples, on Tahiti. The "natives" clung to their idols. The missionaries, although sheltered by the robustly heathen king, Pomare I, could not feed themselves. Temporarily abandoned in 1808, the first Tahitian mission failed to save a single soul.

Meanwhile, the *Duff* had sailed on to Tonga and the Marquesas, depositing agents in both island groups. These missions proved still more ineffectual, collapsing in 1800 and 1799, respectively. Adding scandal to incompetence, the Tongan episode featured two LMS men who settled down with indigenous women and three more who were murdered after rashly choosing sides in a local civil war. Such fecklessness was not the stuff of martyrs.[61] When the *Duff* set out on her second voyage in late 1798, she was captured by a French privateer. Her evangelists were packed off to France, only to be recaptured, this time by the Portuguese, upon their release. It may have been the case, as one advocate insisted, that such disheartening accounts "tended doubtless to increase the interest" of Dissenters in the missionary cause.[62] But it is certainly true that the tone of LMS propaganda changed perceptibly over the course of its first twenty years. By the time that John Williams ventured into the Pacific in 1816, the assertive confidence of Reverend Ha-weis had given way to reminders that "patience and perseverance" marked the successful missionary.[63]

For several years after John Williams settled on Raiatea, his sponsor con-tinued to draw sharp criticism. The LMS could take comfort from its orga-nizational growth over the first quarter of the nineteenth century, growth nourished by numerous "auxiliary societies" that sprang up throughout England, especially in the industrial North. Then too, after a new Tahitian king, Pomare II, spurned his idols in 1816, the LMS could at last point to tangible progress in its assault on Oceanic unbelief.[64] But such headway was slow, expensive, and, according to some reports, threatened to transform a once-joyous people into righteous prigs. Captain Otto von Kotzebue, lead-ing a Russian voyage of discovery, spent eleven days near the LMS settle-ment at Matavai Bay during the early spring of 1824. Kotzebue repaid the missionaries' hospitality with what they saw as malicious lies. In *A New Voyage Round the World* (1830), the Russian explorer blasted the faith he encountered on Tahiti: "A religion which consists in the eternal repetition of prescribed prayers, which forbids every innocent pleasure, and cramps or annihilates every mental power, is a libel on the Divine Founder of Christi-anity."[65] First, Europeans had brought disease and alcohol to paradise; now, under LMS direction, they were banning the flute, native dance, long hair, and tattooing. Rephrasing Kotzebue, a modern indictment declares, "Smash went everything that stood in the way of Jehovah and English customs as the missionaries waged a war against Satan that knew no quarter."[66]

To the dismay of British evangelicals, Satan, in the form of French Ca-tholicism, eventually crowded the LMS out of Tahiti. Yet the Society's de-fenders clung to the belief that missionaries were meant to wield "a power over the [indigenous] people."[67] Charles Darwin, by no means a religious zealot, extolled the civilizing force of the LMS. Impressed with the "merry, happy faces" of the Tahitians surrounding him at Papiete, Darwin lashed out in late 1835 at those critics who "expect the Missionaries to effect what the very Apostles failed to do." The shipwrecked sailor "on some unknown coast," Darwin famously observed, "will most devoutly pray that the lesson of the Missionary may have extended thus far."[68] Actually, the shores of such island groups as Tonga and Samoa had by then been cleared of those who might once have dined on the shipwrecked. This had been the work of En-glish Methodists and self-directed Islander evangelists—not, as the LMS wished to claim, through its own exertions.[69] Still, the Society's best-known agent had personally visited Samoa in 1830, and the growing fame of Rev. John Williams did not encourage measured praise.

The story of Williams's modest roots—the London ironmonger's apprentice whose "blind eyes" opened to "God's law" at seventeen[70]—fascinated his contemporaries and has continued to intrigue modern scholars. The latter have generally emphasized Williams's liminal social status. He was, supposedly, one of those marginal men in their own cultures who achieved social distinction back home by breaking idols abroad. In the most ideologically charged reading of this story, Williams belonged to a "dominated fraction" of the "dominant class," ever eager to elevate himself.[71] Certainly John Williams was both personally ambitious and hyperactive. But his roots were petit bourgeois, not proletarian. Through his apprenticeship he learned the commercial side of the hardware business, "exempt[ing] him from the manual labour of the forge and the furnace." What impressed his contemporaries is that Williams's "mechanical instinct" (as Samuel Smiles phrased it) was the product of curiosity, not necessity. He loved to handle tools: Williams so enjoyed the "practical arts" that he often volunteered for labor "such as could neither be asked nor expected of him." This eagerness to "don [the] workman's apron" was the evidence of a superior mind. Allied with a spiritual compulsion to convert the pagans, it would soon make Williams an evangelical legend.[72]

The legend began to build on Raiatea. Located 120 miles northwest of Tahiti, Raiatea was a mountainous, reef-encrusted riot of green. When Williams and his wife crossed its beach in September 1818, the island was home to roughly 1,500 souls. According to the LMS instructions that Williams would have read, the defining feature of most Polynesians was sloth. With fish in the lagoon, fruit overhead, and root crops thriving in rich volcanic soil, the Raiateans supposedly knew not the stimulus of want; they were, as the poet William Cowper imagined, "inert through plenty," the "victims of luxurious ease."[73] Williams therefore viewed it as his duty to demand changes of habit as well as of heart. Hence by building his family a comfortable home, the missionary aimed to rouse the "imitative faculties" in his flock. The resulting object-lesson was a fine, seven-room house overlooking the harbor that boasted solid wood framing, walls plastered with coral lime, shady verandahs, a spacious flower garden, and a full complement of handcrafted furniture. It was literally an awe-inspiring example. And it served its purpose. For gradually, the Raiateans abandoned their "sordid huts" in the interior and built European-style homes near the shore.[74]

Although still in his early twenties, John Williams yearned to tread a wider stage. His declaration to LMS headquarters in 1823—"[F]or my own part I cannot content myself within the narrow limits of a Single reef"[75]— could be interpreted as the ravings of a megalomaniac or, alternatively, as a cry of frustration with the cheeseparing caution of LMS headquarters. The available evidence suggests that whatever his private fantasies may have been, Williams regarded the question of expansion as a fundamentally practical matter, one whose imperatives were as familiar to the prudent businessman as to the evangelical in a hurry. On 7 June 1820, less than two years after reaching Raiatea, Williams informed the LMS directors that his talents were being squandered: "I know that one soul is infinitely more valuable than my body or a thousand bodies, but how does the merchant act who goes in search of goodly pearls? Supposing he knows where there is one pearl which would pay him for his trouble, and he knows where there are thousands of equal value, to which place would he direct his course?"[76]

Williams's course, he decided early on, lay to the west, among those island groups where sailors still feared to sail. Any such mission would require a ship, however. The first attempt to secure one ran afoul of Williams's London masters. In 1822, while on medical leave in Sydney, the enterprising missionary bought a small schooner, the *Endeavour*, partly with an inheritance from his mother. This vessel would, Williams reasoned, pay for itself by carrying island-grown tobacco and sugar to market in Australia, while still leaving time to explore the pagan western isles. Uneasy with the way Williams had involved the LMS in commerce, headquarters forced him to sell the *Endeavour* in 1823. Four years later he resumed his nautical quest under very different circumstances. This time Williams found himself temporarily stranded on Raratonga, the largest island in the Cook Group, a "splendid" place that he (mistakenly) claimed to have "discovered" and on which he had landed Raiatean teachers.[77] Now, in 1827, Williams sought a way back to Raiatea. His solution was to build a ship from the materials at hand. Williams would later claim that he "yielded" to the wishes of his Raratongan hosts and allowed them to help with the unskilled portions of the job. But the construction of the sixty-foot *Messenger of Peace* in just fifteen weeks was mostly a feat of ingenuity. Wooden pins sufficed for nails; a mixture of coconut husks and dried banana stumps served as caulking; hibiscus bark made first-rate rope; and the fiber mats on which the Islanders slept, much enlarged, became sails.[78] A fellow LMS missionary lauded Williams's "perfect genius for mechanical contrivance."[79]

The myth of the self-sufficient man resonated powerfully in an ever more interdependent British economy, and Williams fully understood the atavistic charm of his Pacific regime. No man was an island, but some islands could draw out the best in men. As for the missionary and his people on remote isles, "it must be at once obvious, that the simplicity of the means used two or three hundred years ago would better suit both his condition and theirs than the improvements of modern times."[80]

By the time John Williams returned to London aboard a whaling ship in 1834—the first glimpse of his homeland in nearly eighteen years—much had been accomplished on Raratonga. The "repulsive deformity of rude idolatry" had been banished, as had polygamy. The sincerity of the conversion experience among some Raratongan men was demonstrated by confessions of cannibal pasts.[81] The Tongans and Samoans had joined the Protestant fold, if not always as Congregationalists. Only dangerous Melanesia remained beyond Christian reach.

Before Williams could attack that last bastion of sin, however, there was a reputation to enhance at home. It would be unduly cynical to say that no British missionary worked harder than John Williams to win applause if one did not add that he probably could not distinguish between his personal fame and the health of the Pacific mission field. While his three sons acclimated to city life and his wife recuperated from years of poor health at their lodgings in Bedford Square, London, John emerged as a star on the lecture circuit. Some of the same LMS leaders who had once chided their man for his blinkered devotion now colluded in his celebrity. For the best antidote to critiques of LMS policy in the South Seas was the magnetic appeal of Williams on a public platform. There, his abrupt phrases, "sonorous" voice, and command of the telling detail packed chapels, town halls, and private chambers.[82] He seldom spoke for less than an hour, often five times per week, reportedly with undiminished "freshness of feeling." The talk he gave at Birmingham late in 1834 would become his set piece. The text was Psalms 74:30—"The dark places of the earth are full of the habitations of cruelty." After flattering local benefactors, Williams put flesh on the "pitiable condition of the degraded heathen" by telling of his longtime servant, a woman who before embracing Christ had specialized in strangling unwanted babies while they "writhed in her arms." At Hull, Williams "awakened the greatest interest" and opened the pockets of local merchants who were then battling a trade depression. At Glasgow, in late 1835, he aroused "unusual excitement" with his scheme to evangelize the New Hebrides. At Bristol, he breakfasted with the future penal reformer Mary Carpenter who, along with several other young ladies, judged him to possess a "gift of tongues."[83] After his widely read *Narrative of Missionary Enterprises* appeared in April 1837, his demand as a speaker soared. Williams, now the LMS's most compelling public figure, became a fixture at both branch ("auxiliary") festivities and the parent body's carefully choreographed annual general meetings.[84]

The furlough lasted nearly four years (Figure 2.2). During that time he not only spoke incessantly but also published his manuscript of the New Testament in Raratongan; testified before Parliament's Select Committee

Figure 2.2 The ambitious Reverend John Williams. In 1823, Williams warned LMS headquarters, "I cannot content myself within the narrow limits of a Single reef."

SOURCE: Ebenezer Prout, *Memoirs* (1843).

on Aborigines (during which appearance Williams maintained that even completely "degraded" savages were "capable of receiving instruction"); and basked in the praise for his new book.[85] *Missionary Enterprises* sold 38,000 copies, in various editions, over five years. Illustrated by the evangelical printmaker George Baxter, it soon became the most popular portrait of the South Seas since Cook's *Voyage to the Pacific Ocean* (1784).[86] It appealed to several audiences, armchair scientists and dry-land sailors as well as staunch evangelicals. Both Lyell and Darwin welcomed the missionary's account of the exceedingly slow formation of coral reefs. The ethnographically inclined applauded Williams's willingness to let his Islander informants "speak for themselves," a noteworthy anticipation of modern fieldwork practice however naïve its claim to unmediated reportage.[87] Williams could not bear to let his book speak for itself. The first edition, a handsome octavo priced at twelve shillings, was dedicated to the King. The LMS directors gave their famous agent fifty copies, all of which, accompanied by personal letters from Williams, were presented to members of the British elite. Princess Victoria received her copy one month before she ascended the throne.[88]

The mighty, as well as the readers of the later cheap editions, learned that Williams had fixed his gaze on the "several millions" of savages who supposedly occupied "Western Polynesia." Here, in New Guinea, the Solomons, the New Hebrides, and Fiji, where "copper-coloured" peoples gave way to the "negro race,"[89] he would labor last and best—provided, of course, that a proper ship could be found. The LMS leadership forbade Williams to petition the central government directly (because "public property" should not finance private ventures), but, in a peculiar suspension of that same logic, allowed him to solicit the Corporation of London. Its resulting grant of £500 proved to be the largest of a great many gifts totaling nearly £4,000. With this sum the LMS bought and fitted out a 200-ton brig, the *Camden*. This became the Society's first missionary vessel, although Williams irked some of his coworkers by treating it as his personal ship.[90] All that remained was to orchestrate a rousing exit.

That send-off surpassed even Williams's expectations. On 8 October 1837, he delivered a sermon at Surrey Chapel entitled "The Missionary's Return." There is something "transcendentally sublime" in the missionary spirit, he reminded the congregation, since it "regards the globe . . . as its parish." In his own future parish, the persistence of "horrible cannibalism" was "enough to make the missionary weep." But such painful facts at least made plain the "contrast between your mercies and their miseries."[91] Six months later it was the missionary's farewell that transfixed evangelical London. "There is in fact no observance on earth more heart-stirring than that of the . . . sending forth of missionaries to the heathen," Harriet Martineau would concede in 1856.[92] This certainly proved true for the metropolis in the spring of 1838. Williams's packed last speech at Moorfields Tabernacle on 4 April gave him the chance to wonder out loud whether he would ever see his birthplace again, whether he would be "entombed in the ocean" or sent to rest "among the graves of my children."[93] The *Camden* lay moored at the West India export dock, open to viewing by the Christian public. "Immense throngs" inspected her.[94] By 11 April, departure day, the *Camden* had been moved downriver to Gravesend. To board her, the missionary party took a steam launch from London Bridge. Reverend Williams waved to the "multitudes" lining the wharfs and eastern walls of the bridge, and was gone. When Robert Moffat, LMS agent among the Bechuana tribes of South Africa, reached London on furlough in early June of 1839, the "missionary heart of England" was still "stirred to its depths" by the figure of John Williams.[95]

What Rev. Moffat could not have known was that his brother missionary had then just over five months left to live. The *Camden's* passage to Australia proved uneventful, as did her subsequent visits to LMS settlements on Samoa, Raratonga, Tahiti, and Raiatea.[96] Several nineteenth-century accounts of Rev. Williams's last days find dark portents. There was, above all, the final sermon at Upola, Samoa, where Williams, his mind "beclouded with a presentiment of coming danger," took as a text Acts 20:36–38, Paul's farewell to the Ephesian Elders.[97] The disaster that did in fact befall Williams at the New Hebridean island of Erromango on 20 November 1839 is more difficult to understand today than it was during the Victorian era. We know that he exercised caution when approaching reputedly hostile shores, as for example when he reconnoitered "Savage Island" (Cook's name for Niue) around 1830. Yet his landing at Erromango seems to have been the one time when he approached a strange island without either Polynesian teachers or returning locals to smooth the way.[98] One reconstruction of events suggests that Williams blundered into a coastal community then preparing to hold a religious feast, thus annoying Islanders who already associated white men with the rapacious sandalwood trade. But this is conjecture, and in any case LMS agents were apt to blame the crews of commercial vessels for much "native" violence.[99] We can be reasonably sure that as the whaleboat containing Williams, his fellow missionary James Harris, and seven more men rowed toward the head of Dillon's Bay, it neared a canoe holding three Islanders. These appeared "wild" and "extremely shy"; their refusal to come closer and accept gifts signaled further cause for concern. Yet Williams would not wait. He is alleged to have told the *Camden*'s captain, just before wading ashore, "You know, Babel was not built in a day—if we can only make a good impression *now*, we must be content to do a little and come back another day and leave teachers."[100]

These words, if indeed they were uttered, do not portray John Williams as a man courting death. But die he did, along with James Harris, when club-wielding natives rushed them from the bush that fringed a steep and stony beach. George Baxter's color print of their slaying vastly exaggerates the number of attackers and strategically poses Williams in the surf to recall images of Cook's death.[101] The senior missionary's body, riddled with arrows, could not be retrieved. An eyewitness (and near victim) of the attack, William Cunningham, vice consul at Sydney, later lamented that had those in the whaleboat possessed a single musket, Williams could have been saved.[102] But perhaps better that he had died a righteous death, better that, in the hero's own words, his "happy spirit" had "quit its tenement of clay." It was very rare, the *Evangelical Magazine* pointed out, "that any death produces the deep, the general, the thrilling impression which that of Williams did." Theologically speaking, sorrow for the mere man was "profitless." Yet his "blessed enterprise" would presumably inspire other workers to still nobler triumphs.[103]

The relics of Victorian Britain's first missionary martyr largely vanished into rumor. His clothes were stripped from the body and the corpse hauled into the bush as his friends watched helplessly from the whaleboat. At the end of February 1840, a British warship dispatched from Sydney sailed into Dillon's Bay; its captain was assured that both Williams and Harris had been eaten. All that remained of the former, it appeared, was his skull and a few bone fragments, buried shortly thereafter at Apia, Samoa. The authenticity of even these few bits would be cast into doubt a generation later when descendants of the original killers confessed that their kin had simply handed over random bones scattered across a native burial cave. A club, reputedly the instrument of death, found its way back to the LMS's Missionary Museum in London—where for a generation it bore mute witness to the corporal fact of Christian sacrifice.[104]

Mainly, though, what endured of John Williams was a legend. His wife, Mary, whose grieving retreat to London fascinated the evangelical press, prolonged interest in her husband's fate.[105] His name lived on, gracing LMS ships in the Pacific from 1844 until 1971. Rural districts back home grew accustomed to the "John Williams Missionary Van" spreading the good news at a statelier pace. He would long be compared to both Cook and Livingstone. Williams would serve as the model of male mechanical savvy for R.M. Ballantyne's juvenile classic *The Coral Reef* (1858). And, tragically, he would inspire three more white missionaries to be butchered on the same deadly island. "Alas poor Williams," one prescient LMS agent exclaimed in April 1840: "It appears he was the arch deceiver."[106] We cannot know what the indigenous people of Erromango thought of Rev. Williams, or of those who followed him to an early grave. We certainly should not assume, as the hagiographers do, that their deaths enhanced the prestige of Europeans in Islander eyes. "[T]hose wild eyes that watch the wave / In roaring round the coral reef" (as Tennyson conceived the Pacific savage) may well have viewed such risk-taking as foolish.[107] There can be little doubt, however, that the apotheosis of John Williams did much to advance the missionary cause at home and abroad.

THOMAS BAKER: ALL BUT HIS BOOTS

No subsequent missionary martyr in the Pacific achieved the fame of John Williams. Indeed, one of them, Thomas Baker, died largely unmourned by his natal land and has only now resurfaced as a Victorian curiosity, a hapless trigger of unintended consequences. Born in England, reared mostly in New South Wales, Baker would meet a gruesome end in the mountainous center of Viti Levu, Fiji's largest island. His name appears in few biographical dictionaries; his murder excited comment mainly in Methodist periodicals and a few Australian newspapers. But Baker's death, more than that of any other Victorian messenger of grace, has framed discussion about what "Christian duty" entailed in the British Pacific.

Thomas Baker arrived in Fiji on 25 April 1859, keen to enlarge the Christian foundation that his predecessors had so laboriously built. Two months earlier, upon learning that the Australasian Wesleyan Methodist Missionary Society would send him to toil in this notorious den of vice, Baker had been elated. To Fiji, he told his diary, "I have felt my spirit irresistibly drawn, and now I have my hearts desire. My glory rejoiceth." Then, as if worried that these islands had already been domesticated beyond the point of salvific challenge, Baker added, ominously, "May I not be disappointed."[108] It is useful to keep in mind that by midcentury such evangelical exuberance was hardly typical of the average Australian settler—or, for that matter, of the average citizen back in Britain. Just seven years before Baker set foot on Fijian soil, Charles Dickens had lampooned the "telescopic philanthropy" he saw sustaining much missionary work abroad: Mrs. Jellyby could in good conscience lavish time and money on the Africans of "Borrioboola-Gha" yet ignore the perishing classes all around her.[109] One month after Baker's mission began, a London newspaper attacked "cannibal-civilizing societies" in general, and the LMS in particular, for wasting "enormous sums" on the conversion of "barbarians."[110] Plainly, the fate of John Williams had not silenced the critics of foreign missions.

But Thomas Baker had become a Methodist, not a Congregationalist, and in Fiji at least his brand of Dissent had made remarkable progress. The early Methodist agents in Fiji understood the value of a lurid tale. Sir Edward Belcher, captain of HMS *Sulphur*, had predicted in 1840 that the tiny band of Methodist brethren then at work on Lakemba, Viti Levu, and Taveuni "will find these people far beyond their powers." The Fijians that Belcher had encountered were "at the present moment far too ferocious to submit to any restraint."[111] The Methodist pioneers, however, saw this ferocity as their raison d'être. In his 1838 "Appeal to the Sympathy of the Christian Public, on Behalf of the Cannibal Fegeeans," Reverend James Watkin merely teased. These savages, he lamented, were "enslaved by vices too horrid for minute description." The Reverend David Cargill was less coy. In a letter to mission headquarters in London dated 2 July 1838 but not published until October of the following year, Cargill sought to shock:

> Let your ears be pierced with the dying groans of strangled widows, and the wild shrieks of the victims of a horrid superstition, who are either roasted alive, or otherwise cruelly murdered. Paint to your imaginations the awfully horrifying spectacle of multitudes of human beings fattened and slaughtered to be roasted and eaten! Look at enraged warriors cutting out the tongues of their fallen enemies, and eating them raw! See some of them quaffing the still reeking blood, and proudly retaining the skull of their vanquished foe as a drinking vessel![112]

If a more debased people cried out for conversion, they were not of this world.

It may be generally true, as one historian has argued, that the tenets of the evangelical revival remained at midcentury "but a dim light in the conception of the [South Sea] islanders."[113] In Fiji, Thomas Baker's first impression—"there seems to be a very great lack of heartfelt religion"—appears to support this generalization.[114] But for Baker, as for his predecessors in Fiji, imperfect faith demanded greater resolve. Methodists embraced John Wesley's "Arminian" form of Protestantism, one that stressed the role of free will in the attainment of grace. This was the motor of both Methodist optimism and Methodist anxiety. For those who could win divine forgiveness through moral self-discipline might also, through spiritual complacency, revert to a state of sin. The fear of backsliding expressed itself in several ways, not least importantly in the expectation that Methodist missionaries would welcome hardship. Jabez Bunting, for eighteen years secretary of the Wesleyan Missionary Society in London (and a stranger to empathy in almost any form), set out four "maxims" for his agents abroad:

1.   A missionary ought to be able to live anyhow and die anywhere.
2.   The missionary will not be murdered though he may be assassinated.
3.   All persons taken into the work for mission stations are to remain abroad for life.
4.   So long as a missionary has no wife the heathen people must have no gospel.[115]

Bunting, it should be added, never entered the foreign field.

Those who did often endured severe trials, especially in Fiji. Ever since their late eighteenth-century emergence as a distinct Protestant community, Methodists had worried that they were making "too great advances towards conformity to the world." Seeking to avoid moral enervation, their leaders as early as 1792 had decried dancing school instruction for children, "superfluity" of dress for adults, the consumption of alcohol, and all "unprofitable conversation."[116] Exhorted to shun outward forms of vanity while constantly scanning the soul for signs of wavering faith, the pious Methodist missionary could rarely have felt comfortable in his own skin. During much of his ten years in Fiji (1838–1848), John Hunt, perhaps Methodism's most effective emissary there, was haunted by a sense of his own worthlessness. Another agent, probably the Reverend Thomas Jaggar, wondered in 1844,

"I am this day 30 years of age. How many of these have I spent in the service of the wicked one?"[117] David Cargill, among the first missionaries in Fiji, broke under the psychic strain. His wife and two children having died, Cargill sought oblivion in brandy and later, fatally, in a bottle of laudanum. Methodism's pioneers in Fiji earned scorn from some European observers. For example, both the missionaries' rigid opposition to Islander polygamy and their almost hysterical suspicion of the Catholic presence in Fiji drew fire.[118] More often, criticism came from white traders, a scattered community whose commercial hub in the 1850s and '60s was Levuka, on the island of Ovalau, where mammon appeared to rule. If mainline Methodism grew more receptive to imperial values toward the close of the nineteenth century, its Fijian agents treated "trade" as a dirty word. Such primness infuriated planters, merchants, and Levuka's small tradesmen.[119]

Despite their peculiar blend of sanctimony and self-doubt, however, Methodist missionaries transformed the religious face of Fiji. In some of its foreign arenas, such as among Native Americans west of the Mississippi, Methodism's advance proved slow and uneven.[120] Among the fabled "Cannibal Isles," it exceeded all expectations. The intrepid Cargill and Cross had arrived in 1835; a generation later, 106,000 Fijians out of an estimated indigenous population of 120,000 were thought to be regularly attending public worship. In 1867, the year of Thomas Baker's death, 481 Methodist chapels and 238 "other preaching places" dotted the archipelago. By 1922, a resident magistrate could reasonably declare that "Wesleyanism, to all intents and purposes, occupies the position of the established religion of Fiji."[121]

Here, then, was a Christian triumph to which a godly young man like Thomas Baker might cleave. Whether he was temperamentally suited to the work in Fiji is another matter. Rev. Walter Lawry, General Superintendent of Methodist missions in New Zealand, visited both Fiji and Tonga in 1847. His tour prompted Lawry to reflect on the two "classes" of men who should "never dream of entering upon South Sea Mission work." The first, he held, were "those who feel a thirst for popularity, and who would like to shine before the people." The second sort of misfit was he who had been "bred and cooped up all [his] days in artificial society," a stranger to rugged travel and the carpenter's plane.[122] Thomas Baker may have been safe on the second score but not, unfortunately, on the first.

What we know about Baker's route to the islands derives largely from a diary he began on 25 August 1850, eight months after his conversion at the age of seventeen. Through this evangelical lens only the outline of a poor, emigrant childhood can be glimpsed. Thomas, born on 6 February 1832, was the second of five children in a "humble class" family whose breadwinner was a carpenter. Just short of the boy's seventh birthday, his father decided to leave their parish of Playden, near the East Sussex town of Rye, and start over in Australia. The rough passage from Gravesend to Sydney seemed to confirm Mrs. Baker's fears about the move: en route, her eldest child was swept overboard. The bereaved family reached Sydney on 17 March 1839. Illness soon descended on Thomas and his parents, and carried off two new babies. Eventually, though, health returned, the family moved to the "Glebe" (then a southwestern suburb of Sydney), and the parents joined a local Methodist meeting. Alas, just as Mr. and Mrs. Baker were discovering the depths of their depravity, their son rebelled, "being led captive by the Devil." At the age of fourteen, Thomas abandoned Sunday school and turned to taunting outdoor preachers. "Next came night walking, and from that to smoking and the ale house and gambling, swearing, fighting." But the life of a young rough left Thomas "miserable beyond degree." Apprenticed to a shoemaker, he relinquished most of his profligate ways and "found myself in a spider's web, quite secure." Mere security could not ease his "sin burdened conscience," however, so Thomas's search for spiritual peace continued until midday on 1 December 1849, as he was walking up a hill. Recalling the Hill of Difficulty in *Pilgrim's Progress*, the simplicity of true faith suddenly overwhelmed the young man, who was saved there and then in the middle of the Morpeth Road.[123]

Baker's New Nature nevertheless remained embattled, since his mind could not ignore the material world. Some prayer sessions proved uplifting, others felt "slack." Local Methodist fellowship meetings—"lovefeasts"— gave Baker the confidence to try preaching. Yet even this new outlet for his faith failed to banish the "great sluggishness of soul" that paralyzed him from time to time. By the autumn of 1858, Baker had come to "feel very deeply . . . about the Fijians"[124] at least in part because service in this risky arena promised to erase lingering self-doubt. Enthusiasm alone did not immediately sway his superiors in the Australian Wesleyan Conference. Having no theological training, indeed little more than a fractured elementary education, Baker was not the first choice of a committee that still looked askance at "colonial" recruits. But Thomas did, finally, get his wish. In a letter to his experienced agents in Fiji dated 11 April 1859, Rev. John Eggleston, General Secretary of the Conference, reported that the elders had just sent some freshly ordained missionaries and their partners "to share in your toils and triumphs."[125] Thomas Baker and his new wife formed part of this relief column.

Once in the field, Baker found that everyday chores left little time for the sort of epic labor he had envisioned. "Fiji is before me," he announced in an early letter to headquarters, "and I resolve to spend and be spent for its salvation." But his house near Bua on Vanua Levu, Fiji's second largest island, required constant repair, his halting Fijian demanded improvement, and perverse winds constantly delayed the small vessels used for most travel. Moreover, if Baker savored the idea of saving souls, he often found the attached bodies "dirty," occasionally "horrible-looking."[126] Drama, not pious routine, compelled him. Late in 1862, the missionary and several teachers had to slip past the notoriously violent village of Macuata. The sight of sails being raised in the much faster canoes thus induced a shudder: "I thought[,] Fiji has never stained its shores with a Missionary's blood yet, and am I to be the first[?]"[127] Not then and not there, it so happened. But Baker's transfer from the Bua Circuit of Vanua Levu to the upriver station of Davuilevu in the Rewa Circuit of Viti Levu during June of 1865 brought him closer than any other Methodist preacher to the big island's craggy center, and to its mountain tribes that had thus far refused to *lotu* (embrace Christian worship).

Now officially designated "Missionary to the Interior," Baker continued to find certain local habits unsettling. He resented the traffic in his house at all hours. Nor did he welcome the stares: one day when soaking wet he was forced to change clothes "before a full bure [thatched house] of heathen, who feasted on me with their eyes."[128] The missionary nevertheless appeared to relish the long and often uncomfortable journeys that went with his new territory. Baker estimated that between mid-1865 and mid-1866, his remote posting at Davuilevu had necessitated 1,800 miles of boat travel, or roughly thirty-five miles per week.[129] Geographic isolation alone may not have accounted for all this movement. The last entry in his diary, for 31 July 1866, mentions a "considerable altercation with Bro[ther] Carey" over the distribution of teachers. Methodist agents were expected to maintain among themselves "unity of affection, which will not fail to produce unity of action."[130] It appears that theory and practice were increasingly at odds on Viti Levu, however. Baker must have communicated his growing disenchantment to mission headquarters, because in a letter dated 12 July 1867, one of the brethren in Sydney wrote urging him to persevere "for a few more years."[131] Rev. Baker never saw this letter. He was dead before it reached Fiji.

Precisely why he died remains unclear. But a spasm of ambition, possibly a reaction to growing conflict with his colleagues, was the impulse that placed him in harm's way. Viti Levu's size—nearly as large as Jamaica—and mysterious interior made it attractive to European explorers. It was not until late 1865 that J.B. Thurston, then a cotton planter and later governor of the colony, led what he called "the first expedition across Fiji," by which he meant Viti Levu. Its formidably steep inland hills, violent rains, and sometimes "insolent" tribesmen had provided all the challenge Thurston could handle on his south-to-north trek.[132] How much more impressive, Rev. Baker reasoned, if he could traverse the island by canoeing up the Rewa River and then pushing west, across the staunchly heathen Navosa Plateau, down to the coast at Vuda. The hazards of this plan were such that Baker did not alert his wife when he left. On Friday evening, 19 July, he finally put pen to paper, assuring Mrs. Baker that he had already completed half of the journey and anticipated no trouble ahead, save perhaps at Navosa. And even if the "natives" there "do not lotu, I believe they will not venture to kill me." The potential glory was worth the risk, he calculated. "If I accomplish this trip," Baker told his wife, "I shall be the 'Lion of the Day,'" a boast that would be carefully erased from the official Methodist account of his death.[133]

He became, instead, a kind of Pacific holy fool whose murder rekindled debate over the conduct of missionaries among "savages." Earlier, on Wednesday, 17 July, Baker, the Fijian minister Setareki Seileka, two teachers, and six students had reached the Dawarau district where they enjoyed the hospitality of a friendly chief. Their host accepted a *tabua*, the sperm whale tooth that in Fijian custom obliged the recipient to honor an accompanying request. The request was for guides who could show the way to Navosa. Most of the subsequent accounts of "The Baker Tragedy" agree that although willing to provide guides, the chief implored Baker to avoid the Navosa district. The missionary may well have interpreted this warning as one tribal leader's reluctance to share a prestigious visitor with rival tribes.[134] Yet the weight of contemporary, non-Methodist opinion would be less charitable: Baker brought on his own death, and that of seven companions, through "imprudent zeal" or "sheer fanatical obstinacy."[135]

The party's last rest came at the village of Nagagadelavatu, perched 3,000 feet above sea level where the headwaters of the Sigatoka River rush south through deep ravines. Their reception was chilly. Nawawabalavu, the village chief, offered no yams to the strangers and expressed contempt for their faith. Accepting a *tabua*, he agreed to show Baker's group the path to Vuda next day. But allegedly just before the missionary's arrival, Nawawabalavu had accepted another *tabua* from the chief of an eastern village who wished the entire party killed. This melodramatic rendering of events, besides inspiring one of Jack London's more obscure short stories,[136] is at least plausible. For at this time, Thakombau, who had converted in 1854, was trying to consolidate his influence throughout Viti Levu. Resentful mountain tribes, long accustomed to independence, would reasonably have linked Thakombau's meddling with the Methodist *lotu*.[137] An alternative explanation for the missionary's demise paints Baker as a cultural buffoon. First sketched by Thomson in 1894, embellished by Brewster in 1922, and now widely accepted as accurate, it has Baker either playfully trying to comb Nawawabalavu's tangled hair or else indignantly snatching his borrowed comb from the chief's "verminous" locks.[138] Thomas Baker may have had tunnel vision, but he was not a moron. For a missionary with eight years' experience in Fiji to touch a chief's head would have been unthinkable. Furthermore, if the repeated cultural gaffes that Rev. Thomas Williams committed at Somosomo in the early 1840s are any indication, Fijian chiefs may have been quite tolerant of pale men in black coats.[139]

Whatever its motivation, the killing of Thomas Baker and most of his party on Sunday morning, 21 July 1867, was premeditated. After early prayers, the Methodists and several villagers set out single file along a track bordering the Sigatoka gorge. Just outside the village, Nawawabalavu, his axe-bearing guides, and a second group of armed natives suddenly turned on the visitors. Baker was among the first to fall, followed shortly by Setareki, the Fijian minister, who caught his fatal blow while stooping to kiss Baker's bloody face.[140] The only survivors of this ambush were two students who escaped by burying themselves in the tall grass that bordered the track; they would separately stagger back to the east coast, carrying with them the grim news. Although the two guides who had brought Baker's party to the Navosa district had been detained in the village, they later saw the corpses piled up, Baker's on top. The preparation of the *bakola* took place a short distance away at Cubue. In rumor and in verse, the diners would be demonized:

They slay, they cut, they cook, they eat;
  For days the feast is spread;
Nor guilt they feel, nor sin, nor shame;
  Nor pity for the dead![141]

The legend of Reverend Baker's exotic demise built quickly. When A.B. Brewster landed at Suva less than three years after the fact, children in Methodist schools there had already composed their own "dirge":

Oh! Dead is Mr. Baker,
They killed him on the road,
And they ate him, boots and all.[142]

His killers went unpunished. Thakombau's punitive expedition of April 1868, even with support from John Thurston, failed to dislodge the "mountaineers" from their aeries.[143] And the Methodist mission in Fiji remained unusually quiet about its slain agent, as if Baker's bid for personal glory had sullied a church known for its "self-denying and unostentatious labours."[144]

Yet remorse, if not retribution, would haunt the highlands of Viti Levu. Baker's murder left a widow and three fatherless daughters. It also launched a quest for atonement, a campaign of expiation that lasted 136 years. The afterlife of this missionary death began even before the tribes of the Navosa Plateau were fully "pacified." Having eaten a white man and defeated Thakombau's warriors, Nawawabalavu and his highland allies went on an extended rampage, slaughtering hundreds of lowlanders in mid-1870, then killing and cooking two white planters, Spiers and Macintosh, on the Mba River a year later.[145] But by the late 1870s, the former "devil tribes" had been defanged and partially Christianized. Nagagadelavatu, the village where Rev. Baker had earned his "martyr's crown," was abandoned. Henceforth the missionary's murder would be associated with nearby Nabutautau, to which some of the killers moved.[146] Body parts allegedly belonging to Baker—a sliver of arm bone here, three skulls there—remained in short supply compared to the many cannibal forks and war clubs sold as the true tools of dispatch.[147] Baker's telescope, now part of the Mitchell Library's collection in Sydney, and his ordination Bible, on display at the Fiji Museum in Suva, may be the only authentic relics to survive.

Then there are the boots. Or rather, there are the leather fragments that remain of footwear "recovered from near where [Baker] was murdered years after the event," as the display case in Fiji's national museum explains.[148] Just before resident magistrate A.B. Brewster left Fiji in 1910, the people of the Navatusila area, some of whose parents had feasted on the Baker party, held a council at which they issued a formal apology, an *isoro*, for what their kin had done. But these early twentieth-century apologists "hotly resented the accusation of having eaten the boots." After all, "they knew quite well" that boots "were adjuncts of the *vavalongi* [white men] . . . in the same category as their guns, powder, axes, knives, etc." Never mind that the curled leather soles look very much as if they had been boiled.[149]

The interesting point here is not that Brewster's Fijian informants resented being cast as ignorant—an entirely reasonable sensitivity. Rather, it is their residual guilt. On the basis of more than twenty years' experience as a colonial judge in the highlands of Viti Levu, Brewster concluded that Protestant Christianity had reinforced, but certainly not created, a cultural belief in the need to compensate for past injuries inflicted. What Brewster called "conscience" could not be salved entirely through the confession of personal sin and perpetual self-examination. A communal expression of regret for a communal wrong needed to supplement prayer. Officials of the Fijian Methodist Church reasoned in 1913 that the monument to Rev. Baker erected by highland villagers near the site of the massacre constituted "the fullest atonement possible."[150] Apparently this gesture, too, was insufficient, because over the next several decades, people of the Navatusila district continued to endure land disputes, leadership struggles, wretched roads, inferior schools, and rising rates of teen pregnancy, incest, and suicide. The "generational sins of their fathers, particularly the bloodguilt of the murders," demanded a traditional forgiveness ceremony, a *matanigasau*.[151]

Thus it happened, after months of planning and a barrage of newspaper publicity, that 600 people gathered on 13 November 2003 at Nabutautau village to watch what may prove to be the last act in the martyrdom of Thomas Baker. The missionary's great-grandnephew had flown in from London, as had eight other relatives from Australia. To them, the chief of Navatusila, Ratu Filimoni Nawawabalavu, presented thirty whales' teeth. Only if publicly forgiven, Ratu Filimoni announced, could the people of his district escape "the bondage and curse" that had oppressed them since

1867.[152] The ensuing hugs and tears seemed sincere all around. Forgiveness was granted. A few of the highland villagers told perplexed reporters that the rationale for their elaborate penance was biblical: "[I]f my people who are called by my name humble themselves . . . then I will hear from heaven, and will forgive their sin and heal their land" (2 *Chronicles*, 7:14).[153] This much the headstrong Reverend Baker would have understood. But he probably would not have grasped that the descendants of Nawawabalavu and his warriors had combined pagan and Christian imperatives to acknowledge their cannibal past.

JOHN COLERIDGE PATTESON: PATRICIAN SAINT

If it was the postscript that preserved Reverend Baker's name, the fame of Bishop John Coleridge Patteson owed more to pedigree than "native" penance. Whereas Baker brought very modest social credentials to the work of conversion, J.C. Patteson emerged from a cocoon of privilege to find death in the western Pacific. Indeed, it was Patteson's renunciation of status and security that made his martyrdom so poignant. Unlike Thomas Baker and John Williams, Patteson would be neither dismembered nor eaten; a body known to be the bishop's was retrieved from his killers and buried at sea. However civilized his obsequies, Patteson's death would nonetheless serve as the single most compelling proof of the need to rein in the Pacific labor trade. Savagery, his murder seemed to show, knew no color.

Patteson's story struck the comfortable classes as at once "picturesque" and "touching," as full of "holy charm [as] that of any saint of ecclesiastical legend."[154] His childhood and youth had been quintessentially genteel. Born in London in 1827, "Coley" was the elder son of Sir John Patteson, for over twenty years one of the most learned judges in the civil law court of King's (later, Queen's) Bench. The boy's mother, Sir John's second wife, was the sister of a still more famous judge, Sir John Taylor Coleridge, and it was through this side of the family that Coley traced his kinship with the great poet.[155] Both clans thought of rural southwestern England as home, favored a "high church" form of Anglicanism, sent their boys to Eton, their young men to Oxford or Cambridge and, well before "a healthy mind in a healthy body" became Victorian scripture, encouraged athletic pursuits for their males. Coley followed this arc. Although his academic performances at Eton and Balliol College, Oxford, were lackluster, he excelled at such "manly" games as cricket and football. More importantly, Patteson's arrival at Balliol in 1845 coincided with John Henry Newman's conversion to Catholicism. Although Patteson remained within the Anglican fold, some features of the "Tractarian" movement—especially its emphasis on prayer, prescribed by liturgy and celebrated by the ordained clergy—made a lasting impression on him.[156]

Intending to take holy orders, Patteson left Oxford with an undistinguished degree but a growing sense that foreign languages would enrich study of the New Testament, and so make him credible as a preacher of God's word. While touring Western Europe, he quickly acquired German and French, whereas brief forays into Hebrew and Arabic proved more demanding. This Continental interlude convinced him that he had a linguistic gift, a gift that would later be realized as a preternatural facility with Melanesian tongues.[157] But the welcome prospect of serving as a parish priest in Devonshire preceded any yearning for the South Seas. For seventeen months Coley threw himself into showing the people of tiny Alfington that spiritual renewal was as much a concern of Anglicanism as of any Dissenting sect. The reappearance of George Selwyn in Patteson's life altered the young curate's vision, however. In 1841, as a fourteen-year-old boy at Eton, Coley had been impressed with the newly appointed bishop of New Zealand. A great oarsman at Cambridge and himself an Old Etonian, George Augustus Selwyn (1809–1878) had sung the praises of self-sacrifice on the eve of his departure for the Antipodes. Thirteen years later, in the summer of 1854, Selwyn was back in England to raise funds for a missionary schooner and plead the cause of Melanesia. Why, Selwyn asked during several sermons, should young gentlemen rush to volunteer for war in the Crimea yet hesitate to enlist for more noble service among the heathen isles? Patteson, for one, would not hesitate. Now intent upon a missionary career, he left England with the bishop in March 1855, arriving at Auckland in July. Nine months later he sailed for the first time to Melanesia as Selwyn's missionary chaplain.[158]

In Bishop Selwyn, Patteson gained the sort of powerful patron that neither John Williams nor Thomas Baker ever knew. Privilege begat privilege. Yet Selwyn's patronage required agreement with his brand of expansionist Anglicanism. During his first six years as bishop of New Zealand, Selwyn had alienated some white settlers by championing Maori land rights under the Treaty of Waitangi (1840); he had vexed a sponsor, the Church Missionary Society, through his insistence on the rigid separation of church and state; and he had seized on a clerical error in the "Letters Patent" of 1841— Selwyn's ecclesiastical marching orders—to define the Diocese of New Zealand as including much of Melanesia.[159] Even without this technical excuse to do so, the bishop probably would have looked north, toward the equator. Writing to his father from Tonga in early 1848, Selwyn explained, "Lest you should think that I have gone out of the range of my own duty, I must tell you that the Archbishop of Canterbury in his valedictory letter to me, commended to my notice the progress of Christianity 'throughout the Coast and Islands of the Pacific'; a charge which the troubled state of New Zealand has hitherto prevented me from attempting to fulfil."[160] The bishop was capable of considerable generosity toward other evangelists. He admired John Williams, for example. But he never ceased to regard Dissenters as theological renegades, and he longed to reclaim Melanesia from the white traders, many of them British, who had transformed these western isles into a "field of mischief."[161] This was the formidable mentor in whose hands Patteson had placed himself.

Selwyn found an able student in Patteson. Fortunately, the acolyte could match the master in physical strength. Selwyn had at first allowed no one to land with him on an unvisited island; the bishop insisted on swimming ashore alone from a whaleboat, presents stowed in a top hat. Shortly after Patteson's arrival, however, both men swam through a gap in the reef surrounding Bellona, a Polynesian outlier near the Solomon group, somehow hauling two adzes and two hatchets between them.[162] Patteson moreover embraced Selwyn's plan to use island converts as evangelists. Other missionary societies had of course relied on Polynesian "teachers" to conduct much of the routine work on heathen islands, but Melanesia posed special problems. Its bewildering diversity of languages, malarial climate, and fragmented, egalitarian social structures rendered hopeless any scheme centered on European agents and a top-down conversion strategy. The bishop therefore proposed bringing potential converts to his headquarters at St. John's College in Auckland. Once they had grasped the core precepts of Christianity, these "boys" (some of whom were mature men) would return to their home islands as Anglican proselytizers. The implementation of Selwyn's plan began in October 1849, when he returned to Auckland with five young men recruited in the southern New Hebrides. Arriving at St. John's, Selwyn triumphantly announced to his wife, "I've got them."[163] The Melanesian Mission had been launched.

Although the Mission's growth would prove all too gradual, its supervision rapidly passed from Selwyn to Patteson. By the end of 1859, the latter had established a routine: five months in New Zealand each year interspersed with two long voyages among the New Hebrides and the Solomons.[164] One measure of Patteson's effectiveness throughout this vast territory came in 1861 when, Selwyn having pulled the right political strings back in Britain, Coley was consecrated "Missionary Bishop of Melanesia." The duty daunted Patteson, then just thirty-three (Figure 2.3). He asked the worshippers in St. Mary's Church, Auckland, "[P]ray for me, called too

Figure 2.3 John Coleridge Patteson, bishop of Melanesia, circa 1865.

SOURCE: Courtesy, Auckland Institute and Museum.

young, so in years so in all else, to an office of which I dare not say that I realize the responsibility."[165]

Taking time and place into account, a more humane appointment could not have been made. The new bishop's renowned kindness to Islanders within and beyond his ministry flowed from racial egalitarianism. Advocating "deep compassion" for the Pacific Islander and warning against "self-complacent assumption[s] of superiority"[166] among his white supporters, Patteson never underestimated the cultural dislocation that religious teaching entailed. He understood, in part, because he could converse with nearly all the "boys" he recruited. Patteson seems to have spoken four Melanesian languages fluently (Mota, Bugotu, Arosi, and Negone) and to have had some skill in at least sixteen others. Armed with a remarkable vocabulary, it was true that he possessed an unmatched "feeling [for] the native ways."[167] One of these was an aversion to cold. Patteson had realized early on that St. John's College, built atop an exposed hill outside Auckland, made a poor site for instruction; the change from a constant 84° climate to a springtime 56° at St. John's shocked Melanesian bodies. Moving the central school in 1859 to Kohimarama, a more sheltered spot on the south shore of Auckland Bay, helped.[168]

But Patteson had long dreamt of shifting Mission headquarters to sub-tropical Norfolk Island, 600 miles closer to Melanesia than Auckland, warm enough for his scholars yet pleasant also for Europeans. In 1855, Norfolk had been abandoned as the empire's most brutal penal colony. Shortly after the last convicts decamped, most of the surviving "Pitcairners," descendants of unions between *Bounty* mutineers and Tahitian women, took their place. Concern in Britain over the fate of the Pitcairn "half-castes"—a romance of preservation through isolation at a time of debate about "dying native races"—had frustrated first Selwyn's and later Patteson's plans. But at last, in 1867, the Mission managed to buy about one-ninth of Norfolk Island.[169] This crucial relocation paid one more dividend, the services of Robert Henry Codrington. Like Patteson the fellow of an Oxford college, Codrington (1830–1922) was a learned man who at first regarded his work as head of Mission education on Norfolk as an intellectual exile. He would stay for twenty years, however, running St. Barnabas as a bare-bones public school and winning wide acclaim for his pioneering contributions to Pacific anthropology and linguistics.[170] The benighted isles could now receive the bishop's undivided attention.

That attention, unusually, was accepting of much indigenous behavior. As Patteson put it to his uncle in March of 1866, "[W]e ought surely to change as little as possible—only what is clearly incompatible with the simplest form of Christian teaching and practice."[171] To be sure, Patteson agreed with his British missionary predecessors that the conversion of a primitive people necessarily involved exposing them to new social and economic values. But unlike, say, John Williams, who gloried in the belief that right religion created new material needs, Patteson insisted that Christianity must accommodate itself to local habits. It is difficult to know precisely what the bishop meant when he referred to the "Oriental tendencies" of Melanesian minds.[172] Those minds were unambiguously Other. Still, a good shepherd ought not order his flock to adopt strict Sunday rituals, or to stop smoking, or even to wear clothes. What was the likely message of a ban on nakedness, Patteson wondered, if not to imply that simply wearing a yard of unbleached calico signaled salvation?[173] After the bishop's death, Mission officials, particularly Islander agents possessed of an "evangelizing ferocity," would grow far more intolerant of nakedness and unmarried couples living together.[174] So long as Patteson remained in command, however, the Anglican imprint on Melanesian culture was comparatively light.

The strain of authority nonetheless told on Patteson. It was gratifying that by the late 1860s a model Christian village had been established on Mota (Sugar Loaf) island. Part of the Banks group, an island cluster situated between the New Hebrides to the south and the Santa Cruz group to the north, Mota had contributed not only the first indigenous deacon, George Sarawia, but also the language of instruction for all Mission schools. To Mota could be transported promising recruits from the turbulent central Solomons, where Christian influence remained nearly invisible.[175] Even so, the long voyages on the *Southern Cross*, an unrelenting yam-based diet while living ashore, and the loss of close colleagues aged Patteson alarmingly. In August 1864, a surprise arrow attack at Graciosa Bay, Santa Cruz island, wounded two of his trusted assistants. The slow, agonizing deaths from tetanus of Edwin Nobbs and Fisher Young caused the bishop "one of the deepest sorrows I have ever known."[176] He never married, refused to consider taking an extended leave, and rarely saw Auckland acquaintances once Mission headquarters moved to Norfolk Island. Selwyn's return to England in 1868 to become bishop of Lichfield caused further regret. By 1870, save for the lively correspondence he maintained with his family and friends,

Coley had become remarkably isolated. Yet the obvious antidote for isolation, resuming his work as a parish clergyman at home, held little appeal.
"I am not the man," Patteson assured his mentor, "to stand up and fight
against . . . many-headed monsters."[177]

Ironically, it was just such an evil, the Pacific labor trade, that most of
Patteson's admirers would identify as the underlying cause of his murder.
Some of the Islanders among whom Patteson sought recruits for his schools
were "unpredictable." That is to say, the rare European visitor had no way
to gauge the impact of events, recent or remote, on such people. The bishop
appreciated that he was often working blind—or, expressed in more Christian terms, from faith. His multiple landings on Santa Cruz island during
the summer of 1862 amid "exceedingly friendly" (if heavily armed) men gave
no hint of the hail of arrows that would be unleashed on his boat two years
later.[178] Moreover, what Patteson first identified in late 1867 as "a semi-
legalized slave trading between the South Sea Islands . . . and the white settlers in Fiji" was deepening distrust of strangers arriving in large vessels. He
grew incensed about this human traffic. In a five-page memorandum dated
11 January 1871, the bishop warned his Anglican colleagues in New Zealand
that neither the government of Queensland nor Her Majesty's consul at
Levuka, Fiji, had done anything to protect people on their home islands.
Thus, "we are now obliged to be very cautious" even at islands where the
Mission was already on "intimate terms" with the local folk. Native retalia-
tion was inevitable, Patteson wrote. When it occurred, the perpetrators must
not be punished unless and until evidence proved that their violence had no
connection to "outrages first committed by white men."[179]

He dismissed the rumor that at least one unscrupulous labor recruiter had
been landing on islands dressed as a bishop with a Bible in his hand. But the
blow that fell soon thereafter at the small coral atoll of Nukapu, near Santa
Cruz, was all too real. Around noon on 20 September 1871, the bishop
landed in a canoe at low tide, having left his boat and its crew of four outside
the exposed reef half a mile from the beach. Nukapu was known territory.
Patteson had visited its Polynesian-speaking people on at least three previous
occasions and hoped now to enlist an interpreter for help with the vexing
language of Santa Cruz. The bishop had been ashore and out of sight for
about forty minutes when suddenly the Islanders in the canoes near the
whaleboat began shouting and firing yard-long arrows at the visitors. Three
of the four men in the boat were wounded yet managed to reach the *South-*

ern Cross. Joseph Atkin, a missionary most recently based in the eastern Solomons and one of the wounded, led what he hoped would be the rescue of his leader. As Atkin crossed the fringing reef he could see through his glass one apparently empty canoe being towed toward him by another. Cut adrift, this canoe was found to contain the bishop's body, naked except for his shoes and socks, wrapped in a mat. The right side of his skull had been shattered. On his chest rested a sago palm frond tied in five knots. "Beside all this ruin," marveled C.H. Brooke, another agent posted in the Solomons, "the sweet face smiled as of old, with the eyes closed as if in prayer."[180] Patteson's corpse was consigned to the deep next day.

The bishop shared his fate with two others. Stephen Taroaniara, a new convert from San Cristobal in the eastern Solomons, and Atkin, the son of an Auckland settler, both died in the convulsive grip of tetanus seven and eight days later, respectively. Their deaths were vaguely unsatisfying, as was C.H. Brooke's account of them. For "no word bearing upon religion," no expression of "faith and hope" passed their lips.[181] That Patteson had left the world equally mute mattered less since a life of self-denial provided grist enough for any martyr's mill.

The production of a legend began immediately despite ambiguities surrounding both the motive for Patteson's murder and the efficacy of his work. In Brooke's report to the Anglican Church of New Zealand, he declared that the killing of the bishop could only have been "an act of revenge" against white kidnappers. Codrington, shortly after the news reached Norfolk Island, agreed that the slave trade was, with "very little doubt," behind the attacks. Lorimer Fison, like Codrington an ethnographically astute missionary, sketched a similar picture, speculating that "for tribal reasons" the warriors of Nukapu had killed "a great chief" who belonged to their enemies.[182] Speculation congealed into certainty. Five Nukapu islanders had supposedly been snatched to toil on a Fijian plantation, and the reminders of this crime were the five knots tied in the palm frond on Patteson's chest. The identities of the five kidnapped men were never established, however, a detail that troubled none of the bishop's hagiographers. Nor did they dwell on the very limited success of their saint's work. Under Patteson's regime, the only place in Melanesia to approach complete Christianization was Mota, a dot of land with brackish water located in a minor island chain. After Patteson's death, R.H. Codrington soldiered on, refusing to succeed him as bishop but persevering with teaching on Norfolk and fundraising among genteel supporters in England.[183] The Santa Cruz and Reef islands would long remain the "weakest part of the whole Mission." As of 1910, after a generation of contact with Anglican agents, perhaps a hundred out of the Santa Cruz group's estimated 8,000 inhabitants were believed to be living under Christian influence.[184]

If anything, the generally "sullen" resistance of these people to Western ways burnished the legend. Santa Cruz became the late-Victorian Erromango.[185] Just as the island of John Williams's death would later claim three more white victims, so Santa Cruz destroyed another English gentleman, James Graham Goodenough. An "honourable, true, [and] tender-hearted" schoolboy at Westminster, Goodenough had gone on to carve out a distinguished naval-cum-philanthropic career, helping to capture Canton in the Anglo-Chinese conflict of 1856–1858, distributing food to war-ravaged French villagers in 1870, and eventually, as commodore on the Australia Station, seeking to suppress the worst abuses of the Pacific labor trade.[186] During the summer of 1875, Goodenough took HMS *Pearl* through the New Hebrides and Santa Cruz groups, hoping to "open up friendly intercourse with the natives." On 12 August at Carlisle Bay, Santa Cruz, Goodenough and five of his crew received a sudden volley of arrows in exchange for the presents they had just distributed. Before succumbing to tetanus a few days later, Goodenough insisted that his men do no more than burn the offending village. In their different ways the commodore and the bishop had each turned the other cheek.[187]

The murder of Patteson became "the absorbing topic" throughout New Zealand and the eastern states of Australia.[188] In Britain, the grim details produced anguish among the mighty. Gladstone wrote early on that reports of the tragedy had caused him "extreme grief," although the prime minister confessed to a devastated Selwyn that more direct government control of the Pacific labor trade aroused "much misgiving." Three years later, now out of office, Gladstone concluded his review of Charlotte Yonge's massive *Life* of her cousin with words that approached rapture: "The three highest titles that can be given to man are those of martyr, hero, saint; and which of the three is there that in substance it would be irrational to attach to the name of John Coleridge Patteson?" In the autumn of 1878, as he was preparing several essays for reprinting, Gladstone dove back into the Yonge biography. As he confided in his diary, "Reperusal of Patteson moves even me to tears."[189] The same study also stirred Gladstone's most regal critic, the

Queen herself. Victoria recorded in her journal for 30 November 1874: "[Princess Beatrice] read to me after tea, the most sad death of the really saint like Bishop Patteson, whom one might call a martyr, & who was killed by savages. It is so dreadful, for it was due to the wickedness of others who had killed and kidnapped the poor natives, till they thought every white man was their enemy!"[190] Max Müller, the eminent philologist and one of Patteson's regular correspondents, told *The Times*, "His bones will not work childish miracles, but his spirit will work signs and wonders by revealing even among the lowest of the Melanesian savages the God-like stamp of human nature." Later, during a lecture delivered in the Nave of Westminster Abbey, Müller resumed his panegyric. "It has been my privilege to have known some of the finest and noblest spirits which England has produced during this century," he observed, "but there is none to whose memory I look up with greater reverence . . . than [to] that true saint, that true martyr, that truly parental missionary."[191]

The outcry over Patteson's death expressed itself in legal reform as well as eulogy. The Queen's Speech at the opening of Parliament in 1872 mentioned his murder and called for legislative remedy.[192] The killing of a Christ-like innocent mobilized humanitarian sentiment in the imperial hub and hastened passage of the "Pacific Islanders Protection Bill." Speaking to the House of Lords, the Earl of Kimberly, Gladstone's Colonial Secretary (and Patteson's contemporary at Eton), pointed to the murder as "the crowning atrocity" in a traffic that could go unpunished no longer.[193] Thus, June of 1872 saw passage of the so-called "Kidnapping Act." As the next chapter will discuss, the 1872 act would prove woefully inadequate. But in the short term, law appeared to have vindicated an exemplary life.

That life would continue to be celebrated, in the small and the large, for decades. There was awkward poetry:

Floating along from the island,
    Look at that silent canoe;
Scarcely a ripple 'tis making
    Over the deep shining blue.
What is it bearing so gently,
    Gliding along to its rest?
The motionless form of the martyr,
    A palm on its lifeless breast![194]

Memorials multiplied. Coley's silver cross, marked with the initials of his governess, would be fixed into the altar at Selwyn College, Cambridge; his image, rendered in stained glass, would shine down on the boys in chapel at Sedbergh School, Cumbria; the ornate sandstone and Devonshire marble chapel at St. Barnabas School, Norfolk Island, became a shrine.[195] Numerous articles and popular biographies compared the fate of the bishop with that of Livingstone, and within the Established Church the murder of this refined Christian did much to enhance the prestige of foreign missions. It is no accident that among Anglican communities in Melanesia today, "Patteson" is a common first name. There is more at work here than the residue of cultural deference, or the remnants of what one anthropologist has called the "infantilization" of evangelical colonialism.[196]

. . .

Britain's modern missionary project has not yet fully shed what one historian terms the taint of "postcolonial disgrace."[197] It is certainly true that the Oceanic murders discussed here tended to reify a discursive realm of savagery named "Melanesia." It is also true, however, that the men and women who gave their lives for a set of Protestant precepts recognized differences among the cultures specific to individual islands and settlements. These Christian emissaries, then, should not be held hostage to a scattershot critique of racism.[198] Nor should we assume that the Islanders of the western Pacific viewed British missionaries as disembodied numbers in a calculation of otherness. No doubt overgeneralizing himself, an early twentieth-century agent of the Melanesian Mission cautioned new recruits to remember that "Natives never generalize. They seldom have a name for their island, but only names for each tiny headland, and bay, and village."[199] Given their eagerness to move, by boat and boot, between place-bound tribes, the missionaries discussed in this chapter all became well known throughout their districts. Their murders, with the possible exception of Bishop Patteson's, occurred precisely where a missionary was *not* known. Clerical familiarity rarely bred contempt, although neither did it necessarily win converts.

John Williams, Thomas Baker, and John Patteson played deceptively important parts in a vast drama. The year of Queen Victoria's death, 1901, found roughly 10,000 British missionaries, representing some 154 societies and auxiliaries, toiling overseas. Britain at that time contributed about

£2 million annually to support Protestant missionary ventures, a sum equivalent to almost two percent of the central government's gross yearly expen-
diture.[200] The Pacific Islanders attracted more foreign missionaries, per
capita, than any other indigenous population except the North American
Indians.[201] Such a concentration of religious resources was attributable as
much to stirring propaganda as to an abundant harvest of souls. This propaganda, in turn, derived a good deal of its emotive force from accounts of
missionary lives lost to violence.

But the western Pacific was not simply a place where white missionaries
went to die at the hands of black savages. It was, additionally, a quasi-
colonial sphere in which the construction of Christian heroes must complicate what we think we know about the impact of evangelization. In Oceania,
as for example among the Xhosa peoples of southern Africa, missionaries
provided information—"colonial knowledge"—to the imperial state.[202] Yet
much of this knowledge was not directly useful to those who may have
dreamt of a British-dominated Pacific. Williams's observations on coral
reefs; Baker's accounts of the upper Rewa River; and Patteson's philology:
these contributions fascinated naturalists, explorers, and linguists, although
such information possessed little strategic value. Moreover, the sharp contrasts that are so often drawn between the job of the missionary and that of
the anthropologist tend to blur where Melanesia is concerned. Daniel
Hughes, who served the western Pacific in both capacities, has offered a neat
distinction: "The missionary is essentially a teacher and, to some extent at
least, an agent of cultural change. The anthropologist is an observer and
preserver of culture."[203] But what of Patteson and James Chalmers, Victorian New Guinea's own "Great-Heart"? Both men vigorously resisted most
efforts to Anglicize their people. And what of those local mythologies that
described a hero-stranger? Did the coming of British evangelists affirm or
subvert such myths? That is, to what extent was Protestantism indigenized?[204]
Finally, the butchered missionaries of Erromango, Viti Levu, and Nukapu
became revered elders for the denizens of those islands, as well as for a large
Christian-activist minority in the British Isles. The sacrifices of these martyrs would provide stories to think with throughout Melanesia.

THREE

Indentured Labor and the White Savage

The murders of British missionaries on western Pacific islands reinforced stereotypes of their inhabitants as "treacherous," too impulsive to be trusted. But such violence also advanced a key humanitarian counterclaim. As the prominent Anglican missionary-cum-ethnologist Walter Ivens put it, "[I]n most cases of wrong done to whites in Melanesia there has been some antecedent cause, some evil associated with a white person somewhere."[1] Ivens, for whom the killing of Bishop Patteson offered the ultimate proof of this dictum, was no sectarian zealot. On the contrary, his belief that the Islanders were, in King Lear's well-worn phrase, "more sinned against than sinning" became the core assumption in an exculpatory discourse centered on the Pacific labor trade.

Between 1863 and 1900, roughly 100,000 Pacific Islanders left their homes to work for European employers abroad, especially in Queensland and Fiji. By contemporary European standards, most of these migrants were "savages," products of rude barter economies and practitioners of the crudest kind of retributive justice. Yet to many white contemporaries the *lex talionis* of these people seemed less brutal than the all-consuming greed that drove some European traders to snatch "boys." Savagery, as Jane Samson has observed, was partly a moral state from which an Islander might be raised or to which a white man could just as easily fall.[2] Humanitarian activists denounced the indentured labor traffic, insisting that it constituted a thinly disguised form of slavery. If slavery must require overt physical coercion, then the humanitarians' case was weak in certain respects, as we will see. The Pacific labor trade nonetheless served up several spectacular examples of white savagery in action, however unrepresentative of the trade they may have been. Consider the disturbing story of the *Young Australian.*

In the late spring of 1868, the *Young Australian,* a three-masted schooner of 190 tons sailing under the British flag, left Sydney bound for Melanesia.

The vessel carried a general cargo of supplies for the planters, traders, and missionaries who clung tenaciously to outposts scattered throughout the island groups lying to the northeast of Australia. But the true purpose of this voyage involved a different commodity. Two Sydney businessmen had recently formed the South Seas Trading Company, a speculative venture whose aim was to supply manpower for the labor-starved cotton planters of Fiji by recruiting workers from among the island populations of the New Hebrides. The demand for cheap labor was just as strong in Queensland, where both sugarcane and cotton flourished in a semitropical climate. But the Queensland Assembly had, in March of 1868, passed the Polynesian Laborers Act,[3] legislation designed to prevent the outright kidnapping of naïve Islanders by regulating the conditions of their recruitment, transport, and employment. Fiji, not yet anyone's colony, seemed a safer labor market. So the South Seas Trading Company chartered the *Young Australian,* hired an experienced master, Albert Ross Hovell, to sail her, and appointed one Hugo Levinger, a Bavarian by birth, to serve as "supercargo," the company's agent and the man in charge of recruitment. The ship's crew was a polyglot assortment of Australians, Frenchmen, and Pacific Islanders. Referring to the murders later committed in this schooner's quest for cheap labor, the *Sydney Morning Herald* would protest that "the originators of a dark deed are shielded [by the law], while the men they have employed as their tools are seized upon, and now await the award of justice—death for death."[4]

The voyage began quietly. Captain Hovell established a base of operations at Port Resolution on the still turbulent New Hebridean island of Tanna. Hugo Levinger opened a trading station at the head of the harbor. Buying pigs, coconuts, and sulfur in exchange for muskets, ammunition, tobacco, and cotton cloth, Levinger encountered no hostility from the Tannese. This happy circumstance may have resulted from the fact that the Islanders were too busy killing one another with their newly acquired guns. Thomas Neilson, the young Presbyterian missionary stationed nearby, tried to halt this "mutual destruction" by appeals to conscience. The moral high road took Neilson nowhere: Captain Hovell still had 300 pounds of bullets left to trade and Levinger announced that he would make more of the same by melting down the lead linings of tea chests.[5] Such single-minded pursuit of profit was of course not on display when, in early October, the captain sailed to Levuka, Fiji, and asked his friend J.B. Thurston, the acting British consul, for a license to recruit laborers in the New Hebrides. Thurston liked

Hovell. Besides, as a former cotton planter himself, the acting consul recognized local labor needs. Hovell's license was therefore granted and the ship sailed west to troll for recruits. Five months later it would be a furious Thurston who alerted both the Royal Navy and the governor of New South Wales about news that the *Young Australian* had perpetrated an atrocity in the New Hebrides, "the particulars having oozed out from members of the crew [later] left in Fiji." It would also be Thurston who sent three Islander witnesses to give evidence at the sensational trial in Sydney.[6]

That trial sought to apportion blame for what occurred off the island of Paama in late October 1868. By this point in its voyage, the *Young Australian* had about seventy recruits aboard, most of them obtained from the southern New Hebridean islands of Tanna and Erromango. Erromangans and Rotumans also served as oarsmen in the two whaleboats that brought recruits from shore to ship. While rowing toward Paama one morning, these whaleboats intercepted a canoe carrying three Islanders, all of whom attempted to escape by swimming away. The terrified Paamese were wrestled into the boats, one of them reportedly with the aid of a gaff hooked through his cheek.[7]

The capture of these three "strange coloured men" (as the white first mate later described them) took place in silence, for neither the crew nor the oarsmen understood the Paamese tongue. Mutual incomprehension could only have heightened the captives' anxiety. They were presented with loincloths and given yams to eat on the poop deck, but were then forced down into the hold where several Tanna men lounged around mocking the newcomers' obvious confusion. Whether motivated by fear or rage or a blend of both, the Paamese began pelting the Tannese with coconuts and chunks of wood. After the latter threw open the hatchways and escaped to the main deck, the three Paamese discovered a cache of Tannese bows and arrows in the hold. Seizing these, they began shooting at anything that moved above them. Amidst the escalating violence the words and actions of Captain Hovell and the company agent, Levinger, would remain matters of dispute among witnesses at trial. The weight of the evidence, however, suggested that Levinger eventually ordered a few trusted crewmembers to fire into the hold through gaps in the bulkhead. When even this countermeasure was judged inadequate, the second mate, a Frenchman nicknamed "Bob," ordered the cook to tie a kerosene-soaked wad of hemp to the end of a long pole and, using this makeshift torch to illuminate the hold, the musketmen granted Levinger's wish to "quieten" the Paamese. Three corpses were retrieved from the hold and tossed overboard next morning. The *Young Australian* sailed back to Fiji, where its recruits disembarked as arranged at Levuka and a handsome payment of £1,200 was received.[8]

Although several men, perhaps as many as seven, assisted in the killings off Paama, just three could be located when, six months later, evidence sufficient for prosecution had been gathered. Captain Hovell and an Islander from Rotumah, "Rangi," were tried for murder on the high seas at Sydney's Central Criminal Court. Levinger faced the same charge in Melbourne. The *Sydney Morning Herald*, having provided detailed coverage of the first trial, took grim satisfaction in the guilty verdict that a jury had very reluctantly delivered against Hovell and Rangi: "let it be observed that in the eye of the law of England murder is the same whether the victim be black or white."[9]

But this was Australia, not England, and white colonial doubts about the reliability of black witnesses ran deep. The governor of New South Wales had urged Thurston in Fiji to send only Islander witnesses who were "sensible of the obligations of an oath from religious sentiment and belief."[10] Nevertheless, after the verdict had been rendered and a sentence of death imposed on both Hovell and Rangi, defense counsel argued before the state Supreme Court that "Josiah," one of the witnesses from Rotumah, should not have been allowed to give evidence. Josiah explained during the trial—through a sworn interpreter—that he had been baptized; that he had learned about Jesus from a Methodist missionary; that he could read the "Rotumah book," as he called the New Testament translated into his language; and that he knew he would go to hell if he told lies. Yet these assurances meant little to Sir James Martin. Learned counsel for the defense objected that Josiah, "being of a savage race which was not shewn to have any system of religion or morality of its own," should have been required to offer proof "as to the nature and extent of the religious knowledge [he] . . . had acquired."[11]

A better illustration of legal hair-splitting it would have been difficult to find. But other forces combined to make Martin's argument attractive as the way out for a governor under mounting public pressure. First, a petition signed by 1,746 "respectable" citizens of Sydney listed twenty reasons why the trial of Hovell and Rangi had been unfair.[12] Second, on 8 May 1869, the secretary of the Presbyterian Missionary Society, Robert Steel, had published a letter in the *Herald* that was later deemed to have "disturbed the free course of justice" by damning the actions of Hugo Levinger in advance of a trial. Dr. Steel was officially reprimanded and fined.[13] Taken together, these post-trial developments persuaded the Earl of Belmore to commute the death sentences to penal servitude for life. Just two years later he released Hovell and Rangi.[14]

Hugo Levinger, who quite likely had orchestrated the slaughter off Paama, also escaped severe punishment. Tried in Melbourne, the supercargo was found guilty of manslaughter rather than murder and sentenced to seven years' penal servitude. Although during the subsequent appeal at least one justice on Victoria's Supreme Court refused to accept that Levinger's ship had engaged in kidnapping, the conviction stood.[15] As in Sydney, however, a legal nicety thwarted the course of justice. Under the Colony of Victoria's criminal procedure, Levinger, a foreigner, enjoyed the right to be tried before a "mixed" jury. Since the requisite number of Bavarians had not been impaneled, the Privy Council moved to quash Levinger's conviction, leading shortly thereafter to his discharge.[16]

Both Australian opponents of indentured labor and humanitarians back in Britain regarded the *Young Australian* scandal with deep concern. Writing to Her Majesty's consuls in the Pacific, Britain's Foreign Secretary warned that "a slave trade with the South Sea Islands is gradually being established by British speculators for the benefit of British settlers."[17] Neither the *Young Australian* case nor the even more heinous *Daphne* incident that followed hard on its heels can be taken as typical of the treatment of Islander migrants. But such horror stories, widely noted in the British as well as the Australasian press,[18] tended to create a presumption of malice on the part of labor recruiters. These stories, moreover, should remind us today that the focus of postcolonial scholarship on sexual and intimate relationships as the main axis of interracial relations is sometimes misleadingly narrow. In the western Pacific, it was above all the world of work where the quotidian violence of colonial rule expressed itself. Stubborn European stereotypes about life in the Pacific Islands heightened concerns over reports of exploitation. After all, these Islanders were thought to inhabit an earthly paradise free from the curse of work. Why would they willingly quit paradise to toil on a white man's plantation?

MONSTERS REAL AND IMAGINED

Between 1863 and 1906, debate over indentured labor in the Pacific featured few measured words. Those who recruited Islanders for plantation work found themselves stigmatized as "heartless," "inhuman," even "monstrous." In return, champions of the "poor native" earned scorn as "demented" philanthropists and "hysterical" pawns of Exeter Hall. The unedifying venom of such rhetoric has understandably driven some historians to push beyond the obsessions of rival European interest groups toward a more "island-centered" reading of the Pacific past. Although this scholarly shift of focus has enriched our appreciation of the Islander-as-actor, matters of scale and context, easily overlooked, must also be kept in mind. The Pacific labor trade, for one, represented a tiny fraction of the global migration of labor during the nineteenth century, constituting perhaps three percent of the whole.[19] For another, the condemnation of unscrupulous recruitment ("blackbirding") in the Pacific mirrored contemporary critiques of labor markets in China (the "pig trade") and India (the "coolie trade").[20] Indeed, by the late nineteenth century, "coolie" (probably derived from the Hindi *kuli*) had become a generalized label for any Asian-Pacific unskilled laborer hired at or near a subsistence wage—whether the person so labeled picked cotton in Queensland or cut sugarcane in Louisiana.[21] Most importantly, however, we need to remember that the Pacific labor trade was predicated on an assumption of indispensability: without Islanders to endure its scorching fieldwork, plantation-based agriculture was widely believed to be unsustainable.

This reliance on "native" labor in the western Pacific was not new and had never been trouble-free. Apart from brief and widely spaced contacts with European vessels of exploration, most South Sea Islanders first encountered white men as whalers or collectors of *bêche-de-mer*, the "sea slugs" whose smoked flesh was prized in China. The ships chasing sperm whales were largely self-sufficient, since the flensing and boiling down of carcasses took place at sea. Whalers obviously had to find fresh water, trade for food, and replace masts; and Melville's literary depictions of the business were accurate in their references to Islanders joining ships' crews. Still, the success of a whaling voyage did not hinge on local labor. The harvesting and curing of the edible species of *bêche-de-mer*[22] was, by contrast, local labor-intensive. Valued in China partly for their supposed aphrodisiac qualities, these marine creatures, varying in length from six inches to nearly two feet, littered coral reef shallows throughout much of Melanesia. Only Islanders waded or dove for them. The slugs then had to be dried, and here again indigenous help proved vital. Local labor built and thatched the long curing sheds and, under white supervision, gutted, boiled, and smoked the holothurians over closely watched fires. "Too much heat," warned one trader, would "cause [the slug] to blister, and get porous like a sponge; whereas too little heat . . . will make it spoil, and get putrid."[23] Profits from the sale of properly cured *bêche-de-mer* in Manila or Canton could be handsome. But the weeks and sometimes months during which black labor continuously served white needs created workers with a shrewd understanding of their own commercial value, and employers who rued this emerging sophistication.[24]

The sandalwood and pearl shell trades were, according to the reports of missionaries and naval officers, more brutal. Pearl shell, or mother-of-pearl, referred to the iridescent lining of certain warm water oysters. The fancy buttons and fine knife handles made from this substance came at a considerable human cost. Although as early as 1825 London entrepreneurs had tried to fabricate an air-filled "bell" to replace the slow and dangerous job of free-diving for pearl shell, it was not until 1874 that the cotton twill and rubber "diving dress," complete with heavy copper helmet and air hose, reached the Torres Strait. South Sea Islanders did nearly all the underwater work before 1874, and predominated among the "dressed" divers until Japanese competitors displaced them in the mid-1890s.[25] Throughout the second half of the nineteenth century, freelance "pearlers," mostly Australians, earned an evil reputation for abusing their black divers.[26]

The sandalwood atrocity stories, worse yet, should be treated with caution. One of several authorities to recount the emblematic Efate (Sandwich) island massacre of 1842, Commander Albert Markham noted simply that the "reckless" crews of two British vessels had shot down twenty-six Islanders while collecting the aromatic trees. Later, lighting brushwood fires at the mouths of caves where other Efatese had taken refuge, the crews suffocated several more. "This is merely one instance of the barbarities perpetrated by . . . Englishmen," Markham was "ashamed" to say.[27] What actually occurred on that New Hebridean isle in 1842 is far less certain. The crewmen sent ashore to cut sandalwood were all Tongans, and the fighting apparently broke out over an exchange of insults. Whether those who employed the Tongan musketeers deserved equal blame for the killings may be argued, but it is noteworthy that no white man set foot on shore.[28]

The sandalwood trade, in any case, became permanently associated with what the *Nautical Magazine* termed "all kinds of excesses." Cruel treatment at the hands of sandalwooders was popularly thought to have reignited the "fiendish ferocity" of some Islanders, thereby launching an undeclared tropical war between savages black and white.[29] As Dorothy Shineberg has shown, the denizens of sandalwood-rich islands (like the indigenous mainstays of the *bêche-de-mer* business) quickly grasped their own economic worth, since they were often needed to cut trees growing far inland.[30] The Islander-as-victim image nonetheless remained unchallenged in the eyes of most humanitarians. Missionaries were particularly keen to connect the sandalwood trade with the later resort to indentured labor. Clerics alleged that both enterprises wallowed in "awful depravity," both depended on "collecting cannibals," and the advocates for both spread vicious lies about the servants of Christ.[31] There was, in fact, a famous capitalist whose career bridged the two trades. Robert Towns, a Sydney merchant, had joined the search for sandalwood in 1844, and nearly two decades later, his ship, the *Don Juan,* recruited the first laborers for Queensland. Australians today still debate whether Towns deserves to be branded a "blackbirder." They frequently forget that even the fair-dealing James Paddon, one of Towns's main rivals in the sandalwood boom, believed that Melanesians worked better when removed from their home islands and made dependent on their employers for food.[32] Ironically, in at least one respect antipodean critics of the sandalwooders helped to sustain a robust triangular commerce: they drank tea. Australia's unquenchable thirst for the beverage drove its rising merchant class to exchange tobacco, steel axes, and muskets for Islander-harvested sandalwood; and sandalwood, which China burned as incense in Buddhist ceremonies, bought a great deal of Chinese tea.

If the extractive trades of early Pacific commerce called into question the ethics of their white undertakers, the plantation-based cotton and sugarcane industries sharpened these questions. Cotton grown in coastal Queensland and Fiji at first appeared to offer the brightest prospects. As early as January 1860, eight months after Queensland won recognition as an independent colony, its new governor was urging London to help turn northeastern Australia into the world's leading producer of luxurious "sea island" cotton. Featuring unusually long fibers, a silky texture, and high market value, the sea island variety was then grown mainly by slave labor along the coasts of South Carolina and Georgia. But Queensland boasted at least six hundred miles of rich alluvial soil where this crop had been shown to flourish. And the moral stench of slavery need never pollute the land, for indentured Chinese or Malay or Indian laborers would tend fields in the torrid north, while in the milder south British emigrants would build a prosperous cotton-growing yeomanry.[33]

The onset of the U.S. Civil War sparked an explosive transformation in global cotton production. When Union ships imposed a blockade on Confederate ports, the resulting "cotton famine" in Lancashire's textile mills suddenly energized growers large and small around the world, from the Nile delta to the northern shores of Brazil.[34] The direction of British interests seemed clear. By turning to her "loyal dependencies . . . in the Southern Hemisphere," the mother country could avoid any future reliance on foreign nations (or "half-civilized" people) for her raw fibers. Such at least was Bobbie Towns's thinking when he bought 4,000 acres of prime agricultural land south of Brisbane.[35] Fiji, unlike Queensland, was not yet a British possession. Still, most of the European settler-adventurers who had rushed there to cash in on cotton were now demanding swift annexation.[36]

Whereas the cotton boom proved fleeting, the lure of sugarcane endured. The end of the American Civil War and the reopening of the South's cotton pipeline eventually drove down world prices for the fiber. Moreover, the two violent storms that flattened crops throughout central Fiji in early 1866 brought ruin for many planters who were already deeply in debt for the land and equipment they had purchased.[37] The nimbler planters, both in Fiji and in Queensland, managed to shift from cotton to cane, having already begun to import South Sea Islanders for the former crop. Cane growers had the additional advantage of feeding a local addiction: sugar and molasses consumption in Australia was reportedly then the world's highest, a formidable 78.7 pounds per capita in 1878.[38] (All that tea had to be sweetened.) As with any farming scheme, the success of cane growing hinged on labor costs, as well as on weather and market price. In Fiji, where powerful rulers tended to control the labor pool, planters found it difficult to enlist enough local help. In Queensland, the Aboriginal peoples had long frustrated settlers who expected an improbable marriage of docility and initiative in their hired hands.[39] As one sugar-farmer observed, just ten days by sail from Brisbane lay the New Hebrides, islands "densely crowded with a population who, having nothing to do and sometimes very little to eat, spen[d] their whole time killing one another, not as we do in Europe, for the sake of an idea, but for the sake of a dinner."[40] The planters would save the cannibals from themselves and turn a profit in the bargain.

This simple solution masked what was, in fact, a complex debate about the requirements of tropical labor. Those eager to see Australia provide a home for the respectable surplus population of Europe abhorred the idea of importing either Chinese or Indian "coolies." As for South Sea Islanders, in modest numbers they might prove useful on small farms. But the European immigrant, as exotic plants and animals had already done, would learn to acclimate to the rigors of a new environment; so long as they blocked the sun's harsh rays, British immigrants would flourish in Queensland.[41] Eventually, of course, whites did adapt to raising cane in the high heat and humidity of coastal Queensland, making Australia's the only sugar industry in the world to rely on workers of European origin.[42] However, this distinction was not achieved until the early years of the twentieth century, when exclusionary "White Australia" legislation made a virtue of necessity. For a generation before that, Islander muscle, commonly called "Polynesian" or "Kanaka" labor, did all the punishing fieldwork, from "trashing" (trimming) the cane plant's lower leaves to manhandling the sheaves into carts or tramway cars. The growers of Fiji were less particular about where their laborers originated, so long as they came cheap: "Let John Chinaman once scent a new field for accumulation, and he will undergo any amount of privation . . . to pile up a few dollars."[43] It was nevertheless on Islander backs that Queensland's sugar production rose from 388 tons in 1867 to 21,000 tons in 1880, and expanded almost as impressively in Fiji.[44] The critical question therefore became not "Will they work?" but "Will they come?"

To make sure they did, recruiters began in 1863 to entice able-bodied Islanders with "gifts" and the promise of more such wealth once a specified term of labor had been completed. Even where interactions between blacks and whites did not appear to involve physical coercion, opponents of this rapidly expanding labor trade denounced it as "disguised slavery." Such accusations greeted the docking in Brisbane on 15 August 1863 of Towns's *Don Juan*. Within a week the *Courier* had declared that this "traffic in human flesh" was "palpably rank" and brought "a crying disgrace upon the colony."[45]

Such invective stemmed from two related concerns. There was, first, the issue of Queensland's racial identity. "We want to make this colony different from those of the West Indies," proclaimed the *Courier*. An influx of "coloured" labor would constitute a giant stride in the wrong direction.[46] Then there was the record of white violence in the Pacific to consider. Some Australians still remembered the cruel conduct of the schooner *Velocity* in

1847. Seeking Islanders as shepherds for New South Wales, its captain had shot a Rotuman chief and several of his followers when they dared to protect a group of abused recruits.[47] Much more recently, international pressure had been brought to bear on the Peruvian government, which throughout 1862 and early 1863 had licensed private recruiting ships to scour the eastern Pacific for workers. Having abolished slavery in 1855, Peru needed bodies not only to cultivate its cotton fields but also to mine guano, its most valuable export. Through outright abduction, diseases introduced during transport, and meager rations, this brief but disastrous experiment had ravaged Easter Island and the coral atolls of Polynesia. Now, it appeared, Queensland was poised to enter a commercial field that Peru had just abandoned in shame.[48]

Robert Towns's enduring notoriety as a blackbirder, it should be added, was mostly a matter of guilt by association. He had not originally tried to recruit Islander labor. But his attempt to hire "coolies" at Madras and Calcutta had run afoul of India's colonial government, and his subsequent plan to engage German immigrants had unraveled when these "useless" Europeans demanded higher wages.[49] Granted, Towns could never have been mistaken for a diplomat. In an open letter to missionaries that accompanied the *Don Juan* on its first recruiting voyage, this lion of commerce sought clerical help with his "worldly mission," noting that picking cotton in Queensland "will do more towards civilizing the natives in one year than you can possibly [do] in ten."[50] Towns's most glaring defect, though, was employing Ross Lewin, one of the mythical monsters of the Victorian Pacific.

Among them, Lewin, Dr. James Murray, and William "Bully" Hayes personified the worst of white savagery. Exactly because their careers remained shrouded in unknowns, they could bear the weight of rumor, providing the "slave trade" with human faces and, in the long recounting of their evil acts, perpetuating a crude villain/victim dichotomy. Prior to the large-scale recruitment of Islander labor for Queensland and Fiji, white savagery in the western Pacific had often been associated with "beachcombers," a catchall category that included shipwrecked or abandoned seamen, deserters from whaling ships, escaped convicts, and nearly any masterless man who appeared to have "gone native."[51]

The monsters of the 1860s and '70s seemed to be an altogether more calculating lot. In the eyes of their enemies at least, they combined pretensions to gentility with a cold-blooded pursuit of wealth. Ross Lewin, once a Royal Navy seaman and possibly a deserter, was said to have honed his man-stealing skills in the brief but lethal Peruvian labor trade. By his own reckoning, Lewin had taken up trading in the South Seas around 1842.[52] Robert Towns's recruiting agent between 1863 and early 1867, Lewin was widely believed to be a blackbirder, an imputation he denied almost as vehemently as his alleged rape of a Tanna girl aboard the *Spunkie* in 1868.[53] The rape charge against Lewin failed for lack of a white witness. Nor did his subsequent ownership of the *Daphne*, a small schooner that R.N. Captain George Palmer found to be "fitted up precisely like an African slaver, *minus* the irons," result in anything more penal than revocation of his Queensland recruiting license.[54] Yet a harsher judgment awaited him. Lewin boasted that the best proof of his kindness toward savages was his flourishing estate on Tanna: "Had I been the wholesale and unprincipled kidnapper . . . represented by those who can know nothing of the circumstances . . . I should not have dared to land upon the island, much less make arrangements to live there." It was on Tanna, in April 1874, that this demonic figure was shot in the back while strolling about his heavily fortified plantation—rough justice for killing a local banana thief.[55]

James Patrick Murray vanished before he could be rewarded in the manner of Ross Lewin, although not before winning a reputation for diabolical cruelty. Born in Ireland and raised in New Zealand, this one-time health officer for Sandhurst, a borough in the Australian colony of Victoria, abandoned medicine for the lucre of the labor trade. Having bought the brig *Carl*, Murray set sail from Melbourne in June of 1871. The doctor's savagery began in the New Hebrides but reached its peak off Buka in the western Solomons. There the crew of the *Carl* was ordered to drop cannonballs, iron spars, and lengths of heavy chain on the canoes of Islanders who had paddled alongside to trade.[56] Those fished out of the sea were added to the "recruits" already locked in the ship's hold. Repression bred resistance. On the second night of rioting in the hold, worried crew began firing down the main hatchway (Figure 3.1). Far from halting this massacre, Murray joined the shooters, reportedly serenading them with the callously upbeat "Marching Through Georgia" (which celebrated, among other marvels, "How the darkeys shouted when they heard the joyful sound" of Sherman's army approaching).[57] A large fraction of the estimated seventy Islanders killed were wounded men tossed overboard after having their hands and feet bound. Dr. Murray, the "monster in human shape" who had orchestrated these atrocities, dodged all legal sanctions by turning Queen's evidence at the

II.—BLACKBIRD TAMING

Figure 3.1   The *Carl* atrocity, 1872. "Blackbirders" shoot into the *Carl*'s hold to silence terrified Islanders.

SOURCE: *Illustrated Monthly Herald* [Melbourne] (28 December 1872).

subsequent murder trials of four crewmembers. Lest it abet a lynching, the *Town and Country Journal* waited until Murray fled Australia before publishing his likeness. Murray's own father agreed that this brute ought to hang, should capital punishment be considered.[58]

If, as one historian has suggested, the enormity of James Murray's crime served to distance the *Carl* massacre from its "enabling colonial context" of labor exploitation,[59] such spectacles of inhumanity nonetheless cast a moral pall over the most upright recruiters. As for South Sea outlaws, a resort to blackbirding was assumed to be irresistible. William "Bully" Hayes, for example, topped any Oceanic rogues' gallery. American by birth and a brawler by nature, Hayes, from the mid-1850s through the mid-1870s, made the Pacific his pond, surfacing unpredictably in San Francisco, Honolulu, Sydney, Hong Kong, and a great many of the island groups in between. He somehow managed to stay a step ahead of the naval authorities and swindled the merchants hunting him.[60] Hayes's reported kidnapping of Islanders dismayed the Aborigines' Protection Society, caused consternation in the House of Lords, and allowed Fijian planters to denounce the "tyranny and rapacity" of ruffians who had given labor recruitment an undeserved bad name. In 1877, his murder at sea by an enraged mate wielding a marlinspike—a "deserved extinction," R.L. Stevenson called it—ended a famously larcenous life.[61] And yet there exists no solid evidence that Bully Hayes was a blackbirder. Such conflation of theft and slave-trading occurred in part because humanitarian activists encouraged it.

These activists argued, rightly, that the labor trade was fast reshaping island life, although they often lacked the statistical data to prove it. Thanks to patient demographic reconstruction, we now have a far clearer sense of the scale of Pacific labor migration. Between 1863 and the end of Queensland's recruiting in 1904, roughly 61,000 Islanders, primarily from the New Hebrides and the Solomons, arrived in northeastern Australia. The years 1864 to 1911 saw another 27,000 go to work in Fiji.[62] Several thousand more were obtained to toil on the coconut plantations of German Samoa, in the nickel mines of French New Caledonia, and as crew aboard European ships sailing under many flags. It has been estimated that in 1882, during the peak period of labor recruitment, there were about 14,000 New Hebrideans working abroad out of a total population of 100,000. Their absence represented not merely fourteen percent of the New Hebridean population but an alarming share of its young men. British missionaries railed against this denudation. They could not have known, as we do today, that as a proportion of their combined populations, the central Melanesian islands furnished more migrants than China during the last third of the nineteenth century.[63]

Other aspects of the labor trade struck humanitarians as no less repugnant. The distinguishing feature of indentured labor was its contractual character—an agreement to serve an employer for a fixed period at a fixed wage rate with penal sanctions to enforce these terms. The length of service specified for Islanders migrating either to Queensland or Fiji was initially three years, although in 1877 Fiji adopted the five-year indenture more common in British colonies. On paper the agreements looked fair. Beyond his wages (paid in the form of trade goods), the migrant was entitled to free food, clothing, and shelter, as well as passage back to his island at the end of service. But when profit margins shrank, unscrupulous employers were known to skimp on these benefits, sometimes with deadly consequences.

For example, the captain of a recruiting vessel might save himself considerable time and expense by dumping returning workers on the first island sighted or, far worse, among their traditional enemies.[64]

Even without evidence of callous neglect, humanitarians were disposed to view indentured labor in the Pacific as a stain on Christian civilization. The timing, admittedly, seemed suspect: no sooner had slavery been abolished throughout the British Empire in 1833 than indenture schemes had arisen in its place. And this was a new sort of servile labor. Whereas the indentured servants of the seventeenth and eighteenth centuries had been poor Europeans seeking better lives in the New World colonies, the indentured poor of the mid-nineteenth century were now all nonwhite. Those twin pressure groups forged in the fires of abolition, the Aborigines' Protection Society (1837) and the British and Foreign Anti-Slavery Society (1839), believed that planters everywhere would "inevitably" oppress the "negro" so long as right-thinking citizens remained silent.[65] Neither organization in fact slowed the destruction of black communities in South Africa, Australia, or Tasmania. Indeed one could argue that their humanitarian ideology, which often posed British Christianity as the only practical alternative to extinction, smacked of white supremacist thinking.[66] But the activists backing the Aborigines' Protection Society (APS) in particular managed to heighten public awareness of the dangers facing indentured Islanders. Civilization, declared one APS leader in 1872, had little to do with "machines, steam-ships, and electric telegraphs," and everything to do with extending the "civil rights of mankind." To this end APS delegations not only haunted the Colonial Office and the halls of Parliament, but also operated a global network of correspondents—merchants, clerics, and colonial civil servants, in the main—whose identities were cloaked.[67] So, when rumors of skullduggery aboard a labor recruiting ship spread in a Levuka hotel or on a Brisbane wharf, there was a fair chance that they would eventually reach London.

Whether aligned with the APS or not, the foes of the labor trade saw threats to dark strangers nearly everywhere. In Queensland, the articles of indenture derived from its 1861 Masters and Servants Act, legislation that devoted far more attention to the duties of employees than to those of employers. This was worrisome enough. More disturbing still, such agreements began as oral contracts with illiterate men and women. Admirably flexible instruments for recruiters, who could alter the terms of service before they were fixed in ink, these contracts impressed humanitarians as hopelessly flawed.[68] Where brute force trumped the letter of the law, protecting indigenous peoples came down to the might of the Royal Navy. Unfortunately, Britain's Australian Division, organized in 1859, was too occupied with New Zealand's racial strife to provide meaningful oversight of labor recruitment until 1866, and long thereafter, as we will see, legal restrictions continued to hamper effective action against blackbirders.[69] Nor was action to shield vulnerable Islanders likely to originate in the Colonial Office, especially after 1871 when the deeply religious permanent undersecretary, Frederick Rogers, retired. Only the prospect of imperial "dishonour" appeared likely to rouse torpid civil servants.[70] Thus, the enemies of indentured labor sought to make their case using a moral register from which moderation was missing.

Moral absolutism proved a potent weapon, to be sure. But the humanitarians' fevered rhetoric often outstripped their facts, and their zeal to "humanize savage and cannibal races"[71] struck defenders of the labor trade as irresponsible. Whereas the murder of J.C. Patteson became an abolitionist parable, planters in Fiji pointed out that, although the martyred bishop had expressed grave doubts about renegade recruiters, he never proposed to halt the traffic.[72] Planters and merchants in pre-cession Fiji were widely depicted as thugs, it is true. Their contempt for most missionaries seemed complete, and their tiny commercial hub, Levuka, served as headquarters for the "British Subjects' Mutual Protection Society," better known as "the Ku Klux."[73] Still, they had good reason to complain that the humanitarians tarred all labor recruiters with the same sanctimonious brush. Especially in the Presbyterian-dominated southern and central New Hebrides, abolitionist claims could be far-fetched. Hence the charge that recruiting had increased infanticide by separating husbands and wives for several years, the latter growing desperate to eliminate proof of their infidelity.[74] Early in 1872, 10,000 copies of a pamphlet on the "slave trade" were mailed to Presbyterians in Scotland, Nova Scotia, and the Australasian colonies. Subtlety did not muddy its message. To speak of Islander recruits as "free labourers" was "simply to prostitute words, pervert the English language, and turn it into a vehicle of deception."[75]

Conspicuously missing from these mutual recriminations was any Islander assessment of the labor trade. Recruits published no tracts and delivered no speeches. They did act, however, and their actions, although often difficult to interpret, suggest a lively appreciation of injustice.

AGENCY AND OUTRAGE

Both during the years of the Pacific labor trade and among those who later studied it, questions about Islander participation have stirred fierce debate. Could a "savage" gauge the probable consequences of near-term decisions? What, in the context of nineteenth-century Melanesian cultures, marked a "free" decision? Assuming that they did behave as rational actors, how much decision-making power did Islanders actually wield when depraved white men stood in their way? And if Oceanic subalterns *did* speak, can we, products of vastly different worlds, hear them?

Even to frame these questions is to impose retrospective clarity on what often must have seemed a spider's web of possibilities; choices and consequences, expectations and results, were never so neatly formulated either for Islander recruits or for those who spoke and wrote about them. Assessments of "native character," to take an obvious example, varied widely among self-styled friends of the Aborigine. According to one such ally, the South Sea Islander was "in mental capacities and development on a par with . . . the English schoolboy"—impetuous, trusting, naïve. The Islander also resembled the "simple English country girl in London" who "rushes into the snares awaiting her!"[76] Here, popularly dressed, was J.S. Mill's only exception to the sovereignty of the individual: when "backward" peoples were in their "nonage," they, like children, must be protected against their own actions, as well as against external harm.[77] Another staunch supporter of "these uneducated savages" depicted them as perfectly sensible people who would never have agreed to leave their homes for three years if the true length of their service obligation had been disclosed. Deception, the abolitionists maintained, wore many masks. "The horrid trick of putting remorseless savages in charge of recruiting [whale]boats" was among the most cynical because it channeled the presumed appetite of the cannibal into procuring bodies for plantations to devour. Eternally divided among themselves by an inveterate lawlessness, island folk were easily turned against one another, or so it appeared to their would-be protectors.[78]

At the same time, however, some late-Victorian defenders of the labor trade imputed to the savage a basic business acumen. William Wawn, an English expatriate who took up labor recruiting for Queensland, allowed that the early years of the trade had witnessed several egregious cases of kidnapping. But such misbehavior would be "extremely impolitic on the part of a recruiter who expected to be engaged for any length of time," since, once deceived, indigenous communities would rebuff all future overtures. A like-minded writer complained that semi-Christianized Islanders became "learned in the trading tricks of the white man, drive hard bargains, and having lost much of their respect for the European by intimate association with him, are apt to regard themselves as his equals."[79]

Modern revisionist historians have been blunter. Hugh Laracy declared in 1975 that to represent labor recruitment as thinly veiled slavery "involves the assumption that Melanesians were so stupid that for more than forty years tens of thousands of them stood around on island beaches waiting to be kidnapped."[80] Similarly, it has been argued that as Islanders grew more familiar with the recruiting process, kidnapping was rendered "at once unnecessary and impossible."[81] Seeking to reconfigure the labor trade as a set of willing negotiations between Europeans and Melanesians, the revisionists have tended to downplay the coercive conduct of the former as "petty acts of duress,"[82] and to emphasize the initiative, or agency, of the latter. After the mid-1880s, many scholars have agreed, the forcible recruitment of Islanders grew increasingly rare. To account for this shift in the nature of the trade, revisionists accept that stricter state oversight, particularly the presence of government inspectors aboard all British-registered recruiting vessels, was a contributing factor. But the explanatory key to the normalization of recruiting, they insist, lay with the accommodation and resistance of the migrants themselves. The volunteering of Islanders for second and third periods of indenture has thus been cited as proof that they were making a free and informed choice. The revisionists have pointed out that laborers returning to their islands after three (or more) years toiling on European-owned plantations brought back a wealth of knowledge about the material rewards to be gained abroad and the physical price to be paid for them. In short, after a turbulent start the labor trade created its "own harbinger."[83]

Depicting Melanesian recruits, like E.P. Thompson's early industrial workers, as "present at [their] own making"[84] does not, of course, suffice to explain why these tropical migrants left their homes in the first place. To the extent that it can be answered at all, the question of motivation must be approached largely by inference. Leaving aside those Islanders who were abducted into indentured service, several considerations could have made paid labor abroad attractive. Discussing Solomon Islanders, a leading revisionist historian discerned four "stimuli": the lure of European goods; the novelty of travel; the example set by others who had returned and apparently prof-ited from their experiences in a variety of ways; and pressures within their own society.[85] Certainly the tobacco, cloth, steel axes, and, in the early years, firearms that recruiters gave to the friends and relatives of men willing to sail away provided material lubrication. Enemies of the labor trade were wont to see such transactions as "bribery." But because Western concepts of buying, selling, and gift giving rarely carried the same connotations in isolated island communities, the abolitionists' case was weak on this score.[86]

The enticement of the new is another "push" factor that can easily lend itself to distortion. Ironically, imagining the Islander as a free agent keen to see distant lands can also infantilize, conjuring up "a Pacific Sambo, mind-lessly lusting for the bright lights of civilisation."[87] The spectacle of return-ing workers laden with white men's goods would have made a lasting im-pression for at least two reasons. First, on islands that produced no cash crops, indentured labor constituted one of the few forms of negotiable cur-rency; unless an employer reneged on a contract or a recruit died on the job, cutting cane for three years would yield a predictable cash-equivalent. Sec-ond, the treasures that a young man brought home in his "trade box"—typically a rectangular pine chest with a lockable lid—could have invested him with a tribal status disproportionate to his tender years. The prospect of lavishing trade box wealth on his elders might have proven irresistible to a young mind.[88] Finally, fixed-term immigration to Queensland or Fiji would have offered a convenient escape for individuals out of favor in fish-bowl villages. Queensland, the missionary-ethnologist Walter Ivens ob-served, was a "veritable refuge" for Solomon Island pariahs: "murderers, sorcerers, adulterers, . . . thieves, discontented wives, rebellious children, all hailed the coming of a labor-vessel as a chance to be freed from the likeli-hood of punishment or from the irksomeness of home restrictions."[89]

The reasons why Pacific Islanders would voluntarily, even eagerly, seek passage on recruiting ships must have been as varied as the migrants them-selves. Surely desperation, as well as calculated advantage, drove Islanders overseas. For example, famine produced by local crop failures would have chased some to distant plantations, while others, suffering from chronic disease, reportedly saw their only hope for cure in European settlements.[90] But in their campaign to resuscitate the Islander-as-agent, revisionist schol-ars of the labor trade have sometimes failed to acknowledge that the line between coerced and free labor must often have been blurred. Formerly indentured workers, once back on their islands, sometimes acted as middle-men ("passage masters") in the recruiting business. The careers of enterprising brokers such as "Kwaisulia" of Ada Gege, northeastern Malaita, can be offered to show that the give and take of the labor trade became an accepted rhythm in Islander life.[91]

Yet some "volunteers" for Fiji and Queensland were captives of local custom if not of white monsters. Where social expectations called for the repayment of one clan's debt to another, a senior member of the obliged side might have felt great pressure to enlist himself, or to lean on a younger relative, when the recruiter's boat arrived. Although such mechanisms of clientage and control operating unspoken within island communities probably escaped the notice of most government inspectors, they would certainly have limited the free choice of recruits. Volition, then, was a contingent state. Or, put another way, Islander agency did not preclude the existence of constraining forces within local cultures.[92]

If trying to square revisionist accounts of the labor trade with the ongoing grievances of its descendants is apt to be an exercise in frustration, the fact remains that affected island populations usually had options. This assertion flies in the face of much abolitionist evidence. Rev. R.H. Codrington of the Melanesian Mission, for one, would have disputed any such claim. Referring to the Mission's stronghold in the Banks Islands, he lamented in late 1872:

> There are six "labourers" returned from Queensland now at Mota; not a single one of them was a free agent entering into a contract with the colonial Government or employer. Everyone had been deceived into going as he thought for three months to some country they call Sydney, without any notion of work or wages. They were generally well treated, it is true, but their [understanding of] their condition in the Colony is simply that they were bought and sold.[93]

Codrington, normally an astute observer of island life, was then reeling from the news of Bishop Patteson's murder—ostensibly a product of unfocused revenge for the brutality of white labor recruiters. Had this trauma distorted his perception of the Mota men and their innocence?

By late 1872 such naïveté would have been rare in central Melanesia (although not in New Guinea or on its adjacent islands). If an Islander was willing to migrate, there often arose a choice between Queensland and Fiji. Since Queensland paid indentured men £6 per year, twice Fiji's wages, and asked three rather than five years of service, recruiters for the latter worked at a disadvantage. Fijian ships also retained the onus of the pre-cession years, when struggling planters had often been unable to return Islanders on time. Once it became a crown colony in 1874, however, Fiji enacted a comprehensive set of labor regulations that conduced to the Islanders' benefit. Migrants usually preferred Fiji's yam ration to Queensland's rice. Fiji, well before Queensland, made sure that wages were paid into a government-supervised fund every six months (thereby minimizing the wages lost through planter bankruptcies), and earlier recognized the justice of sending what was owed a deceased laborer to his next of kin.[94]

Whether their young men and, much less often, young women chose Fiji or Queensland, Melanesian villagers would eventually have learned that indentured labor entailed serious risks. Captain William Wawn declared that Islanders who had recently spent three years cutting cane in Queensland stood out on any New Hebridean beach: "They would present a healthier aspect, possess more muscular frames, and be devoid of the furtive, 'wild dog' expression which the genuine savage usually wears." Another champion of the Queensland trade held that "habituating" Islanders to prolonged hard work "infuse[es] into their minds the germs of civilization, viz. a knowledge and a feeling that they have rights, and are protected by law."[95]

Alas, an appalling proportion of these lucky laborers never lived long enough to savor the rule of law, or to glimpse the beaches of home. Compounding the mortality of the Pacific's own Middle Passage, roughly a quarter of the Islanders who reached Queensland between 1863 and 1904 died in that colony.[96] Most—over seventy percent—of these deaths occurred among people in the prime of their lives, a period spanning the mid-teens to the mid-thirties. Between 1880 and 1883, the mortality rate among this demographic segment was about five times higher for Pacific Islanders than for Queensland's European population as a whole. The foes of indentured labor sketched a still more damning profile, estimating the "Polynesian" male death rate at nine to eleven times that of English males between ages sixteen and thirty-two.[97] Mortality rates for Islanders working in Fiji, although more difficult to ascertain, would have been little, if any, lower. Physical exhaustion rendered Melanesians in both places highly susceptible to dysentery, influenza-pneumonia, and tuberculosis. Acknowledging a link between overwork and the severity of infectious disease, the Fijian government in 1890 prohibited the employment of Islanders on sugar plantations where new land had to be cleared. Yet 12.5 percent of those recruited between 1891 and 1900 perished on the job all the same.[98]

The continuing sacrifice of Melanesian recruits on white men's lands must have deterred an unknowable number of Islanders from accepting terms of indenture, or from reenlisting. But where death or injury resulted from perceived malice, Pacific Islanders were often keen to settle scores. They did not need European employers, missionaries, or colonial administrators to explain their "rights." Seeking revenge against an aggressor was both permitted and expected in many Melanesian cultures. The British imperial view was naturally far different. Particularly where Islanders succeeded in killing Europeans, newspapers habitually referred to the perpetration of an "outrage"—that is, an act of violence constituting "a gross or wanton . . . indignity," as the *Oxford English Dictionary* defined this emotive noun.[99] The dignity of presumed racial superiority was nearly always violated when blacks slaughtered whites. Only where black men organized large armies and demonstrated tactical cunning on the battlefield, as the Zulus did on the South African veldt and the Ashanti in the dense forests of West Africa, might "savages" become "warriors." The South Sea Islanders, by contrast, were merely "treacherous" because their tactics involved the false smile and the hatchet blow from behind. Regardless of means, however, striking against an enemy, or against those who resembled that enemy, constituted the most dramatic form of Islander agency.

Although defenders of the labor trade praised the usual docility of Islanders employed in Fiji and Queensland, meekness was not a defining feature of the aggrieved Melanesian. White traders based in the New Hebrides knew this all too well. Surrounded as they believed themselves to be by compulsive thieves, these pioneers placed their faith in fortified compounds and drastic action against trespassers. Such belligerence had not preserved Ross Lewin. Nor did it save George de Lautour, whose small coconut and maize farm on Aore island, off the southeastern coast of Espíritu Santo, was stoutly fenced and gated, each gatepost adorned with a human skull. On a tree close to the gate hung a warning that presumably pleased the trader, even though it would have been meaningless to his illiterate neighbors:

Notice.

Dogs and Niggers are Forbidden to enter inside the
Portals of [these] Gates. Any Dogs or Niggers

found therein will suffer the Penalty of Death.
By order of George de Lautour, British Resident.

Unluckily for de Lautour, one day in the late 1880s his son left the gate ajar, allowing an embittered local to creep toward the main house and shoot the master through its cane walls.[100] Aore, and indeed many of the tropical islands located between the Dutch East Indies and Tonga, formed one of Britain's most turbulent colonial frontiers, as exotic as her African enclaves and just as dangerous.[101]

It was at the interface of ship and shore where this turbulence was most apparent. (See Figure 3.2.) European captains began to take precautions against Islanders swarming aboard their vessels long before the labor trade commenced. In early 1846, for example, a Marist priest wrote to his brother about the "vast net-work of ropes which rose up above the bridge of the ship . . . & which formed a kind of wall" to repel the Solomon Islanders

Figure 3.2   Labor recruiters at work in the New Hebrides, circa 1878. To discourage an ambush by opportunistic Islanders, the covering whaleboat remains at a distance.

SOURCE: Courtesy, Dixson Library, State Library of New South Wales, DL 90_672, no_6.

among whom they were cruising.[102] But the hunt for indentured help plainly did multiply the points of potential friction: between 1863 and its end in the early twentieth century, the Queensland labor trade alone generated over 700 voyages to or from Melanesia.[103]

We will never know how many deaths resulted from Islander attacks on labor vessels. One gentleman-tourist who spent a few months sailing through the Solomons and New Hebrides in 1880 later compiled a list of thirty-four "outrages" that had claimed 114 lives between early 1875 and early 1881. This catalog clearly understated the actual loss of European life because it failed to disaggregate what "murder of crew" meant for several attacks.[104] In any event, naval and colonial officials knew where trouble lurked. The Admiralty's *Sailing Directions* for the western Pacific offered indispensable advice about the locations of dangerous reefs, potable water, and protected anchorages. Tellingly, the 1885 edition also warned of the Santa Cruz group that "too much caution cannot be used in dealing with the inhabitants of these islands."[105] Lieutenant-Commander Moore, upon completion of a peace-keeping voyage through the Solomons and New Hebrides aboard HMS *Dart* in late 1883, pinned much of the blame for civil unrest on former Queensland laborers. Their "moral welfare" having been neglected abroad, they had supposedly returned as brazen enemies of all whites. "It is the most daring of these men who are the leaders in all the conspicuous cases of massacre," Moore declared. By 1892, John Thurston, now high commissioner for the western Pacific, had grown inured to the fact of violence in this region, where "ships of war are almost constantly cruising at a cost to the Imperial Treasury wholly incommensurate with the interests involved." Regrettable as the killing of a white man on Espíritu Santo may have been, "all that has happened is that a British subject has adventured himself among barbarians, notorious for their savage propensities. He has been murdered. . . . Nothing is certain but uncertainty."[106]

Quite sure at least was the emergence of Malaita, largest island of the Solomon group, as among the most hazardous recruiting grounds. If familiarity did in fact breed contempt, then Malaita simmered with disaffection. After all, at least half of the 30,000 Solomon Islanders obtained for plantation work abroad hailed from this place. And in many cases such widespread exposure to European society seems to have made them no less truculent.[107] Malaita had long known intra-island raiding between the bush people of its hilly interior and the "saltwater" folk of the coast. With the tantalizing wealth in trade goods now available aboard recruiting ships, raiding turned outwards. John Gorrie, the Western Pacific High Commission's chief judicial officer, could see no reason for the *Borealis* outrage of mid-September 1880 "except the desire for plunder." Anchored a quarter of a mile off a small island in Mamana Bay, this recruiting vessel was quietly overrun by eighty Malaitans in canoes once the whaleboat carrying the ship's captain and nearly all its firearms had rowed ashore. Only the cook survived the slaughter that ensued, a slaughter in which one crewman's leg was found hacked off and gnawed to the bone.[108] Two years later the *Janet Stewart* was seized under similar circumstances at Kwai.

When a recruiting vessel managed to beat back an attack, the losses it inflicted might just steel the Islanders' resolve. The case of the *Young Dick* suggested as much. In late May of 1886, Captain Rogers foolishly left too few men aboard his labor vessel anchored in hostile Sinerago Bay. This mistake was compounded when his skeletal crew allowed several local men to feast their eyes on the trade gear spread across the deck. The so-called "cupidity of natives" soon launched an attack. But for the quick thinking of able seaman Thomas Crittenden, all aboard the *Young Dick* would have been lost. Once the axes began flashing, however, Crittenden fought his way up to the topsail yardarm, Snider rifle in hand and pockets stuffed with cartridges. From this perch he managed to pick off more than a dozen of the "seething, screeching mob of brutal devils" below. This halted the attack but not the bloodshed. To avenge their lost men, the Sinerago people offered a reward of 100,000 porpoise teeth to any village that could capture a ship. The residents of Manaoba earned a smaller prize two years later by killing the government inspector of the *Ariel*, whom they lured ashore with pleas for medical aid.[109]

Why did Royal Navy "gunboats," Britain's best weapon in the Pacific, not punish such Islander aggression? Sometimes, of course, they did. Eighteen days before the attack on the *Young Dick*, tomahawk-wielding men had waylaid the ship's boatswain. Blood streaming from his face and scalp, the mate had barely survived to tell his tale of treachery. The captain of HMS *Opal*, then visiting nearby Port Adams, decided that the offenders ought to learn a "salutary lesson." Captain Brooke therefore shelled a village said to be sheltering them. One coconut palm perished, but none of the assailants—all of whom, having been warned by the resident Anglican missionary, watched this administration of naval justice from the safety of a distant beach. As for those who later swarmed the *Young Dick,* the likelihood of apprehending the culprits struck Rear-Admiral Tryon as remote. The declaration of an "act of war" against the offenders seemed inappropriate because the captain and crew of the *Young Dick* had, essentially, invited disaster. Moreover, since the Islanders of the eastern Malaitan coast could readily distinguish among trading vessels, labor ships, the mission schooner, and men-of-war, few naval craft would ever enjoy the element of surprise. And to order a landing party meant asking sailors to walk "Indian file" along narrow jungle tracks where the danger of ambush loomed large. Thus, if they could not persuade or pressure a local strongman to give up the architects of an "outrage," naval officers had little room to maneuver.[110]

Adding to these tactical constraints was the ambivalence of public opinion about such attacks and the appropriate response to them. "Exeter-Hallism," as supporters of the labor trade dismissed all philanthropic concern for Islander welfare, covered a wide range of humanitarian thought. Few were as doctrinaire as Rev. John Inglis, for nearly three decades the chief guardian of Presbyterian values in the New Hebrides. According to this missionary, a "small, wealthy, influential, bold, bouncing, unscrupulous class of men" would soon exterminate the "natives" unless enlightened naval officers kept these race-killers in check.[111] With J.C. Patteson's martyrdom fresh in his memory, Commander Albert Markham later explained that he had "determined to do all in my power to shield and protect the Islanders." Yet Markham's enlightenment arrived too late for the Reverend Inglis's taste: the commander's destruction of two villages on Nukapu when his own men drew a hail of arrows impressed some self-appointed friends of the Aborigines as rash.[112] Markham's reprisal was unusual for its time. Between the start of regular Pacific island patrols in 1829 and the cession of Fiji in 1874, just eight Royal Navy ships fired on indigenous settlements.[113] True enough, at the height of the labor trade, stepped-up recruiting provoked more Islander "outrages" and correspondingly more punitive policing methods from naval authorities. But as the *Sandfly* affair suggests, it usually required spectacular violence to ignite the Royal Navy's wrath.

HMS *Sandfly* was one of five Sydney-built schooners launched in 1873 and 1874 to survey the backwaters of Melanesia and monitor the labor traffic. Light and nimble, they were well suited to ply reef-strewn seas.[114] The *Sandfly's* log for 13 October 1880 mentions only that its captain, Lieutenant-Commander James Bower, and five crew left in the whaleboat at 6:30 a.m.

to explore the tiny islands near Florida, in the central Solomons. It had been a placid cruise so far, the only mishap recorded being the loss of a hammer overboard. Calm gave way to consternation, however, when six days elapsed without word from the captain or his crew. A search party finally located the missing men on uninhabited Mandoleana Island. All save one were dead, their headless bodies baked black by the equatorial sun. Only seaman Francis Savage had managed to swim away at dusk and hide on a neighboring islet.[115]

Although conceding that the *Sandfly's* captain and his men had been unwise to relax—brewing tea and bathing—on a strange beach, the same Sydney newspapers that normally urged restraint in dealing with wayward Islanders now demanded "sharp justice." The attack, it appeared, had been entirely unprovoked. The assailants were headhunters, single-minded killers about whose deeds Lieutenant Bower had already warned his superiors. The victims, four of them Londoners, exemplified the best qualities of the English "tar." No trade goods had stirred envy in savage breasts. The *Sandfly* murders, moreover, roughly coincided with at least four other massacres of Europeans in the Solomons and eastern archipelagoes of New Guinea.[116] At the hub of empire, as well as on its Australian periphery, smug letters still praised the Royal Navy's measured response to such "cowardly" acts. Subsequent searches for the ringleaders of the *Sandfly* tragedy yielded just two culprits. Rushed shipboard trials featuring unchallenged witnesses had prefaced both executions, one of which saw local men compelled to hang their own comrade. If this was naval justice at work, one skeptic observed, then Britain was waging a most peculiar war.[117]

The strangeness of the conflict forced colonial administrators, as well as admirals, to temporize. Established in 1877 and headquartered in Fiji, the Western Pacific High Commission had been saddled with vast responsibility backed by what its historian has termed "ludicrously inadequate" resources. The Colonial Office, on the far side of the globe, hoped that Sir Arthur Gordon, the first high commissioner, would somehow harmonize race relations throughout 8,000,000 square miles of ocean and sand.[118] Gordon and his successors were authorized to punish British subjects for a wide variety of crimes. But over the denizens of uncolonized islands, a high commissioner had no legal authority.

How to discourage "native aggression," therefore, posed a vexing problem. Sir William Des Voeux, Gordon's immediate successor, was generally content to let Her Majesty's ships deal with Melanesians accused of murder. When the latter were inconveniently delivered to Fiji, however, Des Voeux took cover behind legal fiction, treating the suspects not as "prisoners" (for fear that "some busybody might obtain a writ of *habeas corpus*") but as "convicts."[119] Arthur Gordon's chief judicial commissioner, John Gorrie, proved equally creative with the law. A political radical, Gorrie viewed the traders and planters around him very much as he had viewed the white colonists of Jamaica—as bigots bent on their own enrichment. Gorrie therefore set out to weight the scales of justice. In the 1879 case of *Regina v. Kilgour*, the captain of a Queensland labor vessel was slapped with a heavy £100 fine for burning native huts on the New Hebridean island of Aoba. Charles Kilgour testified that Aoba men had stolen one of his whaleboats on a previous recruiting trip, and that it was only after coming under musket fire while trying to recover his property that he had registered his displeasure. For Commissioner Gorrie, though, nothing excused a resort to private war: "It is the sovereign power alone which has the right to say when a recourse shall be had to arms."[120] Gorrie failed to mention that the High Commission possessed no such power where Islanders were concerned.

Aoba produced another case that displayed Gorrie's legal legerdemain at its most artful. There was no question that "Aratuga," a resident of that island, had "treacherously decoyed" the *Mystery*'s whaleboat, urging its recruiting agent to land where Aratuga's friends lay in wait. During the melee that followed, Aratuga hacked to death at least one member of the landing party and later confessed his deed to a missionary. Judge Gorrie addressed his thirty-six-page opinion not to intent, however, but to the issue of jurisdiction. If Aratuga had acted as an individual while committing homicide in a British boat, then, Gorrie reasoned, this Islander would have been solely responsible for his crime. But Gorrie chose instead to regard Aratuga's deed as part of a "general and tumultuous onslaught," an "act of the community." Since Britain enjoyed no diplomatic relationship with this community, Britain had no right to punish members of it, at least not in a court of law.[121] Aratuga returned to Aoba unscathed.

Their enemies charged that Judge Gorrie was a "protégé" of the Aborigines' Protection Society, and that his superior, Sir Arthur Gordon, was a "pet" of Exeter Hall.[122] Both charges were unfair. Nonetheless, the tendency of the Western Pacific High Commission to rationalize Islander attacks clearly did stir resentment among many Europeans living or working on a dangerous frontier. As one Royal Navy officer wrote in exasperation, the concept of "native practice" could be advanced to excuse almost any "savage outrage":

> To take a willing recruit off the beach without giving a
> gun for him, is "stealing," according to "native practice";
> to shoot a man from behind a rock because your
> mother-in-law had died is a "native practice";
> to shoot any white man because one of your tribe
> has died a natural death in the white man's country
> is "native practice"; to hack a man's head off
> with a tomahawk because your daughter has run
> off to Fiji is "native practice." "Native practice" will
> account for every brutality committed in the South
> Sea Islands, because "native practice" means to kill
> whenever the opportunity . . . presents itself.[123]

Through the 1890s and on into the new century, Islanders continued to shoot at the sails of recruiting ships. Whether these volleys represented self-conscious defiance or merely target practice, it is impossible to say.[124] What can be shown is that a parallel form of skirmishing over the labor trade played out in Australian courtrooms.

THE MISRULE OF LAW

What British colonial administrators, naval officers, missionaries, and moral reformers of all hues found most galling about the labor trade was that legal ambiguities too often shielded predators. Captain George Palmer's widely noted exposé of "kidnapping in the South Seas" drove home the point that, as of 1871, "You may hire a vessel and fit her up precisely the same as an African slaver"[125] without fear of interdiction. Palmer certainly stood to gain by demonizing the recruiting process. After all, his aggressive move against the labor ship *Daphne* in 1869 had landed him in serious legal trouble. But considerations of self-interest aside, Palmer's argument impressed humanitarians at home and abroad as credible. "Let any intelligent man read Captain Palmer's book," challenged one letter to *The Times*, "and he will see that for a long time the British law was at fault."[126] British law did render it nearly impossible to try Islander "kidnapping" cases as crimes under the old anti-slavery statutes, an anomaly discussed below. Of greater practical conse-quence, though, was the refusal of some Australian courts, and many Aus-tralian juries, to deal severely with the misdeeds of labor recruiters.

As far back as 1828, Britain's Parliament had granted Australian supreme courts the authority to hear criminal cases originating in New Zealand, Ta-hiti, or any other Pacific island not under the control of a European state.[127] On the rare occasions when this power was exercised, the judicial outcomes had generally sickened humanitarians. The November 1849 murder trial in Sydney of Captain John Charles Lewis, for example, served to "embarrass the march of justice." Lewis had shot and killed a male adult, name un-known, on Maré, one of the Loyalty Islands located near New Caledonia. With no Islander present to rebut the captain's account, a jury found that Lewis had acted while under the impression that his life was in danger. Little over a month after his "triumphant" acquittal, Lewis and the entire crew of his cutter, the *Lucy Anne*, were captured and butchered off Maré. A higher justice had intervened, or so it seemed to some humanitarians.[128]

Six years after Queensland gained self-rule in 1859, Britain enacted legisla-tion that allowed colonial assemblies to pass laws without obtaining prior approval from London.[129] This meant that, short of meddling with a self-governing colony's constitution (a step bound to ignite settler resentment), Britain could no longer dictate how "natives" should be treated. Colonial officials in the mother country envisioned a partnership with local leaders in the autonomous reaches of the empire. For this partnership to succeed, however, both administrative costs and notions of good government would have to be shared. Unfortunately, neither in London nor in Brisbane or Sydney did those who greased the wheels of colonial justice wish to pay for refinements in that mechanism. Thus, in early 1871, when contemplating new legislation to protect Pacific Islanders from deceptive recruiting prac-tices, an economy-minded Colonial Office pressed the Australian colonies to guarantee payment of expenses associated with transporting witnesses from and back to Melanesia. Down Under, this request smacked of coercion.[130]

But the quality of justice delivered in cases involving Pacific Islanders suffered more from notions of racial inferiority than from administrative penny-pinching. Was it the oppressive heat, wondered Captain Palmer, that transformed "a certain class" of white men into crazed persecutors of dark-skinned peoples? "It is like flourishing a red flag before a bull," Palmer observed, "to show an aboriginal of the South Sea Islands to some Englishmen, with the thermometer at 90° in the shade. They go mad."[131] Yet even in the cooler months of an Australian winter, racialized thinking generated a kind of courtroom madness. Kanakas—a general term for Pacific island laborers—were widely believed to occupy a higher branch on the evolutionary tree than the "ineradicably savage" Australian bushman. The distinguished English novelist Anthony Trollope, who toured the antipodes in 1871 and 1872, spoke for many white settlers when he wrote of the Kanakas, "Civilisation is within their reach—in spite of their island homes, their dusky colour, their various languages, and old cannibal propensities—because they will work."[132] Australia's first people, however, were presumed hostile to steady labor of any sort and, until the late 1880s, often stood ready to resist European occupation of their ancestral hunting grounds. Such supposedly extreme cultural backwardness went far toward excusing judicial disregard of violence committed against indigenous Australians. The conviction of a white man for the rape of an Aboriginal did not occur until 1883, and not before 1888 were convictions for killing Aboriginals secured in Queensland courts.[133]

If the failures of law to protect Pacific Islanders from European violence were less blatant, they were just as improbably justified. Here, in "a matrix of abstract legality," can be found support for the postcolonial charge that liberal imperial values masked a bedrock authoritarianism designed to perpetuate the exploitation of subject peoples.[134] Take the exclusion of Islander evidence at trial. It had long been a presumption of English criminal procedure that before offering testimony, a witness must grasp the cultural underpinnings of "truth." In theory, the compromise was elegant: understanding the religious consequences of a lie would dispel further epistemological doubt. But in practice, those who judged whether an Islander witness understood the meaning of an oath might have had personal interests in this determination. Hence John Fenwick, one of the justices of the peace who dismissed a charge of rape against Ross Lewin in 1868, was himself engaged in the labor trade and had been one of Lewin's employers.[135]

Should an Islander's claim of conversion be trusted? Did nominal membership in a Christian community erase the savage propensity to deceive? In the Babel that was Melanesia, could an interpreter from one island accurately convey the words of a witness from another? Australian judges and juries asked these questions, and often answered them in the negative. As an enemy of the "slave trade" reasoned, "If the testimony of the South Sea Islanders is not to be received in our courts of justice because they are heathens and savages, they are thereby placed beyond the pale of the law, and debarred from the common rights and privileges of civilization, justice, and humanity."[136]

At last, in 1876, legal barriers to the acceptance of Islander and Aboriginal evidence at trial began to crumble. By this time, with white settler fears of vengeful blacks ebbing in Australia's Outback, the old exclusionary practices now seemed less vital. By legislation passed in 1876, New South Wales allowed a witness to make a "declaration" in lieu of an oath on a Bible; no longer would belief in a "power which can punish or reward after death" be demanded.[137] But Queensland, where the majority of Australia's Islander immigrants worked and from whose ports most of the recruiting ships set out, did not start to relax its own oath standard until 1884. Unqualified acceptance of witness declarations would need another seven years.[138] That Pacific Islanders in Queensland had much to say about their lives became poignantly clear through interviews conducted by the so-called "Kidnapping Commission" of 1885. Literally hundreds of Islanders recruited for northern sugar plantations told of deep confusion over their terms of indenture and grief over separation from their loved ones. This voluminous testimony is peppered with confessions of ignorance ("I no savez") and bristles with the linguistic ambiguities created through frequent double translations (from an Islander's native tongue into Pidgin, and once more from Pidgin into the Anglicized Pidgin of the white interviewer).[139] Yet these voices, however filtered, were eloquent. And their exclusion from Queensland's courtrooms until quite late in the labor trade era rendered that colony's rule of law suspect.

Partly to preempt stricter imperial legislation, and partly perhaps to salve some tender consciences,[140] Queensland lawmakers passed the Polynesian Laborers Act in March 1868. Although a Liberal majority on the Colony's Legislative Council had sponsored it, the act hardly qualified as a beacon of racial justice. It is noteworthy that "securing to the employer the due fulfillment by the immigrant of his agreement" shared pride of place in its preamble with "securing to the laborers proper treatment and protection."[141] The 1868 act helped. By requiring each Queensland labor ship to obtain a license, to post a bond for the proper engagement and return of workers, and to provide them adequate food and accommodation during transit, it clarified obligations for conscientious captains and recruiting agents. One year after the act took effect, a Queensland review committee declared it a success, although the committee recommended the placement of a government inspector on each recruiting vessel.[142] As the scandals of 1869–1871 would soon show, however, the rapacious continued to pursue their prey undeterred.

The prospect of being punished under Queensland's new legislation was, at worst, irksome. Kidnapping, if proven in court, would be treated as a breach of government regulations, punishable by a maximum fine of £500, whereas conviction for the same crime under Britain's old antislavery statutes would have meant penal servitude for life and forfeiture of the offending ship. Since profits from a large recruiting haul, such as the 240 Islanders snatched by the barque *King Oscar* in 1867, could exceed £2,000, such a fine held little terror.[143] To avoid fines entirely, of course, some recruiting vessels licensed in Queensland simply unloaded their catch in Fiji—which, prior to 1874, had no capacity of its own to monitor the traffic. Bad luck, not stringent policing, would bring down those in command of the *Young Australian* and the *Daphne*, ships synonymous with white savagery. Rumors of a massacre at sea eventually caught up with the former, as we have seen. The *Daphne*, licensed to carry fifty laborers to Queensland, had collected a hundred when she arrived at Levuka to find HMS *Rosario* lying at anchor. What Captain George Palmer discovered aboard the *Daphne* savored of slavery. In the convoluted legal drama that followed his seizure of this ship, however, it emerged that the law saw "blackbirding" and slavery as different crimes.

As early as the 1820s, the "equipment clauses" in Britain's antislavery treaties had enabled Royal Navy vessels to detain and condemn private ships as slavers even when no victims were discovered aboard. The paraphernalia of slave-trading alone—leg irons, structural modifications to increase a ship's carrying capacity, excess stores of food, water, or matting—might justify a vessel's seizure.[144] In 1869, Captain Palmer not only found telltale accommodations aboard the *Daphne* but also a hundred recruits (who were, he had to admit, free to move about the ship). The master of the *Daphne*, John Daggett, and Ross Lewin's agent, Thomas Pritchard, had plainly violated the terms of their Queensland recruiting license, a violation for which they probably would have been fined if dealt with at Brisbane. But the zealous Palmer, a veteran of antislavery patrols off the West African coast, spurned caution. He sailed to Sydney, and there, invoking the stern majesty of British justice, charged the *Daphne*'s master and agent with having "knowingly and willfully . . .remove[d]" Islanders to be used as slaves.[145]

Captain Palmer's initial seizure of the *Daphne* at Levuka, and the subsequent trial of Daggett and Pritchard in Sydney's Water Police Court, drew detailed press coverage throughout New South Wales and in several British cities. Widespread consternation, therefore, greeted the court's dismissal of charges against Daggett on the grounds that the existence of an agreement for a finite period of service nullified the presumption of slavery.[146] His legal position undercut, Palmer now became the quarry: the *Daphne*'s owners sued him for false imprisonment plus damages. How had British justice failed so completely, poised as it was to ruin a righteous man? "Where," asked one of Palmer's many allies, was the "slightest flash of that frenzy of indignation not long since exhibited in the case of the Jamaica black?"[147] In an opinion that closed the case but pleased few, Sir Alfred Stephen ruled that although Captain Palmer had been wrong to regard the *Daphne* as a slaver, he did have probable cause to seize her, and thus should be spared further litigation.[148] The inapplicability of slave trade legislation to conditions in the western Pacific would wait for judicial confirmation until 1880.[149] Well before that date, however, humanitarians were beseeching the mother country to lift this legal fog.

Britain's attempt to clarify the criminal law as it pertained to labor recruitment was the Pacific Islanders Protection Act of June 1872, better known as the "Kidnapping Act." The impetus for its passage derived from the intersection of two tragedies. We have seen that the murder of John Coleridge Patteson at Nukapu Island on 20 September 1871 sent a shock wave through the imperial heart, as well as its Oceanic appendages. The bishop's killing alone would probably have wrung some legislative response from Parliament, given that his murder was framed in the sort of Manichean terms that a censorious Victorian public preferred. As one biographer summed up this tragedy, "slavery slew Patteson."[150] The Queen's Speech at the opening of Parliament on 6 February 1872 sounded the same note: "The Slave Trade, and practices scarcely to be distinguished from Slave Trading," had "dishonoured" the British Empire "by the connexion of some of my subjects with these nefarious practices."[151] Dr. James Patrick Murray, the Irish-born instigator of the *Carl* massacre, was just such a subject. Indeed, the *Carl* revelations, which unfolded in the courtrooms of Sydney and

Melbourne during the autumn and winter of 1871–72, first broke upon the British domestic scene one month after Patteson's slaying (although one month before British newspapers announced the bishop's death).[152] This confluence of barbarities, wherein one saintly Briton and seventy bewildered Pacific Islanders were metaphorically burned on the same pyre, made calls for new law irresistible. Bishop Selwyn would not get an "armed steamer . . . constantly cruising among the Islands" to suppress man stealing.[153] But Patteson's mentor, and those who shared his anguish, could at least hope that the 1872 Kidnapping Act would halt the ruin of Melanesia.

If hope they did, disappointment followed. The imperial legislation of 1872 made it a felony for British subjects to decoy, carry away, confine, or detain without his or her consent, any native of an uncolonized Pacific island.[154] It also provided for the seizure of any British ship causing "such outrages." Building on Queensland's 1868 statute, the new act required all British vessels engaged in the labor trade to take out a license, and obliged the masters of these vessels to pledge a bond of £500 against violation of its terms. Usefully, Australasian supreme courts were now empowered to compel the attendance of witnesses from outside British territory, and to exercise discretion in accepting Islander evidence. Yet the act fell well short of the comprehensive shield that ardent humanitarians had been demanding. Not by accident was the word "slavery" missing from the new legislation: its framers knew that to equate labor recruitment, even at its most vicious, with the old transatlantic slave trade was to invite protracted legal dispute. At most, imperial law could target "particular forms of inter-insular kidnapping."[155] Nor did the 1872 act address deliberate misrepresentation of the work Islanders were expected to do, the duration of that work, and precisely where workers would be returned once their terms of service had ended. Above all, the Kidnapping Act's narrow jurisdiction limited its influence. Until 1874, the "anarchical condition" of Fiji put British ships flying other flags beyond the Royal Navy's reach. Since, for example, French law on labor recruitment was now considerably less exacting than British law, *le tricolore* gained sudden popularity.[156]

The Kidnapping Act of 1872 would be amended six times over the ensuing twenty years.[157] An awkward division of responsibility for policing the labor traffic would come to frustrate both the navy and the new Western Pacific High Commission. Friends of the trade could now point to a multitude of protective regulations that specified everything from the duration of recruiting voyages to the minimum distance between berths. But the enforcement of these regulations remained loose—a crucial advantage for a speculative business. As one Queensland planter's association observed, "a certain amount of laxness from the regulations was necessary as if these rules were strictly adhered to no islanders at all would be recruited."[158] Necessity was the mother of evasion.

Even the best-positioned eyes, those of the government inspectors assigned to all British labor vessels, might wink. Queensland's colonial government began appointing shipboard inspectors (or "agents," as they were commonly known) first, in 1871; four years later, when Fiji gained a colonial administration of its own, a similar requirement was instituted there. Although berthed and fed at the expense of ship owners, these agents should have been the Islanders' best friends. That is, in addition to explaining the conditions of service to each prospective recruit, a government agent was adjured to "be most careful in seeing that no coercion, undue influence, unfair play, false representation, or treachery of any kind, is employed in procuring laborers, and that perfect freedom of action is allowed to those open to engagement."[159] At least in the early years of their service aboard Queensland labor vessels, it is doubtful how effectively agents could have discharged these duties because, until 1874, they were not obliged to accompany the landing boats from which coercion would have been most visible.[160] Thereafter, some agents, on some Queensland ships, surely did give Islander well-being their full attention. Douglas Rannie, a Scot who had yearned to visit "long-dreamt-of South Sea isle[s]," realized his dream and became a hero at the same time: off Bougainville he allegedly saved a captive Buka man from becoming dinner by buying him.[161] The diary of John Renton, another Scot drawn to the Pacific, documents the gentle care lavished on a New Hebridean man sick with consumption.[162] But those government agents who tried to honor their appointments often found themselves "in a chronic state of warfare with the cook, the mate, or the recruiter," not to mention the captain. The pressure to overlook recruiting violations, combined with poor pay and exposure to ambush along inhospitable coasts, encouraged more than a few agents to seek comfort in a bottle.[163]

Some, sober or drunk, were prepared to ignore the worst treatment of Islanders. The conduct of a British captain found guilty of murder and kidnapping in a French court at Noumea, New Caledonia, in 1882, had recently been rated "satisfactory" by the agent aboard. As the *Pall Mall Gazette* exclaimed to its London readership, it was humiliating to find French colonial officials branding a British crew "the scum of the sea."[164] In Fiji, the Immigration Department generally gave its inspectors better support than did Queensland's Immigration Board. Still, the surviving journals of Fiji's government agents reveal much obstruction: captains who sneered at pleas for humane handling of Islanders in canoes; who denied requests for deck awnings during heat waves; who refused to send back child "recruits"; and who ignored demands for the ending of marathon voyages.[165] Such contempt for the letter of the law mocked the Pacific's "free trade in labor."

A full decade after Britain imposed the Kidnapping Act on its Pacific possessions, another round of scandals gave renewed force to the claim that only total suppression of this trade would halt its parade of horrors. Commodore John Crawford Wilson echoed the experience of many naval officers assigned to the Australia Station when he identified some of the legal loopholes through which recruiting ships continued to sail. The Kidnapping Act, Wilson noted, applied narrowly to Islanders hired for plantation work in Britain's colonies; it offered virtually no protection to "many thousands" of men who lived aboard British commercial ships while diving for pearl-shell and sponges, or during the curing of *bêche-de-mer* and copra (dried coconut meat, from which coconut oil is extracted).[166]

As for those Islanders destined to cut cane in Queensland or Fiji, their pursuers could not be denied a recruiting license unless hard evidence of their unfitness was produced. The commodore ridiculed defenders of the labor trade who cited "old hands"—Islanders who had agreed to work abroad beyond their three-year term of service—as proof that plantation life was agreeable. A lot could go wrong in three years, Wilson observed. Wives might find new mates. Abandoned huts might collapse. Gardens might revert to jungle. The man returning to face such disasters found himself "an alien and an outcast." Once his trade goods had been distributed among his people, the returnee could be left with little more than a rifle and one shabby European suit. Under these circumstances, the semi-stranger might have no practical option "but to return to a life which probably he heartily detests."[167]

A cluster of widely publicized recruiting abuses did eventually compel Queensland's government to ban all labor recruitment in the western Pacific. The mayhem that occasioned this drastic step began with the *Ceara* case of 1882—a calamity in which "Nomoo," a Tanna man-turned-recruiter, stole an Erromangan chief's daughter, shot her father, and later casually executed a Presbyterian teacher. The killer, in one missionary's acid assessment, had spent sixteen years soaking up the "boasted civilizing influence" that the labor trade "brings to bear on savage character."[168] British missionaries were not alone in assailing greed gone wild. The conviction and early release of William McMurdo, Queensland's government agent aboard the recruiting ship *Stanley*, stunned humanitarians in Britain as well as Australia. The main charge against McMurdo and his captain, Joseph Davies, had been malicious destruction of native property, but it was their calm, cost/benefit defense of violence that seemed so unnatural.

In April 1883, the *Stanley* anchored off a small island near the southeastern tip of New Guinea. The enlistment there of "boys" for the sugarcane fields of Maryborough went well until a rival German trader began spreading rumors about the ship's secret plan to keep its recruits in permanent bondage. Mass desertion followed. McMurdo, supposedly the Queensland government's best check against recruiting crimes, eagerly participated in a punitive raid to burn the nearest village and smash its canoes. As McMurdo noted in his journal, the raid was simply a "set off," a business decision to ensure against the potential loss of £325 in negotiable manpower, "exclusive of expenses and delay." This bottom line logic also justified the captain's subsequent threat of war should his "boys" not return to the *Stanley*.[169] They returned. Although the *Stanley* delivered its living cargo to Queensland as arranged, news of McMurdo and Davies's conduct resulted in their arrest at Brisbane, extradition to Fiji, conviction on all charges, and sentencing to three months' imprisonment. What flummoxed humanitarian foes of the labor trade was the judicial sympathy shown to McMurdo. Never mind that this government agent had resorted to "ruthless intimidation" of the Lachlan Islanders: the "unfortunate" McMurdo had somehow been led to believe that his official duties "included the securing as well as [the] protection of recruited labourers."[170] His sins absolved, McMurdo won immediate release from a solicitous William Des Voeux, acting high commissioner for the western Pacific. "If the truth were to be understood," snarled one critic of this resolution, "the real savages, the treacherous villains, the brutal human animals who will shoot men with dusky skins as they would slaughter sheep . . . do not carry black faces."[171]

Miscarriages of justice at trial, combined with a judicial disinclination to hold ship owners accountable for the crimes of their crews, made Queensland's regulation of the labor trade seem farcical. If juries refused to condemn outright kidnapping, as the *Jessie Kelly* verdict of April 1884 appeared to prove, and if judges insisted that a labor vessel could not be confiscated just because "the consent of the natives" had not been clearly established, as the *Forest King* decision of October 1884 signaled, then of what use were laws to protect the Islanders of uncolonized Melanesia?[172] This question gained added urgency when recruiting ships began visiting the little known island groups that bend in a great arc around the eastern tip of New Guinea. New Britain and New Ireland in particular were found to be full of comparatively innocent "boys" and "marys" (as trade Pidgin designated women). By the early 1880s, Islanders throughout most of the New Hebrides and the Solomons had become familiar enough with the recruiting game to spot at least some of the tricks that might be used to "gammon" (fool) them.[173] But on New Britain, for example, where Queensland vessels first materialized in early 1883, the Islanders knew only the routine of a Hamburg firm, Hernsheim and Robertson. Since Hernsheim's agents typically hired plantation workers on brief, three-month "contracts," three fingers held aloft by a Queensland recruiter were bound to mislead.[174]

Misrepresentation, though, was the least damning charge leveled against the New Guinea trade. No fewer than fourteen of the thirty-two labor voyages from Queensland to that region in 1883 and 1884 became targets of official enquiries.[175] Among these stains on colonial commerce, none was more horrific, or more widely denounced, than the 1884 voyage of the woefully misnamed *Hopeful*. Not until a month after this schooner's profitable return with 123 laborers from the D'Entrecasteaux and Louisade island clusters did the "hideous crimes" of seven white savages come to light. As the *Brisbane Courier* revealed in graphic detail, two fleeing Islanders had been casually shot dead, a third had his throat slit, and a little boy, too young to be recruited, had been left to drown in the surf. For their parts in this carnage, the *Hopeful*'s chief recruiter and another crewmember were condemned to hang, its captain and government agent earned life imprisonment, and three more seamen received long jail terms.[176] Yet except for the government agent, Harry Schofield, a drunk who died after less than two years behind bars, all of the convicted men would later be released in 1890—an act of clemency that made sense only to those who placed radically different values on lives black and white.

Still, the labor trade had been wounded. The *Hopeful* revelations, a growing awareness of the terrible death rate among Melanesian laborers in

Queensland, and the ascent of S.W. Griffith to that colony's premiership in late 1883 virtually guaranteed a new, more critical investigation of the trade.[177] The son of a Congregational minister, Griffith detested the traffic in human toil, as well as the plantation society based upon it.[178] His rank-and-file Liberal Party supporters may have been more concerned about the threat that island labor posed to the white workforce, but Griffith's electoral mandate was, for the moment, secure. Not surprisingly, then, the Royal Commission that launched its probe of labor recruitment around New Guinea on 6 January 1885 proved exceedingly thorough. After thirty meetings, during which the translated testimony of 480 Islanders was obtained, the Commissioners learned that very few of the men and women recently brought to Australia had grasped the nature of their engagements.[179] The clarity of this conclusion gave Premier Griffith the leverage he needed. In November of 1885, his Liberal government announced the banning of all recruiting licenses after 31 December 1890. Five years, surely, would be time enough for Queensland's planters to find an alternative workforce. The era of the Kanaka appeared to be ending.

THE UNHAPPY AFTERLIFE OF INDENTURED LABOR

Contrary to most expectations, Britain's Pacific labor trade received a long stay of sentence. By the late 1880s, with Queensland's blanket ban on Islander recruitment drawing near, a common toast among Mackay planters was "D.S.G."—"Damn Sam Griffith."[180] Yet this purported tool of the "Anti-Slavery party"[181] would soon pull a stunning volte-face. In a newspaper manifesto published on 13 February 1892, Griffith defended his decision to resume the colony's labor trade. The Premier's rationale was tortured. His concern supposedly centered not on "the colour of men's skins" but instead on the long-term viability of Queensland as "a home for the British race." By relying on Islander sweat, the colony's sugar industry had called into existence a "large servile population" that was not only antithetical to "free political institutions" but also denigrated tropical agriculture as "unworthy of the white races." If Queensland were to become a haven for the small, independent farmer, European immigrants would have to take over from Kanaka men and women. But until the former could be acclimatized, the

latter needed to carry on as the least objectionable sort of "coloured labour."[182] A ten-year extension of Islander recruitment, minutely supervised,
was thus essential.

The resumption of Queensland's labor trade drew immediate protest.
Dr. John Paton, chairman of the Presbyterian Church's New Hebrides Mission, cut straight to the heart of the matter, as he saw it: if capitalists did not
care about the depopulation of Melanesia, God did; and His judgment
would be terrible.[183] Half a world away in the imperial hub, Dr. Paton's
concerns, shorn of their prophecy, found broad support. Although John
Selwyn, recently retired as bishop of Melanesia, knew full well that the western isles could not be "wrapped up in cotton-wool" and preserved, he worried that their fragile cultures would soon collapse under the weight of renewed commercial exploitation. Both Vice-Admiral James Erskine and Sir
Arthur Gordon believed that a catastrophic reopening of the New Guinea
labor corridor was almost certain.[184] Queensland's lobbyist in London,
James Garrick, assured the British public that his colony would impose the
most stringent conditions on all future recruitment. The Royal Navy's con-
fiscation of the licenseless Fiji labor ship *Emma Fisher* in late 1891 suggested
that the general regulatory climate had indeed grown stricter.[185]

But the trade remained morally suspect. Queensland's importation of
Pacific island labor finally ended not because most Australians came to share
the humanitarians' disgust, but rather because the old dream of a white
yeomanry now seemed feasible under a federal government. Beginning with
Victoria in 1855, the separate Australian colonies had already passed statutes
restricting the entry of Chinese immigrants. Once these colonies merged to
form the Commonwealth of Australia in 1901, the Immigration Restriction
Act of that year made the exclusion of most non-Europeans a nationwide
policy. The 1901 Pacific Island Labourers Act addressed the closely connected issue of Kanaka immigrants. Under its terms, the number of Islanders allowed into Australia would steadily decrease until 31 March 1904, at
which time immigration would cease. All Pacific Islanders still resident in
the Commonwealth on 31 December 1906 would risk deportation. Exemp-
tions were later granted for those who could prove long, continuous residence in Australia, had married there, or were elderly. Such extenuating
circumstances nevertheless applied to few: of the 6,389 Islanders in
Queensland in 1906, just 691 were deemed exempt from deportation. The
prospect of forced repatriation apparently panicked many Melanesian im-

migrants. As early as 1901, some 3,000 of them signed (or marked) a petition to Edward VII in which they assured Britain's king that to be shipped back to certain "entirely heathen and cannibal" isles would mean giving up their lives or their new Christian faith.[186] Meanwhile, a Commonwealth subsidy of £2 per ton of refined sugar had been offered to producers who employed only white labor. The Melanesian no longer fit in this new colonial order.[187]

Among some of Britain's western Pacific territories the recruitment of indentured labor continued, although in highly varied forms. Fiji, unlike Queensland, never expelled its Melanesian field workers. It had no need to do so because Indian "coolies," first introduced in 1878, impressed planters as more efficient (if also slightly more expensive) workers. By 1909, Pacific Islander immigration to Fiji had virtually ceased.[188] Local circumstances, not imperial edicts, also shaped the Solomon Islands' labor regime. The "protectorate" that Britain established over half of the Solomon archipelago in 1893 gave its colonial administrator considerable power to regulate recruitment. C.M. Woodford, the Solomons' first resident commissioner, proved to be an activist in this regard. Concerned that the siphoning off of "natives" to distant plantations was stunting the growth of local copra production, Woodford finally persuaded the western Pacific high commissioner to halt all recruiting for labor outside the Protectorate as of 31 December 1911. Labor shortages within the group would persist, but not because Solomon Islanders were being shipped abroad.[189] In the New Hebrides, finally, long-standing tensions between British and French residents made comprehensive labor regulation impossible. Well into the twentieth century, influential Presbyterian missionaries wore their "Galliphobe" prejudices proudly, infuriating French settlers.[190] British commercial as well as clerical interests, for their part, denounced what they regarded as the criminal sloth of the French Navy in policing rogue labor recruitment.[191] France and Britain's perplexing joint control—the Condominium Government—of the New Hebrides, ratified in 1907, did little to silence these cries.

On the eve of the First World War, indentured Islanders still bore the brunt of plantation work throughout central Melanesia. That these laborers were now restricted to toiling within their own island groups hardly guaranteed kind treatment, however. The Solomons remained a violent backwater whose isolated plantations attracted managers disposed to counter both loneliness and the fear of attack by maintaining strict discipline among their "boys." When it came to controlling local labor, one seasoned manager assured Jack McLaren around 1910, the secret was simple: "Treat them as muck. Remember that a white man's the only human being and that there isn't any other kind. That's the only way to get anything out of them."[192]

After, as well as before, the end of recruitment for Queensland and Fiji, the prolonged drudgery of plantation work had robbed Islanders of "that interest in life which . . . forms the most essential factor in maintaining the health of a people." Or so argued W.H.R. Rivers.[193] Writing in the immediate postwar period (and fresh from treating soldiers with shell shock), this pioneer neurologist and anthropologist sought to illuminate the "psychological" dimensions of Melanesia's alarming population decline. The labor trade, Rivers believed, was deeply implicated. "Voluntary restriction"— abortion and traditional birth control techniques—had far more to do with Melanesia's plummeting birth rate than did the sterility sometimes caused by venereal disease, he held. Ventriloquizing his New Hebridean informants, Rivers asked, "Why should we bring children into the world only to work for the white man?"[194]

William Rivers's speculation must remain just that. Nor is it possible to confirm a related claim that children born in Queensland to Islander parents rarely survived very long after moving to Melanesia and "relaps[ing] into savagery."[195] But we can be confident that for many indentured laborers, homecoming was an event filled with as much dread as joy. If their ship did not sink (as the *Young Dick* did in 1886, when it struck the Great Barrier Reef and drowned 130 Kanakas[196]), some of these workers would have been unable to help locate their home islands because, as people of the inland bush, they had probably glimpsed their own shorelines just once before, three (or five) years earlier. Provided that the right spot on the right island was sighted, heavy surf might force a captain to deposit his returnees elsewhere. Such unfortunates, Commodore J.C. Wilson explained, could be seen "gesticulating and wild with despair as the [whale]boat pulls away." Even if an Islander landed with an armed escort a mere mile from his village, determined robbers still might grab his trade box, as happened at Losa Lava, Banks Islands, in 1882.[197] These dangers were magnified by haste. As of March 1904, nearly 6,000 Solomon Islanders still toiled in Queensland. Since by law most of these men and women stood to be deported starting on 1 January 1907, the odds against an orderly repatriation were long.[198]

We can be confident as well that labor trading accelerated the flow of alcohol and firearms into Melanesia, further rending the fabric of traditional island societies. Like the germs they introduced, the guns and gin that Europeans carried to Oceania arrived decades before Robert Towns's *Don Juan* sailed for the New Hebrides in 1863. But the intensity of the labor traffic, along with its resistance to regulation, created a pipeline for contraband. The tiny pre-cession white population of Fiji had swilled legendary quantities of cheap German gin (four gallons for £1), and this habit spread among Islander crews across the western Pacific. But missionary fulminations against absinthe-dealing Frenchmen notwithstanding, alcohol abuse in late nineteenth- and early twentieth-century Melanesian communities seems to have been rare.[199]

Their preoccupation with guns, on the other hand, proved ruinous. Muskets, ball, and powder became the main Marquesan currency after about 1813. The labor that these eastern Polynesians were willing to perform in exchange for the muzzle-loading weapons of the *aoe* (strangers) made warfare deadlier than ever while undermining the power of the *haka 'ika* (nobility) and the purpose of *koina* (feasting).[200] Muskets later found their way into the hands of Melanesians by way of *bêche-de-mer* and sandalwood traders. Yet it was the conjunction of the indentured labor traffic and advances in rifle technology that unleashed an acquisitive frenzy throughout the western isles.

In the 1850s, Jacob Snider of Philadelphia showed how the British Enfield muzzle-loading musket could be converted into a breech-loading rifle. Shortly thereafter armories in Birmingham and Liège, Belgium, began mass-producing this far more versatile weapon. With each successive refinement of the Snider design, older model breech-loaders were snapped up by Australian middlemen and resold to eager Islanders.[201] By 1870, rumors of Fijian "mountaineers" awash in Sniders had driven one planter to predict the outbreak of a Maori-like rebellion unless some way to stop "tempt[ing] the desires of a savage people" were found.[202] Islander "outrages" against British ships, if not coordinated rebellions, did employ these precision weapons effectively. And the ammunition for them was all too available. While leading a punitive raid on Api (Epi) in 1881, Commodore Wilson found at least 150 rounds of Snider ammunition in every hut he burned; the metallic cartridges had come to serve as "a sort of coinage" there. On Malaita in the north-central Solomons, the flood of breech-loading weapons turned homicide from a selective sanction against witchcraft, adultery, and other major crimes into raw gangsterism.[203]

Had it been the imperial government's decision alone, tough restrictions on Snidermania would have been imposed soon after the 1872 Kidnapping Act took effect. But London's view of the weapons question was not Brisbane's, and Queensland, not Britain, supplied most of Melanesia's rifles. In 1878, over objections from planters and merchants, the colony bowed to imperial pressure by halting the sale of arms to Pacific Islanders.[204] This restriction was at best loosely enforced, however, since those tied to the labor trade saw rifles, cartridges, and dynamite as their trump cards in the competition with other colonies for a scarce human resource. These obstructionists were right. When, in 1884, Queensland and Fiji finally got serious about staunching the flow of guns into Melanesia, both German traders hiring for Samoa and French agents recruiting for New Caledonia quickly filled the void.[205] Britain's subsequent efforts to slap an international arms embargo on the western Pacific never moved beyond vague statements of principle.[206]

In any case, weapon bans deterred few returning Islanders. They became masters of concealment. Cartridges could be stashed almost anywhere: in a furled sail, under a woman's skirt, packed with tobacco, mixed with the soil beneath plants. Bulky rifles, their barrels cut short or their stocks removed, were often hidden under false bottoms in the Islanders' trade boxes. During government inspections, these prizes could be submerged in large water barrels, secreted in sheep pens, or lowered over the side of the ship. For a fee, Islander crews might hide weapons aloft in the rigging or down below with the ballast.[207] Although legally denied access to firearms after 1884, many returning Kanakas brought home their Sniders regardless.

This gun-hunger further threatened already vulnerable island communities. At the village level, Melanesians were in effect trading manpower for a commodity that did nothing to enrich local agriculture, thereby making subsistence yet more dependent on indentured labor abroad.[208] Unlike the indentured Indian "coolies" who eventually shouldered so much of the plantation work in the West Indies, British Guiana, Mauritius, Malaya, Natal, and, after 1878, Fiji, the Islanders of the western Pacific seemed set on a collision course with extinction. Cutting cane in Queensland or on Viti Levu had mostly failed to instill white values—or rather, the right kind of white values—among Islander veterans. Once all but intra-archipelago labor recruitment had ceased, a lethal lack of purpose seemed to cloak Melanesians like a shroud. One naval officer hoped that learning cricket would revitalize the young men of Malekula, in the northern New Hebrides. Discouragingly, they asked to be paid for this new form of work.[209]

By no means all European commentators believed that island peoples were doomed, or agreed on the forces pushing them toward ruin.[210] But for those who did accept that the "inevitable destiny" of Melanesians was oblivion, a moral dilemma arose. Referring specifically to the Pacific "savage" as a casualty of "Mr. Darwin's law," an unnamed ethicist wondered, "[I]s it either necessary or wise to prolong the dying agonies of the moribund by legislation, designed to protect him from one only of his numerous foes?" The answer was of course "yes"; "humanity and justice" demanded action. From the "lawless [labor] trader, that foul blot upon our national honour, prostituting his knowledge to the vilest purposes and giving the lie to our boasted civilization, we can and must preserve him."[211]

The Aborigines' Protection Society reasoned similarly when it declared that Britain and her colonies should treat their black subjects with "such justice as will make allowance for their defects."[212] Even the defect of a cannibal pedigree could not excuse the gulf between ethical theory and everyday practice, however. Britain and, more clearly still, her settler colony of Queensland had done too little too late to guard Pacific Islanders from predatory Europeans. The social-imperialist sage Benjamin Kidd argued at century's end that Britain's tropical colonies warranted firm rule; in an age of heightened rivalry among the world's colonial powers, a long leash for dark peoples in hot lands was irresponsible.[213] The labor trade's slipshod regulation would have provided Kidd a dramatic example of the cost of imperial neglect. The lure of large profits had, it appeared, brought out the beast in some Britons. As judged by one of their own, the British were "capable of a vulgarity, a coarseness" in the presence of beauty. And "this coarseness becomes savagery in many an isolated trader or settler far from religious influences and family ties."[214] The savages had met their match in the likes of Hugo Levinger, James Murray, and Ross Lewin. Indeed, the labor trade's much discussed brutality served to rationalize "native" violence, thereby releasing some white observers to mourn the passing of Melanesia's most martial folk, its headhunters.

FOUR

The Twilight of Headhunting

The so-called headhunting "cults" of Oceania simultaneously repulsed and thrilled a British public fascinated with the exotica of empire. To read about island societies where the taking of human heads marked a way of life was to feel a frisson of relief tinged with pride: relief that such bloodlust occurred half a world away, pride that Britain's imperial reach extended even to these benighted shores. The severed head was a potent symbol of savagery. After all, parting body and mind with the flash of a blade involved more than murder. What remained of the person after beheading was a self-mocking mask whose eyes stared but could not see.

The disembodied head's power to shock served the travel writer well. W.T. Pritchard, born in Tahiti and later stationed in Samoa as Her Majesty's consul, sailed to Britain in 1863 with only a South Seas upbringing to sell. His *Polynesian Reminiscences,* published shortly thereafter, made strategic use of a head-brandishing Samoan buck. Readers learned that "The excitement of the successful warrior is intense as he passes before the chief with his bleeding trophy, capering in the most fantastic evolutions, with blackened face and oiled body, throwing his club high in the air."[1] For Pritchard, as for many others in the business of cataloging savage rites, headhunting rivaled cannibalism as the best spice for a dull tale.

It was however in Melanesia and Borneo, not Polynesia, where Victorian headhunting flourished. A "diabolical" pact between labor recruiters and Solomon Island "skull-hunters," for example, had reportedly erased several villages during the 1870s. Secondhand accounts alleged that certain recruiting ships had agreed to land headhunting parties at undefended settlements, wait while the slaughter took place, and then return the killers with their gory prizes—all in exchange for a cargo of confused young men who dared not protest.[2] Modern historians, too, have often stressed the grotesque otherness of head-taking. Among the Solomon Islands, Britain's quintessential "backward and forgotten" colony, headhunting is said to have constituted "the most spectacular and macabre kind of native violence."[3]

Moral relativists demur, of course. Why denigrate the headhunters of colonial times, one might ask, when American troops eagerly collected enemy ears, teeth, fingers, toes, and penises in Vietnam?[4] Anthropologists, particularly those specializing in the traditional cultures of Southeast Asia, have been equally emphatic. They insist that headhunting should be seen as part of a complex web of ritual rather than as a form of "primitive" warfare or as a feature of the "inevitable" violence that occurs when stateless societies compete for scarce resources.[5] And for those scholars who have focused on the "discourses" surrounding headhunting and cannibalism, what matters are the genealogies of misrepresentation in which these practices are embedded. European preconceptions about the customs of colonial peoples thereby emerge as the subject for analysis, not the customs themselves. It is enough that shrunken heads—"food for thought and also for vultures"—decorate the posts outside Kurtz's hut in *Heart of Darkness*: they betoken a white man's descent into madness. How these heads were gathered is largely irrelevant.[6]

Actually, the provenance of hunted heads *did* matter, not only to the indigenous communities from which they were snatched, but also to missionaries seeking shelter for their flocks, to anthropologists bent on documenting fragile cultures, and to colonial administrators charged with taming unruly peoples. Severed heads could encode very different messages. Although such emblems of depravity served to widen the moral chasm that supposedly separated European and Islander, they might also function to domesticate the wild. David Cannadine has suggested that the British Empire was about "the familiar and domestic, as well as the different and exotic."[7] Strange to say, late-Victorian and Edwardian discussions of headhunting often depicted the aggressor as a doting father and a loyal husband, thereby linking metropolitan Britain's deification of the domestic sphere with apparently similar impulses on the imperial periphery. *The Wild Man at Home* (1879), *The Home-Life of Borneo Head-Hunters* (1902), and *Quaint Subjects of the King* (1909) were only the most obvious illustrations of this peculiar fusion.[8] Walter Bagehot famously praised the role of the monarchy in disguising the real levers of political power: "A *family* on the throne is an interesting idea. . . . It brings down the pride of sovereignty to the level of petty life." If a "princely marriage [was] the brilliant edition of a universal fact,"[9] then the headhunter as family man was the rude exemplar of a global home truth.

But the most noteworthy feature of British headhunting narratives was the distinction they often drew between the "vile" act and the sad passing of a way of life. The artifacts themselves, whether elaborately tattooed Maori faces or plain bleached skulls, often ended up in museum collections throughout Europe. According to at least one literary account, these objects of "hideousness" could also be found in some of East London's "dingy little shops."[10] They would have been no less suitable for display in the ethnographic exhibitions so common during the latter half of the nineteenth century, exhibitions whose eagerness to demonstrate the "varieties of mankind" smacked of the freak show.[11] Such icons of barbarity generated little moral uplift.

Yet the gradual suppression of headhunting in Melanesia, Borneo, and along India's northeastern frontier would give rise to a literature of regret. Between roughly 1880 and 1910, during the twilight of headhunting, travel writers, ethnologists, and even the odd colonial administrator would acknowledge ritual head taking as an important "zest" in the lives of these remote peoples. Indeed, in western Melanesia the precipitous decline of birthrates on several islands would be ascribed partly to Britain's eradication of a practice once widely maligned. A form of "proleptic elegy," wherein a lost essence is mourned before it is completely lost,[12] came to enshroud Pacific headhunting. The practice predeceased the practitioners. But the latter also seemed bound for extinction. Before that happened, those who had made it their mission to document vanishing lifeways embraced a fieldwork rhetoric of urgency,[13] and by so doing romanticized the headhunter.

HEAD MARKETS

The late-Victorian and Edwardian twilight of headhunting fascinated metropolitan audiences because they had long read about, or more recently seen, the human skull treated as a commodity. British explorers, merchants, and ethnologists became keen hunters of heads, traffickers in savage souvenirs. Their first acquisitions were Maori heads. Britain's demand for these South Sea artifacts set in motion what must rank as the Empire's most disturbing commerce.

It was no accident that New Zealand (Aotearoa) became the earliest site for a head market. Whereas indigenous peoples throughout much of Southeast Asia pursued this treasure, high heat and humidity encouraged practitioners to skin, boil, or smoke away the flesh on a victim's head, leaving only bone and teeth. In New Zealand's more temperate climate, however, it was feasible to dry the whole head.[14] The Maori custom of intricate facial tattooing (*moko*) rendered their preserved heads irresistible "curios" for many white mariners. Two generations before Melville's Queequeg took to selling "'balmed New Zealand heads" on the streets of New Bedford,[15] European ships were buying them Down Under. Sir Joseph Banks, the leading gentleman-naturalist on Cook's first voyage to the South Pacific, showed the way. On 20 January 1770, while HMS *Endeavour* lay at anchor in Queen Charlotte Sound near the northeastern tip of New Zealand's South Island, Banks met an old Maori who had earlier promised to show him how the heads of enemies were treated. Those of four recently slain people amazed Sir Joseph and his companions: "the hair and flesh were entire, but we perceived that the brains had been extracted; the flesh was soft, but had by some method been preserved from putrefaction, for [they] had no disagreeable smell." The one specimen that Banks managed to obtain—in exchange for a pair of his old linen drawers—appeared to be that of a teenager whose skull had been fractured from several blows. Based on such thin evidence, Cook's chief scientist concluded that "these Indians give no quarter."[16]

As commercial contact with them grew more regular, so too did a trade in human heads. What jumps off the page in a twenty-first-century reading of this exchange is the consistency with which early British accounts condemn an alleged Maori thirst for revenge. The Maori were known to the British as Polynesians and purportedly shared a Polynesian preference for war-by-annihilation, "a system of ruthless butchery, of horrid carnage."[17] But the Maori supposedly added a mad hypersensitivity to the usual viciousness of Polynesian conflict. For "the very slightest injuries are never passed by unnoticed or unatoned for in New Zealand: the remembrance is kept up from generation to generation, as a plea for aggression, should an opportunity be presented." It was this Maori fixation on revenge, "fostered by cupidity and a spirit of pride, which leads them to preserve the trunkless heads of their enemies, as trophies of their victory."[18] *Pakeha* (white) scholars, as well as British missionaries, have probably exaggerated the level of internecine mayhem among Maori descent-groups during the first third of the nineteenth century, and have tended to misconstrue such violence as the product of "treachery."[19] Still, fractious these people surely were. War among the Maori aimed not only to acquire new land or supplies of the coveted greenstone (nephrite jade) but also to obtain *utu* (compensation) for both material harm and perceived slights. An insult unavenged diminished the *mana*, or efficacy, of the descent-group as well as of the insulted individual.[20] And the coming of European firearms to this culture undeniably increased the destructive power of raiding bands.

The musket did not immediately replace the greenstone club in New Zealand, nor were guns the only objects of desire among trade-minded Maori.[21] But preserved heads did constitute their most liquid asset. Some British commentators found the facial expressions on these artifacts oddly attractive. Major-General Horatio Robley, an avid collector of tattooed heads, savored their "beautiful arabesques in moko patterns"; the "life-in-death" look of these visages was something "which once seen can never be forgotten." Others, among them the censorious Reverend Samuel Marsden, saw only "ghastly grin[s]." Beyond dispute, though, was the sardonic individuality of Maori heads: although their eyes were usually sewn shut, these were clearly real people who had been torn from life with stunning ferocity.[22]

Despite much clerical condemnation of this business, it prospered. Rev. Marsden's missionary politics, in fact, probably accelerated the harvesting of heads. A lash-loving magistrate as well as Sydney's evangelical Anglican chaplain, Marsden had been impressed with the innate dignity of the Maori whom he met in Australia. His dream of launching a mission among the heathen of New Zealand had to wait until 1814, however, when at last a mixed party of godly craftsmen and their wives, three Maori chiefs, and one earnest schoolmaster landed at the Bay of Islands. Soon thereafter Marsden questioned a local leader about the art of preserving enemy heads "not to discover the nature of a practice so revolting to humanity, but to develop more fully the character of the individual." When the "calculating" Pomare interpreted these queries as trade talk, the chief reportedly offered to shoot the men who had murdered his son and use their heads in an embalming lesson—so long as Marsden supplied the gunpowder. The missionary, we are told, was repulsed, commanding his settlers never to "countenance such a shocking exhibition." Yet by insisting that these pioneers remain self-supporting, Marsden in effect pushed them into the musket trade.[23]

The Church Missionary Society would wait ten more years for the first Maori convert to be baptized in 1825. Well before then, Anglicans at home and abroad learned that a musket-enhanced slaughter had begun to ravage New Zealand.[24] The gun-lust of certain Maori chiefs was insatiable, it seemed. Hongi Hika, who initially struck missionary Thomas Kendall as a man of "very mild disposition," came to epitomize the Maori preoccupation with *utu*. Hongi visited England in 1820, care of the CMS. Although he "charmed the religious world by acting the part of a devout Christian," this warrior apparently left London with one overriding impression: that Britain was powerful because it had a single ruler possessed of many weapons. (Hongi's aggression had supposedly been "excited" during a trip to the Tower of London's armory.) Returning to New Zealand by way of Sydney, Hongi exchanged most of King George's presents for the muskets, pistols, and gunpowder he would need to pursue his quarrel with rival North Island descent-groups. We will never know how many of his outgunned enemies were destroyed in Hongi's campaign of 1822.[25] But all the anecdotal evidence points to a direct connection between the advent of the so-called Maori "musket wars" and an expansion of the head market.

It is true that many Maori clans preserved the heads of relatives and friends, as well as those of enemies. Only the latter became a commodity, however. Dubious tales swirling through New Zealand's still small white settler community told of slaves tattooed in order to fetch a better price upon slaughter. No more reliable was the hearsay account of one missionary who claimed that now and then the heads for sale included those of the European agents commissioned to buy them.[26] The trade that appalled Reverend Marsden was largely opportunistic. That is, the captains of some schooners engaged in loading New Zealand flax let it be known that they were always eager to buy "a really good head," although the more cold-blooded among these entrepreneurs may occasionally have paid in advance for a still-animate specimen. William Yate assured the 1836 Select Committee on Aborigines that he knew of at least one case where Europeans had exchanged land for slave heads. Another witness told of watching a predatory captain selling heads "with a bit of Candle in them" on dark nights.[27]

From about 1818 to 1831, steady supply met high demand. Hongi's first great raid against the Bay of Plenty clans in 1818 had featured a *taua*, or war party, of over 900 men, fifty of whom wielded muskets. They returned triumphant with canoes full of heads. Hongi's expedition of 1822 proved to be far more destructive, armed as it was with a thousand guns, many of which he had bought in Sydney upon his return from England. These and several smaller Maori engagements fed both the sailor's appetite for *moko*-embellished souvenirs and the acquisitive ardor of museums and medical societies (Figure 4.1). As of 1896, Robley tells us, no fewer than five London institutions owned fine specimens, as did collections in Halifax, Hull, Sheffield, Devizes, Exeter, Oxford, Cambridge, Dublin, and several Continental

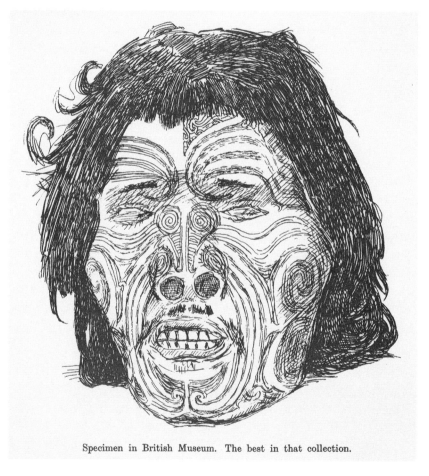

Specimen in British Museum. The best in that collection.

Figure 4.1   The tattooed head of a Maori male, probably sold during the 1820s. A brisk trade in these "curios" continued until the governor of New South Wales outlawed it in 1831.

SOURCE: H.G. Robley, *Moko* (1896).

towns.[28] The pleasurable horror of ownership meshed smoothly with the higher purpose of scientific study. That those Europeans who bought Maori heads were only savages once removed rarely drew comment.

An outraged Australian governor eventually sought to kill this commerce. During the late 1820s, suggestive references to New Zealand "curiosities" occasionally appeared in the "Sales by Auction" column of the *Sydney Gazette*.[29] Britain's Colonial Office was not in the habit of intervening based on rumored impropriety. But Ralph Darling, the Governor of New South Wales, moved swiftly after learning that the schooner *Prince of Denmark*, a veteran of the flax trade, had recently brought several tattooed heads into port. Darling's Order No. 7, issued on 16 April 1831, banned any further such cargoes. In a revealing protest against his Order, the *Sydney Gazette* noted that there was "no reason whatever for supposing that the master and crew [of the *Prince of Denmark*] have been in any respect more blameable, or more engaged in the traffic complained of, than those of other vessels engaged in the New Zealand trade."[30] "The traffic complained of," in other words, had become a standard feature of antipodean barter. It certainly declined, but did not vanish, in the wake of Governor Darling's menacing response to this "disgusting" practice. As late as 1840, the U.S. Exploring Expedition found that a few European ships still offered Maori heads, although now in "the most perfect secrecy." Using religion as his cover, the steward on a missionary brig sold the Americans two "beautiful specimens" for £10 the pair.[31]

Britain's interest in primitive heads persisted. Quite apart from the shock value of specimens preserved in alcohol,[32] those with scientific ambitions also sought skulls to illustrate the range of human "types." Working separately, Johann Blumenbach, professor of medicine at Göttingen, and Franz Joseph Gall, a Viennese physiologist, established the late eighteenth-century analysis of skulls and faces that launched craniology as a respectable field of enquiry—and along the way legitimized race classification based on measurement. In Britain, their cerebral science expressed itself as phrenology. It would be misleading, as Roger Cooter has shown, to dismiss phrenology as "pseudo-science," the playground of mere cranks. Phrenology's basic assumption that the mind was the sum of discrete mental functions produced by specific cerebral "organs" seemed plausible enough given the state of anatomical knowledge during the first quarter of the nineteenth century.[33] Champions of this new discipline believed that skull shape gave the trained observer a topographic map of the mind within. Where phrenologists tended to disagree, however, was over the cultural implications of cranial structure. The Australian Aboriginal head, for example, was usually, but not always, viewed as "proving" the inability of these peoples to join settler society. Moreover, debate among phrenologists over the fit between Aboriginal form and social function led in turn to the systematic plunder of indigenous burial sites. Science trumped the sacred.[34]

Although the middle decades of the nineteenth century saw this enthusiasm for skull science fade, British naturalists continued to regard cranial shape as a vital part of any racial inventory. By 1867, John Crawfurd, an early mainstay of London's Ethnological Society, could reject as "entirely arbitrary" the use of skull configuration to distinguish one race from another. A.R. Wallace concurred. The co-discoverer of natural selection found that wide variations in cranial characteristics among theoretically homogeneous races rendered skull type an unreliable marker of difference.[35] Even so, Wallace (if not Crawfurd) remained a headhunter of sorts. He neither detached heads nor gathered skulls. But Wallace was certainly a keen cataloger of heads among denizens of the Malay Archipelago, capturing in words the "moral features" of the peoples he met there.[36] His focus on the savage skull placed him in the scientific mainstream. Thus in 1854, the British Association for the Advancement of Science published *A Manual of Ethnological Inquiry*, which urged naturalists to seek "facts . . . not inferences." And first among the facts to be ascertained was the "character" of the "whole head" in uncivilized lands.[37]

This pursuit of exemplary heads involved the Royal Navy as well as genteel ethnologists. The Admiralty's *Manual of Scientific Enquiry*, first published in 1849, built upon a tradition of seaborne science stretching back to then-Lieutenant James Cook's astronomical and cartographic voyage of 1768–71. Thereafter, the Admiralty's Hydrographic Department played a pivotal role in exploring both Arctic ice floes and African rivers.[38] It was James Pritchard, physician-philologist, who wrote the "Ethnology" section for the Admiralty *Manual*'s second edition of 1851. Pritchard advised that when encountering a "barbarous" tribe, naturalists should record superstitions and examine weapons. But above all they must obtain skulls. If the latter were unavailable, plaster casts of living heads would do.[39] Ethnological advice varied on preservation. The British Association recommended that a head procured "after a battle, or other slaughter" should be brought home "perfectly closed up in a small keg filled . . . with spirit, or brine thoroughly saturated with salt.[40] But all the field guides continued to urge the collection of skulls, with or without the "soft parts" attached. If anything, the "rapid extermination of savages" demanded an intensified search for heads.[41]

Britain's participation in an ethnological head market was hardly unique, as the histories of German and Portuguese anthropology suggest.[42] An obsession with collecting and categorizing non-European crania nevertheless emerged early in Britain because this commerce evolved out of the trade in Maori heads. English-speaking visitors would later land on Melanesian islands armed with measuring tapes and index calipers. They used these tools, and a nomenclature borrowed from phrenology, to classify island peoples as either "brachycephalic" (short-headed) or "dolichocephalic" (long-headed). Such scrutiny no doubt dehumanized the Islanders, subjecting them to a kind of discursive dissection.[43] Equally important, though, both naturalists and colonial administrators would carry into the Oceanic arena a set of expectations about headhunting folk created by developments elsewhere in the East. Britain's last "real" headhunters, in New Guinea and the Solomon Islands, were by savage affiliation the progeny of Borneo.

RAIDERS OF THE CORAL SEA

If headhunting had a home in Britain's romance of empire, it was Borneo. "[F]or two or three generations," noted Harriet Martineau in 1862, English students had been taught (wrongly, we now know) that Borneo was the world's largest island. Its size awed naturalists as well as schoolchildren. In the opening pages of his acclaimed *Malay Archipelago*, A.R. Wallace treated readers to an arresting map of the British Isles superimposed on Borneo: nearly all of the former fits inside the latter, with a "sea" of equatorial jungle left over.[44] Still, the mystique of this distant place derived at least as much from its peculiar fauna as from its size. Here, a short sail east of Singapore, lay "caves beyond caves" lined with edible birds' nests, voracious leeches, the long-limbed orangutan, stronger than three men, and remote tribes living in longhouses, "where everybody's ways, from the great chief's to the spoiled child's, may be observed."[45] Literary voyeurism might explain part of Victorian Britain's fascination with Borneo. After all, its communal living customs allowed one culture that glorified domestic privacy to gawk at the family intimacies of another, legendarily savage culture. But what made the peoples of Borneo savage in the first place was their enthusiasm for taking heads.

By the end of the nineteenth century, the headhunters of Sarawak—that portion of western Borneo whose rulers for most of the Victorian era were Englishmen—had become colonial celebrities. The so-called "Dayak" peoples of both Sarawak and Dutch Borneo occasionally appeared in traveling shows, their hunger for skulls purportedly coexisting with an obsessive regard for honesty.[46] More sedate were the Dayak warriors-turned-policemen who impressed crowds as they marched in the vast colonial procession at Victoria's 1897 Diamond Jubilee. Wearing their trim khaki uniforms, "[n]othing of the barbarous [was] left about them save the black and white feathers on their scabbards."[47] These Dayaks had been "civilized." That is, their relentless pursuit of heads had been rechanneled into an equally fierce loyalty to Her Majesty, or so those who extolled "our Imperial union"[48] wished to believe. Yet what could be called the Dayak Story involved more than a straightforward account of colonial pacification. Simply put, Borneo's "wild men" would never have gained the notoriety they did save for their ties to the improbable figure of Sir James Brooke, the white raja of Sarawak. Brooke's success in transforming headhunters into his personal shock troops had earned both admiration and condemnation at the imperial center.[49]

As a major London weekly observed in 1881, "Brooke" and "Sarawak" had become "household words." The same could not be said of the Solomon Islands. As late as 1905, these green specks strewn across the Coral Sea comprised "among the least known and perhaps the least important of British possessions."[50] The allure of the Solomons, if allure they possessed in European eyes, derived from their geographic and cultural isolation. To a British reading public that revered Captain Cook and the sort of methodical marine exploration he epitomized, it was curious news that the Solomon archipelago had been "completely lost" for 200 years. Indeed, there existed no stranger story in the history of maritime discovery.[51]

Apart from New Guinea, which Portuguese and Spanish navigators spied early in the sixteenth century, the Solomons were the first islands in the South Pacific to receive Europeans. In 1567, two Spanish ships under the command of Alvaro de Mendaña left the Peruvian port of Callao in search of the great southern continent that cosmographers of the day declared must exist to balance Europe and Asia. Three months on, having crossed 7,000 miles of uncharted ocean in his worm-eaten craft, Mendaña sighted what he would later christen "Ysabel" (Santa Isabel) island. The gold he expected there and elsewhere in the Isles of Solomon could not be found. The "Indians" greeted him with stones and arrows. So, six dispiriting months later, Mendaña sailed back to Peru vowing that he would return with colonists. Not until 1595 did his promised second voyage materialize, however. It proved disastrous. Disease, dissension, and the death of Mendaña himself drove the survivors from their settlement on Santa Cruz island to seek safety at Manila, in the distant Philippines. Partly because no account of either voyage would be published until the mid-nineteenth century, and partly also because Mendaña's crude navigational tools misled him about the location of these verdant isles, they remained invisible—literally fabulous—to European geographers. Only in 1768 did the French explorer Louis-Antoine de Bougainville reach their western shores, thereby "re-discovering" the archipelago.[52]

The cultural isolation of the Solomons was no less profound. Basil Thomson, a former magistrate in Fiji, declared that these Islanders had defied time. When Bougainville chanced upon them in 1768, he allegedly observed customs that "in every particular, down to the pettiest detail in their dress," had not changed since Mendaña's day. Robert Codrington, Victorian Melanesia's most astute missionary-ethnologist, held that when Europeans reentered these people's lives, "all memory and tradition of white men had died away."[53] Both experts probably exaggerated. Rev. Codrington may have wished to explain his Melanesian Mission's lack of spiritual purchase in these islands by depicting their residents as obdurate. Thomson may have been overly eager to dramatize the "decay of custom" everywhere else in the western Pacific.[54] It was nevertheless clear that neither nature nor "native" conduct encouraged carefree rambling around this long-overlooked region. Naturalists such as the intrepid Henry Guppy found the Solomons' mix of searing heat and inch-an-hour rains oppressive. Europeans who ventured beyond the beaches encountered jungle where huge spider webs waited to snare their faces and limestone slopes to shred their boots.[55]

And then there were the "natives." After the decapitation of Lieutenant-Commander Bower and most of his mapping party in 1880 at Mandoleana Island, it was unsurprising that when the Hydrographic Department's surveyors were ordered to set up a theodolite on an unknown Solomon shore, they did so glancing nervously over their shoulders. Inviting scientific study

of the group, a one-time deputy commissioner for the western Pacific assured plucky Britons that they would meet people here who clung to "atro-
cious superstitions, in the exercise of which human life is sacrificed by every
ingenious torture that a savage can invent."[56] How far some forms of ceremonial inhumanity—cannibalism, live burial, and infanticide—flourished
in this backwater was debatable. But few Europeans doubted that a "perfect
passion" for headhunting inspired the Solomon warrior. Very much like the
Sea Dayak of Sarawak and the Naga of eastern Assam, he reportedly dreamed
of adding to his village's "ghastly cluster" of trophies. Whether belonging to
young or old, to the dark or the fair, each head was precious. His fixation
had allegedly rendered the Solomon Islander "the most treacherous and
bloodthirsty of any known savage." At least until the arrival of Methodist
missionaries after 1900, the male residents of the Marovo Lagoon (Map 4.1)
were by all accounts "utterly insensible to kindness."[57] No indigenous force
could stop these saltwater assassins.

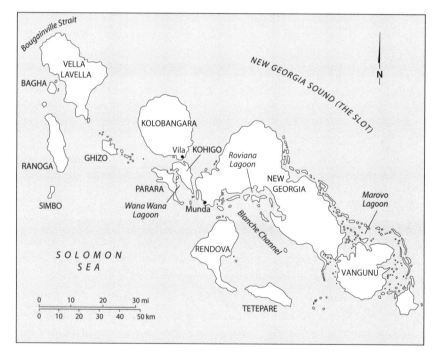

Map 4.1   The New Georgia Group, Solomon Islands.

Several British writers who denounced Solomon Island headhunting speculated on its cultural purpose. Predictably, John Thurston, then assistant high commissioner for the western Pacific, viewed headhunting through a judicial lens. For Thurston, the "principle of individual liberty," which allowed punishment only after proof of guilt had been obtained, was useless in the Solomons. Far better to abandon such rights-based reasoning in favor of what, in penological terms, might be called group liability: "Only when the villages, canoes, and crops of a tribe are threatened will that tribe give up an offender." Hence headhunting originated in a sense of communal solidarity, and had to be attacked as such.[58]

Thurston's thinking of course begged the question of causation. Before he, too, became a colonial administrator, the naturalist C.M. Woodford offered a conventional explanation: headhunting was a response to sacrificial demands. Particularly in the western parts of the archipelago, it appeared that the launch of a new war canoe, or the inauguration of a canoe house, required the presentation of a stranger's head. If a slave—usually someone captured during a previous raid—was not available for sacrifice, then another expedition might be needed to acquire the essential head.[59] A Canadian trader, John Macdonald, purportedly witnessed this consecration rite in 1883. A boy captured during a raid on Ysabel had been brought back to a coastal village in the New Georgia group.[60] When the time came for the opening of a new canoe house, an old man seized the child and first exhausted him by repeated duckings in the lagoon. Next:

> Nono, the chief . . . took a twelve-inch trade-knife, and with one gash across the child's throat, and then a chop, the head was off and the blood streaming from the neck. . . . The [old] man . . . carrying the child on his back, then ran round and round the [canoe] house . . . scattering the blood on the house and ground till the body ceased to bleed. It was then thrown down in front of the house.

Shortly thereafter, Macdonald recalled, the boy and a stolen pig were cooked and eaten together. The child's head later went on display in the canoe house. Woodford, who recorded Macdonald's account in his diary, explained that it was "so minutely circumstantial that I entirely believe it."[61]

A key concern here, scholars then and now agree, was *mana*. For Robert Codrington, who introduced this concept into the anthropological literature, *mana*, used as a noun, referred to power or influence in daily life. The

"Melanesian mind," Codrington wrote, was "entirely possessed" by this notion. And the human head, in the words of one Solomon Islander, contained
more *mana*, more "soul value," than anything else.[62] Modern anthropologists would later refine Codrington's concept. A specialist on the customs of
the Marovo Lagoon, for example, has argued that *mana* should be understood as a stative verb meaning to be blessed or to work well.[63] Still, there is
broad agreement that in traditional Solomon Islands culture, to be without
mana was to endure a purposeless life. For the assailant, then, the sacrificial
head carried with it the possibility of a richer existence in this world and
the next.

Although early European contacts with these people served to reinforce
their reputation as a "much dreaded" race, such contact likely *increased* both
the scope and the destruction of their headhunting forays. In one respect
this dynamic seems self-evident. As we have seen, the early years of indentured labor in Queensland and Fiji enabled some Islanders to buy muskets
and rifles. With them, the men of Savo in the central Solomons and of Vella
Lavella in the west became better killers.[64] But trade relations with white
men also altered the course of head taking in less obvious ways. Whaling
ships had to exercise special care around the Solomons, for these deep draft
vessels were ill suited to maneuvering among coral reefs. (As late as 1925,
sections of the New Georgia group—headhunting's epicenter—appeared as
dotted lines on the Admiralty chart.)[65] For the smaller ships in search of
"tortoise-shell" rather than whales, however, the Solomons beckoned. The
creature they sought was not a true tortoise but the hawksbill sea turtle, a
species whose shell, once polished, had long been prized for use as jewelry,
luxurious combs, and inlaid decoration on fine furniture. At least during the
first half of the nineteenth century, the hawksbill thrived in the archipelago's
sheltered lagoons. Its shell fetched high prices in Sydney and London. Better
yet, this valuable commodity could be purchased in exchange for cheap
beads, red cloth, and empty bottles. Above all, though, the Islanders hoped
to barter for iron. First offered in the form of barrel stays ("hoop" iron) that
sailors with basic blacksmithing skills could beat into cutting implements,
the metal later arrived as manufactured knives and long-handled tomahawks.[66] The iron-for-shell trade proved mutually advantageous until, inevitably, the hawksbill population began to decline. Thus, intensified competition among Islanders for control of the best remaining turtle habitats
probably encouraged more frequent headhunting raids.[67]

The coming of iron to Solomon Island societies unquestionably transformed the rhythm of everyday life.[68] Headhunting expeditions had always been male rituals. The substitution of iron for stone and shell tools meant that other traditionally male tasks such as clearing jungle and building houses now occupied roughly a third less time. (Women, whose main tool was the digging stick, realized fewer time savings.)[69] If what has been observed about the arrival of iron in highland New Guinea cultures applied to the Solomons,[70] then this sudden expansion of male leisure permitted greater ceremonial activity—of which the headhunt would have been a central element. Around the New Georgia group and perhaps elsewhere in this region, hoop iron saws simplified the job of carving local "money" out of fossilized clamshell.[71] Differential access to iron thus accentuated economic power imbalances among different tribes and accelerated the formation of inter-island alliances. Given larger headhunting fleets equipped with iron (later, steel) tomahawks, both conquest and self-defense grew more consequential than ever. And the war leaders who successfully rode this inflationary wave emerged as feared regional "big-men." The toll of their headhunting raids could be staggering. Around 1850, one big-man from the western island of Vella Lavella hurled a thousand war canoes against diminutive Bagha, virtually wiping out human habitation there.[72] The ferocity of such raids both horrified and intrigued the Europeans who learned of them.

The observations of Andrew Cheyne underscore this ambivalence. A Scots trader in everything from tortoise-shell and sandalwood to sharks' fins and birds' nests, Cheyne made four voyages through western Melanesia between 1841 and 1844. Dorothy Shineberg, who has painted the clearest portrait of an otherwise shadowy figure, contends that while Cheyne may have been a humorless and judgmental man, his journals carefully distinguish between what he saw and what he was told.[73] What he saw in the Solomons distressed him. On 3 February 1844, Cheyne had just set several Eddystone (Simbo) Islanders to work gathering *bêche-de-mer* when he entered a nearby canoe house. Therein he became "quite sick" at the sight of fresh heads, all bearing the unmistakable chop marks of tomahawks, festooning the rafters. "Dornin," the village big-man, boasted that his warriors had recently returned from an expedition with ninety-three heads of all ages.[74] About the "general character of the New Georgia natives," Cheyne concluded elsewhere, "*nothing* can be said in their favor." Then, contradicting himself,

Cheyne went on to praise the workmanship of these master builders who designed the swiftest canoes in the Pacific.[75]

More than any other product of material culture, the magnificent *tomako* called into question the purportedly bestial state of these Islanders. Although iron adzes shortened the time required to build a war canoe, both its design and its ornamentation were immemorial. In 1568, Mendaña had praised these craft as "very well made and very light." What stunned the Spanish captain, though, was their speed. These crescent-shaped canoes, powered only by paddle, could within an hour overtake one of Mendaña's ships under full sail and allowed a five-mile head start.[76] Unlike indigenous oceangoing vessels elsewhere in the South Pacific, the *tomako* employed neither an outrigger nor a sail (although some small Solomon canoes, restricted to calm waters, used both). Rev. Codrington understood why a large war canoe might take three years to complete: this was no hollowed-out log. The *tomako* would instead be built from carefully planed-down planks that slid into grooves on a V-shaped keel. Along each seam between the planks a series of small holes would be bored through which craftsmen wove tough vines. All seams were then caulked with a resin obtained from the kernel of a jungle nut. Once it hardened, this resin ensured a watertight fit. Finally, mangrove wood ribs added stiffness to the whole.[77]

With its bow and stern curving upwards as high as fifteen feet, a large Solomon war canoe struck one British observer as "more exquisitely graceful" than any Venetian gondola. However reprehensible its purpose, the *tomako* was, according to an otherwise restrained navy officer, "a most astonishing revelation of scientific art in a people little removed from complete savagery."[78] Remarkable also was the decoration of each canoe's exterior with mother-of-pearl inlays representing sharks, turtles, and frigate birds. Strings of white cowrie shells adorned the *tomako*'s soaring prow, near whose base protruded a carved wooden figurehead meant to ward off the water devils.[79] Such extraordinary vessels were peculiar to the Solomons, providing the most elegant transport for headhunters anywhere.[80]

Both lethal and elegant, the *tomako* spread a "reign of terror" (as one popular ethnography phrased it) throughout the western and central parts of the archipelago. Inter-island raids occurred most often in November and December, a calmer season between the end of the southeast trade winds and the start of the northwest monsoon.[81] Expeditions of a hundred miles or more might be undertaken if, for example, a big-man based in the New

Georgia group decided to attack settlements along the coasts of Guadalcanal; so long as his war canoes could avoid spending their nights in open ocean, few targets would have appeared too distant. The motivations for raiding varied widely. In addition to procuring heads for the sort of ceremonial uses already discussed, expeditions might seek these *mana*-rich prizes to end a period of mourning (as on Simbo), to avenge an insult by another tribe (which drove the warriors of Gao, on Ysabel, to slaughter the Mala men of Ada Gege around 1850), or less commonly, to establish a new settlement abroad (as Roviana fighters managed to do at Buin, on the southern tip of Bougainville island, 160 miles away).[82] The loci of mid- and late-nineteenth-century headhunting in the Solomons were the Roviana and Marovo lagoons of New Georgia, together with the nearby islands of Simbo, Vella Lavella, and Rendova. The raids these predators launched against one another proved traumatic enough. But their more ambitious campaigns against Ysabel, Choiseul, and the Russell islands obliterated settlements along parts of those distant coasts. The survivors of headhunting attacks either fled into the bush or, as at the southern tip of Ysabel, built elaborate tree houses sixty to ninety feet above sloping ground. The only way to reach these bamboo and palm-thatched dwellings was by means of swaying rattan ladders, easily retracted (Figure 4.2). For Europeans, and especially for leaders of the Melanesian Mission, the tree houses of Ysabel bore witness to the deadly impact of large-scale raids. Once the raiders began to acquire rifles after 1870, even these redoubts failed to protect their tenants.[83]

Missionaries and traders remonstrated with the big-men of the western isles, although for very different purposes. In Bugotu, the southernmost district of Ysabel, the late 1860s saw the rise to notoriety of "Bera." This big-man's prestige hinged not only on his audacity as a headhunter but also on the defense of his home district and his skill in attracting European traders to Thousand Ships Bay. As the "passage master" of Bugotu—the middleman through whom labor vessels recruited plantation workers—Bera amassed "numberless trade guns and old rifles." Legend said that when the doors to *Sopelae*, his canoe house, opened, Bera's enemies trembled.[84] One would have been hard pressed, therefore, to choose a less promising site for evangelization. Yet it was to Bugotu that the Melanesian Mission's Mano Wadrokal moved in the mid-1870s. Originally from Mare in the distant Loyalty Islands group, Wadrokal had become a "teacher" under the watchful eye of Bishop Patteson. Bera never embraced the good news that hectoring

Figure 4.2   Tree house, Ysabel, Solomon Islands, early 1880s. Retractable rattan ladders offered some protection against headhunting raids. Once the raiders
acquired rifles, however, these aeries became death traps.
SOURCE: Walter Coote, *The Western Pacific* (1883).

Wadrokal bore; trust in human sacrifice to appease the *tindalo* (ghosts)
trumped the gospel. Still, Bera in his last months took the unusual step of
ordering that his death should occasion no killing.[85] Bera died in 1884. His
son and successor, "Soga," at first honored the old headhunting customs.
But after 1886, when Bishop John Selwyn nursed Soga during an influenza
epidemic, the heir of Bera began to heed the Mission's message. Particularly
following the settlement of the medical-missionary Dr. Henry Welchman
on Ysabel in May 1890, Soga turned his authority to punishing murderers
and, ultimately, to forbidding the acquisition of heads.[86] Soga's much-
praised epiphany, it should be added, was rare among big-men of the western isles prior to 1900.

Relations between traders and the archipelago's headhunting people were likewise fraught. Contrary to the enduring image of the Pacific trader as a libidinous lout whose lucre came from swindling clueless Islanders, in the Solomons these gamblers led hard lives. Few realized handsome profits. They were beholden to the Sydney merchants who expected strong returns on the capital they lent them to buy trade stock. When prices dropped abroad for tropical products, it was the lone trader who sustained most of the loss.[87] Solomon Island traders tried to play one native settlement against another. Nor did traders maintain a united front among themselves. Norman Wheatley, an entrepreneur based at New Georgia's Roviana Lagoon, withheld information about the Bulani village people who had snatched the heads of two European competitors, David Kerr and John Smith of the ketch *Amelia*. Had Wheatley helped the Royal Navy punish those responsible for this "outrage," his business dealings around the lagoon would have suffered irreparable harm.[88] The gamesmanship worked both ways, of course. Just as eager to sell their tortoise-shell, *bêche-de-mer*, and copra as white traders were to buy these commodities, the Islanders often resorted to disparaging "these other people down the coast" in order to monopolize a useful barter relationship.[89] As late as 1896, three years after Britain declared a protectorate over half of the Solomon Islands, there were a mere fifty white residents in the entire group. Only two of this tiny minority were farmers, the rest being either missionaries or traders. The latter quite simply "carried their lives in their hands." It was folly, one veteran remarked, to pass an axe to a Solomon man handle first: "always handle away from him, so as to give the trader time to pull out his revolver." Radiating three hundred miles from its stronghold at New Georgia, and constantly shifting as economic and technological opportunities arose, the Solomon Islands headhunting zone aroused panic among those who lived therein and curiosity among European connoisseurs of savagery.[90]

Violence, especially of the sort endemic to the western Solomons, fascinated a certain sort of leisured European. Proximity to behavior as grotesque as headhunting carried a hint of risk, a chance, however fleeting, to escape the prescribed routines of civilized society. Hence the starry-eyed characterization of a trader's life as "beautiful uncertainty."[91] What headier holiday could there be than to cruise the same waters as the fearsome *tomako*? Dangerous primitives could be glimpsed at a safe remove: "An amateur traveler, if he goes in a yacht, could, in the most luxurious manner, and without a single hardship to endure, see life here [in the Solomons] as thoroughly savage as any in the world, and if he be of an adventurous turn of mind, he might perhaps penetrate a short distance into the bush, and add to our scanty information concerning the natives who live there."[92] The maritime *flâneur*, that is to say, might now and then play ethnologist.

But the romance could easily sour, as the fate of an English eccentric named Childe reminded the impetuous. In May of 1885, R.J. Childe, an "elderly gentleman" suffering from elephantiasis, booked passage to the Solomons aboard a Sydney-based schooner, the *Princess Louise*. It was to be a reconnaissance mission as well as a pleasure cruise, for the Englishman dreamt of starting a farm on some uninhabited isle. Just in case such a place was found, Childe brought along a "native boy," several pigs, and farming tools. The schooner's captain tried and failed to dissuade Childe from his dangerous plan. An apparently empty island adjacent to the headhunting center of Vella Lavella out west intrigued this frail pioneer. The schooner's crew stayed only long enough to build him an agreeable thatched hut. Alas, Childe's "boy" soon ran away and told nearby people about the white man's wealth. The result was all too predictable. A dozen or more Islanders ambushed Childe, took his head, cooked and ate his body, and made off with his goods. The Royal Navy captain obliged to investigate this murder wasted little pity on the victim: "Mr. Childers [sic], by his foolishness, actually courted death."[93] Yet the underlying question remained unanswered. How long could Britain limit its oversight of the Solomons to occasional—and generally futile—visits from a man-of-war?

The late 1880s and early 1890s witnessed a parade of "outrages" against traders and unwary Islanders alike. The headhunting mania of the western districts had infected smaller islands further east. Consider Savo. Although one might walk around tiny Savo in just four hours, by 1886 this headhunting satellite could assemble a raiding force large enough to annihilate entire settlements along the coast of next-door Guadalcanal.[94] Out west around New Georgia, navy ships could do little to punish offenders other than bombard their villages and burn their war canoes. Some of the headhunting big-men, such as the wily "Ingava" of Sisieta, behaved as if they were hereditary rulers when in fact their power was provisional, hinging on continued success in trade as well as war.[95] Tippett offered what is probably the most accurate description of these marauders when he referred to "the emergence of master tribes" during the last third of the nineteenth century.[96]

Their headhunting confederations seemed impervious to after-the-fact policing.

Thus, reluctantly, British colonial officials agreed that a more consistent discipline must be imposed on this remote archipelago.[97] The focus of any such discipline would need to be the great lagoons of the west. These represented a peculiar battlefront, with their "dazzling blue" waters "studded with thousands of islands." Here orchids vied for space with coconut palms and banana trees. A "splendid luxuriant bush" pressed against "labyrinthine reefs" that amazed with their own "feast of color."[98] The Islanders seemed equally exotic. Earlobes sporting wooden discs inlaid with mother-of-pearl complemented the amulets and chest pieces fashioned from the shell of the giant clam. Black bodies, many etched by ringworm, housed an unusually vigorous temperament, or so European observers remarked. Indeed, the vigor of the New Georgia people reminded Robert Codrington of wild men living still farther west: "No visitor can fail to feel himself nearer the Asiatic islands [than] when he finds the public hall of each village adorned with heads."[99] How to divert this energy into less lethal channels would become the challenge facing colonial administrators after 1893.

PACIFICATION AND LAMENT

Although their location on the Pacific map appeared far from strategic, the Solomons nonetheless struck some late-Victorian commentators as ripe for annexation. Those who, like James Froude, associated the Empire's health with the density of its new growth believed that colonial acquisition would nurture the mother country. Froude compared Britain's well-being to a free-branching oak: "The life of a nation, like the life of a tree, is in its extremities. The leaves are the lungs through which the tree breathes, and the feeders which gather its nutriment out of the atmosphere." A historian and man of letters, Froude gave voice to the undercurrent of anxiety that was now surfacing, an uneasy recognition at home that "[o]ther nations . . . are treading fast upon our heels." "Happily" though, disaster on the imperial stage could still be averted because "the colonies are not yet lost to us."[100] The Solomons, infested with malaria as well as headhunters, would never support extensive white settlement. After Germany secured by treaty the northeastern corner of New Guinea in 1884, however, the prospect of that power's expansion eastward through the Coral Sea suddenly loomed large. Preemptive colonization therefore grew correspondingly more attractive, especially to the copra merchants of Sydney.

But officially at least, it was the prospect of mass depopulation at the hands of labor recruiters and rifle-equipped *tomako* fleets that finally convinced Britain to declare a protectorate over the southern Solomons—Guadalcanal, Savo, Malaita, San Cristobal, and the New Georgia group—in the spring of 1893. As an official report would retrospectively explain in 1960, a "mounting tide of savagery" had compelled action.[101] One wonders how far humanitarian concerns actually drove colonial policy in this case. The views of Lieutenant Boyle Somerville may have been more representative of Crown personnel on the ground. Somerville, whose service aboard the surveying ship *Penguin* brought him into close contact with the Islanders of New Georgia during 1893 and 1894, reckoned that without some imposition of order there, New Georgia's people would gradually be exterminated. "Except from a scientific point of view," the young officer added, "I think one might be almost reconciled to this disposition." The disappearance of these Islanders would be "no great loss to the world," Somerville concluded.[102]

Such scorn notwithstanding, the process by which Britain's new role was announced revealed much about the task of pacification that lay ahead. An element of the absurd colored this exercise. Captain Herbert Gibson's orders directed him to cruise HMS *Curaçao* throughout the southern half of the archipelago, reading the "Proclamation of a Protectorate" to small clumps of perplexed villagers, hoisting the Union Jack on flagstaffs set among coconut palms, presenting arms to empty beaches, and discharging cannon while the shipboard band struck up "God Save the Queen."[103] At several islands the residents mistook a *feu-de-joie* for a man-of-war's wrath: fleeing into the jungle seemed the only prudent response. At Vella Lavella, a shore party found several heads but not the warriors who had collected them. Because international law then specified that the "protection" of a foreign power could not be established where "the natives are averse to the proceedings," Captain Gibson searched for signs of disaffection. He found few. Only at the Langalanga Lagoon, Malaita, did he encounter people who questioned the new regime. And their questions stemmed not from a principled objection to British rule but from worry about annoying the bush tribes who supplied the lagoon-dwellers with garden produce.[104] British intervention was to be paternal rather than colonial—a key distinction in the minds of those who expected that local revenues would support all, or at any rate most, policing work. The source of these revenues remained to be determined. More problematic still, until 1896 the Colonial Office refused to consider appointing even a deputy commissioner to oversee the administration of justice. Leaderless and cash-strapped, the early protectorate possessed no reliable means by which to civilize fragmented political units, each of which would have to be convinced to keep the British peace.[105]

The last years of the nineteenth century saw the start of large capital investment in the Solomons. With the advent of Burns, Philp and Company's regular steamer service between Sydney and the Solomons in 1895, copra production gained a reliable outlet to the Australian market. Under optimal conditions of tree growth and meat curing, the annual nut harvest of between twenty and twenty-five coconut palms was required to yield a ton of copra.[106] Eventually, therefore, economies of scale encouraged the planting of trees on a plantation basis. Such industrial agriculture would become most closely associated with the arrival of multinational Lever Bros Ltd. in 1903.[107] Before this rationalization of copra making took place, however, frequent clashes between isolated traders and aggressive Islanders angered Australia's white reading public. What good did a protectorate do if, for example, Donald Guy and his two native "boys" could be decapitated with impunity by the Soy River people of the Marovo Lagoon? That Guy's smoked head—reportedly wearing a "pleasant expression"—was relinquished in May of 1894 gave cold comfort to those already incensed over Islander perfidy.[108]

If the perfidious hailed mainly from New Georgia, they existed throughout the six-hundred-mile-long archipelago. Several widely publicized murders underscored this fact. Charlie Atkinson, an English trader known for kindness toward his "boys," was axed to death aboard his schooner in mid-1895. Atkinson's assailants had all been recruited from two coastal villages on Malaita. To the extent that a motivation for his killing could be divined, it seemed to involve payback for the accidental deaths of earlier recruits from these same settlements.[109] Mr. E. Hamilton, who had opened a trading station on the large southeastern island of San Cristobal, was more cautious but no more fortunate. Adhering to what white traders called the "safe plan," Hamilton in July of 1896 relocated his business to adjacent Ugi island. Here his San Cristobal "boys" would presumably hesitate to plot against him while surrounded by strangers. The discovery of his tomahawked corpse, ransacked store, and missing "boys" mocked Hamilton's survival strategy.[110]

But it was the massacre of the Austrian aristocrat Baron Fullon von Nor-
beck and three members of his scientific party in mid-August 1896 that
caused the greatest stir. Lacking any obvious provocation, this slaughter
prompted an early report to suppose, wrongly, that the culprits must be
Guadalcanal headhunters, the same sort of savages "who have given the
[Solomons] so grisly a reputation."[111] The truth, it later emerged, was less
dramatic. Scaling the 8,000-foot "Lion's Head" peak (Mt. Makarakomb-
uru) had been the baron's goal, and the Austrian gunboat *Albatross* had accordingly deposited a thirty-member expedition on the north shore of Guadalcanal. Several hours into their climb the Austrian party unwisely split up,
making both detachments vulnerable to attack from the axe-laden locals
who began to emerge from the bush. In the fracas that soon followed, the
baron—whose "short, stout" figure invited comparison to Britain's own
Prince of Wales—sustained a gaping wound to his neck. His body, too
generous to be carried down to the *Albatross*, was buried beneath the party's
main tent. As one trader observed, the Sydney merchants who controlled
commerce with the Solomons opposed the creation of tax-levying ports-of-
entry in the archipelago. But these big capitalists "run no personal risk from
the want of a thoroughly organised government here to protect life and
property." The fate of the baron would be repeated, with minor variations,
unless and until Britain gave teeth to its protectorate.[112]

Charles Morris Woodford (1852–1927) believed that he could provide
those teeth. Woodford's atmospheric account of 1890, *A Naturalist Among
the Headhunters*, had already won praise in mainstream reviews and applause
from the Royal Geographical Society. Less ethnologically rich than Guppy's
The Solomon Islands and Their Natives (1887), Woodford's book more art-
fully juxtaposed the delicacy of butterflies with the brutality of the Islanders.
In *The Spectator*'s paraphrase, "The first thing a native thinks, when he sees
one of his kind is: 'Will he kill me?' The next: 'Can I kill him?'"[113] Woodford's eighteen years of autocracy in the Solomons marked the end of a
tortuous career path. His middle-class upbringing in Kent apparently left
him impatient to see a wider world. Shortly after leaving his public school
(Tonbridge), therefore, Woodford found work as a collector of tropical
wildlife for Lord Rothschild's private museum at Tring.[114] Although he
served briefly in Fiji's Receiver-General's Office during the early 1880s, it
was to the Solomons that this adventurer gravitated. His three extended

visits in 1886, 1887, and 1888 yielded a trove of new insect species as well as savage facts for his book.

Woodford relished risk. During mid-1886, for example, he lived alone on Alu (Shortland) island for six weeks, shielded from attack by the *tambu* (prohibition) that "Gorei," the local big-man, had placed on the stranger's equipment. Soon thereafter Woodford paid a visit to the Roviana Lagoon. He arrived just in time to witness the departure of a raiding expedition for Ysabel and, while inspecting several canoe houses, saw half-dried heads with their "grinning teeth and sunken eye-sockets." Even at this early stage of Woodford's exposure to Melanesian customs, his diary suggests, the path to civilization looked obvious: "All this [slaughter] could be easily stopped," he wrote. The secret to pacification involved nothing more and nothing less than burning the war canoes and flogging the "chiefs" of any villages found to harbor heads.[115]

That Charles Woodford saw himself as the right man to bring "firm and paternal government" to the Solomons was apparent by 1890, if not before.[116] But an economy-minded Colonial Office at first refused to grant anyone the resources required for such work. Sometime during the summer of 1894, Woodford decided that the islands, not the Home Counties, offered the best platform for advancement. So, taking leave of his chums in the Epsom (Surrey) Angling Society, he sailed for Fiji, seat of the Western Pacific High Commission. Proximity to power proved useful, especially when Woodford himself probably drafted a dispatch to the Colonial Office begging for some semblance of authority in the Solomons.[117] Finally, in mid-1896, Woodford got his wish when he was appointed acting deputy commissioner for Britain's half of the archipelago. Bare-bones funding from London would last just one year. The ex-public schoolboy had to prove his worth quickly.

If Woodford's brief was wide, his power at first was minimal. One historian has suggested that the legend of the British district officer gained credence with the publication of Lugard's *Dual Mandate* in 1922. From this widely noted study, we are told, there emerged a model of the ideal back-country administrator "almost single-handedly managing to preside with fairness and justice over vast regions of the tropics."[118] Although Woodford's archipelagic beat drew less attention, its rigors surpassed what Lugard's men endured in Nigeria. Compared to the "fever-soaked" Solomons with the "black loneliness" of its bush, at any rate, the isolation of colonial service in the central Pacific's Gilbert Islands (today's Kiribati) seemed trivial.[119] Quite apart from the bouts of malaria that would continue to gnaw at his body, Woodford faced immediate crises as he set up government on the small island of Tulagi.

Although he supported capital investment in the new protectorate, Woodford worried about European land speculators in a region where the connection between indigenous ownership and continuous occupancy was often vague.[120] Until the day that taxes on large plantations could defray the costs of government, income from the issue of commercial licenses and poll taxes on the few resident Europeans would have to suffice. Yet the imposition of these duties in July 1897 enraged a previously untaxed trading community.[121] Above all other concerns, however, loomed that of headhunting.

The Royal Navy's notoriously imprecise punishment of suspected headhunting centers had at times been harsh. In 1891, Commander Davis of HMS *Royalist* estimated that his combined operations against the Roviana headhunters had burned 150 canoes and crushed 1,000 skulls. But by leaving the lagoon "absolutely littered with skulls, the stored and cherished of years," Davis only drove the local big-man, "Ingava," to replenish his stock. Such was the impetus for the latter's 500 rifle-toting warriors who soon thereafter devastated Ysabel.[122]

The crafty Ingava, in fact, reminds us that the people of the western Solomons were anything but one-dimensional assassins (Figure 4.3). Ingava could be downright courtly to white men with retributive power or material wealth. When faced with both, this big-man was prepared to use European rules against European enemies. Reading the manuscript notes of Ingava's legal challenge to trader Edmond Prat ("French Peter") in October 1894, one finds a strategic intelligence at work. Having seized land at Munda Point, New Georgia, that Ingava claimed as his own, Prat found himself backpedaling before High Commissioner Thurston. After Ingava explained (in Melanesian Pidgin) that he would never have given up land that had belonged to his father, Prat was reduced to arguing that no deed of sale existed because neither a kilometer nor a compass reading meant anything to an Islander.[123] At the same time, Woodford might have added, Ingava remained a captive of superstition. When this big-man suddenly took ill in August of 1888, his response had been to torture the woman who supposedly bewitched him.[124]

HEAD-HUNTING CANOE AND CANOE-HOUSE. VILLAGE OF SISIETA, RUBIANA LAGOON.

Figure 4.3 Charles Woodford's reproduction of his own photograph, circa 1886–1888. "Ingava," a headhunting big-man from the Roviana Lagoon, stands in front of a thatched canoe house.
SOURCE: Woodford, *A Naturalist Among the Head-Hunters* (1890).

The laudable impulse of modern scholarship to treat Melanesians as active shapers of their own lives has helped to fuel the argument that headhunting collapsed in the Solomons due to indigenous cost/benefit calculations. This interpretive line suggests that by the late 1890s almost universal access to rifles around the archipelago had persuaded the once-better-armed New Georgia people that raiding was now counterproductive. A variation on this theme of "economic pragmatism" posits a link between the rise of copra as the Islanders' main cash crop and the decline of headhunting. Unlike hawksbill turtles and *bêche-de-mer*, which flourished only in specific reef environments, coconut palms thrived throughout the islands. So the old trading and raiding alliances, based as they were on the leadership of regional big-men who could control scarce resources, ceased to fit the new economic order. Headhunting, in short, no longer paid. Britain's efforts to suppress this custom represented just the "final sentence" in a story whose ending the Islanders already knew.[125]

But to account for the demise of Solomon Island headhunting largely in terms of these endogenous forces is to minimize the relentless coercion of Woodford and his staff. In 1899, under the Samoan Tripartite Convention, Britain's protectorate grew to include the formerly German North Solomons—the Shortland Islands, Choiseul, Santa Ysabel, and Ontong Java.[126] Both before and long after this territorial expansion, Resident Commissioner Woodford suffered few doubts about the proper course of conduct. He looked askance at the idea that headhunting raids might be punished through a court composed of local ship captains and "respectable" traders. Such a derogation of authority, Woodford believed, would only inflame racial tensions around the archipelago. The rule of God pleased him still less. For as Woodford saw it, "native teachers," especially those affiliated with the Melanesian Mission, were apt to bully Islanders who resisted gospel truths.[127] Punishment was his prerogative alone—modified on occasion, to be sure, by orders from the high commissioner in Fiji. And the most efficient punishments would be those meted out by Islander police under his command, or that of Arthur Mahaffy, the assistant (later, resident magistrate) he acquired in 1897. The logistics of retribution seemed simple enough. To harry a band of fleeing headhunters often required rapid pursuit through thick jungle. White men seldom excelled here. Since "[t]he speed of a column of men marching through the bush in single file must of necessity be the speed of its slowest member," it stood to reason that Islanders alone should form Woodford's infantry. Punitive expeditions must capture their quarry lest failure "excite the ridicule of the natives and diminish the respect that should be felt for the power of the white man."[128]

In practice, it proved impossible to bar some traders and naval officers from joining Woodford's punishment patrols. Moreover, "two or three loafers" tainted his Islander police. But never before had British intervention against the headhunters of the west been so thorough. When, as often happened, the inland lairs of suspected killers were found deserted, Woodford and Mahaffy usually mounted return patrols, even where this entailed two or more slogs up steep hillsides. Rugged Vella Lavella received close attention of this kind in 1897, after its warriors had reportedly brought back more than 200 heads from Choiseul and Ysabel in recent raids.[129] The *Sydney Morning Herald* applauded the discovery aboard a commercial steamer of a "special strength" portable jail ordered for Woodford's headquarters on Tulagi. (He also splurged on a proper gallows complete with trap door.)[130] A shoestring budget denied the resident commissioner what he needed most, however: a small steamer of his own to chase war canoes through the waterways of New Georgia and, when necessary, north into what remained until 1899 German territory. Lacking this resource, Woodford improvised. Until 1902, a thirty-ton yacht was his main conveyance. Handy enough in a following wind, it proved painfully slow during the region's unpredictable calms. So, Woodford stationed Mahaffy 250 miles to the west on Gizo, an island strategically located close to Vella Lavella and within striking range of New Georgia's lagoons. When not relying on Royal Navy craft to ferry him about, Mahaffy and his Islander police traveled in a stunning *tomako* seized at Kolokongo. With a crew composed largely of Ysabel men—the traditional prey of New Georgia's raiders—Mahaffy's war canoe soon earned a fearsome reputation for pillaging in the name of peace. Here was an embodiment of what Purnima Bose terms "rogue-colonial individualism." As Mahaffy boasted, "To say that the people here [in the central Marovo Lagoon] are frightened of them [his Ysabel police] would be to most inadequately represent their frame of mind."[131]

And no wonder. The rescue of "Bololo" from her headhunting captors in August 1900 made it chillingly clear that for Woodford, Mahaffy, and their Islander police, ends justified means. "Belangana" was the big-man of a village on Marovo Island. At some point in 1897, he and his men raided Gerasi, a settlement on New Georgia, carrying away ten women. Nothing more was heard about eight of these unlucky souls, leading people around the lagoon to believe that their heads had been taken. Two of the women supposedly remained alive, held prisoner somewhere deep in the bush. Although a detachment of navy "bluejackets" managed to arrest Belangana near his village, the two captives had vanished. In order to try this "desperate character" for murder and hang him "near the scene of his outrages," the missing witnesses would have to be found.

There ensued a dogged, two-year campaign to locate the kidnapped women. The second half of 1899 found Woodford and his crew burning the canoes of any settlement remotely implicated in the abduction. Toward the end of that year one of the captives was released into the custody of trader Frank Wickham. But Bololo, who was rumored to have married one of her captors, remained beyond reach. Woodford's periodic wrecking of native property had so far failed to achieve the desired result. On the eve of his departure for Sydney, therefore, the resident commissioner ordered Mahaffy "to squat upon the island in a passive manner until such time as the woman was surrendered."[132]

Although Woodford's energetic assistant did indeed "squat" on Belangana's home island, his occupation hardly proved passive. Mahaffy assured the people "that if [they] assisted me I should spare their pigs and plantations but that otherwise I should destroy everything I could." He could, and did, destroy canoe houses, fruit trees, taro gardens, pigs, and fortifications fashioned from blocks of coral. On 30 May, eight days after his arrival, Mahaffy summarized the mission to date. The Islanders, he explained, had "suffered much loss in their most vulnerable point—their food supply." At last, on 11 June, after yet more destruction, the recalcitrant big-man "Anna" put Bololo in a canoe and sent her home. Three months later Woodford announced to the high commissioner, "the islands [of the central Marovo Lagoon] may be considered to have been pacified."[133]

Thorough pacification of the archipelago would in fact take several more years. Woodford later stated that the last Marovo Lagoon *tomako* to collect heads on Ysabel was confiscated, "fresh from its baptism of blood," during 1899.[134] But small-scale feuding and paid assassinations roiled the waters around New Georgia until at least 1909. These disturbances Woodford and his crew silenced with unseemly enthusiasm. The protectorate opened a new government station in the Shortland Islands in 1908, and it was the police based at this outpost who allegedly delighted in brutalizing Marovo men, women, and children. During one such massacre, which occurred on Christmas morning 1908 and sought to punish the killer of trader Oliver Burns, Malaita-born police reportedly burned and looted with gusto, decapitating at least one innocent woman.[135] Ridding the Solomon Islands of their headhunters called for a "strong hand," Woodford assured the Royal Anthropological Institute. Closer to the mark is the modern anthropologist who has branded the resident commissioner's tactics "devastating and merciless."[136] Doubts about Woodford's approach to pacification reached as far as the Colonial Office in distant London. "I do not much like this raiding sort of Government," confessed one civil servant: "It is all very heroic but it is not administration."[137] These doubts aside, Woodford's work eventually earned him the C.M.G.—Commander of the Order of St. Michael and St. George—in 1912, three years before his retirement.

It would be rash to argue that government repression alone rendered Solomon Island headhunting "a thing of the past," as Woodford phrased it in 1909.[138] Repeated outbreaks of dysentery, for example, certainly disrupted raiding patterns on and around New Georgia. The arrival of Methodist Protestantism in the western Solomons has also been cited as a factor in eradicating these Islanders' most infamous custom. It may be true that Methodism in the person of Rev. J.F. Goldie and his fellow missionaries did transform "bloodthirsty" Islanders into "gentle" Christians.[139] But by the time Goldie reached the Roviana Lagoon in May of 1902, large-scale headhunting had already ceased. Moreover, Methodism's earliest converts in this mission field tended to be refugees or the socially marginal: no convenient top-down flow of influence operated here.[140] Broadly considered, then, Woodford's systematic assault on raiding must stand as the main, although not the only, element in the demise of headhunting.

"Demise," in fact, encapsulates what was presumed to be occurring in this corner of the Pacific. Ritual headhunting had effectively died. Along with its passing, though, numerous European observers detected a "cessation of activity," a loss of will, among the once vigorous Solomon Islanders. Froude offered a striking analogy:

> It is with the wild races of human beings as with wild animals, and birds, and trees, and plants. Those only will survive who can domesticate themselves into servants of the modern forms of social development. . . . The negro submits to the conditions, becomes useful, and rises to a higher level. The Red Indian and the Maori pine away as in a cage, sink first into apathy and moral degradation, and then vanish.[141]

Dr. W. Thorold Quaife, medical officer for Levers' Pacific Plantations, thought he saw this very process unfolding in the Solomons. Why were its people "slowly melting away?" he asked. The answer had everything to do with the suppression of headhunting. "Savage warfare made the people alert, active, wary, and provident," he reasoned. With the coming of peace, however, those qualities no longer served any purpose. Seeking to explain why "his" Islanders so rarely showed any enthusiasm for their copra-making duties, Dr. Quaife implicitly recognized the stultifying monotony of such labor.[142]

Spokesmen for large corporations were not alone in painting a portrait of racial doom. Irony abounded. Having warned the world in 1890 that the

Solomon Islanders' "insatiable taste" for heads would guarantee their "eventual extinction," Woodford went on to become the headhunters' nemesis—and thus drained the martial energy that had kept these people virile.[143] The surviving big-men remained remarkable only for their frailty. Ingava, former terror of the Roviana Lagoon, had by 1906, the year of his death, become "poor, feeble, tottering" Ingava, the wizened drunk whose "hand trembles as he lifts the glass of grog he begs from you." "Where," a travel writer asked rhetorically, "is the great spirit that once possessed him?"[144] The loss of the "spirit" that had animated Ingava in his prime seemed to be the same psychological malaise behind plummeting birthrates throughout the western Solomons. No less respected a social scientist than W.H.R. Rivers stressed the connection. Rivers, as discussed in Chapter 3, suggested that the drudgery of labor on sugarcane plantations in Queensland and Fiji had robbed Islanders of any joie de vivre. President of the Royal Anthropological Institute and one-time lecturer in psychology at Guy's Hospital, London, Rivers was no dilettante. His professional obituary explained that "vague guesses and insufficiently supported hypotheses were abhorrent to him." Pioneering fieldwork on Vella Lavella and Simbo Islands in the western Solomons convinced him that the suppression of headhunting had induced a similar kind of mental torpor.[145]

The Europeans who had devoted themselves to rooting out savage customs in the western isles knew not what cultural toll their campaigns had taken, Rivers maintained:

> Thus, in the Solomon Islands, the rulers stopped the special kind of warfare known as head-hunting, without at all appreciating the vast place it took in the religious and ceremonial lives of the people, without realising the gap it would leave in their daily interests, a blank far more extensive than that due to the mere cessation of a mode of warfare.[146]

Rivers understood that his association of psychology with reproduction might appear "far-fetched." Yet the observable declines in fertility on Vella Lavella and Simbo could not be adequately explained in terms of epidemic disease, alcoholism, emigration, or the arrival of missionaries. It was, rather, when the social scientist turned from "material to mental factors" that these plunging birthrates made sense. Writing about the inhabitants of Simbo, some of whose genealogies he had traced back three generations, Rivers declared that "the zest had gone out of their lives."[147] It was a zest derived from headhunting. The actual fighting might have lasted no more than a few hours, the expedition perhaps a few weeks. Yet the building of a *tomako*, and the ritual feasts surrounding this complex enterprise, stimulated along the way such apparently unrelated activities as horticulture and pig breeding.[148] Indirectly, then, the white man's moral code was allegedly civilizing these Islanders into oblivion.

Rivers's "psychological" theory for declining Melanesian populations earned its share of criticism. Not surprisingly, Charles Woodford, who published a chapter in Rivers's volume on depopulation, preferred to emphasize introduced disease and the "injudicious use of unsuitable clothing" as contributing factors. Ian Hogbin, whose anthropological fieldwork in the 1930s centered on Malaita (no hotbed of headhunting), declared that he had never seen a native die of despair. At least one modern study has waved away the "discredited" proposition that hopelessness in the face of pacification may have depressed western Pacific birthrates: that most Melanesian populations eventually rebounded is seen to prove that the "death-wish" argument was the product of mere speculation.[149] But rapid social change need not result in catastrophe to be traumatic. Nor must the existence of professional anxieties invalidate the observations of the anxious. As George Pitt-Rivers observed in 1928, the "world-shattering changes" wrought by total war and revolution had led British and Australian anthropologists to channel their concerns about an apparent decline in Western civilization into a preoccupation with charting the actual decline of savage societies.[150] W.H.R. Rivers, who had treated shell-shocked men (most famously Siegfried Sassoon) at military hospitals during the Great War, would have been acutely aware of the West's own forms of ceremonial inhumanity. His psychological profile of the pacified Solomon Islander nonetheless meshed with other contemporary observations including, curiously, that of the protectorate's own administration. Its official report for 1912–13 spoke of the "critical" post-headhunting period in these Islanders' culture, a period during which they might "drift into a careless acceptance of the more easy conditions of life."[151] Peace, that is, might invite sloth.

The suppression of headhunting certainly did trigger crude eulogies to a vanishing world. Regret flowed from E.W. Elkington's pen. Published in 1907, his account of South Seas exotica aimed to catalog "the quaint lives of the natives" before "the sturdy head-hunters will be dead, and their sons will be cadging pennies" from white tourists.[152] Three years later, Robert

Williamson mused that the life of a Roviana male must have grown terribly dull; a little fishing and a lot of betel chewing did not a warrior make.[153] To fill the ritual void left by suppression, Rivers proposed substituting pig heads for human: expeditions, of a sort, might then recommence. And canoe races might help save the exacting art of *tomako*-building.[154]

The last scene in this proleptic drama was Edward Salisbury's 1921 reenactment of a headhunt. An American who seems to have done well in the Alaska gold rush of 1898, "Captain" Salisbury found himself in the western Solomons with a motion picture camera and plenty of time to ponder the passing of barbarism. It may be that Salisbury had seen, or heard about, Edward Curtis's 1914 *In the Land of the Head Hunters*. Although this feature film flopped at the box office, its all-Kwakwaka'wakw (Kwakiutl) cast and thrilling war canoe scene did reach audiences in Fairbanks, Alaska; Seattle; and Northern California.[155] Salisbury's own film footage proved marginally more popular, so far as we can tell, although several of his photographs would grace a magazine devoted to "the Orient."

Vella Lavella, once home to some of the fiercest headhunters on earth, served as Salisbury's backdrop. With the reluctant assistance of an Australian Methodist missionary and one of the protectorate's own district residents, Salisbury sought to win over "Gau," the local big-man and, if the tales were true, a headhunting mastermind. Missionary Nicholson's presence notwithstanding, the people of Vella Lavella had reportedly grown "wretched without their principal occupation." Perhaps, if only for a day, Gau and his people could taste again the unholy joy of a successful raid? The staged event was to be based on the return of Gau's last expedition to Choiseul island, probably in 1899. By the time that filming began, Salisbury explained, the locals had grown accustomed to the "magic eye"—his camera—and "the hunt ceased to be acting." (As a precaution, the bone barbs on all spears had been removed in advance.) The waving arms of excited women and children on the beach, the "wild, mournful melody" of the victorious warriors as their canoe neared shore, the skulls that Gau had brought down from his village: all conduced to a vivid, if entirely contrived, spectacle (Figure 4.4).[156]

What the twilight of headhunting in the Solomon Islands meant to its indigenous people is probably impossible to know. After all, most of the relevant evidence has been filtered either through foreign observers or else embedded in the conversion narratives of Islanders keen to embrace the moral imperatives of Christianity. This much at least is certain: the "paci-

Figure 4.4   "Gau," a former headhunting big-man on Vella Lavella, in the western Solomons. An American filmmaker paid Gau to reenact a headhunting raid in 1921. The fine turtle shell pendant (*mbakia*) around his neck signals Gau's high social status, as do the headhunting canoes (*tomako*) in the scene.

SOURCE: *Asia Magazine* (September 1922).

fied" Solomons remained far from pacific, as the lingering feuds between "salt water" and bush tribes on Malaita testified.[157] Certain also is that headhunting's crepuscular phase in New Georgia and its environs gave rise to second thoughts among Europeans about the wisdom of their intrusion. An equivalent lament would not characterize the assault on this practice along Britain's last Oceanic frontier, New Guinea.

PAPUAN CODA

Headhunters in British New Guinea—the southeastern corner of an island larger even than Borneo—rarely earned the notoriety of their cousins in the western Solomons. At least one naturalist, A.S. Meek, spent considerable time in both locations, emboldening him to compare these savage populations. New Guinea's natives, Meek observed, treated the taking of heads quite casually, seldom placing "any very great value on the human skulls that they had collected." (He once purchased three skulls for a single stick of tobacco.) In the western Solomons, by contrast, the Islanders "set a very great value on their human skulls, and will hardly part from them at any price."[158] The peoples who lived on or near the Gulf of Papua seemed just as resourceful as the lagoon-dwellers to the east when it came to weaponry. Sir William MacGregor, the rugged administrator of British New Guinea from 1888 to 1898, admired the 200-yard range of bows used in some parts of his territory. Rev. James Chalmers introduced a metropolitan audience to the "man-catcher," with its rattan loop and brain-impaling spike. This deadly device was the "constant companion of head-hunters," Chalmers claimed.[159] What deflected attention from their conduct was instead the dramatic opacity of their land.

A.R. Wallace noted that Europe's "almost total ignorance" about New Guinea was all the more remarkable considering that European ships had located this island as early as 1511. Since then, not much more had been learned about its interior. An Italian adventurer, L.M. D'Albertis, had ascended the Fly for roughly 500 miles without locating its source. At several points around the Gulf, deep alluvial deposits implied the existence of lofty mountains far inland—some of them, Wallace imagined, exceeding 18,000 feet. No less imaginative was MacGregor's estimate that the 272 European residents of British New Guinea as of April 1891 shared that expanse with some 800,000 "natives" scattered over dense jungle and labyrinthine swamps.[160] How many more Papuans dwelt in the German- and Dutch-controlled regions defied approximation. And what of their racial composition? The Papuan appeared to be most closely related to such other dark, "woolly-haired" peoples as the aboriginal folk of the Philippines, the Andaman Islands, and equatorial Africa. Was British New Guinea therefore the eastern outpost of primitive man's "direct descendants"? If so, then how to explain the elongated "Jewish" noses common among the "high type of Papuans"? Did Semitic blood flow in the veins of people who had only just discovered metal?[161]

These racial questions engaged very few white Australians, whose interest in the unknown land to the North was thoroughly material. What had generated "so universal an interest" in New Guinea among Australians of a

speculative bent were the triple attractions of gold, cheap labor, and un-
claimed land. Although the sprinkling of gold found near Port Moresby in
1877 set off something well short of a stampede, this event did help focus
attention Down Under on New Guinea as a trove of mineral wealth. The
labor hunger gnawing at Queensland planters added to this allure.[162] That
the Torres Strait was growing ever more useful as a maritime corridor between New South Wales and India and China hardened the resolve of some
Australians to grab as much of this primordial space as possible. These acquisitive pressures pushed Britain's Colonial Office into an admonitory role.
Thus, when in 1875 the "New Guinea Colonizing Association" sought Britain's blessing for a harebrained expedition designed to seize a thousand
square miles of New Guinea land, the Earl of Carnarvon, then Britain's
colonial secretary, made plain his displeasure. Subsequent discussion in German newspapers about carving a "German Java" out of New Guinea only
heightened antipodean worries. Late in March 1883, such unease prompted
Queensland's governor, Sir Thomas MacIlwraith, to order the annexation
of all non-Dutch New Guinea in the name of the Queen. Although London
repudiated this rash act, nineteen months later the imperial government
reluctantly assumed the colonial burden it had long tried to avoid.[163] Needed
now was a territorial administrator who could protect both the indigenous
Papuans and any white colonists who might dare to settle in Britain's wildest possession.

William MacGregor filled that need. A doctor by training and, like his
mentor in Fiji, Sir Arthur Gordon, an enemy of the labor trade, MacGregor
had once referred to New Guinea as "the last country remaining in which
the Englishman can show what can be done by just native policy." In hindsight, this comment seems peculiar, and not simply because MacGregor was
a proud Scot. For in New Guinea, the notion of "just native policy" ran
headlong into what Gordon, speaking about Fijian customs, termed the
punishment of cultural "irregularity."[164] With the possible exception of
murder-by-sorcery, the most irregular of Papuan habits was the taking of
heads. This activity occurred far beyond the Gulf of Papua, as a Dutch naval
officer exploring New Guinea's northwest coast learned as early as 1850.[165]
Nor were Papuans the only offenders. In 1877, the naturalist D'Albertis
knew exactly what to do with the head of a Fly River native shot dead during
an attack: into a jar of spirits it went. Similarly, soon after Britain's annexation of the southeast in 1884, a Greek trader, having been asked to provide

"outward evidence" of punishment inflicted on natives, lopped off an old chief's head and brought it aboard a government ship to be photographed. When MacGregor arrived on the scene in 1888, therefore, New Guinea already bristled with admirers of the human head.[166]

Bracketed between appointments in Fiji and Nigeria, MacGregor's decade in British New Guinea saw autocracy clad as humanity. The same iron will that carried this short, sturdy, and impatient man to the crest of the Owen Stanley Range in the spring of 1889 also informed his approach to pacification.[167] No less brutal than Charles Woodford in the Solomons, MacGregor had fewer superiors to appease. And he fought to preserve this independence, objecting for example to a proposed visit from Queensland's governor in 1896: "I will have no 'bigger fellow Governor' here in my day."[168] Sir William's "visits of inspection," which consumed so much of his time, aimed to establish his personal authority throughout this harsh land. British New Guinea was anarchic, MacGregor pointed out. He faced a lawless frontier where "[a]s a rule, each community was an Ishmaelitic centre, either at war, or in armed neutrality, against its neighbours." Hence the Administrator's first task, as he viewed it, was to "teach [the Papuans] an awful lesson that killing is murder & the punishment for it is death."[169] If imparting this lesson meant sending elderly men to the scaffold, criminalizing sorcery (in 1893, the only British possession to do so), recruiting "village constables" from government jails, or holding warriors hostage until their kin relinquished prized skulls, such costs were the price of peace.[170] The "straight paths" that MacGregor cut for his successors in New Guinea involved little anthropological finesse. He did not, as Sir Hubert Murray later would, seek to preserve a "structure of sane and beneficent social practices . . . based upon the cult of skulls" by urging the offending tribes to substitute pig for human heads.[171] MacGregor's pursuit of those who continued to collect the latter can only be termed remorseless.

Intimidating the Wabuda headhunters of the Fly River Estuary in March 1893 proved easy enough, and only minor bloodshed accompanied the taming of the Collingwood Bay raiders two years later.[172] Characteristically, the bellicose MacGregor reserved his highest praise for the headhunting people who caused him the most trouble. These were the Tugeri, whose settlements located barely beyond the border in Dutch New Guinea to the west rendered capture nearly impossible. "Nothing can exceed their ferocity," Sir William informed his mentor, adding, "They are by no means contemptable

[sic] as foes."[173] A pervasive dread had grown up around these killers, who usually descended on British territory during the rainy season. One persistent rumor around the western Gulf told of Tugeri warriors breaking the arms and legs of their prisoners not only to prevent escape but also to stockpile fresh meat for the cannibal feasts ahead. The attribution of cannibalism to these predators drew stout denials, particularly from the Reverend James Chalmers. About their lust for heads, however, there could be no dispute. Eager to obtain "head-names" for their children from the people they slaughtered, the Tugeri made a mockery of Britain's pacification campaign along the Papuan coast. Thus in June of 1896, MacGregor and a heavily armed posse felt fortunate to intercept a Tugeri band on British soil, slaying several raiders and seizing forty-eight enemy canoes.[174] But largely because Dutch officials either could not or would not police their side of the border, Tugeri raids outlasted the man who had vowed to smash them: Sir William left for West Africa well before these adversaries ceased raiding.[175] In 1913, Hubert Murray, lieutenant-governor of what had been renamed the Australian Territory of Papua, summarized the Tugeri head-preparation technique, apparently still being used:

> Tugeri cut incision at back of head draw the skin forwards over the face, rub charcoal and cocoanut oil into head[,] eat all the flesh then fill round the skull with clay[,] fix up eyebrows with pieces of rattan, pierce eyelids with thorns, and succeed in making a good likeness of the original man. The name of the man is taken for the next child of his murderer. . . . Before the enemy is killed he is asked his name—often the answer is not a name at all, merely a cry of pain. Cut the head off very slowly with bamboo knife down above the collar bone[;] when nearly through twist it round and pull it out with entrails attached.[176]

In fiction as well as in fact, the Tugeri remained a compelling symbol of savagery resisting civilization. Indeed, for the sake of colonial romance, these assassins *needed* to survive since the wildness they epitomized was by the start of the twentieth century a fading reality.[177] The severed head would remain a literary trope as well as the corporal expression of a radically strange social order. Long after headhunting expeditions had been suppressed in Melanesia through government-sanctioned violence, the remnants of "gruesome plentousness" [sic]—whether a killing-stone or a bamboo knife— served as talismans of a bygone barbarity. A subgenre of Oceanic fiction conflated the past and present to preserve the fantasy of headhunting survivals. The popular novels of Australian Ion Idriess "cannibalized" the anthropological reports of the Cambridge expedition to the Torres Strait (1904–35).[178] At least one yarn, *Headhunting in the Solomon Islands* (1942), dealt not at all with the dreaded act, chronicling instead one woman's ambition to paint Melanesian portraits.[179] This enduring conflation of past and present was aptly illustrated during Queen Elizabeth II's visit to Port Moresby in 1977. There, amidst a "people's welcome" at the sports stadium, she received an *ariba*, or skull rack. The object was a crouching human figure from whose arms dangled a pair of yellowed skulls, along with the stuffed head of a hornbill. The Queen's skull rack, now in the British Museum, came from Goaribari island and dated to the early twentieth century. The Reverend James Chalmers's head, allegedly taken by Goaribari warriors, may once have adorned it.[180]

That the British monarch should have received so macabre a present suggests something else. The officials of a newly independent Papua New Guinea who selected it were acknowledging their headhunting heritage. They were neither celebrating the "timeless" ritual of early anthropological fancy nor mourning the collapse of a "traditional" way of life.[181] They had instead chosen a graphic reminder of cultural difference. Their advance to statehood had been rapid, astonishingly so in the eyes of the West. Modernity and the archaic, the Queen's skull rack implied, might reasonably coexist.

FIVE

Among "Stone-Age" Savages

Parts of the Pacific remained exotic in Western eyes even after the suppression of such outré customs as headhunting. Several Melanesian frontiers appeared impervious to the technological forces that had been dissolving distance since the 1830s. By 1850, for example, railroads had effectively shrunk Europe and looked ready to perform the same service on other continents. As the *Illustrated London News* wrote about the Great Exhibition of 1851, "The intercourse of nations, caused by the practical annihilation of space and time which we owe to the railway system, has removed a whole world of difficulties."[1] The telegraph—and the transoceanic cables that made it a genuinely global technology—began to penetrate what Stephen Kern has called the "sanctuary of remoteness."[2] With a merchant fleet that still carried forty percent of the planet's shipping in 1914, Britain was especially well placed to vanquish the tyranny of distance.

It seemed all the more remarkable, then, that at least two Melanesian islands, one rather small, the other immense, had eluded the tentacles of modern mass communication. Indeed, so resistant to material modernity were the people of these islands that they came to be labeled "Stone Age." Their cultures appeared "frozen," stubbornly primordial. They were the hidden folk of the bush rather than beach dwellers, inward-turning rather than horizon-scanning. And according to several European commentators, they were the last "pure" savages left on earth.

Before discussing these hidden Islanders, we should understand the original purpose of the "Stone Age" designation. Charles Lyell, geological visionary, was probably the first British naturalist to depict early mankind as occupying an "age of stone," an evolutionary phase during which "the rude aboriginal arts" required no metal of any kind.[3] But a less path-breaking evolutionist made "Stone Age" (usually capitalized) a familiar descriptor.

John Lubbock (1834–1913) was a forward-thinking banker, a Unionist member of Parliament, and a close friend of Darwin—as well as Victorian Britain's chief popularizer of archaeological thought. Lubbock brought into common usage the division of Stone-Age culture into distinct "Palaeolithic" and "Neolithic" eras. Whereas his Palaeolithic people supposedly could do no more than chip flints into cutting tools (actually, as we now know, a delicate process), their Neolithic successors grew adept at grinding and polishing stones to hold sharp edges.[4] Lubbock never went so far as mid-twentieth-century theorists of a "Neolithic Revolution." That is, his Palaeolithic/Neolithic divide fell well short of those archaeological economists who have since drawn stark contrasts between the "poverty" of hunter-gatherers and the "affluence" made possible by superior tools.[5] Lubbock's periodization nevertheless has invited overly schematic understandings of prehistoric culture.

Beyond inventing temporal categories, he published a readable account of ancient ethnology, *The Origin of Civilisation* (1870). The existence of modern savages posed an explanatory challenge for Lubbock. As a champion of evolutionary thinking, he could not accept the "degenerationist" view that modern savages were the unfortunate residues of once-civilized ancestors; such a downward developmental path would threaten the "cheering prospects" for humanity often implied in evolutionary projections. Instead, Lubbock emphasized the differential development of various "races." Sounding thoroughly Hobbesian, he agreed that the condition of early man must have been wretched. Yet most races had, over centuries, "independently raised themselves."[6] Thus, for instance, the savages who once painted animal portraits on the cave walls of the Dordogne had gradually evolved into modern Frenchmen. Contemporary savages, Lubbock surmised, had for many different reasons failed to reach a higher developmental plane, although he insisted that race betterment lay within their reach. His energetic embrace of the Darwinian gospel did not make a savage lover of Lubbock.[7] But he found it scientifically intriguing to consider that some among the most isolated people alive—African Hottentots, Australian Aborigines, the denizens of Patagonia—*still* inhabited Neolithic worlds.

Those who viewed human variation through the lens of John Lubbock's archaeology saw Stone-Age man not as "a creature of philosophic inference" but of "known reality."[8] The Tasmanians, allegedly less evolved than Europe's ancient mammoth hunters, had nearly vanished by the 1870s. The

Andaman Islanders, too, appeared doomed. Hence the sense of urgency pervading late-Victorian and Edwardian "salvage anthropology." Fanning out across the globe to record dying customs, these enthusiasts shared with a broader public the elegiac thrust of imperial nostalgia. For the realm of the modern unknown was shrinking. By the outbreak of war in 1914, "Timbuctoo the Mysterious" had been demystified, both geographic poles had been reached, and the totemic rituals of the Australian Aborigines had been recorded in close detail.[9] Not long after the war, twenty-five million visitors to the British Empire Exhibition at Wembly found little left of the primitive to savor. Whereas the tiny Sarawak Pavilion offered "hairy shields and dancing masks" to recall the wild tribes of Borneo, the wooden cannibal forks on display at the Fiji Pavilion now possessed "only historical interest."[10]

Even so, the equatorial Pacific had not entirely lost its power to fire European imaginations. It has been argued that the carnage of total war helped revive a British fascination with remote tropical lands. For those soldiers who had nearly frozen at Ypres or the Somme, Paul Fussell speculates, South Sea images of warmth and verdure would have held special appeal. Britain's tight wartime restrictions on travel abroad, moreover, gave the Pacific idyll renewed potency.[11] One London gentleman reserved tropical travel lust for the enterprising male: "The 'Go-Fever' is in the blood [of 'us men']. We long to hear again the whisper of the trade-wind in the palms, and the thunder of the surf on far-away coral beaches."[12] But this "fever" also attacked women. As we will see, female travelers between 1917 and 1929 would play key roles in publicizing the existence of one Stone-Age tribe.

The preeminent "lost" tropical land of the interwar era was literally fantastic: "Skull Island" of *King Kong* (1932). Reaching it involved a voyage across three oceans. The freighter carrying the film-within-a-film's crew and cast to a secret location entered the Pacific at Panama, resupplied at Hawai'i, Japan, and the Philippines, and sailed on to the pelagic unknown "way west of Sumatra." A tattered map on whose accuracy the film director, Carl Denham, bets everything seems to show a great wall designed to shield the Islanders from something frightful. Denham reasons that an advanced civilization must have built this imposing barrier. Over the centuries, however, the descendants of ancient engineers had somehow "slipped back into savagery."[13] Cultural degeneration had wrecked the Skull Islanders but not, fortunately, their wall. Of course, once Denham and crew learn that an enormous gorilla is the fright in question, the story (and the film) lurches toward the ludicrous. A reviewer for *The Times* panned the film's post-island narrative: "As any self-respecting, outsize ape would, [Kong] bursts his chains, and New York is in for a reign of terror compared with which revolutions or air-raids are child's play."[14]

Still, the ethnographic premise of the story was not wholly fantastic. Both the island-bound ape and the primitive people who try to appease him could remain changeless because the modern world had "forgotten" them. *King Kong* clearly did borrow from "the scientific time machine of anthropology."[15] No less influential, though, was the quasi-ethnographic sensationalism surrounding a Melanesian backwater. The islands of the northern New Hebrides had long impressed European visitors as reservoirs of savagery. One of these isles, Malekula, became briefly notorious as the last bastion of the Neolithic Age.

MALEKULA: CANNIBAL REDOUBT

The second largest landmass in its archipelago, Malekula (also known to Europeans as Mallicollo or Malikolo) stretched fifty miles long by thirty miles wide at its thickest point—plenty of room for colonial development, one might have thought. But this island's rugged interior and legendarily "cruel" bush people had persuaded all save the most daring whites to avoid it. British missionaries insisted that Christianity had saved souls and tamed wildness throughout the New Hebrides. The transformation of Efaté (Sandwich) Island in the center of the archipelago, for example, had allegedly been miraculous. During the late 1840s, a British ship foundered off Efaté. Twenty-three of the surviving twenty-four sailors were eaten, their dismembered bodies shared among several villages. Thirty years later a very different fate awaited 150 "boys" bound for the sugar plantations of Fiji. After a storm drove them ashore, the Reverend J.W. Mckenzie persuaded his flock to feed and house the "boys" for a month. Among those who saved the refugees of 1879 were several dark Christians who had previously "picked the bones" of the shipwrecked.[16] Other New Hebridean outposts of savagery such as Erromango, site of John Williams's martyrdom in 1839, had been rendered generally safe for Europeans by the close of the nineteenth century. Measles, along with the relentless moralizing of evangelical missionaries, had knocked the fight out of these Islanders. Malekula was different. It remained beyond the mission (and viral) pale longer than any other island in the group. Not until 1893 did a Presbyterian, the Reverend Frederick Paton, establish a spiritual beachhead at Pangkumu, on the island's east coast.[17]

Rev. Paton, like most Protestant missionaries assigned to the western Pacific, decried French influence throughout an archipelago that was, he believed, British by right. The joint administration of the New Hebrides—the so-called Anglo-French "Condominium" created in 1907—earned few English-speaking admirers. By the early twentieth century, Francophone residents outnumbered them three-to-one; the government-subsidized steamships sailing from Marseilles had achieved their aim. The supposed moral laxity of these French immigrants, combined with structural flaws in the Condominium's judiciary, had produced a "complete breakdown" in administration. As a result, guns, gin, and predatory labor recruitment abounded. Such at least was the view from Sydney and London.[18] According to English-speaking critics, had the two powers worked as one to assess the needs of the "natives," even the most primitive people could have been eased into the modern world. But competition trumped cooperation.[19] So the bush dwellers of Malekula had been largely left alone to pursue their peculiar customs.

Under colonial misrule, indigenous people throughout the New Hebrides appeared to be racing toward extinction. Whether this seemingly inevitable fate derived from the Islanders' own "internal decadence" or from exposure to "white civilization" fueled heated debate among those who cared.[20] While the Europeans debated, island populations dwindled. By 1910, according to Morton King, the Condominium's British resident commissioner, Aneityum Island retained just eleven percent of the population present back in 1859. There is reason to believe that King overstated the speed of Aneityum's denudation.[21] There can be no question, however, that the connoisseurs of human wildness reacted to such grim news by intensifying their search for the authentically primitive. In 1913, a Swiss anthropologist, Felix Speiser, published his account of a modern Neolithic tribe on the remote northern peninsula of Malekula island. Here thrived a jungle people known as the "Big Nambas" after their flamboyant penis-sheaths (whose purpose Speiser described with exquisite euphemism).[22] Adding to their barbaric interest, the Big Nambas were reportedly also among the last "true" cannibals on earth.

Whereas Dr. Speiser cared less about their diet than their material culture, most European visitors to Malekula fixated on the man-eating. The prolific travel writer Beatrice Grimshaw toured the New Hebrides in late 1905, a journey born of curiosity. Her questions about the archipelago had elicited from acquaintances in Australia "a remarkable crop of know-nothingness, don't careishness, and simple lie." Besides, the liberated Miss Grimshaw—very much a New Woman without being a suffragist—had not made her way from the North of Ireland to Melanesia only to be told that she should content herself with touring Sydney Harbor.[23] There were stories to write about these "mysterious murderous" isles. As the be-monacled Grimshaw explained to readers of the *National Geographic Magazine,* the locus of savagery in the western Pacific had shifted from Fiji, once the epicenter of cannibalism but now full of polite and well-groomed Islanders, to the New Hebrides and the Solomons, "where life is more like a nightmare than a dream." Her contacts with people whom Grimshaw disparaged as "nearer to monkeys than human beings in aspect," were few and always filtered through intermediaries such as traders and converts. She may have stepped ashore, briefly, at South West Bay on Malekula, where she examined a bushman's arrows. Although Miss Grimshaw never met any Big Nambas warriors, her passing references to "the rudest possible state" of life in the Malekulan jungle piqued the interest of an intrepid few who would later pierce this heart of darkness.[24]

Strictly speaking, Malekula was not terra incognita to Europeans. As early as 1774, Captain Cook and the crew of the *Resolution* had explored this island long enough to notice a deformation of indigenous skulls that produced a peculiar, backward-sloping forehead. More than a century later, another shore patrol persuaded a Royal Navy officer that elderly Malekulans risked being buried alive.[25] Yet the everyday habits of the bush tribes remained unknown, particularly those based in the north. The prospect of finding aboriginal kinship systems intact excited W.H.R. Rivers, Cambridge University's leading anthropologist. It was Rivers who urged John Layard, his student, to settle on Atchin, one of the islets lying just off the northern Malekula coast. Layard would spend a full year (1914–15) among the Atchinese compiling genealogies in the Rivers manner. Layard probably did not meet any Big Nambas people. At least a few of his Atchinese informants had, however, and they assured the young man that cannibalism survived on Malekula's high plateau. Layard, the scientist-in-training, chose to describe anthropophagy in functional terms; he shunned moralistic assessments of this custom, determined instead to analyze cannibalism as "an integral part of a larger and more embracing rite of human sacrifice."[26] But for those Westerners who valued sensation over science, the association of the Big Nambas with cannibalism was too lurid to ignore. In the words of that indefatigable naturalist A.S. Meek, the South Seas on the eve of the Great War had nearly lost their "savage charm."[27] Did the interior of northern Malekula offer the last chance to watch, as in a mirror, the primitive violence of Europe's Stone-Age past?

Among those Westerners keen to answer this question was an eccentric husband-and-wife team determined to film humanity's most transgressive act. Americans Martin and Osa Johnson set out in 1917 to alert civilized society about Malekula's man-eaters. Their two visits to the island marked the fulfillment of a project that had obsessed Martin for a decade. In late 1906, he had volunteered to crew for Jack and Charmian London aboard their fifty-seven-foot ketch, *Snark*. The adventure novelist needed a seaworthy cook for a transpacific cruise meant to last several years. Raised in Kansas, Johnson knew very little about either sailing or cooking. But he was young (twenty-three), eager, and understood photofinishing.[28]

With this midwesterner assigned to the galley, the *Snark* left San Francisco Bay on 24 April 1907. Hawai'i, the Marquesas, Tahiti, Samoa, and Fiji: all proved exotic in a safe sort of way. The New Hebrides and the Solomons offered an altogether different experience. Charmian spoke for her shipmates when she reviled the people of Tanna, in the southern New Hebrides. These Islanders, Mrs. London declared, "excel all expectations" as the ugliest Melanesians alive; their "generally evil, low-browed malformed Black-Papuan faces are curiously repulsive," she explained. Although Charmian never set foot on a northern New Hebridean beach, she added that the "obscene hairy men" from that part of the archipelago were dangerously unwelcoming to strangers.[29]

Human ferocity, nurtured by isolation, was increasingly what drew Martin Johnson. Toward the end of the *Snark*'s voyage, he decided how his own story of Stone-Age survivals would be told. While anchored off Guadalcanal in the central Solomons, Johnson met three "moving picture men" sent from Paris by Pathé Frères to document the reception of an American fleet at Sydney. Having completed their assignment, these French cinematographers were preparing to film the "cannibals" who allegedly lurked in Guadalcanal's jungle interior. Disease intervened, however. One can imagine the secret relief that Johnson probably felt upon learning that malaria had scuttled this daring project: the honor might now be his.[30] The cruise of the *Snark* ended prematurely after nineteen months with Jack London's hospitalization in Sydney. But if those who knew Martin Johnson expected that this South Seas episode had taken "some of the wandering out of his blood," they soon learned otherwise. Well before eloping with sixteen-year-old Osa Leighty of Chanute, Kansas, in 1910, Martin had set his sights on returning to Melanesia.[31]

Piecing together a reliable account of the Johnsons' subsequent travels through the Pacific is an exercise in frustration. Their publications, as well as the lectures with which they embellished their silent films, are at best imprecise and at worst deliberately misleading where scene and sequence are concerned. The Johnsons' flippant assessments of indigenous intent, moreover, lend a cartoonish quality to the people whose secret lives they claimed to reveal for the first time.[32] Still, Martin and Osa possessed three undeniable strengths as creators of ethnographic fantasy. There was, first, the teenage Osa herself. Exuding both pluck and vulnerability (much like King Kong's beloved), she spent the early years of her marriage singing on stage in a faux Hawai'ian costume while Martin showed photographs from his cruise with the Londons. Later, on Malekula, it would be the juxtaposition of this diminutive girl-woman with the scowling hulk identified as the "king" of the Big Nambas that infused the Johnsons' film footage with sexual tension.[33] Second, Martin could make the most of Osa's appeal in part because he understood the technical limits of his equipment. An appreciation of what his hand-cranked Universal camera could, and could not, convey to an audience shaped all his filming. Third, the Johnsons saw themselves as entertainers above all else, with the result that they tended to honor the aberrant over the commonplace. "Local Man with Enlarged Scrotum," "Hermaphrodite Local at Port Sandwich," "Bearded Man, Necrosis of Skin," "Toman Man with Dried Head": such images of deformity supplement those of the sullen Big Nambas men in building an atmosphere of the grotesque.[34]

The Johnsons' first ethnographic fantasy, *Among the Cannibal Isles of the South Pacific*, reached selected American theaters in mid-1918. The distillation of almost 40,000 feet of film shot in the Solomons and the New Hebrides, it followed Martin and Osa's quest for the quintessential savage. Their encounter with some fierce-looking Islanders on Malaita in the Solomons failed to satisfy the couple. "We had come in contact with many wild peoples," Martin recounted, "but none of them were quite wild enough."[35] Thus Malekula beckoned. The warning from Britain's resident commissioner for the New Hebrides ("Such a proceeding cannot but be attended with great risk to yourself and all those who accompany you") helped legitimate the Johnsons' subsequent boast that they had stared death in the face.[36] From Tenmarou Bay, near the northern tip of Malekula, it was an exhausting, four-hour climb up to Tenmarou Village, seat of the redoubtable chief "Nagapate." Here, at last, stood savagery incarnate. In the on-screen texts that knit together Martin's otherwise transitionless film footage, viewers learned that "skulls were everywhere to be seen" along the jungle path to Nagapate's lair; that the chief's "darting eyes never left Mrs. Johnson for a minute"; and that only a "heartbreaking dash" down to the coast amidst a "rain of arrows" had saved the visitors when they tried to leave. Save perhaps for Nagapate's interest in Osa, none of this was true.[37] Nevertheless, the resulting lecture-film that ran for a week at Manhattan's Rivoli Theater in late July earned rave reviews from both the popular press and trade publications. Declared the *Motion Picture News*, the Johnsons' images of primordial humanity were "probably the most unusual that have ever been taken, for they were secured at imminent risk of life."[38] Retitled *Adventures Among Cannibals* and released several months later as an eleven-part serial, the film proved equally popular in Britain. The critics gushed. *Pictures and the Picturegoer* was more astute than it knew when it described as "almost unbelievable" the close-up footage of "wild-looking boys intent on making a meal of the white intruders." The film's few British detractors focused their criticism on the Big Nambas's near-nudity.[39]

Delighted with the popular response to their first film yet convinced that they did not "get all they could out of the Cannibals,"[40] Martin and Osa returned to Malekula in the late spring of 1919. This time, they believed, cinematic proof of man-eating would be theirs. The Johnsons' new expedition was handsomely equipped. They arrived on the beach far below Nagapate's village with twenty-six armed Melanesians, plenty of trade tobacco, new cameras, and a Pathé-scope motion picture projector, which, together with a generator and radium flares, would make possible the filming of "cannibals at the movies." Footage of Nagapate and his warriors gawking at themselves on screen did later fascinate audiences in Western Europe and America.[41] But the Johnsons' second film, *Headhunters of the South Seas*, marked no advance over their first in terms of ethnographic accuracy. The

Big Nambas remained prize specimens in a human zoo. Anachronism defined them. "Here [on Malekula] we . . . made movies of fellow human beings in the same stage of development that our ancestors were thousands of years ago," the Johnsons announced.[42] They were considerably less pleased with the concessions to wildness that had to be endured. Sharing a bamboo water bottle with the chief, for instance, disgusted Martin: "It is not pleasant to drink from the mouthpiece at which Nagapate's great lips had sucked."[43]

Despite such sacrifices, the Johnsons ultimately failed to capture cannibals in the ghastly act. Neither the Big Nambas nor the bush people of Espiritu Santo island would feast on cue. Whether to classify the Johnsons' first two films as "ethnographic cinema" depends upon one's tolerance for invention. They shared with the celebrated *Nanook of the North* (1922) an ambition to encapsulate exotic cultures in story form.[44] Yet the fabrications that riddle *Among the Cannibal Isles* and *Headhunters of the South Seas* render these silent films more comic than compelling.

The cinema-going British public, in any case, greeted both films with extraordinary enthusiasm. Although the American block booking of theaters in Britain threatened the latter's home industry, audiences there cared only about what graced their screens. Looking back at the reception of *Adventures Among the Cannibals* in 1919, *The Times* opined that "it would be a long time before the public forgets the features of the formidable Nagapate, who was to be seen on the hoardings [advertising boards] in every part of the country." The movie-mad working classes shared this enthusiasm with the privileged. "When the film was first shown," recalled *The Times*, "so many members of Parliament were present [at its screening] that the House of Commons was counted out [adjourned for lack of a quorum]—which surely must be a record for any film."[45] Martin's patient "stalking" of the Big Nambas together with Osa's "cheerful sang-froid" around glowering Nagapate continued to dazzle viewers of *Headhunters* (Figure 5.1). By 1925, the Johnsons, "plain people from the prairies," had won acclaim enough abroad that a safari picnic in Kenya with the Duke and Duchess of York seemed somehow fitting.[46]

Through their films and frequent newspaper interviews, then, the Johnsons turned a New Hebridean backwater into a synonym for savagery. Their often-irresponsible pronouncements on the customs of the Big Nambas attracted several more Westerners of varying methodological rigor. A. Bernard

Figure 5.1   Osa Johnson and "Nagapate" in the highlands of Malekula island, New Hebrides, 1917. By juxtaposing the elfin Osa and the glowering chief, Martin Johnson created his most titillating image.

SOURCE: Martin and Osa Johnson Safari Museum, negative 250678_1. Reproduced with permission.

Deacon, a young English anthropologist, spent eleven months on Malekula during 1926–27. Blackwater fever killed him at the age of twenty-four. Lest his meticulous work on social organization be lost, fellow scholar Camilla Wedgewood converted Deacon's field notes into the monumental *Male-kula: A Vanishing People in the New Hebrides* (1934). Deacon thought there was "reason to suppose" that cannibalism prevailed among the Big Nambas, though he probably did not enter their territory.[47] The English entomologist Evelyn Cheesman certainly did. Intrigued by the Johnsons' claims, Cheesman sought the help of a Seventh Day Adventist pastor, several of his local converts, and a labor recruiter to arrange a visit in 1929. "Ringapat," the new chief, remembered the "man belong bokis" (the man with a box) and made a rotary movement with one hand to imitate Martin's vigorous cranking of his camera.[48] Unlike the Johnsons, however, Cheesman tried to imagine human sacrifice in indigenous terms. It was, she confessed, a "rare privilege" to meet "barbarians belonging to the Stone Age." But with this privilege came an obligation to listen. What Cheesman heard—through the usual filters—was that the Big Nambas reserved their most terrifying sanction for dangerous strangers and tribal outcasts.[49] Malekula appeared no less a cannibal redoubt for Miss Cheesman than for those Westerners who had preceded her, but her recognition of tribal imperatives tempered the urge to condemn.

Curiously, the last noteworthy Westerner to seek out Ringapat and company during the interwar years was an English ornithologist who attempted, as he put it, to "go cannibal."[50] Tom Harrisson's elite education at Harrow and Cambridge had only sharpened his sense of social isolation. His need to belong somewhere could help explain why, in 1934, he sailed to northern Malekula after his fellow scientists had completed their wildlife survey on nearby Espiritu Santo. The wildlife he now found most interesting were human; and his obsession with the authentically primitive fueled repeated visits to the Big Nambas over a period of nine months. Dressed in little more than short pants, walking barefoot, dancing and drinking *kava* with his now-notorious hosts, Tom later wrote that he "partook in their lives as fully as I could." His year on Santo, he noted retrospectively, had been a time to harden himself. For the Malekulans would not have "respected" him if he had materialized with shoes and a supply of tinned meat.[51] Stripped of most civilized accoutrements, Tom followed in what he took to be Captain Cook's footsteps. Cook had allegedly possessed a gift for communicating with Pacific Islanders; Britain's greatest navigator had sought out indigenous aristocrats "with the persistence of a gossip columnist." Now, therefore, Harrisson would cultivate Ringapat, about whom Evelyn Cheesman had earlier spoken in London.[52]

This much Tom accomplished. His best-selling account of living among the Big Nambas, *Savage Civilization* (1937), opened with him narrating in the person of a Malekulan tribesman. He deemed such literary license justifiable because Tom had learned to appreciate the tribe's "deepest feelings" and "delicate labyrinths of thought." More improbable still, he supposedly witnessed—and by implication joined in—a cannibal feast: "The taste [of baked Islander] is like that of tender pork, rather sweet." Whether such outlandishness constituted "a form of pornography" admissible in polite households back home may be debated.[53] Tom hardly cared. When not ingratiating himself with Ringapat, the self-made ethnologist busied himself with tribal censuses. As unsystematic as these surveys may have been, Harrisson insisted that their results challenged the "decayist thinking" of what he dismissively termed "Riverism." Over recent decades, Tom agreed, the populations of isolated bush people had declined throughout the archipelago. But imported disease, not some fatal despair triggered by Western cultural intrusion, was to blame. Once resistance to white men's germs had time to build up among these vulnerable groups, however, their futures, he believed, need not be bleak. Harrisson's logic lent support to the idea of creating sanctuaries for "backward" tribes. That is, since some primitive populations remained intact, Western assistance in protecting their lands would be a sound investment in cultural diversity.[54] Harrisson argued his protectionist case before the Royal Geographical Society, in the imperial press, and on BBC radio.

It seems odd, therefore, that this champion of human wildness would jump at the chance to participate in another cinematic invasion of northern Malekula. The temptations were strong, to be sure. Word of Harrisson's rapport with the Big Nambas reached Hollywood via Australian newspapers. Proof of his growing reputation sailed into Bushman's Bay on 16 May 1935. The hundred-foot steam yacht *Caroline* belonged to Douglas Fairbanks, Senior, who had come looking for Tom. The latter may have adopted primitive habits, but he did not hesitate to swill gin slings in the company of "probably the best-known individual in the world—with the possible exception of Jesus."[55] Plainly starstruck, Harrisson agreed to help Fairbanks with a drama about the Big Nambas. It did not hurt that Hollywood's grandest figure just happened to carry aboard the *Caroline* a veteran cameraman, a motor launch, food for two months, and £250 to cover preliminary expenses.[56] At the end of filming on location, the plan called for Tom and the cameraman to return to California, where footage of Fairbanks, cast as "expedition leader," would be added. The project looked sure to eclipse Martin and Osa Johnson's movie-making efforts.

Yet seven weeks of filming on Malekula produced nothing. The "cannibals" failed to meet Hollywood's expectations. They refused to wear what the cameraman wished. Their dancing lacked energy. They balked at retakes. Fairbanks's feature never found its way into theaters. For his part,

Tom returned to Britain at the end of filming. In 1936 he would apply his savage-watching skills to analyzing the working poor of northern England, an impulse to do "anthropology at home" that one year later launched the famous Mass Observation oral history project.[57]

Meanwhile, Harrisson's former "friends," the Big Nambas of Malekula, were left mostly alone save for the occasional proselytizing of coastal missionaries. Not quite three hundred square miles in area, the high plateau that sheltered these people had for decades discouraged Western trespass. In truth, the Big Nambas made poor models of Neolithic culture. They were, as one London newspaper pointed out, "the only cannibals in the world that kill their victims with guns."[58] The Big Nambas nonetheless offered living proof of the cultural gulf that as late as 1935 still split the species. Some of the white people who had advertised this tribe as earth's last man-eaters did so in the pursuit of fortune: there was clearly profit in the primitive. But by the time that Tom Harrisson tried to go cannibal on Malekula, a second and vastly larger front in the hunt for human wildness had opened. The forbidding interior of New Guinea, it turned out, harbored both cannibals and some extraordinary remnants of the Stone Age.

THE "SCIENTIFIC ADMINISTRATION" OF "BACKWARD" PEOPLE

Until the 1920s, the island of New Guinea struck most educated Westerners as a distant place rich only in steep mountains, magnificent birds, and primitive tribes. Without accepting the reductionist dictum that geography rules destiny, one can understand how these impressions would have been mutually reinforcing. Take New Guinea's mountains. Its highest summits rise between 14,000 and 16,000 feet above sea level. The notion of such altitudes on an equatorial island is certainly arresting. For the visual incongruity of a glacier-clad peak rearing out of the sweltering jungle tends to disorient— much as it disoriented the first European to describe this strangeness, Jan Carstensz, in 1623. (Indeed, the Dutch navigator's report of snow "so near the line equinoctial" earned ridicule back home.) The mountains of New Guinea, moreover, are packed into closely spaced parallel ranges running generally northwest to southeast (Map 5.1). These cordilleras are themselves composed of "razor-like ridges in endless succession" separated by extraor-

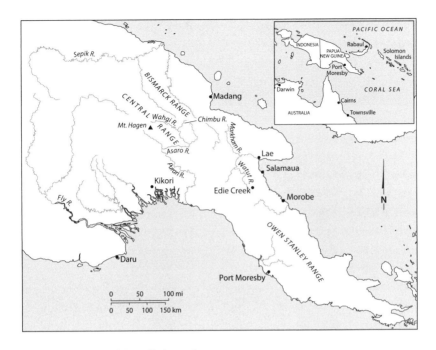

Map 5.1   Eastern New Guinea circa 1930.

dinarily deep and narrow valleys.[59] It would be difficult to invent a more effective barrier to human mobility in an age before widespread air travel.

Sheer limestone slopes are of course less forbidding to birds than humans, and in fact New Guinea's harsh topography offered a measure of protection to the world's most spectacular winged creatures, the birds of paradise. If a Dutch sea captain's sighting of snow in the tropics seemed fanciful, the riotous coloration of several paradise species also strained credibility. Since thirty-eight of the forty-two known species of *Paradiseidae* inhabit only the New Guinea mainland and several nearby islands, it was predictable that collectors would multiply the sites of friction between Papuans and Europeans.[60] When William MacGregor became Papua's first administrator in 1888, therefore, this former medical officer for Fiji found himself wondering how to discipline a wild people without domesticating them. What could be called selective brutality—public hangings, mainly—failed to pacify Papua. Yet MacGregor's decade as administrator did establish the important precedent of using white officers to lead government patrols into Papua's wilderness.[61] Out of this experiment emerged the "discovery" of a twentieth-century Stone Age.

For those Europeans who regarded New Guinea as the last bastion of primitivism, it must have seemed fitting that Hubert Murray, the man who would rule Papua for a generation, rose to power as an indirect result of cannibal mayhem. On or about Easter Sunday, 1901, the Reverend James Chalmers, along with his landing party, vanished into the jungle of Goaribari Island. The missionary's hat later turned up in a nearby village. But it was an eyewitness account of the eating of these careless Christians that stirred debate among colonial officials about the fitting punishment for such barbarism. According to one English observer, Chalmers's martyrdom had generated "exceptional interest" both at home and Down Under. Surely now the reading public's "almost incredible" ignorance about "the world's darkest island" would be dispelled?[62]

Unfortunately, retribution rather than education obsessed the authorities in Papua's capital, Port Moresby. Sir George LeHunt, the colony's administrator, immediately launched a punitive expedition that killed twenty-four Goaribari men. Official vengeance did not end here, however. LeHunt's successor, C.S. Robinson, returned to the scene of the original crime in early 1904 determined to recover the skull of Rev. Oliver Tomkins, Chalmers's companion. When his government yacht drew fitful arrow-fire, Robinson ordered an emphatic answer—a fusillade that may have lasted fifteen minutes and slaughtered as many as fifty Islanders. The newly unified Commonwealth of Australia, under whose control Britain had gladly placed Papua in 1901, could not allow such carnage to go unexamined. The ensuing investigation put Robinson in the wrong. His suicide in June 1904 underscored the rancor that was poisoning Papua's colonial government. This government needed a leader who would put the stability of the state ahead of personal gain. But what visionary could be induced to settle in sweltering, brandy-soaked Port Moresby, whose sixty-six Europeans (all save five of them male) seemed to loathe one another almost as much as their equatorial station? Gavin Souter has offered an apt canine simile, if not exactly an answer: "Into this snarling little community, like an Irish wolf-hound into a terrier's dogfight, came Hubert Murray."[63]

John Hubert Plunkett Murray (1861–1940) possessed a hybrid cultural background that set him apart from most colonial administrators. Australian by birth, his upbringing had been uncommonly cosmopolitan. Hubert's Irish father and English mother elevated learning—preferably of the classical kind—above all other virtues. Although not quite the scholarly equal of his younger brother Gilbert, who went on to become Regius Professor of Greek at Oxford, Hubert flourished at various Australian, English, and German schools. His impeccable education culminated in winning firsts in Classical Moderations and Greats at Magdalen College, Oxford. Unlike Gilbert, Hubert carried a muscular 196 pounds on a six-foot-three-inch frame. This imposing physical specimen rowed and boxed at Oxford; and in 1886, the same year he was called to the bar, Hubert became England's amateur heavyweight champion. Armed with these distinguished credentials, the young man returned to Sydney intent on a legal career. Surprisingly, he failed in private practice, a professional disappointment that some attributed to Oxbridge arrogance. Murray needed a fresh start. Soldiering, he soon discovered in South Africa, could not be his calling: although rock solid under fire, Murray loathed the part he had been obliged to play in burning Boer farms.[64]

By 1904, therefore, the failed lawyer stood ready to accept almost any respectable work that might support his wife and children. Murray's decision to apply for the post of Papua's chief judicial officer perplexed many who knew him. Port Moresby possessed not a trace of glamor. But the advertised position could at least sustain his family, who, he hoped at the start, might join him for substantial parts of each year. As it happened, "the Judge" remained mostly alone not only during his three years as head of the judicial system, but also, discouragingly, throughout his subsequent thirty-two years as Papua's lieutenant-governor.[65] Denied a stable family life, Murray threw himself into what he later termed the "scientific administration" of a frontier colony. Whereas popular accounts of New Guinea rhapsodized about the "spell and mystery" of a land that still "guard[ed] its secrets from the geographer, the naturalist, and the anthropologist,"[66] Judge Murray found himself confronted with the practical problem of trying to reconcile two utterly different understandings of right and wrong.

The first attempts to assess Murray's regime in Papua, offered by those who had either served on his staff or else had been admirers from afar, praised him as a paragon of colonial leadership. Writing in 1940, Professor H.G. Nicholas, an expert on comparative politics, declared that Murray had made Papua a "shining example of the British doctrine of trusteeship and set a standard in the treatment of native races that has been acknowledged to be the highest throughout the British Colonial Service."[67] Lewis Lett wrote two panegyrics about his former boss, and the often testy anthropologist Ian Hogbin conceded that Murray had been a "man of genius" whose humanitarianism improved the lives of many Papuan people.[68] Probably the most influential of his champions was also the first, Beatrice Grimshaw. Miss Grimshaw, a chronicler of tropical danger, has been called the Kipling of Papua's settler community. Whereas some members of that community detested Murray for his strict regulation of commerce as well as his efforts to "elevate" the Islanders, Grimshaw never wavered in her admiration.[69] She had visited Papua in 1907, expecting to stay for a few months at the most. Instead, the hills ringing Port Moresby became her Pacific retreat for the next twenty-odd years. Murray did what he could to make Miss Grimshaw feel at home. She appreciated his encouragement of her writing; he saw in her a kindred spirit—not only educated and daring, but also, as Murray noted in a letter to his brother, "an Irish Catholic and a Fenian." This mutual admiration moved Grimshaw to act as Murray's propagandist-in-chief. Her portrait of Papua's lieutenant-governor as "upright and brilliant" would reach a large and far-flung readership.[70]

Such uncritical praise eventually fueled a revisionist critique. Beginning in the early 1970s, this high-minded ruler of a savage population began to look rather less altruistic. Why, if "the Judge" trusted his dark subjects, did he hesitate to support the creation of tribal courts?[71] Similarly, those who once lauded Murray's resistance to the schemes of predatory capitalists were now urged to look beyond the commercial sphere. As Amirah Inglis's *The White Woman's Protection Ordinance* demonstrated, Murray could bow to cultural hysteria: his ordinance of 1926 exposed the radically unequal legal status of Europeans and Papuans under his regime.[72] At least one indigenous historian, J.D. Waiko, has cast doubt on Murray's administrative vision. Through interviews, Waiko learned that the top-down pressure on his Binandere people to plant coconut palms and pay taxes effectively stole the time needed to conduct traditional ceremonies.[73] Such cultural insensitivity, the revisionists have argued, soils the Judge's reputation as an enlightened colonial ruler.

What then should we conclude about Hubert Murray's invocation of "scientific" administrative principles? And how effectively did his colonial regime cope with earth's "most impressive remaining fragment of the Stone Age"?[74] Murray himself found the "Stone Age" label handy in deflecting demands that he adopt more conventional ruling strategies. Papua's skeletal bureaucracy necessitated unorthodox methods, he often reminded the outside world. In 1907, shortly before Murray was elevated to lieutenant-governor, Papua's government employees numbered forty-nine. Although no one could then know the size of the indigenous population, Papuans were "generally assumed" to number between 400,000 and 500,000 scattered over a landmass larger than England, Wales, and Scotland combined.[75] The onset of world war further skewed this administrative arithmetic. In some British territories, colonial officers were forbidden to enlist for duty abroad. In Papua, however, no such restrictions obtained—with the result that several of Murray's trusted assistants left for France or the Dardanelles, drastically limiting what could be done to tame a turbulent land.[76]

Murray acknowledged the challenge of pacification work in this forbidding place, but his underlying optimism was one reason why the Papuan experiment earned such acclaim. Disputes over land and labor, he recognized from the start, were bound to pit European settlers against the territory's tribal folk. Thus, in aiming to honor what he termed the "British precedent" of placing "the protection and advancement of the native" above all else, the Judge expected bitter opposition from white residents. This he received. Murray nonetheless believed—and repeatedly declared—that over the long term, even the most self-interested settler would learn to appreciate that Australia had shown how "people of the Stone Age" could be brought into the twentieth century "without [cultural] injury."[77]

His confidence stood in stark contrast to the pervasive pessimism that had typified Edwardian discussions of empire. Whereas both pre- and post-war rhetoric tended to identify colonial heterogeneity as a structural weakness, Papua's lieutenant-governor insisted that vast cultural differences could be bridged. As Murray, now Sir Hubert, explained to the Australian and New Zealand Association for the Advancement of Science in 1932, his territory was not "trying to make the brown man white, but to make him a better brown man than before."[78] This noble aim could only be achieved, however, through government policy. Abstractions such as "dual mandate," "sacred trust," and above all "indirect rule" left Murray thoroughly skeptical. He assured all who might listen that Lord Lugard's widely admired strategy of ruling indirectly through Nigerian chiefs or emirs would never work in Papua. For here, as in the Solomon Islands, regional chiefs and traditional councils generally did not exist.[79] Enlisting the cooperation of a "few stray sorcerers" would be worse than useless, Murray observed sarcastically in 1935. Then again, he was not above manipulating the fear of sorcery to obtain voluntary acceptance of smallpox vaccination: informed that a powerful sorcerer from the west was coming to sicken all those who had not yet received the "government mark" on their arms, villagers in several locations eagerly queued for their shots.[80] Murray never tired of reminding his fellow Australians that they went to Papua "solely and simply to serve our own ends." This fact, he argued, carried with it a moral obligation to respect local lifeways.[81]

The actual practice of pacification proved more coercive than Sir Hubert and his acolytes wished to admit. Because Papua was very large and its European rulers very few, the Judge found much to like about the "policy of the oil stain" (*la tache d'huile*). As Murray understood it, French officials in Tonkin and Madagascar had established "certain fixed centers" in the colonial hinterland, centers from which French influence slowly leaked outward. The Papuan variant on this strategy involved building rough outposts that would then become destinations for government patrols. These patrols, usually consisting of one white officer and six to ten Melanesian policemen, were encouraged to blaze new routes between outposts whenever possible. After all, "the ubiquity of the Government" had to be "impress[ed] upon the natives."[82] Patrol officers worked closely with the resident magistrates, whose broad responsibilities ranged from suppressing petty crime and providing jails to clearing trails and supervising public health in their assigned districts.[83] Depending on the magistrate, even a task as seemingly innocuous as improving village hygiene could become an exercise in intimidation. The punctilious A.K. Chignell, for example, was based at Wanigera, on Papua's northeastern coast. He took "pleasure" in announcing new sanitary regulations around 1909: all trees, brush, and rubbish heaps now had to be removed from villages, and all swamps and pools within fifty yards of a dwelling were to be filled. This resident magistrate then explained to the villagers the heavy fines they would bear should there remain "a stick, or a pile of coconut husks and taro parings, or even a single puddle left within the appointed area at the time of the next full moon." If this constituted what Chignell termed a gentle prod, one shudders to imagine his threats.[84]

The methods by which Murray brought law and order to Papua were "as humane as the circumstances permitted," one survey has suggested.[85] The accuracy of this assessment depends on how one views the uncolonized Papuan. Murray attributed his subjects' "backwardness" to geo-cultural happenstance: "It [New Guinea] lay, a fragment of the Stone Age, between Asia and Australia, between Malaya and Polynesia, a part of none of them, unknown to and disregarded by Spaniards, Portuguese, Dutch and English; . . . unexplored and unexploited" down to the late nineteenth century.[86] The Judge dismissed all iterations of the "fatal contact" thesis; however isolated by chance they may have been, his people would, he believed, survive in a world created by and for Europeans.[87] Still, their most brutal customs could not be tolerated. The "Science of Administration," Murray averred, rested on a foundation of common sense. And common sense showed that no sane administrator could discharge a sacred trust to protect "weaker peoples" so long as ritual violence persisted. The Judge would not budge on this point.

> Head-hunting and other atrocities may interest us in a hundred different ways . . . but we must resist the temptation to trifle with our duty. We may sympathise as much as we please with the head-hunter and the cannibal, we may formulate any theories we like about the magic properties of human flesh and the true significance of a severed head; but head-hunting and cannibalism must cease, and must cease at once. And no admiration for the picturesque or the bizarre . . . can excuse a neglect of the essential duty of establishing and maintaining order.[88]

Hence a "violent collision" with those who clung to such customs was unavoidable. Two methods of suppression existed. Either colonial agents could demolish entire settlements where these barbarities prevailed, or else the authorities could concentrate on arresting the individuals deemed most intractable. Although far easier to implement, the first option—"swift injustice," Murray called it—was "unscientific" because it retarded development of respect for the government in savage minds.[89]

Whereas capturing suspected killers in Murray's Papua proved hard enough, trying and sentencing them called for improvisation of a different sort. Occasional reports of black-on-white violence received lurid attention in both Australian and British newspapers. The narrow escape of two settlers from a "horde" of "wild cannibals" on the Kapaina River in 1908, for example, cried out for payback, the *Sydney Morning Herald* thought.[90]

Actually, interracial violence was quite rare in early twentieth-century Papua, a fact that Murray drove home on several occasions.[91] Cases of intravillage and intertribal violence were far more common, however, and they

tested judicial ingenuity. The lieutenant-governor's rough calculus of criminal responsibility involved estimating the accused person's degree of civilization. Thus, a murderer who plainly knew that killing was wrong could
expect to hang, whereas "the absolutely raw savage from the frontiers of
barbarism" might escape with a few weeks' detention. In between these cultural extremes lay endless complexity. What was to be done about the cannibal whose language no one else nearby understood? Could a trial proceed
when an interpreter refused to translate that which he believed to be untrue?
How was a judge to deal with an accused killer whose "horrible desire to
please" tainted much of his testimony? Should a murderer who lashed out
randomly while crazed by grief suffer a harsh penalty?[92] Murray showered
praise on his white patrol leaders and black policemen for their dogged pursuit of malefactors.[93] But his exposure to the peculiar logic of Papuan violence caused him to be both sparing in the use of capital punishment and
curious about how the newly respectable science of anthropology might ease
his colonial burden.

By 1933, Murray could half-seriously complain that the suppression of
headhunting and cannibalism had rendered his annual reports "a great deal
less interesting."[94] As ritual violence declined, however, his search for the
"native view-point" intensified. Those who mocked him for keeping an "anthropologists' zoo" in Papua misunderstood Murray's relationship with anthropology.[95] So did some professional anthropologists, most notably Bronislaw Malinowski, who denounced Papua's anti-sorcery laws as "pernicious"
meddling with venerable customs. Murray cared little about Malinowski's
opinion. If, as the Judge reasoned, anti-sorcery regulations had encouraged
villagers living along the Laloki River to grow food on land formerly regarded as cursed, then these regulations justified themselves.[96] When dealing with indigenous people, "the capacity of 'thinking black' or 'brown'"
never hurt. Here anthropology could help. Yet in a telling qualification,
Murray added, "so long as the student does not allow the charms of that
science to prevail over the claims of duty."[97] He had no patience for the
brand of speculative, evolutionary anthropology that still preoccupied some
scholars. Murray looked instead to the ethnological work of C.G. Seligman,
A.C. Haddon, and, above all, W.H.R. Rivers for guidance. Rivers's focus on
the "complex web of custom and institution" that bound together traditional societies intrigued Papua's ruler, as did the controversial loss-of-
interest-in-life argument.[98] Modern anthropologists no longer spent much

time measuring skulls or collecting curios for museums, Rivers pointed out. They were increasingly turning away from the "physical and material towards the psychological and social aspects" of human existence. This shift in professional focus brought together anthropology and colonial administration as kindred disciplines.[99]

Murray at first entertained high hopes for disciplinary cross-fertilization. He wrote optimistically in 1925 that "I expect from the anthropologist, working with the missionary, no less a result than the bridging of the gulf which separates the Stone Age from the twentieth century."[100] As early as 1914, the lieutenant-governor began pressuring Australia's secretary for external affairs to fund a staff anthropologist. War temporarily shelved this request, but the 1920s saw interdisciplinary thinking assume concrete form: the appointment of government anthropologists for both Papua and the Mandated Territory of New Guinea (formerly German New Guinea); the creation of a cadet scheme to train future colonial officers; and the endowment of a chair of anthropology at the University of Sydney.[101] Murray valued the light that these social scientists sometimes shed on otherwise opaque phenomena. The cultural forces fueling cannibal raids in the Purari Delta now began to make better sense. Probing the spread of nervous symptoms ("Vailala Madness") among villagers in the Gulf Division, F.E. Williams revealed how changes in ancestor-beliefs had disrupted life throughout much of that soggy region.[102]

Murray nevertheless remained skeptical about all anthropologists whom he deemed doctrinaire. The Judge respected F.E. Williams, a Rhodes Scholar from Adelaide, because Murray saw in this young man a commitment to "practical administration." Even so, the mentor hastened to remind the pupil that his task in analyzing the "Vailala Madness" did *not* include propping up dying customs.[103] Murray took quiet delight in reports from London about so-called "pure" anthropologists—that is, hard-line functionalists—whose reverence for "tradition" had obliged them to defend headhunting.[104] Those modern critics who have depicted anthropology as yet another weapon of colonialism would do well to ponder Murray's long regime. Although he welcomed anthropological assessments of indigenous behavior, Papua's proconsul remained acutely aware that the need to maintain order in a "backward" land must always distance the administrator from the academic.[105]

Although Sir Hubert Murray dominated the news from Papua, his was not the only corner of New Guinea that Australia controlled. Shortly after the outbreak of war in 1914, a hastily assembled Australian ground force had captured Rabaul on the island of New Britain, colonial headquarters for German New Guinea. This vast expanse, covering the mainland's northeastern quadrant as well as the Bismarck Archipelago, stayed under Australian supervision until 1921. In that year, what was once Germany's largest Pacific colony became a League of Nations "mandated territory" entrusted to Australia.[106] The league's mandate system created a three-tier classification scheme that reeked of paternalism. Whereas peoples of the "A" mandates, mostly residents of the former Turkish Empire, were judged capable of self-rule after a brief period of Western "tutelage," those of the "B" mandates, concentrated in central Africa, appeared to need indefinite guardianship. The "C" mandates of South-West Africa and some of the Pacific Islands contained peoples deemed so primitive that they likely would never be able to govern themselves. The Mandated Territory of New Guinea, whose rugged interior remained largely unexplored at the end of the Great War, struck Europe's peacemakers as the quintessential dependent land.[107]

Those Australians who salivated at the prospect of getting rich quick in this new territory resented government interference of any sort. One critic denounced the "fanatical regard for the welfare of the native" that officials in Rabaul purportedly displayed. Solicitude seemed wasted on tribal folk who, it was rumored, strangled their sick infants, buried their elderly alive, and ate their enemies.[108] Yet those would-be entrepreneurs who railed against the "mollycoddling" of brutes in the Mandated Territory generally recognized a still greater menace in that "nigger-lover" who ruled Papua. Hubert Murray's restrictions on commercial development there supposedly constituted a "disgrace to the good name of Australia."[109]

Such shrill criticism derived from contrasts in leadership style as well as from substantially different levels of indigenous resistance to colonial authority. Papua's proconsul was just that, a leader whose bold articulation of native policy and unprecedented longevity allowed him great freedom in his day-to-day management of the colony. Not often answerable to higher powers (except on the subject of budgets), Murray could be insufferably smug. For instance, administrators in the Mandated Territory who allowed the "vile gibberish" of Pidgin to infect official business were, Murray believed, lazy.[110] As for the young men whom he trained to be patrol officers, these served as extensions of his own ego; by praising his "outside men" for their physical toughness and sound judgment, Murray was burnishing his own reputation.[111] Moreover, he literally walked the talk. At the age of sixty-nine, Murray could still hike 200 miles through rough country in eleven days. Almost always the tallest man on patrol and partial to a red flannel shirt, he made an ideal target for arrows. An aversion to the use of firearms against threatening groups only added to his stature. The restraint that Murray demanded of his patrol officers earned affectionate parody: "After you've been killed, you may open fire."[112] Although the Mandated Territory attracted some able administrators during the 1920s and '30s, none proved as hands-on, or self-certain, as the Judge.

It must be added that Murray did not have to contend with sustained violence on the edges of his domain. Rabaul, the seat of government for Australia's new mandate, occupied the tip of an island far removed from where Europeans were starting to push west into the mainland interior. That interior held a greater concentration of "uncontrolled" tribes than Papua, along with more unregulated gold prospecting. This combination proved volatile. Probably because of his nationality (English) and unusual training (as a barrister), the spearing of a maverick miner near Madang in 1924 earned mention in the British press.[113] But this same fate would befall several less genteel gold-hunters over the next decade. Arresting their killers consumed much time and treasure. In 1933, for example, after Kukukuku warriors murdered two prospectors on the Tauri River, it took three separate patrols to catch the suspected assassins and haul them back to the coast. The Kukukuku (pronounced "Kooka-Kooka") people kept close guard over some 4,500 square miles of hill country west of the Watut River. In the eyes of Europeans, this fierce resistance seemed "stubborn," as if the Kukukuku had refused to read a memo on tribal submission.[114] The job of the patrol officer or "kiap" may have been attractive to young Australian males eager for adventure and steady pay.[115] It was, though, a more dangerous job in the Mandated Territory. Rather than obey white men, some of the Ramu River people moved their dwellings into cane swamps—sites unreachable to strangers without wading "waist deep in ooze" for miles. As late as 1936, headhunting remained a scourge along upper sections of the Sepik River.[116] Unable to pacify large tracts of the highlands, rulers of the Mandated Territory closed those areas to most European traffic beginning in 1935.[117] In hindsight, this partial closure looks prudent. To the Mandated Territory's missionaries and miners, however, it seemed a confession of administrative weakness in distant Rabaul. To the south, in Port Moresby, one can imagine

Hubert Murray allowing the faint trace of a smile to lighten his stern features.

Despite their bureaucratic differences, however, the Mandated Territory and Papua both embraced the tactic of pacification-by-patrol. Most of the longer patrols added exploration of unknown districts to their policing duties. Indeed, after 1912, when the government of Australia increased its subsidy to Papua by £10,000 per year, Hubert Murray began sending out patrols that pursued geographic knowledge as eagerly as wanted criminals.[118] This repurposing of the patrol entailed considerable risk, as the Judge learned from the Smith debacle of 1911. Late in 1910, Murray had taken his first leave of absence. The man chosen to relieve him, Miles Staniforth Smith, resented Murray's growing stature. The jealous Smith assumed that a display of colonial daring might do his career a power of good. He therefore set out to explore what was then the most mysterious part of Papua, the wall of jungle and mountain lying between the Purari and Fly-Strickland river systems. Smith's quest for glory went terribly wrong. His eleven Papuan policemen and thirty-three carriers, all coastal folk, were unprepared for the cool temperatures they encountered as the expedition gained altitude. When these ill-chosen men complained of hunger, Smith beat them with his walking stick. When they built rafts to bypass precipitous terrain, these capsized. Smith's gamble cost eleven Papuan lives and lasted so long—four months—that three search parties went hunting for the overdue patrol. The *Sydney Morning Herald* lamented the "chaos that has arisen in Papua since the disappearance of its administrator." And all for what? Instead of trekking northwest from the Kikori to the Strickland, Smith had managed to march in a complete circle, ending where he had started on the Kikori. Upon resuming his duties in Port Moresby, Murray could find no silver lining: "the expedition cannot be looked on as other than disastrous."[119]

But there was also much to be gained, he believed, from responsibly led patrols. As Murray's interest in applied anthropology grew, so did the conviction that his patrol officers and resident magistrates were the right sort to make first contact with previously unknown peoples. True, as of 1917 the Judge suspected that much, perhaps most, of Papua's remote backcountry was uninhabited. On an earlier reconnaissance of the Strickland River, after all, no sign of human habitation had been seen for 100 miles, despite the availability of good garden land and a fair number of game animals.[120] Murray's "outside men" nevertheless continued to meet strange specimens of humanity. In 1922, along an arm of the Fly River near Dutch territory, Messrs. Austen and Logan stumbled upon a people who lived in tree houses and wore rattan breastplates, yet designed sophisticated deep-pit toilets. That same year, not far from what appeared to be the headwaters of the Kikori, Flint and Saunders descended into a wide and well-cultivated valley, the Samberigi, whose friendly residents initiated "much handshaking."[121] Perhaps the hitherto unexplored borderlands of Papua and the Mandated Territory contained other rich valleys populated with equally hospitable tribes?

ENCOUNTERING THE STONE AGE

Cultural first contact—that brief "space of wondering . . . where doubt locks horns with fantasy," as Michael Taussig has phrased it—will always be dramatic.[122] For in this liminal moment, the possible obliterates the probable, wonder overwhelms reason. Yet first contact events also invite misrepresentation. Emissaries of modern industrial states are likely to overestimate the befuddlement of isolated people; initially slack-jawed "natives" often size up strangers very quickly. Then too, "advanced" observers will frequently underestimate the cultural connectedness of tribes occupying remote lands. Both errors colored accounts of the New Guinea highlanders whose very existence made front-page news during the late 1920s and 1930s.

In emphasizing the isolation of these "Stone-Age" tribes, Western accounts typically assumed that people who proved so difficult to reach must themselves have been immured in their mountain valleys. One patrol officer writing in the early 1920s claimed that up-country Papua was more daunting than the Himalayas. Attempting to scale 28,000-foot Kangchenjunga was daring, he allowed, but then again Himalayan climbing parties regularly enjoyed fresh goat's milk, butter, and meat. The "outside men" of Papua knew no such luxury.[123] Thus, denizens of the island's almost inaccessible center have long been depicted as living in a cultural cocoon, or, more accurately, in hundreds of small cocoons. A widely read biogeographer has asserted that "most" highlanders in "traditional" New Guinea "never went more than 10 miles from home in the course of their lives."[124] Linguistic barriers presumably also contributed to tribal isolation. As of 1918, the number of mutually unintelligible languages spoken in Papua alone was estimated to exceed 150. By 1965, this estimate had swelled to more than 500 distinct languages in the Australian half of the island. And as of 2003, that figure had climbed again to 750 languages, 150 of which were spoken by fewer than 200 people.[125]

Thought to be both linguistically and physically hemmed in, then, New Guinea's highland folk were for a generation viewed through Western eyes as culturally static. They were literally anachronistic, having survived "against time," temporal oddities whose backwardness was also their fascination. Note the accounts of first contact in New Guinea entitled *The Land That Time Forgot* (1937) and *Patrol into Yesterday* (1963).[126] During the late nineteenth century, earth's last "wild men" had supposedly occupied the rain forests of central Borneo. There, the Penan, gentle nomads who owned nothing except what they could carry, "crystallized" for ethnologists the most rudimentary of cultures.[127] By the eve of World War Two, however, ground zero for primitivism had shifted to the misty, mile-high valleys of central New Guinea. Here, since time out of mind, "Adam in plumes" had pursued a Neolithic existence.[128]

In fact, though, probably some of "Adam's" bird-of-paradise plumes and certainly all his decorative cowries and iridescent oyster shells had arrived through ancient supply lines. For at least 9,000 years, seashells as well as salt and cassowary-bone daggers had found their way from coastal districts up to the highlands via exchange routes that crisscrossed the island.[129] It is often held that the demand for, and appreciation of, iron is a rough measure of a society's grasp of the wider world—since iron is usually the most startling innovation associated with first contact. Hence prospector Michael Leahy's comment about the people living in caves near Lemaki who had been "too stupid to sell a pig for a [steel] tomahawk, instead of for . . . shell."[130] Actually, intelligence, whatever else it might be, has little to do with the swift appreciation of foreign materials. Indeed, Jared Diamond contends—with nearly equal disregard for logical rigor—that the peoples of highland New Guinea are "more intelligent, more alert, more expressive, and more interested in things and people than the average European or American." The highlanders are, Diamond insists, more intelligent because they have had to be; survival in their trying environment demanded exceptional cleverness. Proof of this cleverness resides in the highlanders' survival.[131] Diamond's tautological reasoning aside, it is fair to infer that the highlanders knew through traditional trade activity not only that outsiders existed but also that the world beyond their valleys must be different in several ways. Obvious yet necessary cautions follow: the inhabitants of New Guinea's central valleys were neither "lost" nor "unknown," let alone "forgotten." These people were not "frozen" in time. And to speak of their "discovery" is to accept that Western recognition somehow confers legitimacy.

A corollary of these Eurocentric tropes is that New Guinea's highlanders became "among the most fortunate colonized people on earth." That is, especially compared to Australia's Aborigines whose suffering stretched back 150 years, roughly a million New Guinea "tribals" had remained beyond Western reach until the early 1930s. Their journey from isolation to independence would be stunningly brief; the unified nation of Papua New Guinea won full self-government from Australia in 1975.[132] This narrative celebrated the swift maturation of a "backward race" through the enlightened guidance of Australia, long a colony herself. Yet the celebration masked a darker colonialism. In published records—administrators' reports and patrol leaders' summaries—state-sponsored violence was almost always depicted as regrettable but necessary. Hubert Murray noted with bland menace that "[U]nfortunately, a population of the Stone Age . . . cannot be induced by fair words alone to adopt a more peaceful life."[133] The midnight raids that patrol officers and their police sometimes launched against offending villages would have generated no less terror than "native" attacks. The prisoners led away to become laborers or carriers must have endured an agony of uncertainty about their futures. Patrol officers such as Jack Hides extolled the martial initiative of the "best" policemen. Cannibals and headhunters in their former lives, these "proud and overbearing" Papuans were the antithesis (per Hides) of the demoralized Aborigine begging on the streets of Sydney. Hides's armed constables supposedly kept open "the laneways between civilization and the Stone Age."[134] An indigenous scholar's assessment of these warriors-turned-enforcers credits them with perpetrating "more acts of colonialism than the colonists." Whether such eager complicity derived from ignorance or blind loyalty remains a contested matter.[135]

Nor is it clear what ran through the minds of New Guinea highlanders upon first glimpsing white men and their curious tools. Note, by way of comparison, the eighteenth-century contact experiences of Captain Cook and his crews. In early November 1769, the *Endeavour* sailed into Mercury Bay on the east coast of New Zealand's North Island. Thanks to the detailed account of an indigenous eyewitness, a boy named Horeta Te Taniwha, we know a good deal about how this cultural collision looked through Maori eyes. As Te Taniwha recalled many years later, the elders who watched the pale men rowing toward shore pronounced them "goblins." During their twelve-day anchorage in the Bay, these goblins did some sensible things, such as gathering oysters, but also pursued some strange rituals, among them collecting grasses from the cliffs and inspecting stones on the beach. The goblins caused no harm except for using a thunderous "walking stick" to put a hole in the back of a warrior who had stolen a piece of cloth. Te Taniwha received a present—a small, sharp piece of metal—from a tall goblin of "noble demeanour." That noble goblin was of course Cook, and his present a nail.[136] The *Endeavour* had landed among an unknown people who seemed eager to please and keen to trade.

Westward across the Tasman Sea, Australia's "Indians" (as the English insisted on calling the Aborigines) reacted quite differently to the *Endeavour* and the men it disgorged in late April 1770. Working his way northeast along the Australian coast, Cook anchored in Botany Bay, not far from what is today Sydney Harbor. Whereas the Maoris of Mercury Bay had been curious and accommodating, the "Indians" of Botany Bay seemed supremely indifferent. The ship's gentleman-naturalist, Joseph Banks, observed that even as the landing boats set out for shore, an Aboriginal fishing band "scarce lifted their eyes from their employment." Most of these fishermen scattered as the boats neared land. But two men stayed. As best the *Endeavour*'s crew could tell, this defiant pair yelled out the words *Warra warra wai*. Several years on, English immigrants would learn what these words meant: "Go away."[137]

If the Aborigines' indifference perplexed Cook's crew in 1770, five generations later, uncontacted New Guinea tribes continued to puzzle the Europeans who met them. It was an elaborate Dutch expedition, not an Australian patrol, that first studied a densely settled highland valley. The 1920–22 trek to Mount Trikora in Dutch territory must have made itself known to every indigenous adult through whose districts it climbed. At least 400 participants, including Dayak boatmen, convict carriers, soldiers, and one trained anthropologist, lumbered into the Toli River highlands. Once there, a much smaller contingent went ahead to announce their friendly intentions. Contrary to the "traumatic meeting of cultures" that later expedition leaders would emphasize, this advance party triggered no panic among the Dani women tending their gardens. One of these women calmly left to fetch the men, who then invited the strangers back to their village for a meal.[138]

Michael Leahy, a notoriously impatient Australian prospector, was fond of blanket generalizations. "First contact," Leahy declared, "usually elicits undisguised awe and terror . . . followed by stunned silence and tears, dances of what appeared to be joy, and loud, windy speeches by stone-axe-wielding old men who eventually give all and sundry their visions of the encounter."[139] This condescending portrait of indigenous surprise, especially when reinforced by Leahy's iconic photographs of highlanders in open-mouthed wonderment, implied a one-sided theatricality. Leahy's version of first contact dwelt on the absurdity of the highlanders' overreaction—absurd because Westerners "know" that the "natives" had little to fear from these explorers. But the Australians, along with their policemen and carriers, also resorted to theatrical displays at this tense moment. Though the intruders' carefully restrained hand and head gestures offered a stark contrast to the "wild" gesticulations of the highlanders, the former were no less studied. As Greg Dening has noted about the drama of first contact, *every* participant resorts to stylized actions. The intended meaning of these actions will often be obscure, however.[140] We would do well, therefore, to maintain a healthy skepticism about the constructions of affect and effect contained in New Guinea encounter narratives released between 1928 and 1939.

The first of the three most prominent encounter narratives, that which detailed Karius and Champion's Fly-Sepik patrol of 1927–28, sought in part to settle speculation about the people who might dwell in New Guinea's mountainous heart. Readers of *National Geographic Magazine* had learned in 1908 about the "primitive simplicity" of up-country Papuans, and savored photos of "savages" wearing boars' tusks through their septa.[141] Both Dutch and British expeditions had chanced upon people who used only sharpened rocks and shell edges to fashion their canoes and bows. In 1920, a Dutch patrol spent six weeks among the diminutive Timorini of the western highlands. Possessing neither metal nor cloth, the Timorini proved conclusively that "Stone-Age tribe" was more than a figure of speech.[142] Beyond its original Victorian use as an archaeological descriptor, the compound adjective "Stone-Age" had gradually acquired the additional meanings of "unsophisticated" or "inflexible" (as in General Douglas Haig's limpet-like attachment to horses on a mechanized battlefield).[143] Now, during the interwar years, these meanings were bleeding together to denote humans whose cultural development had been "arrested" long ago.

The Fly-Sepik patrol of 1927–28 proved newsworthy above all for its leaders' resolve. This epic south-to-north traverse of the island at its widest point was from first to last a triumph of the "Murray men."[144] Papua's lieutenant-governor had often dreamed of sending a patrol up the Fly-Strickland river system, across the jagged limestone escarpment wherein these waters presumably originated, and down the north-flowing Sepik River to its mouth. "My idea," Murray confessed, was "to keep hammering away at [this] corner of the Territory," gathering information about the land and its people.[145] The patrol leader he selected for the final push, Charles Henry Karius, hardly looked the rugged sort. Of middling height and reed-thin, Karius, then 34, relied on courtesy rather than fear to motivate. For his second, the Australian Karius chose a short-sighted but uncommonly fit patrol officer named Ivan Champion, who, like several of Murray's "outside men," was Port Moresby–born and reared.[146] These two white leaders, along with thirty-nine Papuan carriers and twelve Papuan policemen, set out in December 1926 knowing nothing about what lay beyond the limestone massif that had repulsed all previous expeditions. They would have to operate on the cheap, moreover, since neither Australia's government nor that of the Mandated Territory wished to underwrite such a gamble.

The patrol consisted of two separate expeditions, the first of which, lasting from December 1926 to July 1927, ran out of food. It was remarkable that Karius and company got as far as they did. After enduring three months of flash floods, disgruntled carriers, and malnutrition, this woefully under-provisioned party found itself 615 miles from the coast. With the dreaded limestone barrier looming ahead, Karius elected to make a "dash" for the Sepik with a small party of his most trusted Papuans. The terrain grew appalling: "broken limestone with knife-like edges, crevices 20 to 30 feet deep, spanned only by a few moss-covered roots, or a fallen tree; sudden, sharp descents and equally sharp climbs, into and out of a series of large 'pot holes,' or depressions varying from 50 to 100 yards in diameter, and from 30 to 100 feet deep, and other obstacles too numerous to mention."[147] Eventually, the arithmetic of survival signaled retreat. Because a carrier could haul no more than about forty pounds over rough country yet ate that weight in rice per month, the range of such parties was quite limited, particularly when local food sources failed to materialize. Karius later estimated that at its turnaround point, this first trek had unknowingly probed to within six miles of the Sepik's source.[148] The "dash" had failed. Yet Karius's bitter disappointment would be salved several weeks later when Champion finally rejoined him. The latter, exploring on his own, had met a friendly highland people called the Bolivip. Intriguingly, their headman, "Tamsimara," told of a stream not far away that flowed north. And he would lead the white men to it.[149]

Buoyed by this news, Karius and Champion wasted little time in launching a second expedition. They left Port Moresby in mid-September 1927, this time accompanied by a core of handpicked carriers from Fergusson Island in Papua's far eastern d'Entrecasteaux group. The accounts of this second Fly-Sepik patrol, published first in Papua's *Annual Report for 1927–28* and later in Champion's *Across New Guinea*, were riveting. The party climbed to 8,000 feet through "needle-pointed pinnacles of limestone" in the Dap Range; strung cane bridges across mountain cascades; and wandered for days through the Upper Sepik's "awful sago swamp."[150] Their providential rendezvous with the government's motor yacht *Elevala* on 18 January 1928, nearly 500 miles up the Sepik, brought to a close one of the twentieth century's greatest tropical adventures. Its audacity cheered Sir Hubert Murray.

So did its restraint. As Ivan Champion noted proudly, not a single shot had been fired at a "native" during either patrol, and on just two nights had sentries been posted.[151] Murray put this achievement down to sound character: "it is generally the timid man who opens fire when he meets with opposition, and the brave man who refrains." By this measure the scrawny Karius was very brave indeed. On 24 December 1927, for example, he and three policemen had entered a village on the Upper Sepik unseen, igniting panic when discovered. The strangers soon found themselves facing a line of warriors with bows drawn. But Karius's soothing gestures and slow, steady advance reportedly transformed a near bloodbath into a village-wide frenzy of welcome.[152]

What such praise tended to obscure, however, was the risk that indigenous peoples assumed in greeting strangers. To his credit, Champion understood how much he and Karius owed to the Bolivip people and their headman, Tamsimara. Without them, the patrol would never have managed the waterless crossing of the mountains that guarded the source of the Sepik. Champion's gratitude was tainted by a sense of cultural superiority, to be sure. Shortly before leading his new friends over the island divide, Tamsimara and the other Bolivip men took shelter in a cave one evening. "[F]rom our beds," Champion recalled, "we could see them sitting round a great fire, stone axes hanging from their shoulders, the flames throwing into relief the peculiar garb of these savages of the Stone Age."[153] Still, for his time Champion must be considered a reasonably perceptive observer of what G.H.L. Pitt-Rivers called "the clash of culture."[154] The "native" reticence, even terror, emphasized in many other first contact accounts is notably missing from Champion's remarks on the Bolivip. These people had been given a half-day's warning about the approach of Champion's subpatrol—time enough, perhaps, to ascertain that the strangers posed no immediate threat. The Bolivip welcome, in any event, was rapturous:

> A crowd of thirty men and youths were round us and fresh numbers were arriving every minute. These would come up to embrace me, shouting the greeting, "Sano!" [Friend!] and our guides had to give them a description of us and our equipment, and they told them, too, of our knives and tomahawks. These were grabbed from the police, and men and boys rushed at every tree and shrub within reach, hacking them down indiscriminately across the path and blocking it. They were madly excited; the din was terrific; it was their first experience of steel.[155]

Both during this initial group contact and later, when alone with Tamsimara, Champion ascribes the wild cordiality of the Bolivip to a hunger for metal. But in subsequent characterizations of Tamsimara, Champion depicts the headman as one preoccupied with honor as much as with blade-envy: "This savage was a gentleman."[156]

THE POLITICS OF FIRST CONTACT

It is doubtful whether the Fly-Sepik patrol did in fact advance "the interest of the Empire," as the Royal Geographical Society proclaimed in 1929.[157] There can be little question, though, that the subsequent highland treks of Michael Leahy and Jack Hides helped to invest "first contact" with troubling associations. Unlike Karius and Champion, both colonial government officers and loyal "Murray men," Michael Leahy was above all an entrepreneur. Gold drew Leahy to the Mandated Territory of New Guinea in August 1926. If this energetic self-promoter's tale is to be trusted, within a few days of hearing about a rich strike at Edie Creek, Leahy, then twenty-four, parked his lorry by the side of a Queensland road and caught the boat to Rabaul.[158] Having spent his first working years in a dead-end job as a railroad clerk, Leahy now turned to the perpetual hope of prospecting; he would remain a miner of fame to the end of his days. The fame is easily explained. It derived from a potent blend of luck, ruthlessness, and an appreciation of how cameras—movie and still—might capture the shock of colliding cultures.[159] Thanks to Leahy, the images of Chuave-area highlanders fleeing, mouths agape, from what they took to be spirits have become the iconic representations of modern Stone-Age people.

Michael Leahy was so sure he could read the "native mind" that the unintelligible speech of highland tribes rarely troubled him. Body language would tell him all he needed to know, Leahy claimed. Shortly after his first failed attempt to coax gold out of an up-country creek, Leahy met the veteran prospector Helmuth Baum. At once polite and crafty, Baum offered advice that confirmed what his young friend had gleaned from a Queensland boyhood: aboriginals are like children, and like children, required a firm hand.[160] Yet the cautious Baum was ambushed and killed in 1931 by the same people, the Kukukukus, who very nearly succeeded in crushing Leahy's skull with a stone club soon thereafter. Henceforth the young miner vowed to punish all thefts of his trade goods. Let just one steel axe go missing, he held, and an entire village would be primed for murder.[161] Such was the sanitized version of Leahy's "native policy." His unpublished diary paints a more troubling portrait. What happened at the village of Korofeigu on the Bena-Bena River late in 1932 occasioned no regret: "Heard there were six nigs killed at Korofeigu in the scrap over the stolen tomahawk."[162] Shooting above heads, or into nearby trees, struck Leahy as dangerous restraint.

Fortunately for the Mandated Territory's eastern highlands, Leahy and Mick Dwyer, another young prospector, did not feel obliged to provide such object lessons during their trek of 1930. Because the Australians sought alluvial gold, it made sense to look for telltale specks of color in the streams located west of the Kratke Mountains, beyond the Markham River watershed. Frequent panning in as many streams as possible would enhance their chances of finding gold-bearing gravel. Leahy and Dwyer therefore moved quickly. Yet as they continued their reconnaissance, the pair were amazed to discover "many thousands of Stone Age natives" living among well-watered grasslands. The indigenous men, clutching bows and arrows, apparently belonged to a "virile race." It was, however, the sight of "symmetrically perfect" gardens full of yams and beans that most impressed the two miners.[163] They kept moving. Finally, in early June, Leahy and Dwyer decided to follow a large river flowing away to the southwest. What they did not at first realize was that they had reached an arm of the Purari, and that by following it down they would eventually reach the Gulf of Papua. This they did on 10 July. Their accomplishment was a product of stamina and persistence on the part of two adventurers who had certainly not set out to fill in the island map.[164]

Leahy and Dwyer's seven-week march of mid-1930 marked the first of several treks through districts whose people flourished in Neolithic isolation. Timorous at first, these people soon put aside their caution and flocked into the prospectors' camps. The villagers of the Bena-Bena region, whom Leahy and Dwyer contacted in late 1930 and 1931, gathered in such crowds around the strangers' tents that campsites had to be roped off and sentries posted to keep the curious at bay. Leahy professed to worry about the human cost of "opening" the highlands.[165] Yet as early as 1929 he had begun experimenting with ways to build landing strips in the bush and signal pilots with smoke. By March of 1933, the combined resources of the colonial administration in Rabaul and the New Guinea Goldfields Company were sufficient to make air power the centerpiece of a thrust into the unknown territory between Bena-Bena and the Hagen Range.[166] Leahy brothers Michael and Dan, along with government officer J.L. Taylor, were poised to enter what would become the most famous highland valley of them all.

Aerial surveys gave these expedition leaders a preview of the region's geology. Still more useful was what the short flight of 17 March 1933 revealed once it reached a great grass plain to the west. There, spread out far below the DeHavilland 50, lay a plateau filled with oblong houses and neat gardens. The evidence of intensive agriculture was crucial. It meant that Taylor and the Leahys would be able to trade for food rather than having to haul it with them. Largely unburdened with the heavy rice rations that the 1927–28 Fly-Sepik patrol had dared not do without, this far better financed team could afford to load up on the pearl-shell and cowries so prized throughout the highlands. And there would still be room left over for the scientific instruments that Karius and Champion could never have afforded. Accordingly, the expedition leaders packed prismatic compasses, barometers, thermometers, cameras, a wireless set, and, in case the people proved tractable, a pair of cranial calipers.[167] Handsomely equipped, a column of four white

Australians and nearly one hundred New Guinea carriers and armed policemen left Bena-Bena camp on the morning of 28 March.

A ten-day march brought this party seventy miles west. Along the way,
Michael Leahy found "amusing" the eagerness with which local people collected souvenirs from the encampments. Everything that the expedition dis-
carded, from empty tins and scraps of paper to the dogs' hair and feces, was
snatched up.[168] It never occurred to Leahy that what he dismissed as the
obsessions of primitive magic might in fact have been a systematic inventory
of the strangers' cargo, their trash being analyzed as a midden. But awe replaced amusement when the prospectors emerged from a thick forest to
behold, spread out in front of them, a "seemingly endless" valley. This was
the Wahgi. As a later survey would establish, it stretched sixty miles long and
twenty to thirty miles wide, mostly suspended 5,000 feet above sea level.[169]

The Wahgi Valley's physical beauty knew few equals. How many people
lived in a "lemon-coloured landscape" encircled by the "ultramarine bulk of
tremendous mountains, rearing their serrated tops . . . into a dome of powder blue!"? The soothing climate varied between 52 and 78 degrees Fahren-
heit over the course of an April day.[170] Despite the Wahgi's natural beauty,
however, what stunned the Australian visitors was the proof, visible in every
direction, of tasteful human design (Figure 5.2). Viewed from above, the
valley's rectangular garden plots (often bordered by "picket fences") resembled a giant chessboard. Where splashes of red or purple best set off the
garden greens, ornamental coleus had been planted. Clumps of bamboo and
small stands of casuarinas added botanic texture. Wild animals, other than
rats, did not disturb this manicured scene: both the pig and the cassowary
had been domesticated. "Park-like" was a description of the Wahgi Valley
that Michael Leahy and his brothers often used.[171]

This proof of aesthetic sensitivity notwithstanding, Leahy insisted on
classifying the people of the Wahgi as "primitive." Their stone axes were
gorgeously polished. And yes, these highlanders appeared healthier than
New Guinea's malarial, low-country folk. But irrational they remained.
When the hurriedly built Wahgi landing strip welcomed its first plane, for
example, the pilot climbed out of his cockpit covered head-to-toe in "shining white." Large, square-cut green goggles rounded out his alien look. The
Australians chuckled. The "kanakas," on the other hand, "simply flattened
into the ground and moaned, and for some moments were afraid to look
upon the white giant from the skies, lest the sight strike them dead."[172]

Figure 5.2   A tidy village atop a ridge near the Marifutiga River, 1934. Here as elsewhere in New Guinea's central highlands, Michael Leahy was stunned to find that "Stone-Age savages" often possessed a keen aesthetic sense.

SOURCE: Courtesy, Mitchell Library, State Library of New South Wales, ML PXA 632, vol_1, item 632.

Leahy's vignette depicts the Wahgi people as hopelessly superstitious. Their fundamental weakness, he argued, was evolutionary:

> I am satisfied that these natives had not as yet developed the brain to cope with conditions . . . that we, with our . . . centuries of technology and culture, find commonplace. The adaptation necessary to survive snowed-in winters in the frigid zones or continual escalating warfare was beyond their ken. Black skins, a hallmark of the sun, have an evolutionary history in the hot tropics, where a bountiful nature rewards a modest effort with all the necessities of life.[173]

Explanations for racial inferiority based on climate or food supply were hardly new. For Leahy in the 1930s, though, this reasoning served two specific purposes. First, since the allegedly stunted highland brain could not grasp the concept of efficiency, it followed that better brains should be entrusted with the task of turning temperate valleys like the Wahgi into highly profitable plantations. "Get Busy or Get Out!" urged one editorial in the development-minded *Pacific Islands Quarterly*.[174] Second and more immediate, the savage impulsiveness that Leahy attributed to New Guineans generally helped justify his resort to force.

In public lectures and newspaper interviews, in magazines, books, and photographs, Leahy proclaimed his startling discovery—that the center of New Guinea, long assumed to be a mountainous waste, supported a million people who for well nigh a hundred generations had lived in ignorance of the wider world. Leahy appeared to believe that because of their profound isolation, these highlanders—dusky "Adams" and "Eves"—could reveal much about human nature in the raw. A fondness for fighting appeared to be their defining characteristic. On its first pass through the Wahgi Valley west to Mt. Hagen, the Leahy-Taylor column had generated much wonderment but little hostility. On its return journey, however, the expedition was "lucky to get out alive." Taylor attributed these utterly different receptions to the "vagaries of human nature."[175] An alternative possibility went unmentioned. Could it be that the "primitive" brains of these highlanders had quickly shed their initial deference? Clearly no longer in awe of the strangers, the Kunimba men looked ready to hurl their spears early one morning. Taylor shot first, killing a warrior. How many more highlanders died in the ensuing melee will never be known.[176]

War, Leahy argued, was an essential outlet for human aggression. Male combatants met highland enemies decked out in pearl-shell necklaces, bird-of-paradise plumes, and opossum fur; their "pugnacious womenfolk" yelled and sang while carrying food and extra weapons.[177] Such belligerence would not cease overnight. Cast as regrettable necessities, therefore, the shootings by Europeans and their Papuan police roiled the highlands between 1933 and 1935. In early 1934, the murder of an Australian mining engineer triggered a particularly brutal response: nineteen highlanders shot dead, seventeen wounded. Michael Leahy played a leading part in this slaughter. By 1934 the Queenslander had ceased believing that nothing more lethal than a walking stick was needed in the Mandated Territory's "Uncontrolled Areas" (Figure 5.3). Sir Hubert Murray deplored Leahy's approach to pacification. So did the Aborigines' Protection Society, which took its case against him to the League of Nations in 1936. Leahy escaped formal sanction although, embarrassingly, Italian diplomats cited his highland reprisals in justifying their nation's assault on independent Abyssinia.[178]

The killings of miners, missionaries, and tribal peoples in the Uncontrolled Areas did produce one important change, however. Keen to staunch

Figure 5.3   Michael Leahy with rifle and dog.

SOURCE: Courtesy, Mitchell Library, State Library of New South Wales, ML PXA 632, vol_2, item 66.

this violence, colonial administrators in Rabaul closed large tracts of the highlands. From mid-1935 until the exigencies of world war forced reconsideration in 1942, only established missionaries and prospectors (such as Leahy) could enter these turbulent districts.[179] Among those of his countrymen and women who admired the principle of retributive justice, Michael Leahy would enjoy "living legend" status until his death in 1979. By that date there were still a few old highlanders who could remember *Taim wait man ikamp pastaim long hilans*, the first coming of the Australians.[180] Some elders recalled benign spirits dressed in human form. The less lucky would never forget how strangers dealt invisible death as they passed through tribal lands.

Whereas the closure of certain highland districts in 1935 caused only minor inconvenience for Leahy, being obliged to share the spotlight with another young and equally hard-charging explorer dismayed him. Jack Hides, born in Port Moresby, a passable speaker of Koiari as well as Motu, and another of "Murray's men," gained widespread acclaim for leading the Strickland-Purari patrol of 1935. Leahy, jealous of Hides's postpatrol adulation, launched an undignified campaign to discredit his rival, a campaign

waged in the tearooms of Sydney and the lecture hall of the Royal Geographical Society in London.[181] Leahy had a point. Jack Hides returned
from his high adventure with an inaccurate map and inflated population
estimates for Papua's "wonderland." Furthermore, thanks to careful ethnographic reconstructions of the Strickland-Purari patrol, we now know what
Leahy did not—that Hides's narrative diverges in key respects from the
memories of indigenous people among whom he moved.[182] Strickland-
Purari nevertheless marked the end of an era in New Guinea. It was the last
large foot patrol to cross the highlands unaided by aerial reconnaissance or
resupply. And through Hides's vivid prose, the incongruity of a Stone Age
persisting into the modern era reached its widest audience.

In case Jack Hides's childhood had not been unconventional enough, the
self-image he fashioned in his publications and interviews played up the
exotic. The son of Port Moresby's head gaoler and sanitary inspector, young
Hides enjoyed ready access to the colony's prisoners. They were "wild men
from all parts of Papua," he recalled, headhunters and cannibals "and savages who told me of their homes in far-away and mysterious places."[183]
From these jailhouse interactions, his public was asked to believe, Jack Hides
learned about racial equality. His mentor, Sir Hubert Murray, would later
praise him for treating Papuans as "men like ourselves." Yet what the young
Hides witnessed growing up in Port Moresby may well have taught him a
different lesson. That is, since the Papuan government was too poor to afford a proper public works department, its prisoners cleaned the streets, dug
building sites, cut roads, and mucked out the town's crude toilet system.[184]
A mature Hides would relish his part in uplifting a "subject race." He may
have liked New Guinea's indigenous people, but he never regarded them as
equals. Hides could summon up something like respect for Papuan males
who behaved with martial dignity. Highland women, however, received no
such dispensation. Virtually naked, they squatted "like apes" on the grass
outside their settlements.[185]

Restless and volatile (as Ivan Champion would later describe him), Hides
joined Papua's patrol service in 1926 at the age of nineteen. His twin strengths
as an outside man were a supposed grasp of Papuan psychology and the
amazing speed with which he could move through dense jungle.[186] No one
could question his courage. In February 1931, for example, Hides found his
patrol under repeated attack from Kukukuku warriors—short, stocky men
dressed in cloaks of beaten bark and armed with black palm bows. These

feared mountain people posed a threat to even the largest patrols. Yet Hides, accompanied by just nine terrified carriers, walked up unarmed to a Kuku-kuku elder and won him over, thereby saving the patrol from probable de-struction.[187] Better known was his pursuit and capture of "Gopa," headman of cannibal raiders called the Loloipa. Assembling a small, mobile posse, Hides set out for the killers' distant lair at the end of 1933. Six weeks later, having executed a "midnight pounce" on the cannibals' village, Hides brought fifteen manacled culprits into Port Moresby after a 500-mile round-trip slog. Gopa was found guilty of man-eating and promptly released. This savage had purportedly glimpsed a better way of life thanks to Murray's rule of law.[188] Prior to his legendary patrol of 1935, Hides could boast that during nearly 150 arrests, not a single Papuan life had been lost. Here, it appeared, was the right man to lead an expedition through the colony's last unknown tract. Jack seemed "a rather restless chap," Murray conceded in a letter to his brother. But if anyone could win over primitive people, it would be Hides.[189]

How Sir Hubert Murray's ambassador could end up implicated in the shooting deaths of thirty-two highland men will always defy easy explana-tion. Hides's biographer dodged the question of blame through resort to banality: "Primitive man is an unpredictable being."[190] A more concrete weakness in the patrol itself deserves mention. It is likely that a dearth of resources placed Hides's party in such compromising positions that preemp-tive action would have been easier to justify. The Strickland-Purari patrol lasted over six months, 1 January to 17 July 1935. For so long a trek over such daunting terrain, the investment was a paltry £290.11.4. This sum, as Hides noted shortly after the patrol's return, included pay for carriers and purchase of canoes, as well as for all food and equipment.[191]

Ponder the contrast. At a time when an American magazine had started searching "Primitive Papua" by seaplane, and New Guinea Airways had begun offering tourists service to remote aerodromes via "giant tri-motored machines," Hides's patrol was strictly boot-and-pack.[192] Taxes on gold min-ing in the Mandated Territory bought *kiaps* such as J.L. Taylor light yet durable silk tents. Lacking this revenue source, Murray's Papuan govern-ment could afford only heavy canvas tents.[193] In constant use and perpetu-ally damp, these literally rotted away. Thus, when heavy rains pounded the patrol above 4,000 feet, hypothermia became a constant enemy. Hides and patrol officer Jim O'Malley were expected to explore roughly 7,000 square miles of still "secret" territory lying between the Strickland and Purari rivers.

They did so following the same minimalist strategy that had worked, barely, for Karius and Champion seven years earlier. It is noteworthy that Karius, Champion, and their "boys" were never refused food. Hides, O'Malley, and company were, at least in the highland Waga River Valley, leaving them "half-starved." Judge Murray could exult in their toughness.[194] But reading between the lines of Hides's brisk narrative, one can discern several points at which both physical and mental collapse would have magnified the perceived threat of "hostile" tribes. Tellingly, the shootings tended to coincide with these periods of acute privation.

Jack Hides's most popular book, *Papuan Wonderland* (1936), focused on the evocative particular. The jagged limestone formations that had earlier tormented the Fly-Sepik patrol now reappeared as Papua's "broken-bottle country." While trekking at an altitude of 6,000 feet, Hides's men encountered fern leeches: "our unprotected skin being cold and numb, we could not feel them crawling to suck the blood under [our] eyelids; it was only when an itching was felt . . . that investigation would reveal the little black and fattening worm." The "brave" deaths of exhausted carriers; the immaculate gardens of the Tarifuroro basin; the short, shy highlanders wearing flowers in their hair and bone daggers in their cane waistbands: Hides's images are sharp.[195] But he deploys them to excuse as well as to edify. Just before his account of shooting a fierce warrior on the upper Rentoul River, Hides escorts the reader through a palm-thatched *dubu* (hut) wherein two smoked human arms hang from the eaves.[196] Cannibalism, we are given to understand, implies a wildness that demands special caution.

Ethnographic reconstructions of the 1935 Strickland-Purari patrol have undermined Hides's version of first contact events. Most glaring is the discrepancy between accounts of a shooting that took place toward the end of the patrol, close to the Erave River. With many of his men suffering from dysentery and all severely malnourished, Hides ordered them to raid a garden and butcher pigs belonging to the Kewa people. One villager, Hides explains, voiced his displeasure by yodeling a "kill call" to his friends. The patrol leader then fired a single round into the rock on which this troublemaker was standing. Obligingly, he "scurried away."[197] The Kewa remember a completely different incident. "Ipitango" did indeed protest this serious theft of food, they agree. But instead of being harmlessly warned, Ipitango was shot between the eyes. If the Kewa testimony (gathered long afterwards in 1985) is accurate, then at the very least it would appear that

Hides had lost control of his police.[198] At worst, the patrol leader soon to be lionized throughout Oceania had participated in murder.

Western exploration of the New Guinea highlands did not end with the Strickland-Purari patrol. The Hagen-Sepik expedition of 1938–39 would prove to be the longest (at fifteen months) and most extensive in New Guinea's history. During its tortuous course, this patrol also encountered perplexed highland people who wanted above all an answer to the question, "Who are you?"[199] But although admirably organized—from its airdropped food to its radio protocols—and handsomely financed, Hagen-Sepik never seized the public imagination as Hides and O'Malley had done.[200] The *Manchester Guardian* likened their discovery of flesh and blood "lost" people to the fictitious *Lost World* (1912) of Arthur Conan Doyle. Oddly enough, *Papuan Wonderland*, which made "better reading than many a novel," was regarded as proof that Murray's men "would sooner resign than rely on force."[201] Not to be outdone, the *Pacific Islands Monthly* observed that "the Australian press—and, in fact, the press of the world—[had given] to Mr. Hides' exploits and discoveries the same publicity as they might have given to H.M. Stanley's travels a couple of generations ago." New Guinea had emerged as the interwar era's "Darkest Africa." And there could be no denying that Australian newspapers had suddenly grown "'Islands conscious.'"[202]

The Strickland-Purari patrol's efforts to complete the map of Papua would not, by itself, have set Australian pulses racing. The much discussed "Japanese menace," however, invested the work of Hides and O'Malley with an importance rooted in worry. Japan's virtual capture of the pearl-shell diving industry along New Guinea's southern and eastern coasts caused consternation Down Under. Suspicious Australians tended to view the influx of motorized sampans as part of a "concerted plan" for Japanese economic expansion around the Coral Sea. Worse, Japan's recent conquest of Manchuria seemed to prove that it sneered at international law.[203] The discoveries by highland patrols in both Papua and the Mandated Territory therefore acquired special significance; they were framed as Australian victories at a time when that nation craved reassurance.

The Strickland-Purari saga appeared to illustrate what the one-time colony wished to believe about itself: that "Stone-Age" people could be shaped into law-abiding citizens through enlightened guidance. Hides's failings as a patrol leader were mostly overlooked because his death on 19 June 1938 seemed shockingly premature.[204] We know now that his habitual risk-taking led to the loss—from exposure and sheer exhaustion—of several carriers and policemen. To Hides, and apparently to most of Australia's reading public, their "sacrifice" savored of heroism, not neglect. These Papuans had supposedly exchanged ritual violence for obedience to the colonial state. They had learned to become, as Hides phrased it, "savages in serge."[205]

First contact exchanges remain a sensitive matter. The "savages" in question can elicit woolly preservationist thinking from their "civilized" champions. Writing about New Guinea's highland tribes in 1938, an Australian zoologist believed it would be "a grand thing if at least one great reservation of wholly natural people could be established before these last Stone Age men are finally dominated by European influences."[206] The issue of trespass on aboriginal lands invariably turns heated. Witness, for example, the acrimony among anthropologists, advocates of economic development, and indigenous rights activists over the Yanomamö. An Amazonian jungle folk whose small encampments had escaped Western notice until the 1950s, the Yanomamö became pawns in an ideological battle. Bitterly at odds have been Napoleon Chagnon, the anthropologist who made them his life's study, and the self-appointed guardians of primitivism. Chagnon used the Yanomamö to illustrate what he believed to be the centrality of war in primitive societies. His critics used the devastating measles epidemic of 1968 to demonstrate the damage that irresponsible contact can unleash.[207] Survival International, a London-based voice for tribal peoples, estimated that as of early 2013, approximately one hundred "uncontacted" groups were left on earth.[208] These pockets of aboriginal culture will continue to fascinate the outside world as living anachronisms. Never again, though, will a "lost" population as large and visually arresting as that of highland New Guinea emerge from its sanctuary of remoteness.

Savage Inversions

Savagery in the colonial Pacific meant different things to different people at different times. Western constructions of Melanesia, especially British stereotypes of its "natives," grew less defamatory over the course of six generations. But as this book has argued, the shift in emphasis from denouncing savage acts to lamenting the domestication of those who committed them should not be confused with racial enlightenment. Nor did the substitution of social science for religious enthusiasm always represent an empathetic advance. Theorizing the ritual role of cannibalism among island peoples, for instance, did not necessarily mark the theorist as superior to the missionary in understanding the Other. We must therefore be cautious about assuming that relations between Europeans and Melanesians improved as the Victorian past gave way to twentieth-century modernity.

An example of what could be called a savage inversion reminds us that images of the Pacific Islander continued to defy neat classification long after Melanesia had been pacified. As used here, an "inversion" refers to a reversal of order, position, sequence, or relation. By extension, an inversion can also refer to a confounding of expectation.[1] White commentary on the conduct of Pacific Islanders during World War Two was noteworthy in this regard. British, Australian, New Zealander, and American accounts lauded the loyalty of "primitive" peoples throughout this testing time. In the words of Sir Philip Mitchell, governor of Fiji from 1942 to 1944, "simple, ignorant, often savage" Islanders proved their "devotion" to Britain under the most trying circumstances.[2] Such commentary was itself fractured. British and Australian accounts of their Islander allies stressed the latter's affection for pre-war colonial rule. American gratitude to these same Pacific peoples ignored the supposed virtues of colonialism, preferring instead to treat the comradeship of "natives" and Yanks as a brotherhood forged in battle.[3] Still, these were variations on a shared narrative. That narrative positioned Pacific Islanders as key allies precisely because their latent savagery could be mobilized against an equally savage foe, the Japanese.

Both the Pacific and the Southeast Asian theaters of conflict generated several stories of one-time headhunters reverting to their martial specialty in dealing with a cruel enemy. Thus, with the catastrophic surrender of Singapore to the Japanese in February 1942, the road to British India lay open save for the hill tribes of Nagaland—tribes whose residual fondness for taking heads at first worried colonial administrators. Fortunately for Britain, the Nagas and kindred peoples spread along the rugged frontier between Burma and Assam mostly became porters and road-builders.[4] Similarly, the Dayak tribes of central Borneo risked their lives to rescue downed American airmen. (A decade after he had tried to "go cannibal" on Malekula island in the New Hebrides, Tom Harrisson, now Major Harrisson, found himself in Borneo coaxing its forest dwellers to report Japanese troop movements.) The Igorots of central Luzon in the Philippines proved no less skilled as jungle fighters. Despite two mistitled books about the Igorots and Dayaks at war, decapitation was for both a rare indulgence.[5]

Although historically linked to man-eating rather than headhunting, Fijians earned a reputation as lethal guerrillas supporting American forces in the Solomon archipelago. British colonial officials seized on the swift recruitment of Fijian volunteers as proof of their affection for "King and Country." Other, less noble, impulses were also at work. For instance, Ratu Sir Lala Sukuna, Oxford educated and widely respected, told young men that "Fijians will never be recognized unless our blood is shed first." (*Eda na sega ni Kilai na i taukei Kevaka e na sega mada ni dave e liu na noda dra.*) This high chief reckoned that if the political demands of Fiji's Indian community were to be resisted, a strong show of loyalty to the Empire would help.[6] White officers—at first British and New Zealanders, later Americans—provided their Fijian recruits with the basics of military discipline and handling small arms. When it came to "bushcraft," though, the young men selected for scout and commando duty often taught their teachers.[7] Later, operating behind enemy lines in such danger zones as Guadalcanal, New Georgia, and Bougainville, these troops excelled at silent killing. Mark Durley, a U.S. Army lieutenant on Bougainville in early 1944, enlisted the help of Fijian scouts with a vital mission: to find a prisoner-of-war camp where captives from the fall of Singapore had been languishing. Whether this camp was ultimately located, Durley does not say. But his scouts certainly found the enemy:

> While on patrol one of the Fijians motioned for us to stop. They stripped down to their shorts and went off into the jungle barefoot. Sometime later they returned. Soon we saw that they had wiped out a Japanese patrol without making a sound. We estimated that they killed seventy Japanese on our trek.[8]

The deadly skills of Fijian scouts would later be turned against "communist terrorist[s]" in the rain forests of Malaya.[9]

Such stories appear to confirm that the alleged "treachery" of Melanesians had been transformed through colonial discipline into fidelity. On closer inspection, however, this savage inversion proved far from complete. Along steep New Guinea trails and amid the sweltering bush of Guadalcanal, European doubts about Islander capacities would linger.

ISLANDER "ANGELS" AT WAR

Seventy-odd years after the fact, it is rarely noted that Pacific Islanders did not always embrace the Allied cause. Long-standing tribal animosities sometimes expressed themselves through proxy slaughter. Thus, acting under Japanese orders, in early 1944 several middle Sepik River (New Guinea) villages massacred nearly a hundred rival villagers at Timbunke—punishment for alleged collaboration with the Australians.[10] Elsewhere, Fijians fought Bougainvilleans, Pohnpei people engaged New Guineans, and Islanders without clear affiliations hid their food stores from troops wearing any uniform. Despite much American praise for loyal Solomon Islanders, U.S. planes did not hesitate to strafe villages on Choiseul and Malaita where support for the Japanese was merely suspected. And at least some of the Papuans who hauled vital equipment and wounded Australian soldiers resented the loads they shouldered.[11]

Even so, the burdens they bore, particularly up and down the seemingly vertical slopes of southeastern Papua, served to invest these men with a qualified heroism. Prior to the start of the Pacific War, white planters, missionaries, and adventurers referred to Papuans by a variety of disparaging names: "boys," "coons," "smokes," and "abos."[12] Once they recognized the strategic value of reliable carriers in a war of endurance, however, Australian troops repurposed an old acknowledgment of savage competence. "Fuzzy-Wuzzy," one of Kipling's most famous poems, appeared in his 1892 collection, *Barrack-Room Ballads.* A salute to Sudanese warriors who had smashed through a supposedly impregnable British formation at the battle of Abu Klea (1885), Kipling's verse linked wild courage with wild hair:

So 'ere's to you Fuzzy-Wuzzy at your 'ome in the Soudan;
You're a pore benighted 'eathen but a first-class fightin' man;
An 'ere's to you, Fuzzy-Wuzzy, with your 'ayrick 'ead of 'air—
You big black boundin' beggar—for you broke a British square.[13]

Apart from the elaborate coiffures of some Islanders, the analogy was weak, not least because Papuan carriers seldom engaged in hand-to-hand combat. But to wounded soldiers from Australia's 39th Infantry Battalion hauled out of harm's way, or to American pilots plucked from behind enemy lines, their jungle-wise rescuers seemed more angelic than savage.

The Kokoda Track campaign of 1942 showed Papua's "Fuzzy-Wuzzy Angels" at their best. The strategic stakes were high. By mid-July, Japanese forces had landed near Gona on the northern side of the Papuan peninsula. From this site, the Allied stronghold in Papua, Port Moresby, lay less than eighty miles to the south. A single-file miner's trail, the Kokoda Track could have been Japan's gateway to Moresby. Had it been captured, the enemy would have won an excellent base from which to strike Australia's populous eastern seaboard. But first there was the Track itself to negotiate. Where it passed through the Owen Stanley mountain range, the Track rose to over 7,000 feet. In addition to braving its torrential rains, knee-deep mud, and dense bush, therefore, both soldiers and porters had to cope with frigid nights. An initial force of between 600 and 800 porters, many of them recruited from local rubber plantations, began carrying supplies to Australian troops stationed in forward areas, then returning for fresh loads. Once the fighting began, however, empty backs vanished; having delivered food and equipment to the shifting front, "Angels" now returned with the sick and wounded strapped to stretchers (Figure C.1). One eyewitness marveled at these porters swinging from branches and clinging to the sides of cliffs "like flies."[14] Since Kokoda's rugged terrain largely ruled out evacuation of the disabled by air, Australia's ability to block advancing Japanese units hinged

Figure C.1   Salamaua, New Guinea, September 1943. Five "fuzzy wuzzy angels" carry a wounded Australian soldier down a steep trail on Buoisi Ridge.

SOURCE: Courtesy, Australian War Memorial, collection number 015758.

on the willingness of exhausted Papuans to carry on while their own villages and gardens were being bombed or requisitioned.

Through a series of tactical retreats along the Track, Australian resistance finally convinced Japan's military planners that an overland assault on Port Moresby was not worth the time and blood it would cost. Between late July and mid-November 1942, Australian casualties on or near the Kokoda Track totaled just over 600 officers and men killed, with another thousand wounded. Sickness probably removed at least twice this number from combat. Compared with Australia's losses at Gallipoli during World War One, the carnage in southeastern Papua proved quite limited.[15] But the latter campaign possessed the distinction of being an exclusively Australian ground action. Not surprisingly, then, Australian veterans and the politicians attentive to them fashioned "Kokoda" into a code word for national valor. To mark the fiftieth anniversary of this campaign in 1992, Australia's theatrical prime minister, Paul Keating, literally kissed the ground next to a memorial on the Track.[16] Only recently have the contributions of Papuans to Australia's success at Kokoda received official notice. And that recognition has retained its colonial tone: honor to the "strength, ingenuity and compassion displayed by the Fuzzy Wuzzy Angels."[17]

This paternalism has lingered in part because no unified voice exists to challenge it. Although independent since 1975, Papua New Guinea remains a polyvocal and culturally diverse state. While Australians have shaped Kokoda into a confident national narrative, the peoples of PNG have tended to regard the dramatic events of 1942 as belonging mainly to the ethnic groups living near the Track.[18] If there has been a reconsideration of the savage stereotypes once central to European images of New Guinea, therefore, it has been partial. In 1944, when news of brave Papuan porters was still fresh, a "New Deal for the Fuzzy Wuzzies" seemed unlikely among "primitives" reputedly unable to grasp that murder is a crime. By 1960, little had changed within some Australian minds. "We know these natives are utterly incapable of anything like self-government," declared a contributor to the *Pacific Islands Monthly*.[19] Although vital to the Allied cause in Papua, they remain in Australian memory as stoic beasts of burden.

Not far to the east of Papua, the Solomon Islands and their people saw still fiercer combat in 1942 and 1943. Here the course of the war unexpectedly turned one of Britain's most remote colonies into the stage upon which Japan and the United States fought for control of the South Pacific. The Battle of Midway in June of 1942 had damaged Japanese naval power. Deprived of its superiority at sea, Japan now aimed to protect and if possible enlarge its Pacific island "screen" by building well-defended air bases. One move in this direction was the construction of an airfield on Guadalcanal, a base from which the New Hebrides and New Caledonia could be bombed. To counter this threat, American Marines landed on Guadalcanal and Tulagi in early August 1942. By the end of that year some 80,000 soldiers, an estimated 30,000 of them Japanese, were engaged in vicious bush fighting.[20] On both Guadalcanal and the western Solomon islands, American troops received crucial information about enemy movements from British and Australian "coastwatchers." But watching and protecting *them* were Islander scouts whose help proved essential.

When the Australian Navy's coastwatcher service began operating in 1919, it guarded only the home waters. Improvements in radio technology made possible the extension of this shield to Papua, the Territory of New

Guinea, and the Solomons. By late 1939, further recruitment had extended the service over most of Melanesia west of Fiji.[21] Anticipating the invasion of Tulagi, government headquarters for the Solomons, Resident Commissioner William Marchant moved his staff across Indispensable Strait to the larger and densely forested island of Malaita. Nearly all the archipelago's European settlers had been evacuated to Australia by the end of January 1942. Yet a small contingent of colonial officials and plantation owners chose to melt into the jungle on several islands, most importantly Guadalcanal. Some ninety miles long, thirty miles wide, and in its center formidably mountainous, Guadalcanal offered many places to hide, but also many sites for enemy ambush. Only the island's indigenous people could reliably distinguish between refuge and trap. Admiral Halsey, commander of the South Pacific, minced few words when it came to operating behind Japanese lines: "The Coast Watchers saved Guadalcanal, and Guadalcanal saved the Pacific." General Douglas MacArthur allowed that the coastwatchers rendered "spectacular service."[22] Nearly all the "watchers" who have left memoirs depict Islanders as full partners in the dangerous game they played with the Japanese.

But that credit is retrospective. At the start of fighting on Guadalcanal, its people did not inspire confidence among Europeans. The *Annual Report on . . . the British Solomon Islands Protectorate, 1938*, reminded readers that the "natives" had recently occupied "the Neolithic stage of civilization." Before the war, Islanders had led "wild, secluded lives." Some of them supposedly still hunted heads.[23] Even the Scot Martin Clemens, a district officer on Guadalcanal at war's start and eventually the most celebrated of all coastwatchers, did not know what to expect from the local men who agreed to help him. As recently as April 1942, he found himself investigating the murder of an elderly European prospector. In his unpublished diary for 10 April, Clemens wrote: "See photographs of Wilmot's corpse. Badly bashed over the head—queer incident, and rather ominous." Was this an isolated crime or did it presage mass unrest following the flight of most European settlers?[24]

Such doubts vanished once Islander scouts swung into action. Some endeared themselves to American forces by rescuing downed pilots and stranded sailors. In mid-August 1942, for example, two teenage scouts, Biuku Gasa and Eroni Kumana, chanced upon the starving survivors of an American patrol boat that had sunk after colliding with a Japanese destroyer off Kolombangara island. Risking execution if caught assisting U.S. personnel, these young men beached their dugout canoe, shared what little food they had with the strangers, and built them a fire. The survivors of patrol torpedo boat 109 owed their lives to Biuku and Eroni; none knew this more clearly than the skipper of PT-109, Lt. John F. Kennedy.[25] Other scouts proved their worth through direct action as guerrillas. Around New Georgia in the west of the Solomons, former district officer Donald Kennedy built an insurgent force out of colonial policemen and sympathetic locals. These men would not only find the beach near Munda Point later used for Admiral Halsey's surprise landing but also turned the jungle of southern New Georgia into a no-go zone for all save the largest Japanese patrols.[26]

On Guadalcanal as on New Georgia, Western accounts of the coast-watchers have emphasized the speed with which Europeans converted fractious Islanders into obedient soldiers. The official history of the Pacific islands at war notes, "[Martin] Clemens had to conjure [local] troops into existence as best he could."[27] Such depictions of the Solomon Islanders minimize their initiative, reducing them to primitive clay waiting for their betters to sculpt them. This is, to say the least, a peculiar portrait. For when we consider the most decorated Melanesian soldier of the war, we find an Islander whose fame rested on his ability to improvise no less than on his willingness to suffer. If anything, the legendary Sergeant-Major Vouza proved rather too independent for his superiors' comfort.

Long after the Pacific War had ended, U.S. General Alexander Vandegrift, formerly commander of the 1st Marine Division during the Battle of Guadalcanal, remembered Vouza, inaccurately, as "a black and bandy-legged little fellow." This Islander had nonetheless rendered "superb service" to the Americans.[28] Clemens, Vouza's coastwatcher boss, was less restrained, anointing him "the greatest Solomon Islander in recorded history." Vouza's defiant loyalty under torture—"Better I die 100 times than Marine friends die"—assured him an honored place in Allied accounts of the Pacific War.[29]

Vouza's path from belligerent youth to war hero looks improbable in hindsight. "Sale," as his parents called him at first, was born around 1898 in the Guadalcanal village of Pappanggu, near Koli Point. Later receiving the Christian name of Jacob Charles Vouza, he early on earned a reputation for fighting. At seventeen or eighteen, however, this village malcontent made his way to nearby Tulagi island, headquarters of the British Solomon Islands Armed Constabulary. Vouza liked what he saw there: uniforms, drilling, rifles, and strict order. So began his twenty-five-year career as a colonial policeman.[30] The disruptive boy became the rigidly disciplined man. In 1927, when some 200 Kwaio tribesmen slaughtered District Officer W.R. Bell and more than a dozen in his tax-collecting party on Malaita, revenge obsessed those policemen whose relatives had died in this ambush. Vouza, though, forbade his men to shoot prisoners or desecrate their ancestor shrines.[31] Eight years later and now in command of the Santa Cruz District Constabulary, Lance-Corporal Vouza impressed the new British administrator: "You could see at a glance that Vouza was a magnificent specimen of humanity." Perhaps it was this policeman's "perfectly respectful air" that won over District Officer Macquarrie? Perhaps Vouza's eyes—"a little hard and uncompromising when he was not smiling"—set him apart? These eyes "offered a hint that hardly more than a generation earlier his forebears were savages who might live only if they were strong and alert." As with so many British colonial officials posted to "primitive" lands, Macquarrie mixed praise with condescension. After all, Vouza "made a quaint picture" as he strode across the beach in his tartan lava-lava, gazing with "childlike delight" at the wristwatch he had been given.[32]

Vouza at war, however, proved far from child-like. Having retired to grow yams on Malaita in 1941, the sergeant-major returned to his home island shortly after the Japanese threat materialized. At first Martin Clemens did not know what to do with this volunteer. When Clemens labeled Vouza a "startling individualist, who overcame difficulties in original ways," no compliment was intended. These initial concerns never entirely disappeared. As Clemens would later write, Vouza "fought his war as he saw fit."[33]

Nothing better exemplified his stubborn individuality than Vouza's capture in mid-August 1942. By now Clemens's most trusted scout, the sergeant-major fell into Japanese hands while on patrol. The miniature American flag he carried left no doubt about his allegiance. Determined to extract information about Marine defenses, Vouza's tormentors began by baking him in the tropical sun. There followed rifle butts smashed into his face, bayonets thrust into his throat and chest, and staking over a nest of red ants. Left for dead, he somehow managed to chew through the grass ropes that bound him and then crawl three miles to the entrance of a Marine outpost. Vouza had revealed nothing. Against very long odds, he not only recovered but also returned to the detachment of scouts he led.[34]

The narrative of Islander valor—the "ordeal of Vouza"—that built upon these revelations served two purposes. Obviously it celebrated the remarkable courage of one man. The governments of Britain and the United States vied to honor Vouza. Major General Vandegrift personally pinned the Silver Star medal, signifying gallantry in action, to his hospital gown. From the British government he received the George Medal for exceptional devotion to duty and earned membership in the Order of the British Empire (MBE) (Figure C.2). And it would be Vouza who represented the Solomon Islands Protectorate at Queen Elizabeth's coronation in 1953. As late as 1968, the embassies of Britain and Australia made plain their wish to join the planning for this hero's American visit.[35]

But alongside such adulation lay another concern. Colonial Office logic held that if the son of savages could acquit himself so honorably, then British

Figure C.2   Sergeant-Major Jacob Vouza, the most decorated Islander in the South Pacific War. The target of Japanese torture on Guadalcanal, Vouza refused to answer any question concerning Allied troop movements.
SOURCE: Courtesy, Mitchell Library, State Library of New South Wales, PXA 644, 433-453, item 447.

(and Australian) rule in Melanesia must have been enlightened. It was of course worrisome that colonial loyalties in the Solomons had frayed considerably during 1942 and 1943, as Britain's inability to halt the Japanese advance grew all too clear. America's brand of militarism, linked as it was in Islander eyes with wealth, generosity, and the visible mixing of black and white troops, appeared comparatively benign.[36] Britain's residual prestige in the western Pacific now rested on a more abstract discourse about its civilizing mission. Reflecting on that work in 1962, Charles E. Fox, missionary-anthropologist and historian, saw social change in the Solomons as evidence of colonial goodwill: "Fifty years ago there was killing everywhere, killing for cannibal feasts, killing for money, killing for glory and revenge." The passing of these homicidal days was a blessing, Fox declared.[37]

Yet the suppression of such violence earned little gratitude from the "natives." Instead, the advent of the Pacific War had intensified political ferment across the archipelago. Beginning in 1946, the "Maasina [Brotherhood] Rule" movement, partly a quest for cultural regeneration and partly a push for independence from Britain, gave focus to a wide range of local grievances.[38] Set against Maasina Rule demands, Vouza's selflessness would have seemed especially important to honor. Inconveniently for the Solomons' colonial government, however, Vouza was for a time sympathetic to the nationalists' program. Indeed, the war hero was arrested (although never charged) on account of these sympathies.[39] Assorted ceremonial duties kept him too occupied to cause trouble thereafter. Over the rest of a long life—which ended in 1984, six years after the Solomons gained independence—the story of his valor remained compelling in part because Western images of the savage South Sea Islander, like Vouza himself, proved hard to kill.

· · ·

Jacob Vouza could hardly qualify as a typical Solomon Islander. His celebrity nevertheless serves to complicate what savagery signified during the late colonial era. If the Pacific during the 1970s became "the last bastion of [Anglophone] colonialism,"[40] it did so partly because in British, Australian, New Zealander, and American eyes, Melanesians retained the "primitive" cultural sensibilities for which they had been both feared and patronized. The key question, as civil servants in London saw it, had become: Who could best look after these still semi-wild people? Such solicitude, rooted in a persistent underestimation of Islander capacity, remains common among

European elites today. Their condescension rankles Pacific people. And it hinders cross-cultural cooperation at a time of crisis for all Oceania. The deniers of climate change notwithstanding, Pacific island nations now face environmental catastrophe in the form of rising sea levels and bleached coral reefs. Swift action to mitigate such threats demands that the West's long-held views of Pacific "natives" be reconsidered.

It will be difficult to jettison some of these views. Consider, briefly, the fate of an American aristocrat who disappeared into the wilderness of New Guinea. This unlucky adventurer, twenty-two-year-old David Rockefeller, vanished somewhere along the coast of Dutch New Guinea (known today as West Papua) in 1961. Rockefeller's catamaran may have capsized close to the tribal territory of the Asmat people. The Asmat, widely suspected of headhunting as well as cannibalism, may have seized him. We simply do not know. Yet ever since Rockefeller's disappearance nearly sixty years ago, public confidence in the guesswork of sensationalists has not wavered: this young man *must* have been eaten. What would explain such faith in rank speculation? There is of course the guilty pleasure of contemplating the mighty brought low. Few of the super rich go missing in tropical backwaters, after all, and fewer still become meals for fierce primitives. Another possibility merits mention, however. Perhaps some fraction of the reading and viewing public clings to the idea that our planet still supports enclaves of wildness? Mere criminality, in the Western sense of that word, will not do; criminals are too familiar to us, and too numerous, to qualify as exotic. We wish instead to learn about the culturally outlandish, about "true" savages. We share more than most of us realize with the English-speaking mariners, missionaries, and explorers who reckoned that landing on uncharted Pacific shores would prove worth the risk.

This book has emphasized the damaging force of misrepresentation. Since the time of Captain Cook, European visitors to Melanesia have been quick to condemn the customs of Pacific Islanders. Voracious cannibals and stealthy headhunters, strangled widows and ambushed sailors: these were the most recognizable figures in a tableau that served to justify colonial intrusion. The colonizers of Melanesia, one might say, required monsters to banish.

Notes

ABBREVIATIONS USED IN THE NOTES

In citing sources in the notes, short titles have generally been used. Sources frequently cited have been identified by the following abbreviations:

B.L.	British Library
CO	Colonial Office papers
FO	Foreign Office papers
NHBS	New Hebrides British Service records
P.I.M.	*Pacific Islands Monthly*
R.C.	Royal Commission
R.G.S.	Royal Geographical Society archives
S.C.	Select Committee
S.O.A.S.	School of Oriental and African Studies
TNA	The National Archives of the United Kingdom
WPHC	Western Pacific High Commission records

INTRODUCTION

1. Anon., Journal of the sufferings of the Carpenter's Mate, *Northumberland*, 1782: manuscript copy, MLMSS A 1727. Sydney's Mitchell Library has been unable to locate the original manuscript from which its copy came.

2. Ibid. For English-speaking traders, the New Guinea coast remained perilous. Nine years after the *Northumberland*'s encounter with hostile Islanders, an American ship, the *Massachusetts*, nearly lost both its supply boats under similar circumstances. That ship's second officer minced few words: the "wooly headed" people of New Guinea's western straits were "well known to hate white people," a hatred "traceable to our own misconduct toward them." Amasa Delano, *A Narrative of Voyages and Travels* (Boston, 1817), 78–80.

3. Greg Dening, *Islands and Beaches* (Honolulu: University Press of Hawai'i, 1980), 263–64.

4. Andrew Sinclair, *The Savage* (London: Weidenfeld & Nicolson, 1977), 1–2.

5. Bernard Smith, *European Vision and the South Pacific*, 2nd ed. (New Haven: Yale University Press, 1985), 317–32.

6. *Encyclopaedia Britannica*, 11th ed. (New York, 1910–11), s.v. "Humboldt, Alexander von."

7. Alexander von Humboldt, *Personal Narrative of Travels*, 7 vols. (London, 1814), 1: xliv–xlv; William Mariner, *Account of the Natives*, 2 vols. (London, 1817), 1: title page.

8. Rod Edmond explains that the adjective "tropical" did not acquire its extra-geographic meaning of "ardent" or "luxuriant" before the nineteenth century. Edmond, "Returning Fears," in Felix Driver and Luciana Martins, eds., *Tropical Visions* (Chicago: University of Chicago Press, 2005), 175–76.

9. *Oxford English Dictionary* online, 3rd ed. (2012), s.v. "savage"; F.J. Turner, "Significance of the Frontier" [1893], in Turner, *Early Writings of Frederick Jackson Turner* (Madison: University of Wisconsin Press, 1938), 187–88; Henry Nash Smith, *Virgin Land* (Cambridge, MA: Harvard University Press, 1950), 251.

10. Sinclair, *The Savage*, 2; *O.E.D.* online, s.v. "savage."

11. William Yate, *Account of New Zealand* [1835], facsimile ed. (Dublin: Irish University Press, 1970), 130.

12. Lorimer Fison, *Tales from Old Fiji* (London: Alexander Moring [1904]), xiii–xiv.

13. H.M. Stanley, *Great Forest of Central Africa* (London, 1890).

14. J. Beete Jukes, *Narrative of the Surveying Voyage*, 2 vols. (London, 1847), 1: 288–89.

15. J.C. Beaglehole, *Life of Captain James Cook* (Stanford, CA: Stanford University Press, 1974), 394.

16. Christopher Lasch, *Haven in a Heartless World* (New York: Basic Books, 1979). On the ideological interplay among "home," "family," and "privacy," see George Behlmer, *Friends of the Family* (Stanford, CA: Stanford University Press, 1998), 1–28.

17. Thomas Carlyle, *Past and Present* [1843] (Boston: Houghton Mifflin, 1965), 9–10; *The Times* [London] (4–6 August 1841).

18. Cardinal Manning and Benjamin Waugh, "Child of the English Savage," *Contemporary Review*, 49 (May 1886): 688–89.

19. *The Times* (21 December 1872), as quoted in Carolyn A. Conley, "Wars Among Savages," *Journal of British Studies*, 44 (October 2005): 777.

20. Johann F. Blumenbach, *Anthropological Treatises* (London, 1865), 165; "Lord Monboddo's Account," in *Selection of Curious Articles*, 4 vols. (London, 1811), 4: 581–84; Julia Douthwaite, *The Wild Girl* (Chicago: Chicago University Press, 2002), 21–25.

21. James Greenwood, *Wild Man at Home* (London [1879]), 1–2.

22. Charles Darwin, *Journal of Researches* [1839] (New York: Hafner, 1952), 235–36.

23. Satadru Sen, *Savagery and Colonialism in the Indian Ocean* (New York: Routledge 2010), 19–20; James Bonwick, *Daily Life . . . of the Tasmanians* [1870], reprint ed. (New York: Johnson Reprint, 1967), 42–43; Henrika Kuklick, *Savage Within* (Cambridge: Cambridge University Press, 1991), 250–51; Sen, "Primitivism," in Hilary Callan, ed., *International Encyclopedia of Anthropology,* forthcoming.

24. Anthony Ashley Cooper [3rd Earl of Shaftesbury], "Soliloquy, or Advice to an Author," in Cooper, *Characteristics of Men* [1711], ed. Lawrence Klein (Cambridge, 1999), 153–55.

25. Nadja Durbach, *Spectacle of Deformity* (Berkeley: University of California Press, 2010), 22–23; Carrie Yang Costello, "Teratology," *Journal of Historical Sociology,* 19 (March 2006): 1–3.

26. Oscar Wilde, *Picture of Dorian Gray* [1890] (Cambridge, MA: Harvard University Press, 2011), 78–79, 94, 96, 192.

27. William Falconer, *Remarks on the Influence of Climate* (London, 1781), 258–59; Joseph-Marie Dégerando, *Observation of Savage Peoples* [1800] (Berkeley: University of California Press, 1969), 86; J.R. McCulloch, *Principles of Political Economy* (Edinburgh, 1825), 397–98; Everard Im Thurn, "On the Thoughts of South Sea Islanders," *Journal of the Royal Anthropological Institute,* 51 (January–June 1921): 15–16.

28. H. Calderwood, "Moral Philosophy," *Contemporary Review,* 19 (January 1872): 210–12.

29. John Foster Fraser, *Quaint Subjects of the King* (London: Cassell, 1909), v–vi.

30. Ibid.

31. *Prospectus of a Proposed Aboriginal Museum* (London [1850?]), n.p.

32. Patrick Wolfe, "History and Imperialism," *American Historical Review,* 102 (April 1997): 410–11; Antoinette Burton, "Who Needs the Nation?," in Catherine Hall, ed., *Cultures of Empire* (New York: Routledge, 2000), 138–39.

33. Nicholas Thomas and Diane Losche, "Introduction," in Thomas and Losche, eds., *Double Vision* (Cambridge: Cambridge University Press, 1999), 2–3; Jeffrey Auerbach, "Art and Empire," in R. Winks, ed., *Oxford History of the British Empire,* 5 (New York: Oxford University Press, 1999): 578–79; C.A. Bayly, "Second British Empire," in ibid., 70.

34. For a critique of the undifferentiated Other, see Dane Kennedy, "Imperial History," *Journal of Imperial and Commonwealth History,* 24 (September 1996): 354–55.

35. E.B. Tylor, *Anthropology* [1881] (New York, 1898), 23–25.

36. Ter Ellingson, *Myth of the Noble Savage* (Berkeley: University of California Press, 2001), 81–83. Ellingson asserts that the phrase became familiar only after 1859. In that year, John Crawfurd, soon to be elected President of the Ethnological Society of London, wielded the phrase only to destroy it—all part of Crawfurd's "racist agenda." Ellingson, 291, 295–97.

37. Jean Jacques Rousseau, *Discourse upon the Origin and Foundation of . . . Inequality* [1754] (London, 1761), 78; Rousseau, *Émile* [1762] (London: Dent, 1974).

260 NOTES TO INTRODUCTION

38. John Reinold Forster, *Observations Made During a Voyage* (London, 1778), 325.

39. Nicholas Thomas, *Colonialism's Culture* (Cambridge: Polity Press, 1994), 99–100; Patrick Brantlinger, *Dark Vanishings* (Ithaca, NY: Cornell University Press, 2003), 3. The Victorian philologist Max Müller noted the absurdities that could result when people "imagine that the same name must always mean the same thing." Take the three signs of the "true" savage: (1) that he murders his children; (2) that he kills and eats his companions; and (3) that he disregards certain laws of nature. Müller then dismissed this creature. The first man could not have been a savage, "for if he had murdered his children we should not be alive." Similarly, "if he had eaten his fellow-men, supposing there were any to eat, again we should not be alive." Müller, "The Savage," *Nineteenth Century*, 17 (January 1885): 116.

40. Richard Lansdown, "Dark Parts," *Times Literary Supplement* (17 August 2004), 12–13.

41. Charles Dickens, "Noble Savage," *Household Words*, 7 (11 June 1853): 337–38.

42. Anon., "Pacific Islanders' Protection Bill," *Westminster Review*, n.s. 48 (July and October 1875): 81; Dickens, "Noble Savage," 338.

43. K.R. Howe, "Fate of the 'Savage,'" *New Zealand Journal of History*, 11 (October 1977): 137–38, 147–48; Matt K. Matsuda, "The Pacific," *American Historical Review*, 111 (June 2006): 771–72.

44. See especially J.W. Davidson, "Problems of Pacific History," *Journal of Pacific History*, 1 (1966): 5–21; and H.E. Maude, "Pacific History," *Journal of Pacific History*, 6 (1971): 3–24.

45. Jane Samson, *Imperial Benevolence* (Honolulu: University of Hawai'i Press, 1998), 2.

46. James Belich, "Victorian Interpretation of Racial Conflict," *Journal of Imperial and Commonwealth History*, 15 (January 1987): 123–24.

47. Nicholas Thomas, "Epilogue," in Michael O'Hanlon and Robert Welsch, eds., *Hunting the Gatherers* (New York: Berghahn Books, 2000), 274–76.

48. Bronwen Douglas, *Science, Voyages, and Encounters in Oceania* (Basingstoke, Hampshire, UK: Palgrave Macmillan, 2014), 24–26; Douglas, "Art as Ethnohistorical Text," in Thomas and Losche, eds., *Double Vision*, 79–82.

49. John Williams, *Narrative of Missionary Enterprises* (London, 1837), 461–62.

50. Ibid.

51. H.E. Maude, "Beachcombers and Castaways," in Maude, *Of Islands and Men* (Melbourne, Australia: Oxford University Press, 1968), 161–62; Dening, *Islands and Beaches*, 247.

52. S.C. on Aborigines (British Settlements), P.P., 1836, VII (538): 682; Sen, *Savagery and Colonialism*, 2, 27, 42.

53. Alice Bullard, *Exile to Paradise* (Stanford, CA: Stanford University Press, 2000), 72, 93.

54. Ibid., 133–34.

55. [Julian Thomas], *Cannibals and Convicts* (London, 1886), 120–21; *Daily Telegraph* (22 December 1883).

56. Letters 11–15, 22, and 26, Correspondence respecting New Guinea, P.P., 1883, XLVII [C. 3814]; Stuart Ward, "Security," in D. Schreuder and S. Ward, eds., *Australia's Empire* (Oxford: Oxford University Press, 2008), 236–37; Luke Trainor, *British Imperialism* (Cambridge: Cambridge University Press, 1994), 38–39.

57. Lyell, *Principles of Geology*, 3 vols. (London, 1830–33), 2: 255.

58. "Dying Fauna of an Empire," *Saturday Review* (24 November 1906), 635; *Journal of the Society for the Preservation of the Wild Fauna of the Empire*, 1 (London, 1904): 1–6.

59. W.H.R. Rivers, "Psychological Factor," in Rivers, ed., *Essays in the Depopulation of Melanesia* (Cambridge: Cambridge University Press, 1922), 84–113.

60. Sen, *Savagery and Colonialism*, 22, 128–29.

61. H. Ling Roth, *Aborigines of Tasmania*, facsimile of 2nd ed. [1899] (Hobart, Tasmania, Australia: Fullers Bookshop, 1968), 162–63; James Bonwick, *Last of the Tasmanians* [1870], facsimile ed. (Adelaide, Australia, 1969), 61–62, 386–87. Tom Lawson, a self-described "Holocaust historian," has located the Tasmanian story in a wider discussion of genocide in the British world. Lawson, *Last Man* (London: I.B. Tauris, 2014).

62. Ardagh's speech on dumdums, 14 June 1899, as quoted in Barbara Tuchman, *Proud Tower* (New York: Macmillan, 1966), 261–62.

63. Cadwallader Colden, *History of the Five Indian Nations*, 2nd ed. (London, 1750), 9–10; A.M. Hocart, "Warfare in Eddystone," *Journal of the Royal Anthropological Institute*, 61 (1931): 301; *Encyclopaedia Britannica*, 11th ed. (New York, 1910–11), s.v. "tomahawk."

64. Peter Dillon, *Narrative . . . of a Voyage*, 2 vols. (London, 1829), 1: lx–lxi.

65. A.B. Brewster, *Hill Tribes of Fiji* [1922], reprint ed. (New York: Johnson Reprint, 1967), 259–60; John Gaggin, *Among the Man-Eaters* (London: T. Fisher Unwin, 1900), 97–98.

66. *Manual of Scientific Enquiry*, 5th ed. (London, 1886), 231; Clements R. Markham, *Commodore J.G. Goodenough* (Portsmouth, UK, 1876), 33–35; *The Times* (24 August 1875); Goodenough to the Admiralty, letter dictated 13 August 1875, TNA, CO 83/7/f. 427.

67. W.R. Gowers, *Manual of Diseases*, 2 vols. (London, 1886–1888), 2: 623–24, 631–32, 641–46; "Health of the Navy," *Edinburgh Medical Journal*, 23 (May 1878): 1023. In twenty-first-century terms, tetanus is an acute poisoning from a neurotoxin produced by *Clostridium tetani*.

68. F. Milford, "On Tetanus," *New South Wales Medical Gazette*, 2 (April 1872): 196.

69. R.H. Codrington, *On Poisoned Arrows* (London, 1889), 218–19; Codrington, *The Melanesians* (Oxford, 1891), 306–08.

70. A.G. Hopkins, "Back to the Future," *Past and Present*, 164 (August 1999): 198–99.

71. Kathleen Wilson, "Introduction," in Wilson, ed., *New Imperial History* (Cambridge: Cambridge University Press, 2004), 2. Dipesh Chakrabarty, for example, doubts that "Europe" can be unseated as the "sovereign, theoretical subject of all histories." Chakrabarty, *Provincializing Europe* (Princeton, NJ: Princeton University Press, 2000), 27–29.

72. Nicholas Thomas, "Force of Ethnology," *Current Anthropology*, 30 (February 1989): 30.

73. Tracey Banivanua-Mar, *Violence and Colonial Dialogue* (Honolulu: University of Hawai'i Press, 2007), 3, 23–24.

74. Marshall Sahlins, "Poor Man, Rich Man," *Comparative Studies in Society and History*, 5 (April 1963): 286–89, 295; Thomas, "Force of Ethnology," 27–28, 31–32.

75. Epile Hau'ofa, "Our Sea of Islands," *Contemporary Pacific*, 6 (Spring 1994): 153; Matsuda, "The Pacific," 759, 761–62.

76. Clive Moore, *New Guinea* (Honolulu: University of Hawai'i Press, 2003), 4–5.

77. Paul S. Landau, *Popular Politics* (Cambridge: Cambridge University Press, 2010), 1–2; Chris Lowe et al., *Talking about 'Tribe'* (Washington, DC: African Policy Information Center, November 1997), 1–8.

78. W.H.R. Rivers, *Social Organization*, ed. W.J. Penny (New York: Alfred A. Knopf, 1924), 32.

79. Brian Stanley, *Bible and the Flag* (Leicester, UK: Apollos, 1990), 34.

80. Richard Price, "One Big Thing," *Journal of British Studies*, 45 (July 2006): 612–13; Rod Edmond, *Representing the South Pacific* (Cambridge: Cambridge University Press, 1997), 14–15.

81. W.D. McIntyre, "Australia, New Zealand," in Louis and Brown, eds., *Oxford History of the British Empire*, 4: 667.

82. Robert A. Stafford, "Scientific Exploration," in Porter, ed., *Oxford History of the British Empire*, 3: 314–15; Richard D. Fulton and Peter H. Hoffenberg, eds., *Oceania* (Farnham, Surrey, UK: Ashgate, 2013), 1–2.

83. Maude, "Pacific History," 4–5, 24.

CHAPTER I

1. Anna Reid, *Leningrad* (New York: Walker, 2011), 286–92; Yuki Tanaka, *Hidden Horrors* (Boulder, CO: Westview Press, 1996), 126–29; Antony Beevor, *Second World War* (New York: Little, Brown, 2012), 619, 780.

2. "Cannibal Evidence Discovered at Jamestown," *Los Angeles Times* (1 May 2013).

3. "Victim of Cannibal Agreed to Be Eaten," *The Guardian* [London] (14 December 2003); "Mass Murder and Cannibalism Claims Emerge in Congo," *The Independent* [London] (21 May 2003).

4. Alfred St. Johnston, *Camping Among Cannibals* (London, 1889), 230, 228. Italics added.

5. Gananath Obeyesekere, *Cannibal Talk* (Berkeley: University of California Press, 2005), chap. 6.

6. Maggie Kilgour, "Function of Cannibalism," in F. Barker, P. Hulme, and M. Iversen, eds., *Cannibalism and the Colonial World* (Cambridge: Cambridge University Press, 1998), 240–241.

7. W. Arens, *Man-Eating Myth* (New York: Oxford University Press, 1979), 44–45; Lewis Petrinovich, *Cannibal Within* (New York: Aldine De Gruyter, 2000), 4–5. Peter Hulme and Neil Whitehead, eds., *Wild Majesty* (Oxford: Clarendon Press, 1992), 29–34; Hulme, "Introduction," in F. Barker et al., *Cannibalism and the Colonial World*, 18–19.

8. Long, *History of Jamaica* [1774], as quoted in Jean Comaroff and John Comaroff, *Of Revelation and Revolution*, 2 vols. (Chicago: University of Chicago Press, 1991), 1: 123–24.

9. Georg W.F. Hegel, *Philosophy of History* [1822] (Buffalo, NY: Prometheus Books, 1991), 95.

10. George Orwell, *Coming Up for Air* [1939] (San Diego: Harcourt, 1969), 31. Orwell's inept everyman, George Bowling, had it wrong. "King Zog," born Ahmet Muhtar Bej Zogolli, was in fact the Muslim ruler of Albania from 1928 to 1939.

11. John Campbell, *Maritime Discovery* (London, 1840), 436–37.

12. George Cousins, *Story of the South Seas* (London, 1894), 132.

13. John Crawfurd, "On Cannibalism," *Transactions of the Ethnological Society of London*, n.s. 4 (1866): 114; R.L. Stevenson, "In the South Seas," in Stevenson, *Letters and Miscellanies* (New York: Charles Scribner's Sons, 1909), 98–99.

14. Cyprian Bridge, "Cruises in Melanesia," *Proceedings of the Royal Geographical Society*, n.s. 8 (September 1886): 561; Mary Wallis [1851], as quoted in Tracey Banivanua-Mar, "Cannibalism and Colonialism," *Comparative Studies in Society and History*, 52 (April 2010): 263.

15. Cook's journal entry for 23 November 1773 in J.C. Beaglehole, ed., *Journals of Captain James Cook*, vol. 2, *The Resolution and Adventure 1772–1775* (Cambridge: Cambridge University Press, 1961), 294.

16. James Burney, *With Captain Cook*, ed. Beverley Hooper (Canberra: National Library of Australia, 1975), 96–97; Frances Burney, *Early Diary of Frances Burney*, ed. Annie R. Ellis, 2 vols. (London: G. Bell & Sons, 1907), 2: 283.

17. Johann R. Forster, *Observations Made During a Voyage* (London, 1778), 328–32; Jonathan Lamb, Vanessa Smith, and Nicholas Thomas, eds., *Exploration and Exchange* (Chicago: University of Chicago Press, 2000), 92–93.

18. Anne Salmon, *Between Worlds* (Honolulu: University of Hawai'i Press, 1997), 337–38; Judith Binney, *Legacy of Guilt* (Christchurch, New Zealand: Oxford University Press, 1968), 82–83; George French Angas, *Savage Life* [1847], facsimile ed., 2 vols. (Adelaide: Libraries Board of South Australia, 1969), 1: 337–39; Rev. M. Russell, *Polynesia*, 3rd ed. (Edinburgh, 1845), 414–15.

19. Obeyeskere, *Cannibal Talk*, 150.

20. Howard L. Malchow, *Gothic Images of Race* (Stanford, CA: Stanford University Press, 1996), 4–5, 261, n.6.

21. Geoffrey Sanborn, *Sign of the Cannibal* (Durham, NC: Duke University Press, 1998), 16–17.

22. Robert Darnton, *Great Cat Massacre* (New York: Random House, 1985), 64.

23. Rudolf S. Steinmetz, "Endokannibalismus," *Mitteilungen der Anthropologischen Gesellschaft in Wien*, 26 (1896): 1–60; J. Deniker, *Races of Man*, 2nd ed. (London: Walter Scott, [1900]), 148; J.A. MacCulloch, "Cannibalism," in *Encyclopaedia of Religion and Ethics*, 3 (Edinburgh: T. & T. Clark, 1910): 195–96; Napoleon Chagnon, *Yanomamö*, 3rd ed. (Fort Worth, TX: Holt Rinehart & Winston, 1983), 105–06.

24. Eli Sagan, *Cannibalism* (New York: Harper & Row, 1974), 9, 28.

25. Marvin Harris, *Cannibals and Kings* (New York: Vintage Books, 1978), 157–66; Michael Harner, "Ecological Basis," *American Ethnologist*, 4 (February 1977): 117–35.

26. Harris, *Cannibals and Kings*, 165.

27. Marshall Sahlins, "Culture as Protein and Profit," *New York Review of Books*, 25 (23 November 1978): 53; Peggy R. Sanday, *Divine Hunger* (Cambridge: Cambridge University Press, 1986), 18–19.

28. W. Arens and M. Sahlins, "Cannibalism: An Exchange," *N.Y.R.B.*, 26 (22 March 1979): 45; Arens, *Man-Eating Myth*, vi.

29. Arens and Sahlins, "Cannibalism," 46–47.

30. Obeyesekere, "Narratives of the Self," in Barbara Creed and Jeanette Hoorn, eds., *Body Trade* (New York: Routledge, 2001), 69–70.

31. See especially Robert Borofsky, "Cook, Lono," in Borofsky, ed., *Remembrance of Pacific Pasts* (Honolulu: University of Hawai'i Press, 2000), 420–42; and Hulme, "Introduction: The Cannibal Scene," 19.

32. Obeyesekere, *Apotheosis of Captain Cook* (Princeton, NJ: Princeton University Press, 1992), 8–9, 21–22.

33. Sahlins, *How "Natives" Think* (Chicago: University of Chicago Press, 1995), ix, 5–6; Sahlins, "Artificially Maintained Controversies (part 2)," *Anthropology Today*, 19 (December 2003): 21.

34. Obeyesekere, *Cannibal Talk*, 267.

35. Sahlins, "Artificially Maintained Controversies (part 1)," *Anthropology Today*, 19 (June 2003): 3; Sahlins, "Raw Women, Cooked Men," in Paula Brown and Donald Tuzin, eds., *Ethnography of Cannibalism* (Washington, DC: Society for Psychological Anthropology, 1983), 88.

36. Tracey Banivanua-Mar, "Cannibalism and Colonialism," 256–57; Banivanua-Mar, "Cannibalism in Fiji," in Patricia Grimshaw and Russell McGregor, eds., *Collisions of Cultures* (Melbourne, Australia: Melbourne University Press, 2007), 203–04. A modern zoologist holds that there is nothing at all strange about cannibalism. For within every class of vertebrates, Bill Schutt points out, eating one's own kind is "perfectly natural." Schutt, *Cannibalism* (Chapel Hill, NC: Algonquin Books, 2017).

37. Malchow, *Gothic Images,* 63, 66; William Dampier, *New Voyage Round the World* [1729], facsimile of 7th ed. (New York: Dover, 1968), 325–26.

38. *Encyclopaedia Britannica,* 2nd ed. (London, 1778), s.v. "anthropophagi."

39. *Encyclopaedia Britannica,* 3rd ed. (London, 1788–1797), s.v. "anthropophagi."

40. Edmund Burke, *Reflections* [1790] (Harmondsworth, Middlesex, UK: Penguin Books, 1969), 164; Linda Colley, *Britons* (London: Yale University Press, 1992), 332.

41. *Encyclopaedia Britannica,* 9th ed. (New York, 1878), s.v. "cannibalism."

42. Herman Melville, *Moby-Dick* [1851] (Berkeley: University of California Press, 1981), chap. 65, 299.

43. Stevenson, "In the South Seas," 96.

44. Hugh H. Romilly, *From My Verandah* (London, 1889), 68–69.

45. Richard D. Altick, *English Common Reader,* 2nd ed. (Columbus: Ohio State University Press, 1998), 63, 220, 258; Ian Watt, "Robinson Crusoe as a Myth," in Michael Shinagel, ed., *Robinson Crusoe* [1719] (New York: W.W. Norton, 1994), 288–306. George Borrow, Victorian wanderer and philologist, reckoned in 1851 that Daniel Defoe's book had "exerted over the minds of Englishmen an influence certainly greater than any other of modern times . . . and with the contents of which even those who cannot read are to a certain extent acquainted." *Lavengro* [1851] (London: J.M. Dent, 1906), 23–24.

46. Woodes Rogers, *Cruising Voyage* [1712], as abridged in Shinagel, ed., *Robinson Crusoe,* 230–35; Kathleen Wilson, *Island Race* (London: Routledge, 2003), 88.

47. Harry Stone, *Night Side of Dickens* (Columbus: Ohio State University Press, 1994), 60–61.

48. Defoe, *Robinson Crusoe,* ed. Shinagel, 124.

49. Ibid., 112, 119–20, 168–71, 116.

50. Peter Hulme, *Colonial Encounters* (London: Methuen, 1986), 184–85, 211–14; Felix Padel, *Sacrifice of Human Beings* (Delhi: Oxford University Press, 1995), 151–152.

51. Defoe, *Robinson Crusoe,* 152; Frank Lestringant, *Cannibals* (Cambridge: Polity Press, 1997), 137–39; Patrick Brantlinger, *Taming Cannibals* (Ithaca, NY: Cornell University Press, 2011), 2–3; Samuel Patterson, *Narrative of Adventures* [1817], quoted in Sanborn, *Sign of the Cannibal,* 27.

52. Capt. Charles Johnson, *General History of . . . the Most Famous Highwaymen* (London, 1734), 132–33; Richard Charnock, "Cannibalism in Europe," *Journal of the Anthropological Society,* 4 (1866): xxvii.

53. *Notes and Queries on Anthropology* (London, 1874), 45.

54. William Shakespeare, *Richard II,* act 2, scene 1. It is an aged John of Gaunt who offers this island image.

55. Wilson, *Island Race,* 5.

56. John Gillis, *Islands of the Mind* (New York: Palgrave Macmillan, 2004), 112; William Falconer, *Remarks on the Influence of Climate* (London, 1781), 170–73.

57. Charles de Secondat Montesquieu, *Spirit of the Laws* [1748] (Cambridge: Cambridge University Press, 1989), part 3, book 18, chap. 5; Falconer, *Remarks,* 171.

58. Andrew Kippis, *Life of Captain James Cook* (Dublin [1788]), 482; Cook, *Journals of Captain James Cook,* ed. J.C. Beaglehole, 4 vols. (Woodbridge, Suffolk, UK: Boydell & Brewer, 1999), 1: xxii–xxiii.

59. Harriet Guest, "Ornament and Use," in Kathleen Wilson, ed., *New Imperial History* (Cambridge: Cambridge University Press, 2004), 317–19; Greg Dening, *Mr. Bligh's Bad Language* (Cambridge: Cambridge University Press, 1992), 271–73.

60. "Old Stories Re-Told," *All the Year Round,* n.s. 8 (18 May 1872): 12.

61. A.W. Humphreys, *Orpheus, and Concert-Room Companion* (London, 1832); Harold Scott, *Early Doors* (London: Nicholson & Watson, 1946), 20–21; Peter Bailey, *Leisure and Class* (London; Methuen, 1987), 166–67; Henry Mayhew, *London Labour* [1861–1862], facsimile ed., 4 vols. (New York: Dover, 1968), 1: 213; Leslie Shepard, *History of Street Literature* (Newton Abbot, Devon, UK: David & Charles, 1973), 21–22; Martha Vicinus, *Industrial Muse* (New York: Barnes & Noble, 1974), 13–14.

62. Paul Cowdell, "Cannibal Ballads," *Folk Music Journal,* 9 (2010): 729; "King of the Cannibal Islands," *Punch,* 6 (January–June 1844): 79.

63. Barry A. Joyce, *Shaping of American Ethnography* (Lincoln: University of Nebraska Press, 2001), 98; Madeline House and Graham Story, eds., *Letters of Charles Dickens,* vol. 2, *1840–1841* (Oxford: Clarendon Press, 1969), 262–63.

64. Herman Melville, *Typee* [1846] (New York: Viking Press, 1952), 16–17; Henry David Thoreau, *Walden* [1854] (New York: W.W. Norton, 1966), 17; Zack Bowen, *Musical Allusions* (Albany: State University of New York Press, 1974), 97–98; E.W. Hornung, *Amateur Cracksman* [1899] (New York: Charles Scribner's Sons, 1908), 204; *The Times* [London] (27 December 1876); Anon., *Travesty Burlesque of Hamlet* (Slough, Berkshire, UK, 1847); Edward B. Taylor, *Anahuac* (London, 1869), 211–13; *Oxford Dictionary of Nursery Rhymes,* eds. Iona and Peter Opie, 2nd ed. (New York: Oxford University Press, 1997), 249.

65. James Catnach, *Catalogue of Songs* [1832], in Shepard, *History of Street Literature,* 217–21; J. Bruton, "Queen of the Cannibal Islands," in Humphreys, *Orpheus,* 28–30.

66. Edward Reeves, *Brown Men and Women* (London, 1898), 268; Thomas Mayne Reid, *Odd People* (New York: Harper & Brothers, 1860), 164–65.

67. Basil Thomson, *The Fijians* (London: William Heinemann, 1908), 1.

68. Peter Dillon, *Narrative . . . of a Voyage,* 2 vols. (London, 1829), 1: 12–21.

69. Obeyesekere, "Narratives of the Self," 69–70, 84, 101, 111.

70. Ruth Richardson, *Death, Dissection* (London: Penguin, 1989), 221–22.

71. Thomas Carlyle, *Chartism* [1839] (Boston, 1840), 28, 30–31; Patrick Brantlinger, *Dark Vanishings* (Ithaca, NY: Cornell University Press, 2003), 94–95.

72. *The Times* (14 August 1845 and 16 August 1845); S.C. on Andover Union, P.P., 1846, V (666-1): vi, xix; James Vernon, *Hunger* (Cambridge, MA: Harvard University Press, 2007), 18–20; Ian Miller, "Feeding in the Workhouse," *Journal of British Studies,* 52 (October 2013): 593.

73. William Booth, *In Darkest England* (London: Salvation Army, 1890), chap.1; *The Times* (13 March 1850).

74. *Lloyd's Weekly Newspaper* [London] (9 August 1863); *The Times* (6 January 1869); *Northern Echo* [Darlington] (15 March 1880).

75. Tristram Stuart, *Bloodless Revolution* (New York: W.W. Norton, 2007), 182–86.

76. Joseph Ritson, *Essay on Abstinence* (London, 1802), 124–25.

77. Dane Kennedy, *Highly Civilized Man* (Cambridge, MA: Harvard University Press, 2005), 168–70; Mary S. Lovell, *Rage to Live* (New York: W.W. Norton, 1998), 413.

78. Morley Roberts, "True Function," *The Humanitarian*, 4 (April 1894): 284–88.

79. William Makepeace Thackeray, *Works of . . . Thackery*, 22 vols. (London, 1869), 18: 228–29; Cowdell, "Cannibal Ballads," 723–25.

80. A.W.B. Simpson, *Cannibalism and the Common Law* (Chicago: Chicago University Press, 1984); "The Apologists for Cannibalism," *The Spectator* (13 September 1884), 1198–99; "Civilized Cannibals," *Nautical Magazine*, 44 (March 1875): 177–78.

81. Simpson, *Cannibalism*, 96–101.

82. Malchow, *Gothic Images*, 55; Michael Alexander, *Mrs. Fraser* (New York: Simon & Schuster, 1971), 17–18, 114–15, 149, 159–62; Reay Tannahill, *Flesh and Blood* (New York: Stein & Day, 1975), 145–46; Kay Schaffer, *In the Wake of First Contact* (Cambridge: Cambridge University Press, 1995), 3–14, 18, 110–15.

83. "Skulls of the Crew," *Missionary Magazine* (May 1837), 181–83.

84. [James Oliver] *Wreck of the Glide* (New York and London, 1848), 52–53; Obeyesekere, *Cannibal Talk*, 163–67.

85. *Sydney Morning Herald* (27 January 1859); *South Australian Register* [Adelaide] (5 February 1859); *The Times* (30 March 1859); *Lloyd's Weekly Newspaper* (3 April 1859); *The Observer* [London] (4 April 1859); M.V. De Rochas, "Naufrage et scènes d'anthropologie a l'île Rossell," *Le Tour Du Monde* (deuxième semester, 1861), 81–94.

86. J.P. Thomson, *British New Guinea* (London, 1892), 12, 14–17; C.G. Seligmann, *Melanesians of British New Guinea* (Cambridge: Cambridge University Press, 1910), 548, n.1; Basil Thomson, "Rossel Island," *Journal of the Manchester Geographical Society*, 6 (October 1890): 8–11; Hubert Murray, *Papua or British New Guinea* (London: T. Fisher Unwin, 1912), 132–34; diary entry for 2 April 1908, Murray Papers, Mitchell Library, A 3139, vol. 2.

87. Beatrice Grimshaw, "World's Worst Cannibal Island," *Asia,* 34 (June 1934): 348–51.

88. Cătălin Avramescu, *Intellectual History of Cannibalism* (Princeton, NJ: Princeton University Press, 2009), 1–2, 9; Lestringant, *Cannibals,* 100, 147.

89. Stevenson, "In the South Seas," 129; Malchow, *Gothic Images*, 52; Garry Hogg, *Cannibalism and Human Sacrifice* (New York: Citadel Press, 1966), 22–23.

90. Crawfurd, "On Cannibalism," 106–08.

91. H.L. Roth, *Aborigines of Tasmania*, facsimile of 2nd ed. [1899] (Hobart, Tasmania, Australia: Fullers Bookshop, 1968), 97.

92. Hume Nisbet, *Colonial Tramp*, 2 vols. (London, 1891), 2: 133–34.

93. Booth, *In Darkest England*, 10.

94. H.M. Stanley, *Great Forest of Central Africa* (London, 1890), 17–20.

95. Paul B. Du Chaillu, *Explorations & Adventures* (London, 1861), iii–iv, 67, 88–89.

96. R.F. Burton, "A Day Amongst the Fans," *Anthropological Review*, 1 (May 1863): 48–49; James Greenwood, *Curiosities of Savage Life* (London, 1863), 294; W.W. Reade, *Savage Africa* [1864], reprint ed. (New York: Johnson Reprint, 1967), 136–39.

97. *The Times* (12 April 1895); A.B. Lloyd, *In Dwarf Land* [1899] (London: T. Fisher Unwin, 1907), 295–97; *The Times* (14 December 1898); "Excursions and Cannibalism," *Daily Chronicle* [London] (16 September 1895); "African Cannibals," *Saturday Review*, 81 (30 May 1896): 544; "Cannibalism," *Vegetarian Messenger* (October 1895), 309–10.

98. James R. Ryan, *Picturing Empire* (Chicago: University of Chicago Press, 1997), 222–23; Adam Hochschild, *King Leopold's Ghost* (New York: Houghton Mifflin, 1998), 165–66.

99. Reade, *Savage Africa*, preface.

100. Rev. D. Lang, "On the Origin and Migration," *Nautical Magazine and Naval Chronicle, for 1870*, 4, 6–7.

101. John Coulter, *Adventures in the Pacific* (Dublin, 1845), 178–79, 223–25, 229, 231; "Day Among the Cannibals," *Nautical Magazine and Naval Chronicle* (July 1864), 344–47; "Cannibalism in the Marquesas," *The Times* (24 September 1873). Greg Dening has observed that the combined impact of imported alcohol and epidemic disease transformed Marquesan cannibalism from a practice suffused with ceremonial meaning into meaningless violence: drunken *enata* (Marquesans) now "sat amongst their carcases . . . like actors in some mad dream." See Dening, *Islands and Beaches* (Honolulu: University Press of Hawai'i, 1980), 259–61.

102. "South Seas—Mission at Raratonga," *Missionary Magazine* (September 1840), 131–32.

103. "Manua," *Samoan Reporter* (March 1845), 4; T.H. Hood, *Notes of a Cruise* (Edinburgh: Edmonston & Douglas, 1863), 139–40; William Mariner, *Account of the Natives*, 2 vols. (London, 1817), 1: 115–17.

104. Schaffer, *In the Wake of First Contact*, 118–19.

105. Angas, *Savage Life*, 1: vii, and 2: 210–11, 231; J.G. Frazer, *Totemism* (Edinburgh: Adam & Charles Black, 1887), 80–81.

106. Roslyn Poignant, *Professional Savages* (New Haven, CT: Yale University Press, 2004), 10–11; "Among Cannibals," *The Spectator*, 63 (21 December 1889): 884–85; [William Houghton], "Among Cannibals," *Edinburgh Review*, 172 (October 1890): 521, 531–33.

107. W.G. Lawes, "Notes on New Guinea," *Journal of the Royal Geographical Society*, n.s. 2 (October 1880): 613–14, 616; James Chalmers, *Pioneering in New Guinea* (London: Religious Tract Society [1902]), 48–51.

108. George Brown, "Life History of a Savage," *Proceedings of the Australian Association for the Advancement of Science* (Sydney, 1898), 785–86; Brown, *Melanesians and Polynesians* (London: Macmillan, 1910), 152–54; Hydrographic Office, British Admiralty, *Pacific Islands, Sailing Directions*, 2nd ed. (London, 1890), 427–28, 447–48.

109. For Solomon Islands headhunting, see Chapter 4.

110. "Cannibalism in the South Seas," *The Observer* (25 July 1847).

111. *Encyclopaedia Britannica*, 11th ed. (New York, 1910), s.v. "Melanesia."

112. Bronwen Douglas, "Art as Ethnohistorical Text," in Nicholas Thomas and Diane Losche, eds., *Double Vision* (Cambridge: Cambridge University Press, 1999), 79–80; Andrew Cheyne, *Description of Islands* (London, 1852), 6–8; Alice Bullard, *Exile to Paradise* (Stanford, CA: Stanford University Press, 2000), 46–48, 206, 272–77.

113. Rev. M. Russell, *Polynesia*, 281–82; Robert Steel, *New Hebrides and Christian Missions* (London, 1880), 192–93; A.K. Langridge, *Conquest of Cannibal Tanna* (London: Hodder & Stoughton [1934]), 11–12.

114. George F. Angas, *Polynesia* (London [1866]), 352–53; Oscar Michelsen, *Cannibals Won for Christ* (London [1893]), 112–13; George Turner, *Nineteen Years* (London, 1861), 82–83; George Patterson, *Missionary Life* (Toronto, 1882), 160–61; Julius Brenchley, *Jottings* (London, 1873), 226–27.

115. A.B. Brewster, *King of the Cannibal Isles* (London: Robert Hale, 1937), 19; Banivanua-Mar, "Cannibalism in Fiji," 206; E.W. Said, *Orientalism* (New York: Vintage Books, 1979), 6.

116. Thomas Williams and James Calvert, *Fiji and the Fijians* (New York, 1859), 80–81, 166–167.

117. John Erskine, *Journal of a Cruise* (London, 1853), 274–75; *Caledonian Mercury* [Edinburgh] (17 January 1825); Alexander Pearce, "Confessions of Murder and Cannibalism, 1822," microfilm copy, Mitchell Library, ML A 1326.

118. Bertholdt Seemann, "Feejee Islanders," *Nautical Magazine and Naval Chronicle* (1861), 258; Angas, *Polynesia*, 219–20.

119. A.B. Brewster, *Hill Tribes of Fiji* [1922], reprint ed. (New York: Johnson Reprint, 1967), 72–73.

120. John Lubbock, *Pre-Historic Times* [1865], 2nd ed. (New York, 1872), 459–60; James Greenwood, *Wild Man at Home* (London [1879]), 280–81; Walter Lawry, *Friendly and Feejee Islands* (London, 1850), 89.

121. Williams and Calvert, *Fiji and the Fijians*, 123; *Juvenile Missionary Herald* (April 1871), 56–57; Richard Siddons, *Experiences in Fiji*, in *The Journal of William Lockerby*, ed. Everard Im Thurn (London: Hakluyt Society, 1925), 174–75; G. Wright, "Fiji in the Early Seventies," *Transactions of the Fijian Society* (1916–1917), 27; Nicholas Thomas, *Entangled Objects* (Cambridge, MA: Harvard University Press, 1991), 67, 110–11.

122. *Juvenile Missionary Herald* (August 1871), 120–21; Thomas, *Entangled Objects*, 165–67.

123. David Cargill, *Memoirs of Mrs. Margaret Cargill* (London, 1841), 10–11.

124. Brantlinger, *Taming Cannibals*, 32–33; Seth Koven, *Slumming* (Princeton, NJ: Princeton University Press, 2004), 94–95.

125. Joyce, *Shaping of American Ethnography*, 103–09, 114–17; "Special Instructions for the Captains, 1 January 1845," B.L., Martin Papers, Add. Ms. 41463, ff. 121–24.

126. Cook, *Journals of Captain James Cook . . . 1772–1775*, ed. J.C. Beaglehole, 2 (Cambridge: Cambridge University Press, 1961): 452–53.

127. Beaglehole, *Life of Cook*, 349; *Journals of Cook . . . 1776–1780*, 3, part 1: 163–64.

128. William Bligh, *Bligh Notebook, 28 April to 14 June 1789*, facsimile ed. (Canberra: National Library of Australia, 1986), entry for 7 May 1789.

129. Walter Lawry, *Second Visit to the Friendly and Feejee Islands* (London, 1851), iv.

130. W.T. Pritchard, *Polynesian Reminiscences* [1866], reprint ed. (London: Dawsons of Pall Mall, 1968), 370–72; [Herman Merivale], "Christianity in Melanesia," *Quarterly Review*, 95 (June 1854): 175.

131. [Merivale], "Christianity," 170–71; Herbert Spencer, *Principles of Sociology*, 1, part 2 [1874–1875] (New York, 1896), 524.

132. Sahlins, "Raw Women," 81–82. Henry Fowler, a crewmember from the Salem *bêche-de-mer* trader *Glide*, probably wrote the detailed account of Fijian butchery techniques that appeared in a letter to the *Danvers Courier* on 16 August 1845. Sahlins finds no compelling reason to dismiss this account; Obeyesekere terms it "surreal," just another nautical "yarn." Papers of Henry Fowler, Phillips Library, Peabody Essex Museum, MH-102, folders 1–3; Obeyesekere, *Cannibal Talk*, 167–69.

133. Williams and Calvert, *Fiji and the Fijians*, 40–41.

134. David Cargill, *The Diaries . . . of David Cargill, 1832–1843*, ed. Albert Schütz (Canberra: Australian National University Press, 1977), 159–60; Fergus Clunie, *Fijian Weapons and Warfare* (Suva: Fiji Museum, 1977), 6–7; Angas, *Polynesia*, 236; "Proceedings of H.M.S. *Calliope*," *Nautical Magazine and Naval Chronicle* (September 1853), 457–59.

135. Williams and Calvert, *Fiji and the Fijians*, 2–3.

136. Joseph Waterhouse, *King and the People of Fiji* [1866] (New York: AMS Press, 1978), 26–28; Peter France, *Charter of the Land* (Melbourne: Oxford University Press, 1969), 21; I.C. Campbell, "Historiography of Charles Savage," *Journal of the Polynesian Society*, 89 (June 1980): 143–46; David Routledge, *Matanitu* (Suva, Fiji: Institute of Pacific Studies, 1985), 43–47.

137. *Dictionary of Australasian Biography*, Supplement, s.v. "Thakombau"; [C.W. Hope], "Sketches in Polynesia," *Blackwood's Edinburgh Magazine*, 106 (July 1869): 35–36; Mary Davis Wallis ["A Lady"], *Life in Feejee* (Boston, 1851), 30–31; Lawry, *Friendly and Feejee Islands*, 104–05.

138. *The Times* (27 June 1862 and 1 July 1872); Thomson, *The Fijians,* 51–55.

139. Deryck Scarr, *Fiji: A Short History* (Laie, HI: Institute for Polynesian Studies, 1984), 40–51.

140. T.R. St. Johnston, *South Sea Reminiscences* (London: T. Fisher Unwin, 1922), 180–81; R.A. Derrick, *History of Fiji,* 3rd ed. (Suva, Fiji: Government Press, 1957), 235–44; *The Times* (13 February 1875).

141. See, for example, G.K. Roth, *Fijian Way of Life* (London: Oxford University Press, 1953), chap. 2.

142. France, *Charter of the Land,* 108.

143. Brewster, *Hill Tribes,* 25–26.

144. Scarr, *Fiji: A Short History,* 75.

145. Banivanua-Mar, "Cannibalism and Colonialism," 278.

146. *Fiji Times* [Levuka] (18 February 1871); "Fejee Cannibals," *Every Saturday* [Boston], 3 (29 July 1871): 110.

147. Interview with Ratu Isikia Rogoyawa (1978?), in Kim Gravelle, *Fiji's Times,* 8th reprint (Suva, 1992), 111–114; Derrick, *History of Fiji,* 200–01; W.C. Gardenhire, *Fiji and the Fijians* (San Francisco, 1871), 21.

148. On the hapless Rev. Baker, see Chapter 2.

149. G. Wright, "Fiji in the Early Seventies," 17–18; Brewster, *Hill Tribes,* 32.

150. *Fiji Times* (6 August 1873).

151. Ibid. (15 February 1871); Derrick, *History of Fiji,* 211.

152. J.K. Chapman, *Career of Arthur Hamilton Gordon* (Toronto: University of Toronto Press, 1964), 155–56; Victoria Goodenough, *Life of Love and Duty* (London [1891]), 86.

153. *Fiji Times* (20 February 1875); A.H. Gordon to Wood, 14 July–14 August 1876, Stanmore Papers, B.L., Add. MS. 49237.

154. For a provocative account of colonial medicine as social surveillance, see David Arnold, *Colonizing the Body* (Berkeley: University of California Press, 1993).

155. http://www.cdc.gov/measles

156. Andrew Cliff and Peter Haggett, *Spread of Measles in Fiji* (Canberra: Australian National University, 1985), 31–33; Robert Nicole, *Disturbing History* (Honolulu: University of Hawai'i Press, 2011), 24–26.

157. S. Soulter Harwood, "Measles in the Fiji Islands," *Pacific Medical and Surgical Journal,* 18 (January 1876): 352–53; Alan Macfarlane, *The Savage Wars of Peace* (Oxford: Blackwell, 1997), 291–92. Certain northeastern Pacific communities may have suffered just as grievously from another epidemic virus, smallpox, during the late 1770s. Perhaps a third of the coastal Haida, Tlingit, and Salish peoples succumbed to this deadly pathogen. David Igler, "Diseased Goods," *American Historical Review,* 109 (June 2004): 701–02. For the impact of smallpox on the Makah people, see Joshua Reid, *The Sea Is My Country* (New Haven, CT: Yale University Press, 2015), 119–123.

158. Constance Gordon-Cumming, *At Home in Fiji,* 2nd ed., 2 vols. (Edinburgh, 1881), 1: 56–59; *The Times* (18 June, 1 July, and 29 September 1875).

159. *Fiji Times* (27 February, 3 March, and 24 February 1875).

160. *The Lancet* [London] (3 July 1875), 33; Bolton Corney, "Behaviour of Certain Epidemic Diseases," *Transactions of the Epidemiological Society of London*, n.s. 3 (1883–1884): 81–82; Brewster, *Hill Tribes*, 67–68.

161. H. Stonehewer Cooper, *Islands of the Pacific*, 2nd ed. (London, 1888), 34.

162. Arthur H. Gordon, *Fiji; Records of Private and of Public Life*, 4 vols. (Edinburgh: R. & R. Clark, 1897–1912), 1: 198–99, 209–11.

163. "The Abolition of Cannibalism in Fiji," *The Graphic* (17 July 1875), 62–63.

164. "Cannibal Outbreak in Fiji," *Manchester Guardian* (24 August 1876).

165. Wright, "Fiji in the Early Seventies," 34–35; J.H. DeRicci, *Fiji* (London, 1875), 15–16.

166. Banivanua-Mar, "Cannibalism and Colonialism," 258.

167. Chapman, *Career of Gordon*, 185–87; A.H. Gordon, *Letters and Notes Written During the Disturbances in the Highlands*, 2 vols. (Edinburgh: privately printed, 1879), 1: 421–23.

168. James Edge Partington, *Random Rot* (Altrincham, Manchester, UK, 1883), 67.

169. Elizabeth Bisland, "Confessions," *Outing; the Gentleman's Magazine* [Boston], 12 (April–September 1888): 546–51.

170. Melville, *Moby-Dick*, chap. 3, 24.

171. *Morning Courier and Enquirer* (3 September 1831).

172. Benjamin Morrell, *Narrative of Four Voyages* (New York, 1832), 466; Thomas Jefferson Jacobs, *Scenes, Incidents* (New York, 1844), 13–15. For a detailed reconstruction of the fates that befell "Sunday" and "Monday," see James Fairhead, *The Captain and "The Cannibal"* (New Haven, CT: Yale University Press, 2015).

173. Antony Adler, "Capture and Curation," *Journal of Pacific History*, 49 (July 2014): 255–82; Poignant, *Professional Savages*, 83.

174. *Fiji Times* (10 May 1871).

175. P.T. Barnum, *Struggles and Triumphs* (Buffalo, NY, 1875), 760–61; Gardenhire, *Fiji and the Fijians*, 13–17; Jeff Bergland, *Cannibal Fictions* (Madison: University of Wisconsin Press, 2006), 35–36, 39–40, 43; John MacKenzie, "Empire and Metropolitan Cultures," in Andrew Porter, ed., *Oxford History of the British Empire*, 3 (New York: Oxford University Press, 1999): 284.

176. Pamela Scully and Clifton Crais, "Race and Erasure," *Journal of British Studies*, 47 (April 2008): 303, 306, 320–21.

177. Poignant, *Professional Savages*, 28, 1.

178. R.A. Cunningham, "Exhibition of Natives," *Journal of the Anthropological Institute*, 17 (1888): 83–84; Poignant, *Professional Savages*, 16.

179. Catherine Hall, *Civilising Subjects* (Chicago: University of Chicago Press, 2002), 279–80; Robert Moffat, *Missionary Labours and Scenes in South Africa* (London, 1842).

180. Nadja Durbach, *Spectacle of Deformity* (Berkeley: University of California Press, 2010), 148–50; Bernth Lindfors, "Ethnological Show Business," in Rosemarie

Garland Thomson, ed., *Freakery* (New York: New York University Press, 1996), 216–17.

181. Partington, *Random Rot*, 67; Hulme, "Introduction: The Cannibal Scene," 24; George S. Rowe, *Life of John Hunt* (London: Hamilton, Adams, 1859), 104–06.

182. [Merivale], "Christianity," 174; *Fiji Times* (11 September 1869).

183. William T. Wawn, *South Sea Islanders and the Queensland Labour Trade* [1893], ed. Peter Corris (Honolulu: University of Hawai'i Press, 183, 1973), 283–84.

184. "Another Samoan," *P.I.M.* (15 September 1939), 18; Nicholas Thomas, *Colonialism's Culture* (Princeton, NJ: Princeton University Press, 1994), 33–35.

185. Reeves, *Brown Men and Women*, 3, 10–11.

186. The spelling of Frazer's surname varies widely. Contemporary newspapers, magazines, and reference works call him "Frazer," "Fraser," "Gordon-Frazer," and "Gordon-Fraser." I thank Wayne Heuple for familiarizing me with this painting.

187. Alan McCulloch, *Encyclopedia of Australian Art*, 2 vols. (Hawthorn, Victoria, Australia: Hutchinson, 1984), 1: 512–13; Algernon Graves, *Dictionary of Artists*, 3rd ed. [1901], reprint (New York: Lenox Hill, 1970), s.v. "Frazer, Charles E."; *Illustrated Catalogue of the National Gallery* [of Victoria] (Melbourne, 1911), 163, 167.

188. *Table Talk* [Melbourne] (20 November 1891), 6.

189. *Melbourne Herald* (10, 12, 21, 23, and 24 November 1891).

190. Frazer, "Tanna," *Table Talk* (27 November 1891), 6; *Melbourne Herald* (29 December 1891).

191. *The Sun* [Melbourne] (28 April 1893); *Melbourne Punch* (4 May 1893).

192. Amy Woodson-Boulton, *Transformative Beauty* (Stanford, CA: Stanford University Press, 2012), 151.

193. *Liverpool Mercury* (23 November 1895); C.E.G. Frazer, "Paper Read at the Soiree" [22 November 1895], Walker Art Gallery Archives, typescript copy, n.p. I thank Alex Kidson, Curator of British Art at the Walker Gallery, for unearthing this long-misfiled document.

194. Frazer, "Paper Read at the Soiree."

195. "Cannibal Feast on Tanna," *P.I.M.* (March 1989), 41–42.

196. Thomas Beale, *Natural History of the Sperm Whale* (London, 1839), 186–87; Melville, *Moby-Dick*, chap. 96, 418–19; Seemann, *Viti* [1862], reprint (Folkestone, Kent, UK: Dawsons of Pall Mall, 1973), 183–84.

197. Arnold F. Hills, *Essays on Vegetarianism* (London, [1894]), 148; *Oxford Dictionary of Quotations*, 6th ed. (Oxford: Oxford University Press, 2004), 834.

198. Freud's formulation declared, "Where id was, there ego shall be." *New Introductory Lectures on Psychoanalysis* [1933], trans. and ed. James Strachey (New York: W.W. Norton, 1965), lecture 31, 71.

199. Ewan Johnston, "Reinventing Fiji," *Journal of Pacific History*, 40 (June 2005): 23, 29.

200. James Mooney, "Our Last Cannibal Tribe," *Harper's Monthly Magazine*, 103 (September 1901): 554–55; "Confessions of a Cannibal," *P.I.M.* (22 May 1936), 17–19.

201. Shirley Lindenbaum, *Kuru Sorcery* (Palo Alto, CA: Mayfield, 1979), 9–10, 19–22; Robert Klitzman, *Trembling Mountain* (New York: Plenum Press, 1998), 5–6, 22; Arens, *Man-Eating Myth*, 104, 107–09.

202. Peter M. Burns and Yana Figurova, "Tribal Tourism," in Marina Novelli, ed., *Niche Tourism* (Oxford: Elsevier, 2005), 101–10; Dennis O'Rourke, in association with the Institute of Papua New Guinea Studies, *Cannibal Tours* (1987); Paul Raffaele, "Sleeping with Cannibals," *Smithsonian,* 37 (September 2006): 48–59.

CHAPTER 2

1. [Sydney Smith], "Indian Missions," *Edinburgh Review,* 12 (April 1808): 179–180.

2. Lady Holland, *Memoir of the Reverend Sydney Smith,* 2 vols. (New York, 1855), 2: 337.

3. Richard Le Gallienne, *Romantic '90s* (Garden City, NY: Doubleday, Page, 1926), 251.

4. Jeffrey Cox, *Imperial Fault Lines* (Stanford, CA: Stanford University Press, 2002), 8. This historiographical "blind spot" has been the subject of several shrewd critiques. See especially A.G. Hopkins, "Back to the Future," *Past and Present,* 164 (August 1999): 198–243; D.W. Bebbington, "Atonement, Sin, and Empire," in Andrew Porter, ed., *Imperial Horizons* (Grand Rapids, MI: W.B. Eerdmans, 2003), 14–31; and Tony Ballantyne, "Religion, Difference," *Victorian Studies,* 47 (Spring 2005): 427–455.

5. Bernard Porter, *Lion's Share,* 3rd ed. (London: Longman, 1996); Bernard Porter, "'Empire, What Empire?'" *Victorian Studies,* 46 (Winter 2004): 256–57. Porter's controversial stance is fully delineated in his *Absent-Minded Imperialists* (New York: Oxford University Press, 2004).

6. Ballantyne, "Religion, Difference," 449. For a dispassionate critique of Porter's case, see Richard Price, "One Big Thing," *Journal of British Studies,* 45 (July 2006): 602–27.

7. John L. Comaroff, "Images of Empire," in Frederick Cooper and Ann Laura Stoler, eds., *Tensions of Empire* (Berkeley: University of California Press, 1997), 166.

8. Greg Dening, "The Comaroffs Out of Africa," *American Historical Review,* 108 (April 2003): 474.

9. Jeffrey Cox, "Were Victorian Nonconformists the Worst Imperialists of All?," *Victorian Studies,* 46 (Winter 2004): 253–54; Andrew Porter, "Religion and Empire," *Journal of Imperial and Commonwealth History,* 20 (September 1992): 375, 386; Susan Thorne, *Congregational Missions* (Stanford, CA: Stanford University Press, 1999), 49–50. For the argument against depicting British missionaries as agents of cultural imperialism, see Brian Stanley, *Bible and the Flag* (Leicester, UK: Apollos, 1990).

10. Bebbington, "Atonement," 16–17, 19–20. On the centrality of the doctrine of atonement in nineteenth-century thought, see Boyd Hilton, *Age of Atonement* (Oxford: Clarendon Press, 1988).

11. John M. MacKenzie, "Empire and Metropolitan Cultures," in Andrew Porter, ed., *Oxford History of the British Empire*, 3 (New York: Oxford University Press, 1999): 281–82.

12. Cox, "Were Victorian Nonconformists," 253–54; Catherine Hall, *Civilising Subjects* (Chicago: University of Chicago Press, 2002), 84–86, 112–15, 172–73.

13. *Program of Worship*, "Bishop John Patteson Day," 17 September 2006, Holy Trinity Anglican Cathedral, Suva, Fiji.

14. *Vaccination Inquirer* (September 1879), 79; Nadia Durbach, *Bodily Matters* (Durham, NC: Duke University Press, 2005), 99–103.

15. Pamela J. Walker, *Pulling the Devil's Kingdom Down* (Berkeley: University of California Press, 2001), 221–23.

16. William Moister, *Missionary Martyrs* (London, 1885), 9–10.

17. *Encyclopaedia Britannica*, 7th ed. (1842), s.v. "martyr."

18. Ibid., 8th ed. (1857), s.v. "martyr."

19. Ibid., 11th ed. (1910–1911), s.v. "martyr."

20. A.G. Dickens, *English Reformation* (New York: Schocken Books, 1969), 264–65.

21. G.R. Elton, *England Under the Tudors* (London: Methuen, 1965), 220; Brad S. Gregory, *Salvation at Stake* (Cambridge, MA: Harvard University Press, 1999), 137.

22. David Loades, "Introduction," in Loades, ed., *John Foxe and the English Reformation* (Aldershot, Hampshire, UK: Scolar Press, 1997), 3–4; Linda Colley, *Britons* (London: Yale University Press, 1992), 25–28.

23. Andrew Penny, "John Foxe," in David Loades, ed., *John Foxe*, 183.

24. "Buried Alive for Christ," *Quarterly Token for Juvenile Subscribers* (October 1868), 4–6.

25. Preface, *Autobiography of Samuel Smiles*, ed. Thomas Mackay (New York: E.P. Dutton, 1905), vii.

26. Samuel Smiles, *Duty* [1880] (Chicago, 1884), 114, 94–95, 118, 122.

27. Tim Jeal, *Livingstone* (London: Heinmann, 1973), 158–59; B. Stanley, *Bible and the Flag*, 70–72.

28. [Elizabeth R. Charles], *Three Martyrs* (London, 1886), 160–61; Kathryn Castle, *Britannia's Children* (Manchester, UK: Manchester University Press, 1996), 88.

29. David Livingstone and Charles Livingstone, *Narrative of an Expedition* (New York, 1866), 595, 599–600. Dane Kennedy has observed that although nineteenth-century British explorers rarely set out to die, "they certainly expected to suffer, and suffer they did." Kennedy, *Last Blank Spaces* (Cambridge, MA: Harvard University Press, 2013), 88–89.

30. Samuel Smiles, *Self-Help* [1859] (London, 1864), 2, 4.

31. A.W. Murray, *Martyrs of Polynesia* (London, 1885), 3–4; S.F. Harris, *Century of Missionary Martyrs* (London, 1897), ix–xi.

32. Jeffrey Cox, *British Missionary Enterprise* (New York: Routledge, 2008), 105–06.

33. Charlotte Brontë, *Jane Eyre* [1847] (New York, 2001), 299, 304, 355–56.

34. *Oxford English Dictionary Online* (2008), s.v. "romance."

35. Robert Young, *Martyr Islands* (Edinburgh, 1889), 19–21; [Herman Merivale], "Christianity in Melanesia," *Quarterly Review*, 95 (June 1854): 180; Norman Etherington, "Missions and Empire," in Robin W. Winks, ed., *Oxford History of the British Empire*, 5 (New York: Oxford University Press, 1999): 312.

36. Vanessa Smith, *Literary Culture and the Pacific* (Cambridge: Cambridge University Press, 1998), 83; Nicholas Thomas, "Force of Ethnology," *Current Anthropology*, 30 (February 1989): 31.

37. J.F. Pullen, "Some Notes Made During Two Seasons in New Guinea" [1885–1886], 3: Royal Geographical Society Archives, London, J.MSS. 13/233.

38. Rev. Samuel McFarlane, *Among the Cannibals* (London, 1888), 36–37; Peggy Brock, "New Christians as Evangelists," in Norman Etherington, ed., *Missions and Empire* (Oxford: Oxford University Press, 2005), 141; Norman Goodall, *History of the London Missionary Society* (London: Oxford University Press, 1954), 421.

39. W.P. Livingston, *Mary Slessor* (London: Hodder and Stoughton, 1915), 1–17, 57–67; A.J. Streeter, *Mill-Girl Who Conquered Cannibals* (London: London Missionary Society, 1925[?]), 4, 6–7; Clare Midgley, "Can Women Be Missionaries?," *Journal of British Studies*, 45 (April 2006): 335–58.

40. *The Times* [London] (18 September 1861).

41. David Cargill, *Diaries and Correspondence*, ed. Albert J. Schütz (Canberra: Australian National University Press, 1977), 16–17; Gavin Daws, *Dream of Islands* (New York: W.W. Norton, 1980), 52.

42. K.R. Howe, *Where the Waves Fall* (Honolulu: University of Hawai'i Press 1984), 94.

43. John D. Mahoney, "Blood of Martyrs," in Frank Hoare, ed., *Mission and Ministry* (Samabula, Fiji: Columban Fathers, 1994), 40–41.

44. Louis M. Raucaz, *Savage South Solomons* (Dublin: M.H. Gill, 1928), 32–36; *Sydney Morning Herald* (24 April 1846).

45. Livingstone and Livingstone, *Narrative of an Expedition*, 436–38.

46. Sione Lātūkefu, "Impact of South Sea Island Missionaries," in James A. Boutilier et al., eds., *Mission, Church, and Sect* (Ann Arbor, MI: University of Michigan Press, 1978), 92–95; Peter J. Hempenstall, *Pacific Islanders Under German Rule* (Canberra: Australian National University Press, 1978), 122–23; *Weekly Advocate* [Sydney] (28 September 1878), 205–06.

47. Helen B. Gardner, *Gathering for God* (Dunedin, NZ: Otago University Press, 2006), 67–74; *Sydney Mail* (15 February 1879).

48. Edith M.E. Baring-Gould, *Missionary Alphabet* (London, 1894), 35; Edward Reeves, *Brown Men and Women* (London, 1898), 281–83; *The Age* [Melbourne] (27 September 1878); George Brown, *George Brown, D.D.* (London: Hodder & Stoughton, 1908), 97; Wilfred Powell, *Wanderings* (London, 1884), 117–58; Rev. G. Brown to Sir A. Gordon, 5 July 1878: Special Collections, University of Auckland, WPHC 2/VI/12 (a); "Report of Enquiry into Action Taken by the Revd Geo. Brown Against Natives in New Britain," 21 September 1879, WPHC 4/IV/88/1879.

49. Susan Thorne has made this point convincingly. See her *Congregational Missions*, especially 4–5, 43, 55–56, and 156–57.

50. [Harriet Martineau], "Christian Missions," *Westminster Review*, n.s. 10 (July 1856): 35–36.

51. K. Theodore Hoppen, *Mid-Victorian Generation* (Oxford: Oxford University Press, 1998), 453–55; Bernard Porter, "'Empire, What Empire'?," 259–60; Jonathan Rose, *Intellectual Life* (New Haven, CT: Yale University Press, 2001), 347.

52. Richard D. Altick, *English Common Reader* (Chicago: University of Chicago Press, 1957), 102–05; Henry Mayhew, *London Labour* [1861–62], reprint ed. (New York: Dover Publications, 1968), 1: 24–39; Hugh McLeod, *Class and Religion* (Hamden, CT: Archon Books, 1974), 55–57.

53. Martha Loane, a district nurse whose work brought her into daily contact with the "respectable" poor, argued that church attendance was a misleading measure of religiosity: "Many of the poor rarely attend church, not because they are irreligious, but because they have long since received and absorbed the truths by which they live." Loane, *Queen's Poor* [1905], ed. Susan Cohen and Clive Fleay (London: Middlesex University Press, 1998), 27–30.

54. *Catalogue of the Missionary Museum, Austin Friars* (London, 1826), 1–3, 17–22; *Mansell's Guide to the Amusements of London for 1847* (London, 1847), n.p. The LMS's Missionary Museum, which opened in 1814 as a display of "curiosities" for supporters of the foreign field, grew over the next half century into an important repository of ethnographic treasures. Its Tahitian collection was especially praised. On such collections as sites that helped to produce "tacit consent for . . . the imperial project," see Annie E. Coombes, *Reinventing Africa* (New Haven, CT: Yale University Press, 1994), 161, 168, 170.

55. Benjamin T. Butcher, *We Lived with Headhunters* (London: Hodder & Stoughton, 1963), 15–16.

56. *Children's Bible and Missionary Box* (January 1854), 1–2, 6–7; *Gleanings for the Young* (January 1878), 2; ibid. (February 1880), 18. On the financial contribution of children to overseas missions, see Prochaska, *Women and Philanthropy* (Oxford: Oxford University Press, 1980), 75–77, 81–86.

57. Robert Newton Young, *Church and the Children* (London, 1860), pp. 3–4, 10, 16; "Juvenile Missionary Meeting at Exeter Hall," *Missionary Magazine and Chronicle* [hereafter, *Chronicle of the LMS*] (May 1842), 246–48.

58. Niel Gunson, *Messengers of Grace* (Melbourne, Australia: Oxford University Press, 1978), 47–48; Doreen M. Rosman, *Evangelicals and Culture* (London: Croom Helm, 1984), 20–21.

59. T[homas] H[aweis], "Very Probable Success of a Proper Mission," *Evangelical Magazine*, 3 (July 1795): 261–70; John Campbell, *Maritime Discovery* (London, 1840), 202–04.

60. Greg Dening, *Islands and Beaches* (Honolulu: University Press of Hawai'i, 1980), 95, 97–98; Charles Henry Robinson, *History of Christian Missions* (New York: Charles Scribner's Sons, 1923), 447–48; Cox, *British Missionary Enterprise*, 82–84.

61. John O. Choules and Thomas Smith, *Origin and History of Missions*, 2 vols., 6th ed. (Boston, 1842), 1: 394–400; A.W. Murray, *Martyrs of Polynesia*, 9–15. For the story of one LMS agent who tried to "go native" on Tonga, see Michelle Elleray, "Crossing the Beach," *Victorian Studies*, 47 (Winter 2005): 164–73.

62. James Miall, *Congregationalism in Yorkshire* (London, 1868), 176–78.

63. Richard Lovett, *History of the London Missionary Society*, 2 vols. (London, 1889), 1: 98.

64. Ibid., 81–83, 213.

65. Anon., "Voyage of His Majesty's Ship *Blonde*," *Quarterly Review*, 35 (March 1827): 439; Daniel Tyerman and George Bennet, *Journal of Voyages and Travels*, 2 vols. (London, 1831), 2: 86–88; Otto von Kotzebue, *New Voyage Round the World*, 2 vols. (London, 1830), 1: 168, 170.

66. Anon., "Narrative of a Voyage to the Pacific," *Edinburgh Review*, 53 (March 1831): 217–18; Kotzebue, *New Voyage*, 1: 172–75; Louis B. Wright and Mary Isabel Fry, *Puritans in the South Seas* (New York: Henry Holt, 1936), 230–31.

67. W.T. Pritchard, *Polynesian Reminiscences* [1866], reprint ed. (London: Dawsons of Pall Mall, 1968), 25–31, 47–49; Rev. M. Russell, *Polynesia*, 3rd ed. (Edinburgh, 1845), 112–13; William Orme, *Defence of the Missions* (London, 1827), 17–19; William Ellis, *Vindication of the South Sea Missions* (London, 1831), 76.

68. Charles Darwin, *Diary of the Voyage of H.M.S. Beagle*, ed. Nora Barlow, *Works of Charles Darwin*, vol. 1 (London: William Pickering, 1986), entry for 22 November 1835, 323–24; George French Angas, *Polynesia* (London, 1866), 291.

69. Henry P. Van Dusen, *They Found the Church* (New York: Charles Scribner's Sons, 1945), 91–93.

70. Lovett, *History of the LMS*, 1: 239.

71. Dening, *Islands and Beaches*, 170; Gunson, *Messengers of Grace*, 46; quotes are from Pierre Bourdieu, *Distinction* (Cambridge, MA: Harvard University Press, 1984), 316.

72. Smiles, *Duty*, 300; Norman J. Davidson, *John Williams* (New York: George H. Doran, 1925), 9–11; Lovett, *History of the LMS*, 1: 238–39; Anna Johnston, *Missionary Writing* (Cambridge: Cambridge University Press, 2003), 119–20.

73. Daws, *Dream of Islands*, 30–31; William Cowper, "The Task" [1785], in *The Poems of William Cowper*, vol. 2, ed. John D. Baird and Charles Ryskamp (Oxford: Clarendon Press, 1995), Book I, 133.

74. Smiles, *Duty*, 301; Davidson, *John Williams*, 16; Moister, *Missionary Martyrs*, 139–40.

75. Williams to LMS headquarters, 30 September 1823, as quoted in Gunson, *Messengers of Grace*, 145.

76. As quoted in Lovett, *History of the LMS*, 1: 249.

77. John Williams, *Narrative of Missionary Enterprises* (London, 1837), 18.

78. Ibid., 143, 148–49.

79. A. Buzzacott, *Mission Life* (London, 1866), 32–33.

80. Williams, *Missionary Enterprises*, 144–45.

81. William Ellis, *Polynesian Researches*, 2 vols. (London, 1829), 1: viii; Williams, *Missionary Enterprises*, 133–34; Buzzacott, *Mission Life*, 52–54.

82. Ebenezer Prout, *Memoirs of the Life of . . . John Williams* (New York, 1843), 299–300.

83. Ibid., 290–91, 276–79, 280–83, 294–95; James Sibree, *Fifty Years' Recollections* (Hull, UK, 1884), 67–69; James J. Ellis, *John Williams: Martyr Missionary* (London: S.W. Partridge, [1900]), 124–25.

84. Newcastle Auxiliary of the LMS, minutes for 13 July 1836, CWM Auxiliary Records/Box 1, S.O.A.S. archives, London; *Chronicle of the LMS* (June 1836), 5–8.

85. George Cousins, *Story of the South Seas* (London, 1894), 125–26; S.C. on Aborigines (British Settlements), P.P., 1836, VII: qq. 5708–10.

86. Prout, *Memoirs*, 319.

87. Typescript letter from Sir Charles Lyell to Dr. John Pye, 2 June 1837: CWM/Home/South Seas Personal/Box 2/ Folder 11, S.O.A.S. archives; Williams, *Missionary Enterprises*, vii–viii; Christopher Herbert, *Culture and Anomie* (Chicago: University of Chicago Press, 1991), 162–64; Johnston, *Missionary Writing*, 139–40. If John Williams was a proto-anthropologist, he was a strange one. Friends invited to dine with the missionary and his wife often watched as Williams "arrayed his own portly person in the native tiputa and mat, fixed a spear by his side, and adorned his head with the towering cap of many colours, worn on high days by the chiefs." Thus decked out, he "marched up and down his parlor . . . as happy as any one of the guests," Prout, *Memoirs*, 323.

88. Manuscript draft of a letter from Williams to the Duchess of Kent, no date: CWM/Home/South Seas Personal/Box 2/Folder 6, S.O.A.S. archives.

89. Williams, *Missionary Enterprises*, 7, 502.

90. Prout, *Memoirs*, 324, 333–35; *Oxford Dictionary of National Biography* (2004), s.v. "Williams, John."

91. Rev. John Williams, "Missionary's Return," in *The Pastoral Echo: Nineteen Sermons* (London, 1837) 238, 244–45.

92. [Harriet Martineau], "Christian Missions," 3–4.

93. *Missionary's Farewell* (London, 1838), x.

94. Ibid., 104–05.

95. *Chronicle of the LMS* (May 1838), 67–69; *John Williams, The Missionary* (London, 1849), 31–32; John S. Moffat, *Lives of Robert & Mary Moffat* (London, 1885), 225.

96. *Chronicle of the LMS* (April 1839), 60–61; ibid., (January 1840), 3–5.

97. Moister, *Missionary Martyrs*, 151–52; Lovett, *History of the LMS*, 1: 376.

98. Williams, *Missionary Enterprises*, 291–92.

99. Dorothy Shineberg, *They Came for Sandalwood* (Carlton, Victoria, Australia: Melbourne University Press, 1967), 205–07.

100. *Chronicle of the LMS* (June 1840), 81–82; [Rev. George Turner?], "Eromanga": CWM/Home/South Seas Personal/Box 1/Folder 9, S.O.A.S. archives.

101. Sujit Sivasundaram, "Shedding the Body," in Rosemary Seton, ed., *A Mission for the Future* (London: Religious Archives Group, 2000), 21–23; Bernard Smith, *European Vision*, 2nd ed. (New Haven, CT: Yale University Press, 1985), 318–21.

102. William Clark, "William Clark's Journal," entry for 2 December 1839: Phillips Library, M656 1838v, Peabody Essex Museum, Salem, MA.

103. *Evangelical Magazine* (July 1840), 332–33; *Chronicle of the LMS* (June 1840), 89; *Leeds Mercury* (11 April 1840).

104. Constance Gordon-Cumming, *A Lady's Cruise*, 2 vols. (Edinburgh, 1882), 1: 237–38; Cousins, *Story of the South Seas*, 132.

105. Newcastle Auxiliary of the LMS, minutes for 23 July 1840: CWM Auxiliary Records/Box 1, S.O.A.S archives; *Chronicle of the LMS* (December 1842), 187–89.

106. John Campbell, *Martyr of Erromanga*, 226–27; Smiles, *Self-Help*, 176–77; Rod Edmond, *Representing the South Pacific*, 146–47, 149–50; Robert Steel, *The New Hebrides and Christian Missions* (London, 1880), 194–203; *Reformed Presbyterian Magazine* (1 February 1873), 39–41; George Platt to William Ellis, 12 April 1840, as quoted in Gunson, *Messengers of Grace*, 61.

107. Alfred Lord Tennyson, *In Memoriam* [1850] (London, 1880), verse xxxvi, 79.

108. Diary of Thomas Baker, 18 February 1859: Fiji Museum Library, Suva, BV3680.F5.B3. This is a typescript copy of the manuscript original, located in Sydney's Mitchell Library (MOM 222). All subsequent citations refer to the Suva copy.

109. Charles Dickens, *Bleak House* [1852–53] (London: Macmillan, 1924), chap. 4. Similarly, see W. Winwood Reade, "Efforts of Missionaries Among Savages," *Journal of the Anthropological Society of London*, 3 (1865): 163–83. Reade warned, "When you subscribe your guinea to a foreign mission, you defraud some starving Englishman of that money" (168).

110. "Saints of Exeter Hall—Their Cannibal-Civilizing Societies," *Reynolds' Weekly Newspaper* (22 May 1859).

111. Sir Edward Belcher, *Narrative of a Voyage Round the World*, 2 vols. (London, 1843), 2: 53.

112. James Watkins, "Appeal to the Sympathy of the Christian Public" [1838], as quoted in Laurel May Heath, "*Matai-ni-mate*," unpub. Ph.D. thesis, Department of History, Queensland University, 1987, 2; "Extract of a Letter from the Rev. David Cargill," *Wesleyan-Methodist Magazine*, 3rd series, 18 (October 1839): 860.

113. Gunson, *Messengers of Grace*, 334.

114. Diary of Thomas Baker, 4 May 1859.

115. As quoted in G. Elsie Harrison, *Methodist Good Companions* (London: Epworth Press, 1935), 88. On Bunting's "surfeit of disciplinary zeal," see E.P. Thompson, *Making of the English Working Class* (New York: Vintage Books, 1963), 352–54.

116. William Peirce, *Ecclesiastical Principles* (London, 1854), 41–42.

117. "Missionary Among the Cannibals," *Monthly Religious Magazine*, 25 (March 1861): 154–55; Rev. Thomas Jaggar [?], manuscript diary, 11 September 1844: Mitchell Library, MOM 337.

118. Charles W. Rigg, *Digest of the Laws and Regulations* (Sydney, Australia, 1863), 191; Berthold Seeman, *Viti* [1862], reprint ed. (Folkestone, Kent, UK: Dawsons of Pall Mall, 1973), 32–33; W.T. Pritchard, *Polynesian Reminiscences*, 266–69.

119. Stephen Koss, "Wesleyanism," *Historical Journal*, 18 (March 1975): 105, 110–11; Waterhouse to Eggleston, 24 January 1861: Mitchell Library, MOM 98; G.R.C. Herbert and G.H. Kingsley, *South Sea Bubbles* [1872], 5th ed. (London: Macmillan, 1911), 297–98.

120. David Hempton, *Methodism* (New Haven, CT: Yale University Press, 2005), 155–56.

121. Stanley, *Bible and the Flag*, 112; [C.W. Hope], "Sketches in Polynesia," *Blackwood's Edinburgh Magazine*, 106 (July 1869): 40; William Moister, *History of Wesleyan Missions*, 3rd ed. (London, 1871), 545; A.B. Brewster, *Hill Tribes of Fiji* [1922], reprint ed. (New York: Johnson Reprint, 1967), 141.

122. Rev. Walter Lawry, *Friendly and Feejee Islands* (London, 1850), 141–42.

123. Diary of Thomas Baker, prefatory account dated "August 1860." For the visceral impact of early Methodist teaching, see Phyllis Mack, *Heart Religion* (Cambridge: Cambridge University Press, 2008).

124. Diary of Thomas Baker, entries for 25 October 1857, 28 October 1857, 1 October 1858, and 5 October 1858; Peirce, *Ecclesiastical Principles*, 102–03.

125. Diary of Thomas Baker, entries for 10 October 1858 and 18 October 1858; Eggleston to the Fijian District Meeting, 11 April 1859: Mitchell Library, MOM 32.

126. Baker to Eggleston, December 1859: Mitchell Library, MOM 165; Diary of Thomas Baker, entries for May 1860 and 25 July 1860.

127. Diary of Thomas Baker, 3 November 1862.

128. Alfred Harold Wood, *Overseas Missions of the Australian Methodist Church*, vol. 2 (Melbourne: Aldersgate Press, 1978): 159; Diary of Thomas Baker, 20 July 1866.

129. Diary of Thomas Baker, 15 June 1866.

130. Ibid., 31 July 1866; Rigg, *Digest of the Laws and Regulations*, 187.

131. Rabone to Baker, 12 July 1867: Mitchell Library, MOM 35.

132. Rev. Joseph Waterhouse, *King and People of Fiji* [1866], reprint ed. (New York: AMS, 1978), 11; J.B. Thurston, diary, "First Expedition Across Fiji (1865)": Royal Geographical Society Archives, London, LMS (116) T.10.

133. Typescript copy of Baker's last letter to his wife, 19 July 1867, appended to the Diary of Thomas Baker, 96. For the redacted version of this letter, see *Wesleyan Missionary Notices* (26 December 1867), 12–13.

134. "Massacre and Cannibalism at Fiji," *Illustrated Australian News* (26 October 1867), 7.

135. [Hope], "Sketches in Polynesia," 45; Herbert and Kingsley, *South Sea Bubbles*, 299–300; H. Britton, *Fiji in 1870*, 2nd ed. (Melbourne, 1870), 45.

136. In "The Whale Tooth" (1908), Jack London transforms Thomas Baker into "John Starhurst" and Nawawabalavu into "the Buli of Gatoka."

137. *Fijian Weekly News and Planters' Journal* (3 October 1868), 1; A.J. Small, "Story of the Navosa Tragedy," *Transactions of the Fijian Society* (1909), 37; Nicholas Thomas, *Islanders* (New Haven, CT, 2010), 245–46; Robert Nicole, *Disturbing History* (Honolulu: University of Hawai'i Press, 2011), 16.

138. R.A. Derrick, *History of Fiji*, 3rd ed. (Suva, Fuji: Government Press, 1957), 165, n.25; Brewster, *Hill Tribes of Fiji*, 30–31; Jane Samson, "Ethnology and Theology," in Brian Stanley, ed., *Christian Missions* (Grand Rapids, MI: William B. Eerdmans, 2001), 120.

139. Rev. Tevita Baleiwaqa, "Baker Luck," *Fiji Times* (15 July 1995); George W. Stocking, *Victorian Anthropology* (New York: Free Press, 1987), 87–88.

140. *Illustrated Australian News* (26 October 1867), 7; *The Times* (17 December 1867).

141. L. McHugh, "Memoirs of Rev. A.J. Small, Fiji 1879–1925," 21: Mitchell Library, ML MSS 3598; the poem is from J.F.H., "Navosah" (1868): Mitchell Library, MOM 520.

142. Britton, *Fiji in 1870*, 46; the dirge is in Brewster, *Hill Tribes of Fiji*, 26.

143. *Wesleyan Missionary Notices* (25 January 1868), 30–31; Rev. J. Horsley to Rev. S. Rabone, 20 April 1868: Mitchell Library, MOM 98; Derrick, *History of Fiji*, 165.

144. Jane Samson, *Imperial Benevolence* (Honolulu: University of Hawai'i Press, 1998), 112–13; Constance F. Gordon-Cumming, *At Home in Fiji*, 2 vols., 2nd ed. (Edinburgh, 1881), 1: 8.

145. *Fiji Times* (23 July 1870); *Sydney Morning Herald* (27 August 1870); A.B. Brewster, *King of the Cannibal Isles* (London: Robert Hale, 1937), 118–19.

146. *Report of the Wesleyan-Methodist Missionary Society, for the Year Ending April, 1873* (Sydney, 1873), 114–15; Journal of Rev. J. Watkins, entry for 28 September 1867: Mitchell Library, ML A 835. Confusingly, the place names associated with Thomas Baker's death are often treated as interchangeable. "Navosa" should refer to a large province in west-central Viti Levu. "Navatusila" (sometimes just "Vatusila") is both an interior district of Navosa and, in the nineteenth century, a collective name for the people who lived there. Four main villages today comprise the Navatusila district: Mare, Nabutautau, Nanoko, and Nasauvakarua.

147. McHugh, "Memoirs of Rev. A.J. Small," 21; [Arthur Gordon], "An Account of Mr. Walter Carew's Tour of the Island of Viti Levu" (privately printed, n.d. [1876?]), 6; James Edge Partington, *Random Rot* (Manchester, 1883), 75.

148. Next to the boot fragments and the ordination Bible rests the "Dish in which some of Mr. Baker's flesh was presented to one of the highland chiefs." Like much of what could be called "Bakeralia," the provenance of this object is dubious.

149. Brewster, *Hill Tribes*, 27. For the "well-worn story" that one highland chief mistook Baker's boots for his skin, see Basil Thomson, *The Fijians* (London: William Heinemann, 1908), 107, n.1.

150. Brewster, *Hill Tribes*, 98; Rev. William Bennett, "Report Read at the Opening of the Baker Memorial, 14th October, 1913," 3: Fiji National Archives, Suva, Bennett Papers, M/103a.

151. *Fiji Sun* [Suva] (26 October 2006); *Daily Post* [Suva] (16 October 2003).

152. Patrick Barkham, "136 Years On, Fiji Says Sorry for Its Cannibal Past," *The Times* (15 October 2003); *Fiji Sun* (14 November 2003); *Fiji Times* (14 November 2003); *Sunday Times* [Suva] (16 November 2003).

153. *Sunday Post* [Suva] (23 November 2003).

154. "John Coleridge Patteson," *The Nation* [New York] (8 April 1875), 244–45.

155. *Oxford Dictionary of National Biography* (2004), s.v. "Patteson, Sir John"; and "Coleridge, Sir John Taylor."

156. C.S.R., "Bishop Patteson-In Memoriam" *The Spectator* (13 January 1872), 44; Elizabeth Grierson, *Bishop Patteson* (London: Seeley, Service, 1932), 21; Jesse Page, *Bishop Patteson* (London, 1891), 29–31.

157. Charlotte M. Yonge, *Life of John Coleridge Patteson*, 2 vols. (London, 1874), 1: 122–23; Sir John Gutch, *Martyr of the Islands* (London: Hodder & Stoughton, 1971), 20–21.

158. Anon., *The Island Mission* (London, 1869), 83–85; Yonge, *Life of Patteson*, 1: 161–62, 180–81; E.S. Armstrong, *History of the Melanesian Mission* (New York: E.P. Dutton, 1900), 23–24.

159. Andrew Porter, *Religion Versus Empire?* (Manchester: Manchester University Press, 2004), 160–61; [Merivale], "Christianity in Melanesia," 193–95.

160. G.A. Selwyn to William Selwyn, Epiphany 1848: Selwyn College Archives, Cambridge University, Selwyn Papers, 6.25.C.

161. Selwyn to Edward Coleridge, 21 August 1849, as quoted in Darrell Whiteman, *Melanesians and Missionaries* (Pasadena, CA: William Carey Library, 1983), 106–07.

162. C.E. Fox, *Lord of the Southern Isles* (London: A.R. Mowbray, 1958), 9; Yonge, *Life of Patteson*, 1: 273–74.

163. Armstrong, *History of the Melanesian Mission*, 14.

164. Yonge, *Life of Patteson*, 1: 439.

165. Anon., *Island Mission*, 188–89; John Coleridge Patteson, *Abiding Comforter* (Auckland, New Zealand, 1871), 8.

166. *Report of the Melanesian Mission for 1861–1862*, 19.

167. Fox, *Lord of the Southern Isles*, 16; Rev. Walter G. Ivens, *Hints to Missionaries* (London: Melanesian Mission, 1907), 21.

168. Yonge, *Life of Patteson*, 1: 289–91; Armstrong, *History of the Melanesian Mission*, 48–50.

169. Gutch, *Martyr of the Islands*, 92–93; Anon., *Island Mission*, 89–102; Whiteman, *Melanesians and Missionaries*, 122.

170. David Hilliard, *God's Gentlemen* (St. Lucia, Queensland, Australia: University of Queensland Press, 1978), 35–37; Patrick Harries, "Anthropology," in Etherington, ed., *Missions and Empire*, 243; Paul Landau, "Language," in ibid., 201.

171. Patteson to his uncle, March 1866, as quoted in Yonge, *Life of Patteson*, 2: 167.

172. Hilliard, *God's Gentlemen*, 57–58; Patteson's diary for 1 August 1861, as quoted in Yonge, *Life of Patteson*, 1: 531–32.

173. Patteson to his sisters Joan and Fanny, 23 September 1869, as quoted in Yonge, *Life of Patteson*, 2: 272–73.

174. *Auckland Church Gazette* (March 1873), 8; *Southern Cross Log* (February 1897), 5.

175. Fox, *Lord of the Southern Isles*, 124–25; H.H. Montgomery, *Light of Melanesia* (London, 1896), 44–47. It was primarily through Mota that R.H. Codrington acquired his knowledge of Melanesian societies. *Mana*, a Mota word, became one of the organizing concepts in Pacific anthropology. On George Sarawia's role as a teacher of the Mota language, see Jane Samson, "Translation Teams," in Patricia Grimshaw and Andrew May, eds., *Missionaries, Indigenous Peoples and Cultural Exchange* (Brighton, UK: Sussex Academic Press, 2010), 96–109.

176. Patteson to his sister Fanny, 27 August 1864, as quoted in Yonge, *Life of Patteson*, 2: 99–101.

177. Patteson to Selwyn, 27 September 1870, as quoted in Yonge, *Life of Patteson*, 2: 460–61.

178. Typescript copy of "A Letter from the Right Rev. John Coleridge Patteson, D.D. to ***," 11 November 1862: Keble Papers, Deposit 8/5, Lambeth Palace Library, London.

179. Patteson to Selwyn, 16 November 1867, as quoted in Yonge, *Life of Patteson*, 2: 289–90; "Bishop Patteson on the Polynesian Labour Trade," printed pamphlet marked "Norfolk Island, January 11, 1871": Tait Papers, 186, ff. 145–47, Lambeth Palace Library.

180. *Mission Field* (1 February 1872), 35–43; ibid. (1 March 1872), 66–72; Brooke as quoted in A.H. Markham, *Cruise of the "Rosario"* [1873], reprint ed. (Folkestone, Kent: Dawsons of Pall Mall, 1970), 65–66.

181. *Mission Field* (1 February 1872), 40–41.

182. Brooke quoted in *New Zealand Church News* (December 1871), 33–34; Codrington quoted in *Mercury* [Hobart] (18 November 1871); Fison quoted in *Sydney Morning Herald* (18 November 1871).

183. *Melanesian Mission Report, 1872*, 6–7; Codrington to Gerland, 31 December 1874: Codrington Letters, MSS. Pac. s. 4, Rhodes House Library, Oxford University; *Melanesian Mission Report, 1884*, 3–4. For well-reasoned doubts about blackbirding as the underlying cause of Patteson's murder, see Thorgeir Kolshus and Even Hovdhaugen, "Reassessing the Death," *Journal of Pacific History*, 45 (December 2010): 331–55.

184. *Melanesian Mission Report, 1905*, 7; *Proceedings of the General Conference on Foreign Missions* (London, 1879), 268–69; W.C. O'Ferrall, *Santa Cruz and the Reef Islands* (London: Melanesian Mission, n.d.), unpaginated; Hilliard, *God's Gentlemen*, 186.

185. Although Bishop Patteson was murdered on Nukapu, located in the Reef Islands group, several prominent reports misidentified the killing field as "Santa Cruz." The latter became a synecdoche for savagery in the late-Victorian Pacific. See, for example, *The Times* (27 November 1871); *Annual Register for 1871* (London, 1872), 158–59; *The Graphic* [London] (6 January 1872), 14; and *Illustrated London News* (2 December 1871), 519.

186. Clements R. Markham, *Commodore J.G. Goodenough* (Portsmouth, UK, 1876), 6–8, 11–12, 16–18, 27–28, 55–56.

187. Rev. Algernon Stanley, *In Memoriam* (London, 1876), 10–14; Victoria Goodenough, *Life of Love and Duty* (London, 1891), 99–101.

188. *Fiji Times* (22 November 1871); *New Zealand Herald* [Auckland] (1 November 1871); *Sydney Morning Herald* (7 November 1871); *Argus* [Melbourne] (16 and 25 November 1871).

189. Gladstone to the Bishop of Lichfield, November 1871: B.L., Gladstone Papers, Add. MSS., 44540; [W.E. Gladstone], "Life of John Coleridge Patteson," *Quarterly Review*, 137 (October 1874): 492; *Gladstone Diaries*, ed. H.C.G. Matthew, vol. 9, entry for 14 November 1878 (Oxford, 1986), 362.

190. Queen Victoria's journal, entry for 30 November 1874: Royal Archives, Windsor Castle, Berkshire.

191. *The Times* (19 February 1872); Max F. Müller, "Lecture on Missions" [3 December 1873], in Müller, *Chips from a German Workshop*, 5 vols. (New York, 1890), 4: 253–54.

192. *Parliamentary Debates*, 3rd series, 209 (6 February 1872): 3.

193. Ibid., 211 (3 May 1872): 185–86.

194. "A Lady," poem entitled "Bishop Patteson" and dated 25 April 1872: Selwyn College Archives, Cambridge University. See also [Thomas Williamson], "In Memoriam: Bishop Patteson" (Rugby, Warwickshire, UK, 1872); H.A.S., *A Martyr-Bishop of Our Own Day* (London, 1881[?]); Jackson Mason, *In Memoriam: J.C. P*[atteson] (London, 1871).

195. Undated letter from Miss Frances Patteson to the Master of Selwyn College: Patteson Papers, Selwyn College Archives, Cambridge University; John M. MacKenzie, *Propaganda and Empire* (Manchester: Manchester University Press, 1984), 230; Charles E. Fox, *Kokamora* (London: Hodder & Stoughton, 1962), 10–11; Julian Thomas, *Cannibals and Convicts* (London, 1886), 40–41.

196. Nicholas Thomas, *Colonialism's Culture* (Cambridge: Polity Press, 1994), 134–36. On the significance of Patteson's murder for Anglican missions, see David Hilliard, "John Coleridge Patteson," in J.W. Davidson and Deryck Scarr, eds., *Pacific Islands Portraits* (Wellington, New Zealand: A.H. & A.W. Reed, 1970), 199–200.

197. The quote "postcolonial disgrace" is from Thorne, *Congregational Missions*, 24; Rhonda Anne Semple, *Missionary Women* (Woodbridge, Suffolk, UK: Boydell Press, 2003), 234.

198. Samson, "Ethnology and Theology," 120–21.

199. Ivens, *Hints to Missionaries*, 20.

200. James S. Dennis, *Centennial Survey* (New York: Fleming H. Revell, 1902), 257–60; Andrew Porter, "Religion and Empire," 372.

201. Charles W. Forman, "Foreign Missions in the Pacific," in Boutilier et al., eds., *Mission, Church, and Sect*, 38–39.

202. Richard Price, *Making Empire* (Cambridge: Cambridge University Press, 2008), 97. On the role of local informants in the accumulation of colonial knowledge, see Richard Drayton, "Knowledge and Empire," in P.J. Marshall, ed., *Oxford History of the British Empire*, 2: 231–52.

203. Daniel T. Hughes, "Mutual Biases," in Boutilier et al., eds., *Mission, Church, and Sect*, 65–66.

204. Michael W. Young, "Commemorating Missionary Heroes," in Ton Otto and Nicholas Thomas, eds., *Narratives of Nation* (Amsterdam: Harwood Academic, 1997), 93, 98; Nicholas Thomas, *Colonialism's Culture*, 62–63. In his extended preface to Frantz Fanon's *The Wretched of the Earth* (1961), Jean-Paul Sartre treated as self-evident the idea that "colonial aggression" had caused "natives" to turn their fear and fury inwards, further oppressing the oppressed. Selecting an image to capture what he saw as the Islanders' schizophrenic reality, Sartre invoked the religion of the missionaries: colonized peoples, he believed, felt compelled to "dance all night" honoring their traditional "idols," and then "at dawn . . . crowd into the churches to hear mass." Whatever its applicability to the Francophone colonies, Sartre's image of European religious influence bears little resemblance to what occurred in Britain's Melanesian territories. Fanon, *Wretched of the Earth* (New York: Grove Press, 1968), 18–20.

CHAPTER 3

1. Walter G. Ivens, *Dictionary and Grammar* (Washington, DC: Carnegie Institution, 1918), 198.

2. Jane Samson, *Imperial Benevolence* (Honolulu: University of Hawai'i Press, 1998), 40.

3. "An Act to Regulate and Control the Introduction and Treatment of Polynesian Laborers," Queensland, 31 Vict., no. 47.

4. *Sydney Morning Herald* (31 May 1869).

5. Ibid. (8 May 1869).

6. Hector Holthouse, *Cannibal Cargoes* (London: Angus & Robertson, 1969), 33–34; quotation from *Sydney Morning Herald* (31 May 1869); Thurston to Clarendon, 23 March 1869, Correspondence Respecting the Deportation of South Sea Islanders, P.P., 1868–69, XLIII [4222]: 50–51.

7. George Palmer, *Kidnapping* (Edinburgh, 1871), 51–53.

8. *Sydney Morning Herald* (26 May 1869 and 31 May 1869).

9. Ibid. (31 May 1869).

10. Belmore to Thurston, 10 March 1869, enclosure 1 in no. 31, P.P., 1868–69, XLIII [4222]: 52.

11. *Sydney Morning Herald* (23 June 1869).

12. Ibid. (28 June 1869); O.W. Parnaby, *Britain and the Labour Trade* (Durham, NC: Duke University Press, 1964), 20–21.

13. *Sydney Morning Herald* (8 May 1869 and 29 June 1869).

14. Belmore to Kimberley, 6 October 1871, Correspondence between the Governor of New South Wales and the Earl of Kimberley respecting certain statements made by Captain Palmer, P.P., 1872, XLIII [C. 479]: 7; Wal Bird, *Me No Go* (Charnwood, Australian Capital Territory: Ginninderra Press, 2005), 19.

15. *Regina v. Levinger, Reports of Cases Argued and Determined in the Supreme Court of Victoria,* 6 [1871]: 148–49.

16. Belmore to Kimberley, 6 October 1871, P.P., 1872, XLIII [C. 479]: 7.

17. Clarendon to March, 3 August 1869, Further Correspondence Respecting the Deportation of South Sea Islanders, P.P., 1871, XLVIII [C. 399]: 1–2.

18. For critical accounts of the *Young Australian* case published in major British newspapers during the summer and autumn of 1869, see especially *The Times* [London] (9 August 1869); *Glasgow Herald* (11 August 1869); *Liverpool Mercury* (8 September 1869); *Leeds Mercury* (8 September 1869 and 16 October 1869); *Western Mail* [Cardiff] (11 September 1869); and the *Daily News* [London] (11 September 1869).

19. Doug Munro, "Pacific Islands Labour Trade," *Slavery and Abolition,* 14 (August 1993): 88. This rough estimate takes into account not only indentured laborers but also free laborers, slaves, and convicts.

20. David Northrup, *Indentured Labor* (Cambridge: Cambridge University Press, 1995), 5–6.

21. For "coolies" in Queensland, see James L.A. Hope, *In Quest of Coolies* (London, 1872); and for Louisiana, see Moon-Ho Jung, *Coolies and Cane* (Baltimore, MD: Johns Hopkins University Press, 2006).

22. Known as "beech" or "beach le mare" by the Salem-based crews who dominated the trade during the 1820s and 30s, the names for this echinoderm were corruptions of the Portuguese *bicho do mar.*

23. Andrew Cheyne, *Description of Islands* (London, 1852), 58–60.

24. Berthold Seemann, *Viti* [1862], reprint ed. (Folkestone, Kent, UK: Dawsons of Pall Mall, 1973), 227–28; H.H. Romilly, *From My Verandah* (London, 1889), 259–60; R.G. Ward, "Pacific *Bêche-de-mer* Trade," in Ward, ed., *Man in the Pacific Islands* (Oxford: Clarendon Press, 1972), 106–08; *Journal of the "Clay,"* entry for 16 September 1827, Phillips Library, Peabody Essex Museum, Ms. 656 1827C; Mary Davis Wallis ["A Lady"], *Life in Feejee* (Boston, 1851), 135.

25. *Pacific Pearl Fishery Company* (London, 1825), 1–2; Frederick J. Moss, *Through Atolls* (London, 1889), 66–67; Romilly, *From My Verandah*, 268–69; W. Saville-Kent, *Naturalist in Australia* (London, 1897), 205–06; Stanley Wilson, "The Early Days of Pearling," typescript paper (1924), Mitchell Library Q 639.4/W.

26. John Moresby, *Discoveries & Surveys* (London, 1876), 24–27; Peter Corris, "'Blackbirding' in New Guinea Waters," *Journal of Pacific History*, 3 (1968): 86–87; Deryck Scarr, *Fragments of Empire* (Canberra: Australian National University Press, 1967), 119–20.

27. Albert Hastings Markham, *Cruise of the "Rosario"* [1873], reprint ed. (Folkestone, Kent: Dawsons of Pall Mall, 1970), 45–46.

28. Dorothy Shineberg, *They Came for Sandalwood* (Carlton, Victoria, Australia: Melbourne University Press, 1967), 62–63.

29. *Nautical Magazine and Naval Chronicle for 1850* (London, 1850), 427–28; George Patterson, *Missionary Life Among the Cannibals* (Toronto, 1882), 153–54.

30. Shineberg, *Sandalwood*, passim.

31. A.K. Langridge, *Conquest of Cannibal Tanna* (London: Hodder & Stoughton, [1934]), 47.

32. K.H. Kennedy, *Robert Towns' Townsville* (Townsville, Queensland, Australia: Townsville City Council, 2004), 58–59; W.P. Morrell, *Britain in the Pacific Islands* (Oxford: Clarendon Press, 1960), 93.

33. Bowen to Newcastle, 6 January 1860, Papers Relative to the Affairs of Queensland, P.P., 1861, XL [2890], no. 3.

34. Sven Beckert, "Emancipation and Empire," *American Historical Review*, 109 (December 2004): 1405.

35. George Wight, *Queensland*, 3rd ed. (London, 1863), 83, 85–87.

36. H. Britton, *Fiji in 1870*, 2nd ed. (Melbourne, Australia, 1870), 9, 11; *Fiji Times* (12 February 1870).

37. Thurston, "Report on . . . the Fiji Islands for 1866," P.P., 1871, XLVII [435], Appendix, 62–63.

38. Henry Ling Roth, *Report on the Sugar Industry* (Brisbane, Australia, 1880), 93–94; Adrian Graves, *Cane and Labour* (Edinburgh: Edinburgh University Press, 1993), 11. Roth estimated that in 1878, per capita sugar consumption in Australia was at least twenty-five percent higher than in England and Wales.

39. An Adelaide newspaper imagined the "unique specimen of humanity" that Queenslanders wanted toiling in their cane fields: "He must be lively and intelligent, hardworking and assiduous; but at the same time he must not be so enterprising as to endeavour, as the Chinese do, to slip the leading-strings of employers and immigration agents and go off to employments which are regarded as belonging of right to Europeans. He must, in short, be an industrious drudge." *The Register* (3 March 1883).

40. Hope, *In Quest of Coolies*, 4.

41. *Brisbane Courier* (12 January 1869); Wight, *Queensland*, 100–04; Warwick Anderson, "Climates of Opinion," *Victorian Studies*, 35 (Winter 1992): 136, 146–47; Dane Kennedy, "Perils of the Midday Sun," in John M. MacKenzie, ed., *Imperialism and the Natural World* (Manchester, UK: Manchester University Press,1990), 119–20.

42. J.H. Galloway, *Sugar Cane Industry* (Cambridge: Cambridge University Press, 1989), 229, 231–32; Kennedy, "Perils," 133–34.

43. [Flora Shaw], *Letters from Queensland* (London, 1893), 10–12; *Fiji Times* (4 June 1870).

44. R.F. Jeffray, "Queensland Planters," *Fortnightly Review*, o.s. 38 (September 1882): 307; Roth, *Report on the Sugar Industry*, 42–43.

45. *Brisbane Courier* (22 August 1863).

46. Ibid. (29 August 1863).

47. Governor Grey to Earl Grey, 10 March 1848, Further Papers relative to the affairs of New Zealand, P.P. 1847–48, XLIII [1002], no. 29 and enclosures.

48. Miller to Russell, 29 November 1862, Correspondence Respecting Removal of Inhabitants of Polynesian Islands to Peru, P.P., 1864, LXVI [3307], no. 11; H.E. Maude, *Slavers in Paradise* (Stanford, CA: Stanford University Press, 1981), 146–47, xix; Robert Short, *Slave Trade in the Pacific* (London, 1870), 8–9.

49. Robert Towns, *South Sea Island Immigration* (Sydney, Australia, 1863), 2.

50. Ibid., "To any Missionary into whose hands this may come," 8.

51. [Herman Merivale], "Christianity in Melanesia," *Quarterly Review*, 95 (June 1854): 176; W.B. Churchward, *"Blackbirding"* (London, 1888), 10–11; Samson, *Imperial Benevolence*, 24–25, 27, 32.

52. Edward W. Docker, *The Blackbirders* (Sydney: Angus & Robertson, 1970), 42; Maude, *Slavers in Paradise*, 113; *Brisbane Courier* (5 January 1869).

53. Reid Mortensen, "Slaving in Australian Courts," *Journal of South Pacific Law*, 4 (2000): 3; *Brisbane Courier* (5 January 1869).

54. *Brisbane Courier* (13 January 1869 and 16 January 1869); Palmer, *Kidnapping*, 108.

55. *Brisbane Courier* (5 January 1869); K.H. Kennedy, *Robert Towns' Townsville*, 47.

56. A.B. Brewster, *King of the Cannibal Isles* (London: Robert Hale, 1937), 227; O.W. Parnaby, "The Labour Trade," in R. Gerard Ward, ed., *Man in the Pacific Islands*, 132–33.

57. Markham, *Cruise of the "Rosario,"* 117.

58. Ibid., 111, 113–15; *Australian Town and Country Journal* [Sydney] (8 March 1873), 21; G.S. Searl, *Mount & Morris Exonerated* (Melbourne, 1875), 16, 37.

59. Tracey Banivanua-Mar, *Violence and Colonial Dialogue* (Honolulu: University of Hawai'i Press, 2007), 32–33.

60. Frank Clune, *Captain Bully Hayes* (London: Angus & Robertson, 1971), 6–7; Louis Becke, *Bully Hayes* [1913], 5th ed. (Sydney: New South Wales Bookstall, 1923), 29–32; "Re William Henry Hayes," 29 November 1871, enclosure 4 in no. 11, P.P., 1872, XLIII [C. 496]: 37.

61. *Sydney Morning Herald* (8 December 1875); *Parliamentary Debates* (Lords), 3rd series, 216 (3 July 1873): 693–94; *Fiji Times* (1 October 1870); *Samoa Times* (1 December 1877); Robert Louis Stevenson and Lloyd Osbourne, *The Wrecker* [1891]

(New York: Charles Scribner's Sons, 1912), 10–11; Thomas Dunbabin, *Slavers in the South Seas* (Sydney: Angus & Robertson, 1935), 223–24.

62. Deryck Scarr, "Recruits and Recruiters," in J.W. Davidson and Scarr, eds., *Pacific Islands Portraits* (Wellington, New Zealand: A.H. & A.W. Reed, 1970), 225–26; Jeff Siegel, "Origins of the Pacific Islands Labourers in Fiji," *Journal of Pacific History*, 20 (1985): Table 4, 46. Indian migrants were allowed to enter Fiji as agricultural workers starting in 1878. Over the next thirty-eight years, approximately 61,000 Indian "coolies" gradually replaced Melanesians in the sugarcane fields. Brij V. Lal, *Girmitiyas* (Canberra: *Journal of Pacific History*, 1983), 13.

63. Dorothy Shineberg, *People Trade* (Honolulu: University of Hawai'i Press, 1999), 4–5; Northrup, *Indentured Labor*, 78.

64. R.A. Derrick, *History of Fiji*, vol. 1, 3rd ed. (Suva, Fiji: Government Press, 1957), 170–71.

65. *Evangelical Magazine* (April 1838), 188.

66. Patrick Brantlinger, *Dark Vanishings* (Ithaca, NY: Cornell University Press, 2003), 90, 93. The Aborigines' Protection Society early on rejected both the "monstrous doctrine" that "coloured tribes" were incapable of improvement and the notion that Aboriginal extinction was inevitable. See *England and Her Colonies in Relation to the Aborigines* (London [1841]), 1–2.

67. *Aborigines' Friend* (May 1872), 41; APS *Annual Report for 1874* (London, 1875), 121; Charles Swaisland, "The Aborigines Protection Society, 1837–1909," *Slavery and Abolition*, 21 (August 2000): 266–67; James Heartfield, *The Aborigines' Protection Society* (New York: Columbia University Press, 2011), 39–41.

68. Graves, *Cane and Labour*, 138–39; Laurence Brown, "'A Most Irregular Traffic,'" in Emma Christopher et al., eds., *Many Middle Passages* (Berkeley: University of California Press, 2007), 187–88.

69. *Aborigines' Friend* (March 1868), 37–40; John Bach, *The Australia Station* (Kensington, Australia: New South Wales University Press, 1986), 78.

70. Martin Wiener, *Empire on Trial* (Cambridge: Cambridge University Press, 2009), 78; [Edward Knatchbull-Hugessen], "The Fiji Islands," *Edinburgh Review*, 136 (October 1872): 429–30.

71. *Hobart Town Mercury* (24 October 1881).

72. Patteson to Lady Stephen, 19 June 1869, Stephen Family Correspondence, Mitchell Library, ML Mss. 777/11; Extract of a letter from Patteson to Selwyn, 8 July 1871, B.L., Gladstone Papers, Add. Mss. 44299, ff. 181–82; *Fiji Times* (10 September 1870).

73. John Gaggin, *Among the Man-Eaters* (London: T. Fisher Unwin, 1900), 30–31; Deryck Scarr, *I, the Very Bayonet* (Canberra: Australian National University Press, 1973), 163–64; Palmer, *Kidnapping*, 76–77.

74. Rev. Oscar Michelsen, *Cannibals Won for Christ* (London [1893]), 133–34.

75. *Reformed Presbyterian Magazine* (1 February 1872), 77; Rev. John Kay, ed., *The Slave Trade* (Edinburgh, 1872), 11.

76. T.P. Lucas, *Cries from Fiji* (Melbourne [1884]), 65–66.

77. John Stuart Mill, *On Liberty* [1859] (Arlington Heights, IL: AHM, 1947), 9–10.

78. Short, *Slave Trade*, 15; quotation ("The horrid trick . . .") from *Argus* [Melbourne] (29 January 1884); R.H. Codrington, mss. "Journal of Voyage 1872," entry for 20 July 1872, S.O.A.S. Archives, Melanesian Mission Papers, Mel. M. 2/4, Box 9.

79. William T. Wawn, *The South Sea Islanders* [1893], ed. Peter Corris (Honolulu: University of Hawai'i Press, 1973), 12–13; Britton, *Fiji in 1870*, 15.

80. Hugh Laracy, review *of Passage, Port and Plantation,* in *Oceania,* 46 (December 1975): 165.

81. Peter Corris, *Passage* (Carlton, Victoria: Melbourne University Press, 1973), 29.

82. Scarr, *Fragments*, 150.

83. Munro, "Pacific Islands Labour Trade," 91; L. Brown, "'Most Irregular Traffic,'" 199–200; Ralph Shlomowitz, "Epidemiology," *Journal of Interdisciplinary History*, 9 (Spring 1989): 589–90; Scarr, "Recruits and Recruiters," 228.

84. E.P. Thompson, *Making of the English Working Class* (New York: Vintage Books, 1963), 9.

85. Corris, *Passage*, 59.

86. Ivens, *Dictionary*, 197; Wawn, *South Sea Islanders*, 10–11.

87. Adrian Graves, "Nature and Origins," in Shula Marks and Peter Richardson, eds., *International Labour Migration* (London: Maurice Temple Smith, 1984), 114.

88. Northrup, *Indentured Labor*, 72; Adrian Graves, "Truck and Gifts," *Past and Present*, 101 (November 1983): 88; Bishop John Selwyn to the *Guardian* (4 May 1892), as quoted in P.P., 1892, LVI [C. 6686]: 6–9.

89. Ivens, *Dictionary*, 227.

90. Shineberg, *People Trade*, 80–81.

91. L. Brown, "'Most Irregular Traffic,'" 185; David Eltis, "Introduction," in Eltis, *Coerced and Free Migration* (Stanford, CA: Stanford University Press, 2002), 6; P. Corris, "Kwaisulia of Ada Gege," in Davidson and Scarr, eds., *Pacific Islands Portraits*, 257–58.

92. Shineberg, *People Trade*, 83–85; Graves, *Cane and Labour*, 220; Munro, "Pacific Islands Labour Trade," 94; Banivanua-Mar, *Violence*, 45; Tom Brass, "The Return of 'Merrie Melanesia,'" *Journal of Pacific History*, 31 (December 1996): 215–16.

93. *Mission Field* (1 March 1873), 69.

94. Leefe to Gov. Gordon, mss. report on recruiting for Fiji, 28 February 1878, WPHC 4/IV/4/1878; Scarr, "Recruits and Recruiters," 245–46; Wiener, *Empire on Trial*, 75; Committee to Promote the Representation of the Colony . . . *of Fiji, 1880* (Levuka, Fiji, 1880), 75–78.

95. Wawn, *South Sea Islanders*, 124; Jeffray, "Queensland Planters," 299.

96. Parnaby, *Britain and the Labor Trade*, 201.

97. Corris, "'Blackbirding,'" 93–94; Scarr, "Recruits and Recruiters," 230–31; Michael Quinlan, "Australia, 1788–1902," in Douglas Hay and Paul Craven, eds., *Masters, Servants, and Magistrates* (Chapel Hill: University of North Carolina Press,

2004), 232–33; John Wisker, "Troubles in the Pacific," *Fortnightly Review*, 37 (June 1882), 729.

98. Shlomowitz, "Epidemiology," 610; Scarr, "Recruits and Recruiters," 230–31.

99. *A New English Dictionary on Historical Principles*, 7 (Oxford, 1905): s.v. "outrage."

100. Douglas Rannie, *My Adventures* (London: Seeley, Service, 1912), 151–53, 159–60.

101. Banivanua-Mar, *Violence*, 22–23.

102. X. Montrouzier to H. Montrouzier, January/February 1846, Archivo Padri Maristi, Rome. I thank Professor Hugh Laracy for this reference and its translation.

103. Kay Saunders, "The Middle Passage?," *Journal of Australian Studies*, 5 (1979): 38–49.

104. Walter Coote, *The Western Pacific* (London, 1883), 173–77.

105. Pacific Islands, vol. 1, *Sailing Directions* (London, 1885), 5–6.

106. Report of W. Usborne Moore, 7 November 1883, WPHC 8/II/56; J.B. Thurston, "Memorandum [on] . . . the New Hebrides," 1892, WPHC 8/II/35.

107. James Boutilier, "Killing the Government," in Margaret Rodman and Matthew Cooper, eds., *Pacification of Melanesia* (Ann Arbor: University of Michigan Press, 1979), 46.

108. "Papers Relating to Murder [aboard] the *Borealis*," 2–4 November 1880, WPHC 8/III/1.

109. "Correspondence Respecting Outrages by Natives on British Subjects," Tryon to the Assistant High Commissioner, Fiji, 3 July 1886, WPHC 8/III/15; Rannie, *My Adventures*, 195–203; Scarr, "Recruits and Recruiters," 240–41.

110. Rannie, *My Adventures*, 195–97; Tryon to the Assistant High Commissioner, Fiji, 3 July 1886, WPHC 8/III/15.

111. *Reformed Presbyterian Magazine* (1 February 1873), 39.

112. Markham, *Cruise of the "Rosario,"* 55; Bach, *Australia Station*, 41.

113. Samson, *Imperial Benevolence*, 130–31.

114. Brewster, *King of the Cannibal Isles*, 214–15.

115. *Sydney Morning Herald* (30 November 1880); *Sydney Daily Telegraph* (4, 6, and 11 December 1880, 17 January 1881); *Sydney Morning Herald* (21 August 1880, 30 September 1880, 2 December 1880).

116. *Sydney Daily Telegraph* (4 December 1880); Bower to Wilson, 24 May 1880, WPHC 4/IV/99/1880; *Hampshire Telegraph and Sussex Chronicle* (19 January 1881); *Liverpool Mercury* (27 December 1883); Coote, *Western Pacific*, 172.

117. Wisker, "Troubles in the Pacific," 724–25.

118. Scarr, *Fragments*, 115, 35.

119. G. William Des Voeux, *My Colonial Service*, 2 vols. (London: John Murray, 1903), 2: 90–91.

120. Wiener, *Empire on Trial*, 80; Morrell, *Britain in the Pacific Islands*, 334; High Commissioner's Court for the Western Pacific Criminal Jurisdiction, *Regina v. Kilgour*, 29 August 1879, WPHC 2/VIII/3.

121. *Regina v. Aratuga*, 5 April 1880, WPHC 2/VIII/7.

122. See, for example, the irate letter from "The Vagabond" (Julian Thomas) to the *Sydney Daily Telegraph* (11 December 1880).

123. W. Usborne Moore, "Report of Proceedings in the New Hebrides" (1883), WPHC 8/II/55.

124. Peter Corris, "Introduction" to Wawn, *South Sea Islanders*, xix–xx.

125. Palmer, *Kidnapping*, 162.

126. *The Times* (24 June 1873).

127. The Australian Courts Act of 1828 (9 George IV, c. 83, s. 4) permitted Australian supreme courts to "hear . . . all Treasons, Piracies, Felonies, Robberies, Murders, Conspiracies, and other Offences of what Nature or Kind soever" originating in uncolonized Indian and Pacific Ocean lands.

128. [Merivale], "Christianity in Melanesia," 177–78 (including the quotation "embarrass the march of justice"); John E. Erskine, *Journal of a Cruise Among the Islands* (London, 1853), 478–86.

129. See the Colonial Laws Validity Act of 1865: 28 & 29 Vict., c. 63.

130. *Sydney Morning Herald* (21 November 1871); *Brisbane Courier* (28 November 1871).

131. Palmer, *Kidnapping*, 182.

132. Hope, *In Quest of Coolies*, 3; Anthony Trollope, *Australia* [1873], ed. P.D. Edwards and R.B. Joyce (St. Lucia, Australia: University of Queensland Press, 1967), 175.

133. Gary Highland, "Aborigines, Europeans," *Aboriginal History,* 14 (1990): 188.

134. Ranajit Guha, "Chandra's Death," *Subaltern Studies,* 5 (1986): 140–41. For indictments of Britain's vaunted "rule of law" as a colonial smokescreen, see Karuna Mantena, *Alibis of Empire* (Princeton, NJ: Princeton University Press, 2010); and Jordanna Bailkin, "The Boot and the Spleen," *Comparative Studies in Society and History*, 48 (April 2006): 462–93.

135. Short, *Slave Trade*, 37–38.

136. Ibid., 39.

137. Sir James Martin, in *Regina v. Paddy, Reports of Cases Argued and Determined in the Supreme Court of New South Wales*, 14 [1876]: 440–44. As early as 1839, the Aborigines' Protection Society had denounced the exclusion of evidence from "native witnesses" at trial. Nancy E. Wright, "The Problem of Aboriginal Evidence," in Diane Kirkby and Catharine Coleborne, eds., *Law, History, Colonialism* (Manchester: Manchester University Press, 2001), 140.

138. By the Oaths Act Amendment Act of 1891: Queensland, 55 Vict., no. 14.

139. On the widespread confusion over Islanders' length of service, see especially testimony from the "boys" on the Hamleigh Sugar Plantation, Herbert River, 17 January 1885, qq. 201–401, Report . . . [of] the Royal Commission [on] . . . circumstances under which labourers have been introduced into Queensland, *Votes and Proceedings of the Queensland Legislative Assembly*, 1885, 2.

140. See the anti-kidnapping petition from Brisbane residents to the Queen, 16 January 1868, Further Correspondence [on] the Importation of South Sea Islanders, P.P., 1867–68, XLVIII [391][496]: enclosure 1 in no. 4.

141. Preamble to "An Act to Regulate and Control the Introduction and Treatment of Polynesian Laborers," as quoted in Charles A. Bernays, *Queensland Politics* (Brisbane: A.J. Cumming, 1920), 66.

142. Progress Report from the Select Committee on the Operation of "The Polynesian Laborers Act of 1868," *Votes and Proceedings of the Queensland Legislative Assembly*, 1869, 2: 5.

143. Short, *Slave Trade*, 22, 25–26, 60.

144. Mortensen, "Slaving in Australian Courts," 4.

145. Palmer, *Kidnapping*, 132. Captain Palmer was proceeding under the Slave Trade Amendment Act of 1824, 5 Geo. IV, c. 113.

146. *Sydney Morning Herald* (16, 23, 25, and 26 June 1869, 14 July 1869); *Daily News* [London] (11 September 1869); *Western Mail* [Cardiff] (11 September 1869); *The Times* (25 January 1870).

147. Julius Brenchley, *Jottings During the Cruise* (London, 1873), x.

148. In the Vice Admiralty Court, "The Daphne," *Reports of Cases Argued and Determined in the Supreme Court of New South Wales*, 10 [1872]: 37–48.

149. *R. and Loggie v. Casaca and Others*, *Law Times*, n.s. 43 (13 November 1880): 290–99.

150. Jesse Page, *Bishop Patteson* (London [1891]), 145.

151. *Parliamentary Debates*, 3rd series, 209 (6 February 1872): 3.

152. *The Times* (29 October 1871); *Argus* [Melbourne] (20 December 1871).

153. Selwyn to Gladstone, 27 November 1871, B.L., Gladstone Papers, Add. Mss., 44299, f. 175.

154. 35 & 36 Vict., c. 19, s. 9 (1).

155. "Abuses Connected with Polynesian Immigration," confidential report to the Cabinet, 27 January 1872, TNA, CO 881/3, 1–2.

156. Anon., "Pacific Islanders' Protection Bill," *Westminster Review*, n.s. 48 (July–October 1875): 78; Derrick, *History of Fiji*, 176; Shineberg, *People Trade*, 27.

157. *Imperial and Colonial Acts Relating to the Recruiting . . . of Pacific Island Labourers* (Brisbane, 1892), passim.

158. Bach, *Australia Station*, 61–62; Jeffray, "Queensland Planters," 298; Mackey Planters Association Minute Book, 1878–1885, as quoted in Banivanua-Mar, *Violence*, 27.

159. *Queensland Government Gazette* (11 February 1871), 202.

160. Deryck Scarr, "Introduction" to W.E. Giles, *A Cruize in a Queensland Labour Vessel* [c. 1880], reprint ed. (Canberra: Australian National University Press, 1968), 9.

161. Rannie, *My Adventures*, 23–24, 42–44.

162. John Renton, *Adventures of John Renton* (Kirkwall, Orkney, Scotland: W.R. Mackintosh, 1935), 61–62.

163. [Julian Thomas], *Cannibals and Convicts* (London, 1886), 349; Scarr, "Recruits and Recruiters," 238–39.

164. *Pall Mall Gazette* (5 August 1882).

165. Diary of schooner *Daphne*, 3 July 1876 (agent M. Murray); diary of schooner *Jessie Henderson*, 11 July 1876 (agent T. Andrews); diary of schooner *Windward Ho*, 4 June 1881 (agent G. L'Estrange); diary of schooner *Rotuma*, 28 September 1889 (agent F. Otway), Fijian National Archives.

166. J.C. Wilson, "Labour Trade in the Western Pacific," n.d. [1882], WPHC 8/III/48, 2.

167. Ibid., 3, 5.

168. John Inglis, *In the New Hebrides* (London, 1887), 212–15.

169. *Liverpool Mercury* (25 December 1884).

170. Clarke to Des Voeux, 10 August 1884; Des Voeux to Clarke, 18 August 1884, WPHC 8/III/11.

171. *Liverpool Mercury* (25 December 1884).

172. *Sydney Morning Herald* (9 April 1884); *R. v. Owners of the Forest King*, *Queensland Law Journal Reports*, 2 [1887]: 50–53.

173. Romilly to Des Voeux, 15 September 1883, WPHC 8/III/53, 8; *Pall Mall Gazette* (16 August 1884).

174. Romilly to Des Voeux, 15 September 1883, WPHC 8/III/11, 46–47; Parnaby, *Britain and the Labour Trade*, 94.

175. Corris, "'Blackbirding,'" 90–91.

176. *The Times* (24 September 1885); *Brisbane Courier* (2, 4, 5, and 8 December 1884).

177. Corris, "'Blackbirding,'" 93.

178. Bernays, *Queensland Politics*, 72–73.

179. Report . . . [of] the Royal Commission [on] . . . circumstances under which labourers have been introduced into Queensland (1885), *Votes and Proceedings of the Queensland Legislative Assembly*, 1885, xvii–xviii.

180. Bernays, *Queensland Politics*, 125.

181. Wawn, *South Sea Islanders*, 440.

182. Sir Samuel Griffith, "To the People of Queensland," *Brisbane Courier* (13 February 1892).

183. *Brisbane Courier* (23 March 1892).

184. Bishop John Selwyn to the *Guardian* (4 May 1892), as quoted in P.P., 1892, LVI [C. 6686]: 6–9; *The Times* (21 May 1892 and 5 January 1893); *Parliamentary Debates*, 4th series, 4 (16 May 1892): 969–72. After 1892, British New Guinea supervised its internal labor trade with notable care.

185. *The Times* (16 May 1892); *Sydney Telegraph* (29 December 1891); "Report of Solicitor to the Vice-Admiral, Fiji," 29 February 1892, WPHC 2/VI/14(a).

186. Commonwealth of Australia, statute no. 22 of 1906, section ix; Parnaby, *Britain and the Labour Trade*, 198; "Petition Signed by 3,000 Pacific Island Labourers Resident in Queensland," point eleven, P.P., 1902, LXVI [Cd. 1285]: 4. Enforcing

this mass exodus proved more difficult than the champions of a White Australia envisioned. When the Kanaka roundup ended in 1908, between 1,500 and 2,000 Islanders remained behind, some hiding in the Queensland bush. Clive Moore, "Kanakas, Kidnapping and Slavery," *Kabar Seberang*, 8–9 (July 1981): 78.

187. Ralph Shlomowitz, "Marx and the Queensland Labour Trade," *Journal de la Société des Océanistes*, 96 (1993): 16.

188. Corris, *Passage*, 147–48. The higher wages and more costly rations of the Indian "coolie" were partly offset by Fijian government subsidies.

189. British Solomon Islands, *Report to 30th June 1913*, P.P., 1914, LVIII [Cd. 7050–15]: 14–15.

190. Report from Commander Addington, 1902, WPHC 8/II/24, 49; British Resident Commissioner to British High Commissioner, 24 July 1913, NHBS 1/I/145/192.

191. Felix Speiser, *Two Years with the Natives* (London: Mills & Boon, 1913), 54; Shineberg, *People Trade*, 45; Glossop to Resident Commissioner, 6 July 1908, NHBS 1/I/11/1907.

192. Jack McLaren, *My Odyssey* (London: Ernest Benn, 1928), 162.

193. W.H.R. Rivers, "The Psychological Factor," in Rivers, ed., *Essays on the Depopulation of Melanesia* (Cambridge: Cambridge University Press, 1922), 106.

194. *Oxford Dictionary of National Biography*, 47 (2004), s.v. "Rivers, W.H.R."; quotation is from Rivers, "Psychological Factor," 104; Adam Kuper, *Invention of Primitive Society* (London: Routledge, 1988), 152–53.

195. A.I. Hopkins, *In the Isles of King Solomon* (London: Seeley, Service, 1928), 93–94. Hopkins's claim does not square easily with Peter Corris's observation that, due partly to the high protein content of Queensland farm diets, some indentured Solomon Islanders sailed home in improved physical condition. Corris, *Passage*, 115.

196. Clayton to Tryon, 13 November 1886, WPHC 8/III/15; *Sydney Morning Herald* (25 August 1886).

197. Des Voeux, *My Colonial Service*, 2: 92–93; J.C. Wilson, "Labour Trade in the Western Pacific," n.d. [1882], WPHC 8/III/48, 5; Charles M. Woodford, *Naturalist Among the Headhunters* (London, 1890), 15–16; diary of schooner *Mavis*, 3 September 1882 (agent T. Hoyt), Fijian National Archives.

198. British Solomon Islands, *Report for 1903–05*, P.P., 1906, LXXV [Cd. 2684–7]: 24–25. In early 1902, the Earl of Onslow, under secretary of state for the colonies, dismissed as "somewhat exaggerated" British fears that repatriated Islanders might become cannibal fare. *Parliamentary Debates* (Lords), 4th series, 103 (20 February 1902): 552–53. Precisely this fate befell a returning Queensland laborer on the New Hebridean islet of Vao in 1891. See WPHC 4/IV/69/1893, case 61(2).

199. Brewster, *King of the Cannibal Isles*, 68–69; L.M. D'Albertis, *New Guinea*, 2nd ed., 2 vols. (London, 1881), 2: 214–16; Bowie to King, 6 March 1909, NHBS 1/I/7/1908; Bowie to Johnson, 5 December 1911 (no. 106), WPHC 8/II/2, 140, 142.

200. Greg Dening, *Islands and Beaches* (Honolulu: University Press of Hawai'i, 1980), 127–28.

201. C.M. Woodford, "Exploration of the Solomon Islands," *Proceedings of the Royal Geographical Society,* 10 (June 1888): 354.

202. *Fiji Times* (26 February 1870).

203. The quotation "a sort of coinage" is from Western Pacific (Punishment of Natives at Api, New Hebrides), P.P., 1881, LX [355]: 2; Scarr, "Recruits and Recruiters," 249; Walter Ivens, *Island Builders of the Pacific* (London: Seeley, Service, 1930), 43.

204. CO to FO, 27 November 1884, enclosure 1 in no. 13, Correspondence relating to . . . regulating the supply of arms . . . to natives of the Western Pacific, P.P., 1887, LVIII [C. 5240]: 21.

205. Wawn, *South Sea Islanders,* 289, 357–58; Hand to Scott, 6 November 1889, WPHC 8/III/18, case no. 38; O'Brien to the Immigration Agent, Brisbane, 14 January 1895, WPHC 4/IV/88/1895; E.S. Armstrong, *History of the Melanesian Mission* (New York: E.P. Dutton, 1900), 241.

206. FO to CO, 7 May 1885, enclosure in no. 20, P.P., 1887, LVIII [C. 5240]. The United States alone refused to consider an arms embargo. Des Voeux, *My Colonial Service,* 2: 93–94.

207. British Solomon Islands, *Report for 1900–1901,* P.P., 1902, LXIV [Cd. 788–17]: 8; Ivens, *Dictionary,* 225; Alexander J. Duffield, *What I Know* (Brisbane, 1884), 6–7; McLaren, *My Odyssey,* 160.

208. Graves, "Truck and Gifts," 95.

209. Report of Commander Rudolf Bentinck [1907], "Correspondence Respecting Outrages by Natives . . . in the New Hebrides," 51, WPHC 8/II/29.

210. Brantlinger, *Dark Vanishings,* 9–10.

211. Anon., "Pacific Islanders' Protection Bill," 102–03.

212. H.R.F. Bourne, *Claims of Uncivilised Races* (London: Aborigines Protection Society, 1900), 12.

213. Benjamin Kidd, *Control of the Tropics* (New York, 1898), 34–35; Bernard Semmel, *Imperialism and Social Reform* (Garden City, NY: Doubleday, 1968), 20–24.

214. H.H. Montgomery, *Light of Melanesia* (London, 1896), 109.

CHAPTER 4

1. W.T. Pritchard, *Polynesian Reminiscences* [1866], reprint ed. (London: Dawsons of Pall Mall, 1968), 56–57.

2. "Head Hunting," *Preston Guardian* [Preston, Lancashire] (19 May 1872); "Statement by the Rev. Charles Hyde Brook," 19 October 1871 . . . respecting the deportation of South Sea Islanders, P.P., 1872, XLIII (C. 496); Moresby to Stirling, 12 September 1872, enclosure 2 in no. 39, Extracts of any Communications . . . respecting Outrages committed upon Natives of the South Sea Islands, P.P., 1873, L (244).

3. The quotation "backward and forgotten" is from Lawrence James, *Rise and Fall* (New York: St. Martin's Griffin 1994), 249–250; "the most spectacular . . .

violence" quote is from C. Hartley Grattan, *Southwest Pacific Since 1900* (Ann Arbor: University of Michigan Press, 1963), 394–95.

4. Joanna Bourke, *Intimate History of Killing* (New York: Basic Books, 1999), 25–31.

5. Janet Hoskins, "Introduction," in Hoskins, ed., *Headhunting and the Social Imagination* (Stanford, CA: Stanford University Press, 1996), 2–3.

6. Gananath Obeyesekere, "'British Cannibals,'" *Critical Inquiry*, 18 (Summer 1992): 636–37; Robert Dixon, "Cannibalising Indigenous Texts," in Barbara Creed and Jeanette Hoorn, eds., *Body Trade* (New York: Routledge, 2001), 114–15; Joseph Conrad, *Heart of Darkness* [1899] (New York, Norton, 1971), 58; Marianna Torgovnick, *Gone Primitive* (Chicago: Chicago University Press, 1990), 147–48.

7. David Cannadine, *Ornamentalism* (London: Allen Lane, 2001), xix–xx.

8. James Greenwood, *Wild Man at Home* (London [1879]); William Henry Furness, *Home-Life of Borneo Head-Hunters* (Philadelphia: J.B. Lippincott, 1902); John Foster Fraser, *Quaint Subjects* (London: Cassell, 1909), chap. 17, "Head-Hunters at Home."

9. Walter Bagehot, *English Constitution* [1867] (London: Collins Fontana, 1973), 85.

10. James Greenwood, *Adventures of Ruben Davidger* (London, 1865), 24.

11. Nadja Durbach, "London, Capital of Exotic Exhibitions," in Pascal Blanchard et al., eds., *Human Zoos* (Liverpool, UK: Liverpool University Press, 2008), 81.

12. Patrick Brantlinger, *Dark Vanishings* (Ithaca, NY: Cornell University Press, 2003), 4.

13. H.G. Penny, *Objects of Culture* (Chapel Hill: University of North Carolina Press, 2002), 32–34; Renato Rosaldo, *Ilongot Headhunting* (Stanford, CA: Stanford University Press, 1980), 24–25.

14. Mid-Victorian ethnologists were aware that the Jívaro of lowland South America had devised a method for "shrinking" enemy heads despite the stifling jungle heat. See William Bollaert, "On the Idol Human Head of the Jívaro Indians of Equador," *Transactions of the Ethnological Society of London*, n.s. 2 (1861–62): 112–13.

15. Herman Melville, *Moby-Dick* [1851] (Berkeley: University of California Press, 1981), 20.

16. John Hawkesworth, ed., *Account of the Voyages undertaken*, 3 vols. (London, 1773), 2: 391–93; Sir Joseph D. Hooker, ed., *Journal of Sir Joseph Banks . . . in 1768–71* (London, 1896), 247–48.

17. John Campbell, *Maritime Discovery* (London, 1840), 484–85. Campbell was recirculating allegations first made by Mariner about the Tongans in 1817 and subsequently by Ellis about the Raiateans in 1829.

18. William Yate, *An Account of New Zealand* [1835], facsimile ed. (Dublin: Irish University Press, 1970), 130.

19. Angela Ballara, *Taua* (Auckland, New Zealand: Penguin Books, 2003), 41–43.

20. Joan Metge, *Maoris of New Zealand* (London: Routledge & Kegan Paul, 1967), 34–35.

21. D. Wayne Orchiston, "Preserved Human Heads," *Journal of the Polynesian Society*, 76 (September 1967): 301–02.

22. H.G. Robley, *Moko* [1896], reprint ed. (Wellington, New Zealand: A.H. & A.W. Reed, 1969), ix, 151; Marsden as quoted in Christina Thompson, "Smoked Heads," *Salmagundi*, 152 (Fall 2006): 56–57; J.S. Polack, *New Zealand* [1838], reprint ed., 2 vols. (Christchurch, New Zealand: Capper Press, 1974), 1: 232.

23. Claud Field, *Heroes of Missionary Enterprise* (Philadelphia: J.B. Lippincott, 1908), 280–81; Marsden as quoted in John Liddiard Nicholas, *Narrative of a Voyage* [1817], facsimile ed., 2 vols. (Auckland: Wilson & Horton, 1971), 1: 307–12; Judith Binney, *Legacy of Guilt* (Christchurch: Oxford University Press, 1968), 48–49.

24. *Missionary Register* (November 1823), 504–05.

25. Kendall as quoted in Anne Salmond, *Between Worlds* (Honolulu: University of Hawai'i Press, 1997), 438; Alexander Strachan, *Remarkable Incidents* (London, 1853), 154–56; Arthur S. Thomson, *Story of New Zealand*, 2 vols. (London, 1859), 1: 255, 258. Keith Sinclair estimated that about forty thousand Maori people were slaughtered during the "savage civil wars" of the 1820s and early 1830s. See Sinclair, *History of New Zealand*, 3rd ed. (London: Allen Lane, 1980), 42; and Amiria Henare, *Museums, Anthropology* (Cambridge: Cambridge University Press, 2005), 102–03.

26. George French Angas, *Polynesia* (London [1866]), 159–60; Andrew P. Vayda, "Maori Warfare," in Paul Bohannan, ed., *Law and Warfare* (Garden City, NY: Natural History Press, 1967), 374; Richard Taylor, *Te Ika A Maui* (London, 1855), 154–55.

27. Frederick Edward Maning, *Old New Zealand* [1863], reprint ed. (Auckland: Whitcombe & Tombs, 1963), 54–55; S.C. on Aborigines (British Settlements), P.P., 1836, VII, q. 1695; "a bit of Candle" quote from S.C. on the Present State of New Zealand, P.P., 1837–38, XXI (680), 70. I thank Jane Samson for this last reference.

28. Gananath Obeyesekere, *Cannibal Talk* (Berkeley: University of California Press, 2005), 120; Thompson, "Smoked Heads," 65; Robley, *Moko*, 197–205.

29. See, for example, *Sydney Gazette* (7 January 1828).

30. Darling to Goderich, 13 April 1831, *Historical Records of Australia*, series 1, 16 (Sydney, Australia, 1923): 241; Paul Moon, *Fatal Frontiers* (Auckland: Penguin Group, 2006), 87–88; *Sydney Gazette* (21 April 1831).

31. *Sydney Gazette* (19 April 1831); Charles Wilkes, *Narrative of the United States Exploring Expedition*, 5 vols. (Philadelphia, 1845), 2: 399–400.

32. J.C. Beaglehole, *Life of Captain James Cook* (Stanford, CA: Stanford University Press, 1974), 444.

33. Alfred C. Haddon, *History of Anthropology* (London: Watts, 1910), 25, 28–30; Roger Cooter, *Cultural Meaning of Popular Science* (Cambridge: Cambridge University Press, 1984), 16–35.

34. Paul Turnbull, "'Rare Work Amongst the Professors,'" in Creed and Hoorn, eds., *Body Trade* (New York: Routledge, 2001), 4–6, 16.

35. John Crawfurd, "On the Classification of the Races," *Transactions of the Ethnological Society of London*, n.s. 6 (1867): 127–29; A.R. Wallace, *Malay Archipelago*, 2 vols. (London, 1869), 2: 467–68.

36. Sandra Pannell, "Travelling to Other Worlds," *Oceania*, 62 (March 1992): 167; Wallace, *Malay Archipelago*, 2: 178.

37. "Manual of Ethnological Inquiry," in *Journal of the Ethnological Society of London*, 3 (1854): 194–97.

38. Robert A. Stafford, "Scientific Exploration and Empire," in Andrew Porter, ed., *Oxford History of the British Empire*, 3 (New York: Oxford University Press, 1999): 296–97.

39. *Manual of Scientific Enquiry*, 2nd ed. [1851], reprint ed. (Folkestone, Kent, UK: Dawsons of Pall Mall, 1974), 448–50, 441.

40. *Notes and Queries on Anthropology* (London, 1874), 142.

41. *Manual of Scientific Enquiry*, 5th ed. (London, 1886), 225–26, 238; *Notes and Queries on Anthropology*, v.

42. Andrew Zimmerman, *Anthropology and Antihumanism* (Chicago: University of Chicago Press, 2001), 86–87; Ricardo Roque, *Headhunting and Colonialism* (Basingstoke, Hampshire, UK: Palgrave Macmillan, 2010), 8–9.

43. *Notes and Queries on Anthropology*, 3–6; H.B. Guppy, *Solomon Islands and Their Natives* (London, 1887), 103; Pannell, "Travelling," 170.

44. [Harriet Martineau], "The English in the Eastern Seas," *Edinburgh Review*, 116 (October 1862): 400; Wallace, *Malay Archipelago*, 1: 5.

45. [Martineau], "The English," 414–15.

46. *Sarawak Gazette* [Kuching] (1 June 1894); *Pall Mall Gazette* [London] (23 March 1896).

47. *The Times* [London] (23 June 1897). These Dayaks had previously performed "savage dances" at the colonial tournament.

48. Ibid. (11 June 1897).

49. On Raja Brooke and his bloody suppression of the "Sea Dayaks," consult Nicholas Tarling, *The Burthen* (Kuala Lumpur, Malaysia: Oxford University Press, 1982), 27–48.

50. *The Graphic* [London] (19 November 1881); *Morning Post* [London] (23 October 1905).

51. H. Ian Hogbin, *Experiments in Civilization* (London: George Routledge & Sons, 1939), 5.

52. Guppy, *Solomon Islands*, 193; William Amherst and Basil Thomson, eds., *Discovery of the Solomon Islands* [1901], reprint ed. (Nendeln, Lichtenstein: Kraus, 1967), xxxiv, lxix.

53. Basil Thomson, *The Fijians* (London: William Heinemann, 1908), v, viii–ix; R.H. Codrington, *The Melanesians* (Oxford, 1891), 9–10.

54. Between 29 June and 5 July 1768, Bougainville's ships sighted land in what today would be considered the Solomon archipelago. Fog, racing tides, and unwel-

coming "Indians" prevented a landing, however. See *Pacific Journal of Louis-Antoine de Bougainville 1767–1768*, trans. John Dunmore (London: Hakluyt Society, 2002), 112–18.

55. Guppy, *Solomon Islands*, 2, 4, 11–12; A.I. Hopkins, *In the Isles of King Solomon* (London: Seeley, Service, 1928), 20–21.

56. H.H. Romilly, *Western Pacific and New Guinea*, 2nd ed. (London, 1887), 13–14.

57. A.R. Tippett, *Solomon Islands Christianity* (London: Lutterworth Press, 1967), 8–9; C.M. Woodford, "Exploration of the Solomon Islands," *Proceedings of the Royal Geographical Society*, 10 (June 1888): 375; John Gaggin, *Among the Man-Eaters* (London: T. Fisher Unwin, 1900), 161–62; Angas, *Polynesia*, 366; E.W. Elkington, *Savage South Seas* (London: A. & C. Black, 1907), 84–86; Alexander G. Findlay, *Directory for the Navigation of the South Pacific Ocean*, 5th ed. (London, 1884), 839–40, 862.

58. Thurston to Tryon, 17 March 1886, WPHC 8/III/15, case no. 1.

59. C.M. Woodford, *A Naturalist Among the Headhunters* (London, 1890), 154; Guppy, *Solomon Islands*, 67–68; Joseph H.C. Dickinson, *Trader in the Savage Solomons* (London: H.F. & G. Witherby, 1927), 184–92.

60. The names of islands and island settlements around New Georgia remained very imprecise well into the twentieth century. "New Georgia" in the broadest sense referred to a cluster of several large and many small islands located in the west-central part of the Solomon archipelago. But "New Georgia" also signified the largest single island in that cluster. Confusingly, various navigational charts and travelers' accounts sometimes referred to the latter as "Rubiana," "Kusage," or "Marovo" Island. There was no standard indigenous name for New Georgia. Two vast lagoons hug New Georgia island, the Marovo Lagoon on its east coast and the Roviana (Rubiana) Lagoon on its northwest coast. See Edward Hviding, *Guardians of Marovo Lagoon* (Honolulu: University of Hawai'i Press, 1996), 106, 395; and C.W. Woodford, "Further Explorations in the Solomon Islands," *Proceedings of the Royal Geographical Society*, 12 (July 1890): 394–95.

61. Woodford, *A Naturalist*, 155–57.

62. Codrington, *The Melanesians*, 118, n.1; Codrington, "Religious Beliefs and Practices in Melanesia," *Journal of the Anthropological Institute*, 10 (1881): 308–09; B. Gina, as quoted in Tippett, *Solomon Islands Christianity*, 7.

63. Hviding, *Guardians*, 89, 91, 418.

64. Andrew Cheyne, *Description of Islands* (London, 1852), 65; Peter Corris, *Passage, Port and Plantation* (Carlton, Victoria, Australia: Melbourne University Press, 1973), 113; Judith A. Bennett, *Wealth of the Solomons* (Honolulu: University of Hawai'i Press, 1987), 87–88.

65. Hannah Chewings, *Amongst Tropical Islands* (Adelaide, Australia: J.L. Bonython, 1900), 26; Colin Jack-Hinton, *Search for the Islands* (Oxford: Clarendon Press, 1969), 345.

66. Angas, *Polynesia*, 363–64; "After Tortoise-shell," *Australasian Methodist Missionary Review* (4 April 1898), 4–5; J.M. McKinnon, "Tomahawks, Turtles and Traders," *Oceania*, 45 (June 1975): 293.

67. McKinnon, "Tomahawks," 301–02.

68. Early European shipwrecks may have alerted some Solomon Islanders to the virtues of iron. We know that in August 1788, when Lieutenant John Shortland encountered four canoe-loads of "Indians" off Simbo Island, these people expressed a "manifest preference to whatever was made of iron." *Voyage of Governor Philip to Botany Bay* (London, 1789), 196. Either they had an intuitive grasp of the metal's potential or else empirical knowledge gained from flotsam.

69. Bennett, *Wealth*, 34.

70. Richard F. Salisbury, *Stone to Steel* (Parkville, Victoria, Australia: Melbourne University Press, 1962), 118–19.

71. McKinnon, "Tomahawks," 299–300; Martin Zelenietz, "End of Headhunting in New Georgia," in Margaret Rodman and Matthew Cooper, eds., *Pacification of Melanesia* (Ann Arbor: University of Michigan Press, 1979), 94–95.

72. J.M. McKinnon, "Bilua Changes," unpub. Ph.D. thesis, Department of Geography, Victoria University, Wellington, New Zealand, 1972, 62.

73. Cheyne, *Trading Voyages of Andrew Cheyne,* ed. Dorothy Shineberg (Honolulu: University of Hawai'i Press, 1971), editor's intro., 24–25, 27.

74. Cheyne, *Trading Voyages*, 303–04.

75. Cheyne, *Description of Islands*, 65–66.

76. Amherst and Thomson, *Discovery*, 109.

77. Codrington, *The Melanesians*, 294–96; Claude Bernays, "The British Solomon Islands," *Queensland Geographical Journal*, n.s. 24 (1908–09): 38–39.

78. *Pacific Islands (Western Group): Sailing Directions*, 2nd ed. (London, 1890), 51–52; "more exquisitely graceful" quote from Walter Coote, *Western Pacific* (London, 1883), 170; "a most astonishing revelation . . ." quote from Boyle T. Somerville, "Ethnographic Notes in New Georgia," *Journal of the Anthropological Institute*, 26 (1897): 369.

79. Gaggin, *Man-Eaters*, 193–94; Guppy, *Solomon Islands*, 146–47; Bernays, "British Solomon Islands," 40; Somerville, "Ethnographic Notes," 371.

80. W.H.R. Rivers, *History of Melanesian Society*, 2 vols. (Cambridge: Cambridge University Press, 1914), 2: 450–51; Woodford, "Canoes of the British Solomon Islands," *Journal of the Anthropological Institute*, 39 (1909): 50. One other indigenous culture built equally seaworthy canoes, the Haida of Canada's Queen Charlotte Islands (Haida Gwaii). Up to the mid-nineteenth century, Haida warriors also hunted heads and launched long raids across Hecate Strait to find them. Their canoes were also sumptuously decorated. See especially W.H. Collison, *Wake of War Canoes* (London: Seeley, Service, 1915), 88–90; and Douglas Cole and Bradley Lockner, eds., *The Journals of George M. Dawson*, 2 vols. (Vancouver: University of British Columbia Press, 1989), 2: 507–08.

81. Hopkins, *In the Isles*, 174–75; Hviding, *Guardians*, 172.

82. A.M. Hocart, "Cult of the Dead," *Journal of the Royal Anthropological Institute*, 52 (1922), part 1, 89–90; W.G. Ivens, *Island Builders* (London: Seeley, Service, 1930), 185–86; Tippett, *Solomon Islands Christianity*, 154–55; Richard C. Thurnwald, "Price of the White Man's Peace," *Pacific Affairs*, 9 (September 1936): 349.

83. [C.G.S. Foljambe], *Three Years on the Australian Station* (London, 1868), 215–217; Coote, *Western Pacific*, 141–45; *The Island Voyage, 1879* (London, 1880), 89–95; mss. enclosure, "Story for Children," Patteson to Lady Stephen, 31 October 1866, Stephen Family Correspondence, Mitchell Library, ML MSS. 777/11.

84. K.B. Jackson, "Head-hunting," *Journal of Pacific History*, 10 (1975): 67–68; Diary of Rev. Alfred Penny, 22 September 1879, Mitchell Library, ML MS. B 807–817; George Bogesi, "Santa Isabel, Solomon Islands," *Oceania*, 18 (March 1948): 210–11.

85. Codrington, *The Melanesians*, 135–36, 256–57; Ellen Wilson, *Dr. Welchman of Bugotu* (London: Society for the Propagation of Christian Knowledge, 1935), 6–8; Frances Awdry, *In the Isles of the Sea*, 2nd ed. (London: Bemrose & Sons, 1903), 59–61.

86. Jackson, "Head-hunting," 71–73; *The Island Voyage, 1886* (London, 1887), 10–11; David Hilliard, *God's Gentlemen* (St. Lucia, Australia: University of Queensland Press, 1978), 173–74; Diaries of Rev. Henry Welchman, 29 July and 23 August 1892, 31 October 1896, Mitchell Library, ML M 728.

87. Bennett, *Wealth*, 76–77; C.M. Woodford, "Report on the British Solomon Islands," P.P., 1897, LIX [C. 8457], 11–12.

88. Woodford to Thurston, 17 July 1896, WPHC 4/IV/285/1896; *Morning Post* [London] (27 July 1895).

89. Woodford, *A Naturalist*, 176–77; Hviding, *Guardians*, 107.

90. "General Report on the Progress . . . of British Subjects in the Islands," Appendix 3, Australian Station, Solomon Islands, 1896: WPHC 8/III/25.

91. Fraser, *Quaint Subjects*, 248–49.

92. Romilly, *Western Pacific*, 88–90.

93. Clayton to Tryon, 15 November 1885, WPHC 8/III/14; *Sydney Morning Herald* (14 December 1885); G.F. Childe to S. Samuel, 22 February 1886, WPHC 8/III/15.

94. Douglas Rannie, *My Adventures* (London: Seeley, Service, 1912), 188–89.

95. Zelenietz, "End of Headhunting," 104; Elkington, *Savage South Seas*, 89–90.

96. Tippett, *Solomon Islands Christianity*, 148.

97. Minute by F. Fuller, 3 September 1892: "Protectorates in the South Pacific," CO 225/40/6920, copy in Rhodes House Library, Oxford University.

98. A.S. Meek, *A Naturalist in Cannibal Land* (London: T. Fisher Unwin, 1913), 106; Somerville, "Ethnographic Notes," 359–60; Chewings, *Amongst Tropical Islands*, 24–26.

99. Woodford, "Exploration," 370; Guppy, *Solomon Islands*, 169–70; Codrington, "Religious Beliefs," 265.

100. J.A. Froude, *Oceana* (London, 1886), 387–88.

101. British Solomon Islands, *Report for 1957 and 1958* (London, 1960), 59.

102. Somerville, "Ethnographic Notes," 411.

103. "Special Report Declaring Protectorate over Solomon Islands," 10 August 1893, 18–19, WPHC 8/III/22.

104. Ibid., 20; Ripon to Thurston, 20 April 1893, WPHC 8/III/28; Bennett, *Wealth*, 106–07.

105. Hogbin, *Experiments*, 14–15; Deryck Scarr, *Fragments of Empire* (Canberra: Australian National University Press, 1967), 258–59.

106. Corris, *Passage*, 106–07; Pollard to Bridges, 22 June 1897, in "Selected Documents [on] the Declaration of the Protectorate," WPHC 8/III/28.

107. Although Lever Brothers' plantations transformed island life in the Solomons, this firm's soap and margarine factories abroad served the more profitable local consumer markets. See D.K. Fieldhouse, *Unilever Overseas* (London: Croom Helm, 1978), 13, 31.

108. Goodrich to Bowden-Smith, 26 May 1894, WPHC 8/III/23.

109. *Australian Town and Country Journal* [Sydney] (12 October 1895).

110. *Sydney Morning Herald* (3 August 1896).

111. Ibid. (19 September 1896).

112. *The Age* [Melbourne] (18 and 28 September 1896); *Sydney Morning Herald* (18 and 19 September 1896, 25 January 1897).

113. *The Spectator* (15 March 1890), 374–75. See also *All the Year Round* (20 September 1890), 279–80; *Saturday Review* (15 March 1890), 322–23; *Athenaeum* (29 March 1890), 406–07; *Liverpool Courier* (29 April 1891); *Sydney Morning Herald* (19 November 1890).

114. *The Times* (7 October 1927).

115. Woodford, "Exploration," 358; Woodford, *A Naturalist*, 152–53; diary entry for 6–8 October 1886, and draft of letter to Thurston, November 1886, in Papers of Charles M. Woodford, bundle 30, Research School of Pacific and Asian Studies, Australian National University, Canberra.

116. Woodford, *A Naturalist*, n.23.

117. *Epsom Herald* (8 September 1894); Scarr, *Fragments*, 262.

118. Wm. Roger Lewis, "Introduction," in Robin W. Winks, ed., *Oxford History of the British Empire*, 5 (New York: Oxford University Press, 1999): 21–22.

119. Arthur Grimble, *Pattern of Islands* (London: John Murray, 1952), 69–70.

120. Woodford to Thurston, 4 July 1896, TNA, CO 225/500/21654.

121. *Sydney Daily Telegraph* (30 June 1897).

122. Davis to Scott, 17 October 1891, as quoted in Scarr, *Fragments*, 174; Somerville, "Ethnographic Notes," 399–400.

123. "In the matter of a complaint made by Ingava," 22 October 1894, WPHC 2/VI/1(a).

124. Diary entry for 20 August 1888, Woodford Papers, bundle 29.

125. Zelenietz, "End of Headhunting," 92, 105–06; McKinnon, "Tomahawks," 305.

126. In 1897, Lord Salisbury, Britain's foreign secretary as well as her prime minister, and Joseph Chamberlain, the colonial secretary, agreed to implement Thurston's recommendation that the outlying islands of Rennell, Bellona, and Sikaiana (Stewart Island) be added to the protectorate. They balked, however, at including the Santa Cruz group lest France's "Chauvinist" newspapers "get up agitations" over any attempt to absorb this island cluster.

127. Untitled newspaper clipping dated 27 July 1895, Woodford Papers, bundle 30; Woodford to Thurston, 7 September 1896, WPHC 4/IV/415/1896.

128. Woodford, "Report on the British Solomon Islands," 26–27.

129. Woodford to Berkeley, 8 June 1897, WPHC 4/IV/300/1897; Woodford to O'Brien, 17 April 1898, WPHC 4/IV/8/1898.

130. *Sydney Morning Herald* (10 July 1897); C.A.W. Monckton, *New Guinea Recollections* (London: John Lane, 1934), 198–200.

131. O'Brien to Chamberlain, 11 October 1898, WPHC 8/III/32; "Report of the British Solomon Islands for 1899–1900," P.P., 1901, XLV (Cd. 431–12), 15; Arthur Mahaffy, "The Solomon Islands," *Empire Review*, 4 (September 1902): 193–94; Purnima Bose, *Organizing Empire* (Durham, NC: Duke University Press, 2003), 29–33; "Extract from Mr. Mahaffy's Report of Proceedings" [1900], WPHC 4/IV/285/98.

132. Woodford to O'Brien, 24 June 1900, WPHC 4/IV/285/98.

133. "Extract from Mr. Mahaffy's Report," WPHC 4/IV/285/98; Woodford to O'Brien, 10 September 1900, WPHC 4/IV/285/98.

134. Woodford, "Canoes," 511.

135. Scarr, *Fragments*, 266–67; Frank Burnett, *Through Polynesia and Papua* (London: G. Bell & Sons, 1911), 111–14. The 1909 pursuit and arrest of another fighting man, "Zito" of Vella Lavella, earned similar criticism. See Woodford to Thurn, 20 December 1909, TNA, CO 225/91; and *The Age* [Melbourne] (21 and 25 May 1910).

136. Woodford, "Canoes," 510; Harold W. Scheffler, "Social Consequences of Peace," *Ethnology*, 3 (October 1964): 399. David R. Lawrence has recently pointed out that "The process of civilization [in the Solomons] was made imperfect by imperfect agents." Lawrence, *The Naturalist and His "Beautiful Islands"* (Canberra: Australian National University Press, 2014), 217. But to characterize Woodford as an "imperfect" agent is to minimize his responsibility for several heinous acts of colonial discipline.

137. Colonial Office minute of 29 April 1902, TNA, CO 225/63.

138. Woodford, "Canoes," 510.

139. *Australian Methodist Missionary Review* (4 February 1903), 2; Joseph Bryant, *Coral Reefs and Cannibals* (London: Epworth Press, 1925), 106–07; Cyril Belshaw, *Changing Melanesia* (Melbourne, Australia: Oxford University Press, 1954), 55.

140. Nicholas Thomas, "Colonial Conversions," in Catherine Hall, ed., *Cultures of Empire* (New York: Routledge, 2000), 318; Tippett, *Solomon Islands Christianity*, 61.

141. Froude, *Oceana*, 300. See also "The Dying Races," *The Vegetarian* (12 August 1899), 379.

142. "Doomed Islanders," *Sydney Morning Herald* (26 January 1913).

143. Woodford, *A Naturalist*, 188.

144. Elkington, *Savage South Seas*, 98; T.W. Edge-Partington, "Ingava, Chief of Rubiana, Solomon Islands," *Man*, 7 (1907): 22–23.

145. Obituary of W.H.R. Rivers, *Man*, 22 (July 1922): 97; Anna Grimshaw, *Ethnographer's Eye* (Cambridge: Cambridge University Press, 2001), 32–33.

146. Rivers, "Psychological Factor," in Rivers, ed., *Essays in the Depopulation of Melanesia* (Cambridge: Cambridge University Press, 1922), 93; *Nature*, 3 (3 February 1923): 145.

147. Rivers, "Psychological Factor," 101. Echoing Rivers, the German anthropologist Richard Thurnwald observed in 1933 that the suppression of headhunting-by-contract in Buin, on Bougainville Island, had taken the "spice . . . out of native life" there. Thurnwald, "Price," 353.

148. Rivers, *History of Melanesian Society*, 2: 259; Rivers, "Psychological Factor," 102.

149. Woodford, "The Solomon Islands," in Rivers, ed., *Essays in Depopulation*, 69; Hogbin, *Experiments*, 136; H.C. Brookfield, *Colonialism, Development and Independence* (Cambridge: Cambridge University Press, 1972), 25.

150. George H.L.F. Pitt-Rivers, *Clash of Culture* (London: George Routledge & Sons, 1927), xii; Dixon, "Cannibalising Indigenous Texts," 120–21.

151. British Solomon Islands, "Report to 30th June, 1913," P.P., 1914, LVIII (Cd. 7050–15): 5.

152. Elkington, *Savage South Seas*, 15–16.

153. Robert W. Williamson, *Ways of the South Sea Savage* (Philadelphia: J.B. Lippincott, 1914), 62–63.

154. Rivers, "Psychological Factor," 107–09.

155. Bill Holm and George Irving Quimby, *Edward S. Curtis in the Land of the War Canoes* (Seattle: University of Washington Press, 1980), 72.

156. Edward A. Salisbury, "A Napoleon of the Solomons," *Asia*, 22 (September 1922): 707–08, 712, 746; Salisbury and Cooper, *Sea Gypsy* (New York: G.P. Putnam's Sons, 1924), 160–71.

157. The pacification of Malaita, an island bristling with rifles, is often dated to 1927. On 4 October of that year, District Officer W.R. Bell, his white assistant, and thirteen Islanders from their party were massacred at Sinalagu while collecting taxes. The punitive expedition that followed imposed a draconian peace on the Kwaio people of Malaita's hilly midsection. See Roger M. Keesing and Peter Corris, *Lightning Meets the West Wind* (Melbourne: Oxford University Press, 1980).

158. Meek, *A Naturalist*, 53.

159. T.H.H. Richards, "British New Guinea," *Proceedings of the Royal Colonial Institute*, 24 (1892–93): 295; Chalmers, *Pioneer Life and Work* (London, 1895), 61–62;

Michael O'Hanlon, "Mostly Harmless," *Journal of the Royal Anthropological Institute*, 5 (September 1999): 390–93.

160. *Annual Report on British New Guinea, 1889–1890* (Sydney, 1890), 49–50; Wallace, "New Guinea and Its Inhabitants," *Contemporary Review*, 34 (February 1879): 424; Richards, "British New Guinea," 301.

161. Wallace, "New Guinea," 440.

162. Octavius C. Stone, *A Few Months in New Guinea* (London, 1880), 16; J.H.P. Murray, *Papua or British New Guinea* (London: T. Fisher Unwin, 1912), 72–73.

163. Malcolm to Schubert, 30 October 1875, and Schubert to Carnarvon, 3 November 1875, in Correspondence respecting New Guinea, P.P., 1876, LIV (C.1566); *Brisbane Courier* (8 March 1883); Bramston to Maciver, 15 November 1883, in Further Correspondence respecting New Guinea, P.P., 1884, LV (C. 3863); *Sydney Morning Herald* (23 November 1883).

164. MacGregor to Gordon, 18 January 1889, Stanmore Papers, B.L., Add. Mss. 49203, f. 178; A.W. Monckton, *Some Experiences* (London: John Lane, 1921), 10; Nicholas Thomas, *Colonialism's Culture* (Cambridge: Polity Press, 1994), 110–11.

165. G.F. DeBruijn Kops, "Contribution to the Knowledge," *Journal of the Indian Archipelago and Eastern Asia*, 6 (1852): 314–15.

166. L.M. D'Albertis, *New Guinea*, 2nd ed., 2 vols. (London, 1881), 2: 281–83; R.B. Joyce, *Sir William MacGregor* (Melbourne: Oxford University Press, 1971), 129; C.G. Seligmann, "Classification of the Natives," *Journal of the Royal Anthropological Institute*, 39 (1909): 256; Wilfred N. Beaver, *Unexplored New Guinea*, 2nd ed. (London: Seeley, Service, 1920), 249.

167. William MacGregor, "Journey to the Summit," *Proceedings of the Royal Geographical Society*, 12 (April 1890): 199.

168. MacGregor to Griffith, 9 April 1896, as quoted in Joyce, *Sir William MacGregor*, 126.

169. MacGregor, "British New Guinea," *Journal of the Royal Commonwealth Society*, 26 (1895): 318; MacGregor to Gordon, 6 February 1889, Stanmore Papers, B.L. Add. Mss. 49203, f. 187.

170. *Annual Report on British New Guinea, 1893–1894* (Brisbane, Australia, 1895), vi–vii; MacGregor, "British New Guinea," 321–22; MacGregor, *Handbook of Information for Intending Settlers* (Brisbane, 1892), 2; Musgrove to Douglas, 7 September 1886, MacGregor Papers, Mitchell Library, ML MSS 2819/3.

171. *Brisbane Courier* (31 October 1896); Grimble, *Pattern*, 143–44.

172. *Annual Report on British New Guinea, 1892–1893* (n.p., n.d.), xvi–xvii, and Appendix F; *Annual Report on British New Guinea, 1895–1896* (n.p., n.d.), xvi–xvii.

173. MacGregor to Gordon, 21 May 1891, Stanmore Papers, B.L. Add. Mss. 49203, ff. 252–53.

174. A.C. Haddon, "Tugeri Head-Hunters," *Internationales Archiv für Ethnographie*, 4 (1891): 177, 180; John Strachan, *Explorations and Adventures* (London,

1888), 131–33; Murray, *Papua*, 195–96; *Annual Report on British New Guinea, 1895–96*, xix; Mollie Lett, "How the Terrible Tugere Were Suppressed," *P.I.M.* (24 April 1933), 30–31.

175. Le Hunte to Lord Lamington, 15 November 1900, TNA FO 37/866.

176. Diary entry for 20 November 1913, Murray Papers, Mitchell Library A 3140.

177. The Jaqaj people of the Mappi River, an area slightly west of Tugeri territory, were still collecting heads into the 1950s. J.H.M.C. Boelaars, *Head-Hunters* (The Hague: Martinus Nijhoff, 1981), 1–7.

178. Chewings, *Amongst Tropical Islands*, 21–25; W. Charles Metcalfe, *Undaunted* (London [1895]), 108, 112, 170, 184–86; Dixon, "Cannibalising Indigenous Texts," 113–14, 119–20.

179. Caroline Mytinger, *Headhunting in the Solomon Islands* (New York: Macmillan, 1942).

180. *The Times* (25 March 1977).

181. Renato Rosaldo, *Culture and Truth* (Boston: Beacon Press, 1989), 16, 86–87; Anna L. Tsing, "Telling Violence in the Meratus Mountains," in Hoskins, ed., *Headhunting and the Social Imagination*, 189.

CHAPTER 5

1. "The Great Exhibition," *Illustrated London News*, 18 (3 May 1851): 343.

2. Stephen Kern, *Culture of Time and Space* (Cambridge, MA: Harvard University Press, 1983), 213.

3. Charles Lyell, *Geological Evidences* (London, 1863), 10; *Encyclopaedia Britannica*, 9th ed. (New York, 1878), s.v. "Archaeology."

4. John Lubbock, *Pre-Historic Times* [1865], 2nd ed. (New York, 1872), 2–3.

5. On the ideological content of prehistoric categories, see Marshall Sahlins, *Stone Age Economics* (Chicago: Aldine-Atherton, 1972), 1–39.

6. S. Evans, *Nature*, 3 (9 March 1871): 362–65; [H.B. Tristam], review of *The Origin of Civilisation, Contemporary Review*, 15 (September 1870): 311–13; Lubbock, *The Origin of Civilisation* [1870], reprint ed. (Chicago: University of Chicago Press, 1978), 322–23.

7. George Stocking, *Victorian Anthropology* (New York: Free Press, 1987), 152–54.

8. E.B. Tylor, "Preface" to H. Ling Roth, *The Aborigines of Tasmania*, facsimile of 2nd ed. [1899] (Hobart, Tasmania, Australia: Fullers Bookshop, 1968), ix; Tylor, "On the Tasmanians as Representatives of Palaeolithic Man," *Journal of the Anthropological Institute*, 23 (1893): 142–45.

9. "Timbuctoo the Mysterious," *The Spectator*, 77 (26 December 1896): 934; Baldwin Spencer and F.J. Gillen, *Native Tribes of Central Australia* [1899], reprint ed. (New York: Dover, 1968), passim.

10. *Daily News Souvenir Guide to the British Empire Exhibition* (London: Daily News, 1924), 70–71, 54; Jonathan Rose, *Intellectual Life of the British Working Classes*

(New Haven, CT: Yale University Press, 2001), 349; Peter H. Hoffenberg, *Empire on Display* (Berkeley: University of California Press, 2001), 276.

11. Paul Fussell, *Abroad* (New York: Oxford University Press,1982), 7, 9–10.

12. Clifford W. Collinson, *Life and Laughter* (London: Hurst & Blackett, 1926), ix.

13. Delos W. Lovelace, *King Kong* (New York: Grosset & Dunlap, 1932), 42–43, 51–54, 66–67.

14. *The Times* [London] (12 April 1933).

15. Fatimah Tobing Rony, *Third Eye* (Durham, NC: Duke University Press, 1996), 158–59.

16. Robert Young, *Martyr Islands of the New Hebrides* (Edinburgh, 1889), 34–35.

17. George Palmer, *Kidnapping* (Edinburgh, 1871), 55–56; Jeffrey Cox, *The British Missionary Enterprise* (New York: Routledge, 2008), 216; K.R. Howe, *Where the Waves Fall* (Honolulu: University of Hawai'i Press, 1984), 299–300; C.H. Irwin, "On a Cannibal Island," *Sunday at Home*, 13 (1900): 409–12.

18. Cyril Belshaw, *Changing Melanesia* (Melbourne, Australia: Oxford University Press, 1954), 21–22; [Alexander Hume Ford], "Among the Cannibals of the New Hebrides," *Mid-Pacific Magazine*, 22 (July 1921): 35–37; John Harris, "The New Hebrides Experiment," *Nineteenth Century and After*, 75 (April 1914): 932–34; F.H.L. Paton, "Australian Interests in the New Hebrides," *United Empire*, 10 (April 1919): 154–55, 158. As of 1910, the New Hebrides supported roughly 1,000 white settlers and an indigenous population estimated to number 65,000. Harris, "New Hebrides Experiment," 932.

19. [Ford], "Among the Cannibals," 34.

20. Felix Speiser, "Decadence and Preservation," in W.H.R. Rivers, ed., *Essays on the Depopulation of Melanesia* (Cambridge: Cambridge University Press, 1922), 38–39.

21. Christian Kaufmann, "Felix Speiser's Fletched Arrow," in Michael O'Hanlon and Robert Welsch, eds., *Hunting the Gatherers* (New York: Berghahn Books, 2000), 207–08; Jean Louis Rallu, "The Demographic Past," in Joël Bonnemaison et al., eds., *Arts of Vanuatu* (Honolulu: University of Hawai'i Press, 1996), 318.

22. Felix Speiser, *Two Years* (London: Mills & Boon, 1913), 57, 59–61. Speiser informed his readers that the Big Nambas owed their name to "the size of a certain article of dress, the Nambas, which partly replaces our trousers." (60).

23. Beatrice Grimshaw, *From Fiji* (London: Eveleigh Nash, 1907), 166–68; Eugénie and Hugh Laracy, "Beatrice Grimshaw: Pride and Prejudice in Papua," *Journal of Pacific History*, 12 (1977): 156.

24. B. Grimshaw, "In the Savage South Seas," *National Geographic Magazine*, 19 (January 1908): 2; Grimshaw, *From Fiji*, 270–72.

25. J.R. Forster, *Observations Made During a Voyage Round the World* (London, 1778), 242–43; William H. Flower, "On a Collection of . . . Artificially Deformed Crania," *Journal of the Anthropological Institute*, 11 (1882): 75–77; Boyle T. Somerville, "Notes on Some Islands," *Journal of the Anthropological Institute*, 23 (1894): 6.

26. W.H.R. Rivers, *History of Melanesian Society*, 2 vols. (Cambridge: Cambridge University Press, 1914), 2: 88–89; Jeremy MacClancy, "Unconventional Character," in George Stocking, ed., *Malinowski, Rivers, Benedict* (Madison: Wisconsin University Press, 1986), 52–53; John Layard, *Stone Men* (London: Chatto & Windus, 1942), 619.

27. A.S. Meek, *A Naturalist* (London: T. Fisher Unwin, 1913), 191.

28. Jack London to Martin Johnson, 17 November 1906, in Earle Labor et al., eds., *Letters of Jack London*, 2 (Stanford, CA: Stanford University Press, 1988): 632; Charmian London, "Cruise of the Snark," *Mid-Pacific Magazine*, 11 (May 1915): 417–23.

29. Charmian London, *Voyaging in Wild Seas* (London: Mills & Boon, 1915), 325–26; C. London, "New Hebrides Days," *Mid-Pacific Magazine*, 12 (July 1916): 69.

30. Martin Johnson, *Cannibal-Land* (Boston: Houghton Mifflin, 1929), 3; M. Johnson, *Through the South Seas* [1913], reprint ed. (Cedar Springs, MI: Wolf House Books, 1972), 329–31.

31. Jack London to J.A. Johnson, 3 April 1909, in Labor et al., *Letters of Jack London*, 2: 797–98; Martin Johnson, *Through the South Seas*, 268.

32. Pascal and Eleanor Imperato, *They Married Adventure* (New Brunswick, NJ: Rutgers University Press, 1992), xi–xii; Rony, *Third Eye*, 88–89.

33. Ian Aitkin, ed., *Encyclopedia of Documentary Film*, 3 vols. (New York, 2006), 3: 1460.

34. Photographs 250640.2, 250665, 250619, and 108255.1, respectively, in "South Seas I" (1917), Johnson Safari Museum Archives, Chanute, Kansas.

35. Osa Johnson, *Bride in the Solomons* (Garden City, NY: Garden City Publishing, 1946), 1–3; Martin Johnson, *Cannibal-Land*, 6.

36. Martin Johnson, *Cannibal-Land*, 21–22.

37. "South Seas Rough Footage Transfers" (1917), Johnson Safari Museum Archives; Philippa Levine, "Naked Truths," *Journal of British Studies*, 52 (January 2013): 18

38. "Rialto and Rivoli," *Motion Picture News*, 18 (3 August 1918): 737.

39. *Pictures and the Picturegoer* (15–27 February 1919), 189; *The Times* (12 May 1919); *Manchester Guardian* (14 May 1919); *Pictures and the Picturegoer* (14 June 1919), 597; *Manchester Guardian* (20 June 1919).

40. Copy of typescript letter, "C.E.G." to Martin Johnson, 4 November 1919, Johnson Safari Museum Archives.

41. Imperato, *They Married Adventure*, 77–80.

42. "South Seas Rough Footage Transfers" (1919), Johnson Safari Museum Archives.

43. Martin Johnson, *Cannibal-Land*, 76.

44. Rachael Low, *History of the British Film*, 4 vols. (London: George Allen & Unwin, 1971), 4: 289; Karl G. Heider, *Ethnographic Film* (Austin: University of Texas Press, 1976), 19–20; Rony, *Third Eye*, 6–7.

45. Peter Miles and Malcolm Smith, *Cinema, Literature and Society* (London: Croom Helm, 1987), 166; *The Times Supplement* (21 February 1922).

46. "Cannibal-Land," *New Statesman*, 20 (7 October 1922): 22; Osa Johnson, *I Married Adventure* (Philadelphia: J.B. Lippincott, 1940), 9, 289–93. *Punch* must have had the Johnsons in mind when it imagined an American film crew shooting scenes for a "palpitating drama" entitled "Baby, I Could Eat You Whole!" "The Film-Director and the Cannibal," *Punch*, 180 (13 May 1931): 510–11.

47. Deacon, *Malekula: A Vanishing People in the New Hebrides*, ed. Camilla Wedgewood (London: George Routledge & Sons, 1934), 227–30.

48. Evelyn Cheesman, *Backwaters* (London: Jarrolds, 1937), 192, 104, 163–64, 176–77.

49. Ibid., 18–19, 169–71.

50. Tom Harrisson, *Living Among Cannibals* (London: George G. Harrup, 1943), 7.

51. Harrisson, *Savage Civilization* (New York: Knopf, 1937), 3; Harrisson, *Living Among Cannibals*, 10–12; Judith Heimann, *Most Offending Soul* (Honolulu: University of Hawai'i Press, 1998), 79–84. Tom would later remark that he had used "all my experience" to extract information from "these difficult people." Harrisson, "Living with the People of Malekula," *Geographical Journal*, 88 (August 1936): 103.

52. Harrisson, *Savage Civilization*, 116; Heimann, *Most Offending*, 83.

53. Harrisson, *Savage Civilization*, 3–4, 403–04; "Unconventional Scientist in the New Hebrides," *P.I.M.* (23 March 1937), 22–23; "Civilisation the Destroyer," *Illustrated London News*, 190 (23 January 1937): 144; Henrika Kuklick, *Savage Within* (Cambridge: Cambridge University Press, 1991), 13.

54. Harrisson, *Savage Civilization*, 269, 342, 270–75.

55. Ibid., 425–27.

56. Heimann, *Most Offending*, 97. Eager to whet American appetites for his "cannibal film," Fairbanks returned to Hollywood claiming that he, too, had mingled with the Big Nambas. "Hollywood Stars in the New Hebrides," *Quarterly Jottings from the New Hebrides*, 170 (October 1935): 18–20.

57. *Oxford Dictionary of National Biography* (Oxford: Oxford University Press, 2004), s.v. "Harrisson, Tom Harnett," 545; David Hall, *Worktown* (London: Weidenfeld & Nicolson, 2015), 14–17.

58. *Morning Post* [London] (21 December 1935).

59. Osmar White, *Parliament of a Thousand Tribes* (London: Heinemann, 1965), 2; Gavin Souter, *New Guinea* (London: Angus & Robertson, 1964), 6; A.E. Pratt and Henry Pratt, *Two Years Among New Guinea Cannibals* (London: Seeley, 1906), 17. Carstensz must have glimpsed New Guinea's highest peak, Puncak Jaya, whose main summit, still known as the "Carstensz Pyramid," towers 16,024 feet above the Arafura Sea.

60. Pamela Swadling, *Plumes from Paradise* (Boroko, Papua New Guinea: P.N.G. National Museum, 1996), 15–16, 64–65; Clive Moore, *New Guinea: Crossing Boundaries* (Honolulu: University of Hawai'i Press, 2003), 113–14.

61. J.H.P. Murray, "Introduction" to Lewis Lett, *Knights Errant* (Edinburgh: William Blackwood, 1935), ix–x.

62. James Johnston, "World's Darkest Island," *Chambers's Journal*, 6th series, 5 (December 1901): 25, 23.

63. Kenneth MacKay, *Across Papua*, (London: Witherby, 1909), viii–ix; Souter, *New Guinea*, 92.

64. *Oxford Dictionary of National Biography* (Oxford, 2004), s.v. "Murray, Sir (John) Hubert Plunkett"; *Sydney Morning Herald* (28 February 1940); *Australian Dictionary of Biography*, 10: 1891–1939 (Carlton, Victoria, Australia, 1986), s.v. "Murray, J.H.P."

65. One of his first biographers noted the irony that although Murray pined for his family, the Papuan heat eventually rendered him unfit for residence in "cold" climates, such as Sydney's. Lewis Lett, *Sir Hubert Murray of Papua* (London: Collins, 1949), 223.

66. Pratt and Pratt, *Two Years*, 19–20.

67. H.G. Nicholas, "Sir Hubert Murray, KCMG," *Australian Quarterly*, 12 (June 1940): 5. For an overview of Murray's contested legacy, see Roger C. Thompson, "Hubert Murray and the Historians," *Pacific Studies*, 10 (November 1986): 79–96.

68. Lewis Lett, *The Papuan Achievement*, 2nd ed. (Carlton, Victoria: Melbourne University Press, 1944); Lett, *Sir Hubert Murray*; I.H. Hogbin, "Our Native Policy," *Australian Quarterly*, 15 (June 1943): 105.

69. "Miss Beatrice Grimshaw's South Sea Stories," *Manchester Guardian* (6 May 1922); Eugénie and Hugh Laracy, "Beatrice Grimshaw," 154–55.

70. Hubert Murray to Gilbert Murray, 16 December 1907, in Francis West, ed., *Selected Letters of Hubert Murray* (Melbourne: Oxford University Press, 1970), 47; "An Englishwoman Among Cannibals," *Manchester Guardian* (13 May 1922).

71. R.C. Thompson, "Hubert Murray," 81.

72. Amirah Inglis, *White Woman's Protection Ordinance* (New York: St. Martin's Press, 1975), 109–10. The only comparable legislation enacted within a British colony was Southern Rhodesia's 1903 Criminal Law Amendment Ordinance, which made nonwhite male assaults on white women capital crimes. See Jock McCulloch, *Black Peril* (Bloomington: Indiana University Press, 2000).

73. R.C. Thompson, "Hubert Murray," 91–92. Murray was still the colony's chief judicial officer when, in 1906, its government passed legislation that forbade Papuans to wear clothing on the upper part of their bodies. Justified as a sanitary reform, this measure ensured that bare-chested (and bare-breasted) "natives" remained instantly recognizable as Other.

74. Norman Goodall, *A History of the London Missionary Society* (London: Oxford University Press, 1954), 413.

75. M. Standiforth Smith, *Handbook of the Territory of Papua* (Melbourne: J. Kemp [1907]), 9.

76. [J.H.P. Murray], *Review of the Australian Administration in Papua* (Port Moresby, Papua New Guinea: Government Printer, 1920), 9.

77. Ibid., ix–x.

78. Ronald Hyam, "The British Empire in the Edwardian Era," in Wm. Roger Lewis and Judith M. Brown, eds., *Oxford History of the British Empire*, 4 (New York: Oxford University Press, 1999): 50–51; Bernard Porter, "The Edwardians and Their Empire," in Donald Read, ed., *Edwardian England* (London: Croom Helm, 1982), 136–37; "From Cannibalism to Civilization," *The Times* (19 August 1932).

79. Hubert Murray, *Native Administration* (Port Moresby: Walter Bock, 1929), 1–3, 5–6; Murray, "Scientific Aspect of the Pacification of Papua," in *Report of the Twenty-First Meeting of the Australian and New Zealand Association for the Advancement of Science* (Sydney, Australia: ANZAAS, 1932), 8–9.

80. August Ibrum Kituai, *My Gun* (Honolulu: University of Hawai'i Press, 1998), 3; J.H.P. Murray, *Papua of To-day* (London: P.S. King, 1925), 232–33.

81. Murray, *Papua, or British New Guinea* (London: T. Fisher Unwin, 1912), 23–24.

82. Murray, "Scientific Aspect of Pacification," 7.

83. Wilfred N. Beaver, *Unexplored New Guinea* (London: Seeley, Service, 1920), 26–28.

84. Arthur Kent Chignell, *Outpost in Papua* (London: Smith, Elder, 1911), 2. Cf. Kituai, *My Gun*, 8–9.

85. P. Biskup, B. Jinks, and H. Nelson, *Short History of New Guinea* (Sydney, Australia: Angus & Robertson, 1970), 84.

86. [Murray], *Review of the Australian Administration*, vii, 25–27.

87. Murray, *Papua of To-day*, viii–ix; [Murray], *Review of the Australian Administration*, 31.

88. Murray, "Scientific Aspect of Pacification," 8–9.

89. Ibid.; [Murray], *Review of the Australian Administration*, 28.

90. *Sydney Morning Herald* (15 April 1908).

91. [Murray], *Review of the Australian Administration*, 1–2.

92. Murray, *Native Administration in Papua*, 16; Diary for 1905 (18 September 1905), Murray Papers, Mitchell Library, ML A 3139, pt. 1; draft of an address on crime and criminals in Papua (c. 1934), Murray Papers, Mitchell Library, ML A 3138, ff. 14, 11–12.

93. The willingness of government patrols to engage much larger groups of hostile "natives" gratified Murray. The refusal of thrice-wounded H.S. Ryan to abandon his sick orderly during an ambush west of the Kikori River in 1913 ranked with the heroics of many Victoria Cross winners, Murray declared. See Territory of Papua, *Annual Report for 1913–14* (Melbourne, 1914), 10, 170, 178.

94. Territory of Papua, *Annual Report for 1932–33* (Canberra, Australia, 1934), 17.

95. G.H.L. Pitt-Rivers, *Clash of Culture* (London: George Routledge & Sons, 1927), 60; J.K. McCarthy, *Patrol into Yesterday* (Canberra: F.W. Cheshire, 1964), 9–10.

96. Bronislaw Malinowski, *Crime and Custom* (New York: Harcourt, Brace, 1926), 92–93; R.F. Fortune, *Sorcerers of Dobu* (New York: E.P. Dutton 1932), Appendix 3; Murray, "Depopulation in Papua," *Oceania*, 3 (December 1932): 210.

97. [Murray], *Review of the Australian Administration*, 41.

98. I.C. Campbell, "Anthropology and the Professionalization of Colonial Administration," *Journal of Pacific History*, 33 (June 1988): 70–71; Territory of Papua, *Annual Report for 1922–23* (Melbourne, 1925), 15.

99. W.H.R. Rivers, "Government of Subject Peoples," in A.C. Seward, ed., *Science and the Nation* [1917], reprint ed. (Freeport, NY: Books for Libraries Press, 1967), 306–07.

100. Murray, *Papua of To-day*, 242.

101. I.C. Campbell, "Anthropology," 89, 69.

102. F.E. Williams, *Natives of the Purari Delta* [Anthropology Report No. 5] (Port Moresby, 1924), 107–09; Williams, *Vailala Madness* [Anthropology Report No. 4] (Port Moresby, 1923), 1–2, 55–56.

103. Francis West, *Hubert Murray* (Melbourne: Oxford University Press, 1968), 216–17; Murray, "Introduction" to Williams, *Natives of the Purari Delta*, iii; "Memorandum from the Lieutenant-Governor to the Government Anthropologist," in Williams, *Vailala Madness*, vii.

104. Territory of Papua, *Annual Report for 1931–32* (Canberra, 1933), 10; "A London Diary," *New Statesman and Nation*, 8 (11 August 1934): 174–75. Hubert Murray to Mary Murray, 31 March 1932, in F. West, *Selected Letters*, 143.

105. George Westermark, "Anthropology and Administration," in Naomi McPherson, ed., *In Colonial New Guinea* (Pittsburgh: University of Pittsburgh Press, 2001), 46–48; Murray, *Native Administration in Papua*, 9–10.

106. *Official Handbook of the Territory of New Guinea* (Canberra, 1937), 59–66.

107. Wm. Roger Louis, *Imperialism at Bay 1941–1945* (Oxford: Clarendon Press, 1977), 92; *Official Handbook*, 72–73.

108. *Manchester Guardian* (18 November 1938); J.S. Lyng, *Our New Possession* (Melbourne: Melbourne Publishing, 1919), 164–65.

109. A.J. Marshall, *Men and Birds of Paradise* (London: William Heinemann, 1938), 99–100; McCarthy, *Patrol into Yesterday*, 9–10.

110. Lett, *Sir Hubert Murray*, 228.

111. A.I. Kituai points out that several Papuan field officers had an association with the colony before joining its service. These local recruits were therefore more likely than their counterparts in the Mandated Territory to forge personal bonds with the chief administrator. Kituai, *My Gun*, 23.

112. Souter, *New Guinea*, 157–58.

113. *Manchester Guardian* (3 March 1924 and 10 March 1924).

114. McCarthy, *Patrol into Yesterday*, 90–91; J.P. Sinclair, *Behind the Ranges* (Carlton, Victoria: Melbourne University Press, 1966), 7–8.

115. William C. Groves, "With a Patrol Officer in New Guinea," *Walkabout* (1 August 1935), 22, 25; Naomi McPherson, "'Wanted: Young Man,'" in McPherson, ed., *In Colonial New Guinea*, 83–84.

116. *Report to the . . . League of Nations on . . . New Guinea* (Canberra, 1936), 23; Brian Stirling, "In Wild New Guinea," *Walkabout* (1 November 1936), 28–29.

117. *Report to the . . . League of Nations on . . . New Guinea* (Canberra, 1937), 25–26.

118. O. White, *Parliament of Tribes*, 66.

119. *Sydney Morning Herald* (28 February 1911); Souter, *New Guinea*, 103–06; Hubert Murray to Gilbert Murray, 28 April 1911, in F. West, ed., *Selected Letters*, 42–43; Territory of Papua, *Annual Report for 1911–12* (Melbourne, 1912), 9. Recent ethno-historical evidence has confirmed that however inept Smith's leadership, his patrol was the first to enter what would become known as Papua New Guinea's southern highlands. See Edward L. Schieffelin and Robert Crittenden, *Like People You See in a Dream* (Stanford, CA: Stanford University Press, 1991), 39.

120. Territory of Papua, Annual Report for 1916–17 (Melbourne, 1918), 5.

121. Territory of Papua, *Annual Report for 1921–22* (Melbourne, 1923), 8–9.

122. Michael Taussig, *Shamanism, Colonialism* (Chicago: University of Chicago Press, 1987), 101.

123. W.R. Humphries, *Patrolling in Papua* (London: T. Fisher Unwin, 1923), 189–90.

124. Jared Diamond, *Guns, Germs, and Steel* (New York: W.W. Norton, 1999), 306.

125. Walter G. Ivens, *Dictionary and Grammar*, 158; O. White, *Parliament of Tribes*, 11; C. Moore, *New Guinea*, 29.

126. Michael Leahy and Maurice Crain, *Land That Time Forgot* (New York: Funk & Wagnalls, 1937); McCarthy, *Patrol into Yesterday*.

127. Ivor H.N. Evans, *Among Primitive Peoples in Borneo* (London: Seeley, Service, 1922), 17; Odoardo Beccari, *Wanderings in the Great Forests of Borneo* [1904], reprint ed. (Singapore: Oxford University Press, 1986), 363–64; Charles Hose, *Natural Man* (London: Macmillan, 1926), 10, vii–viii.

128. Colin Simpson, *Adam in Plumes* (Sydney: Angus & Robertson, 1955).

129. Aletta Biersack, "Introduction," in Biersack, ed., *Papuan Borderlands* (Ann Arbor: University of Michigan Press, 1995), 8–11.

130. Sjoerd Jaarsma, "Conceiving New Guinea," in McPherson, ed., *In Colonial New Guinea*, 36; diary of Michael Leahy for 6 June 1930, quoted in Keith McRae, "Kiaps, Missionaries and Highlanders," *New Guinea and Australia, the Pacific and South-East Asia*, 9 (March/April 1974): 17.

131. Diamond, *Guns, Germs, and Steel*, 20–21.

132. Donald Denoon and Marivic Wyndham, "Australia and the Western Pacific," in Andrew Porter, ed., *Oxford History of the British Empire*, 3 (New York: Oxford University Press, 1999): 549–50; Bob Connolly and Robin Anderson, *First*

Contact (New York: Viking Penguin, 1987), 9–10; Kate Fortune, ed., *Malaguna Road* (Canberra: National Library of Australia, 1998), 235.

133. Murray, "Scientific Aspect of Pacification," 5.

134. Paula Brown, "Colonial New Guinea: The Historical Context," in McPherson, ed., *In Colonial New Guinea*, 23–24; J.G. Hides, *Savages in Serge* (Sydney: Angus & Robertson, 1938), 8–9, 229–31.

135. Kituai, *My Gun*, 163.

136. John White, *The Ancient History of the Maori*, 5 (Wellington, New Zealand, 1888): 121–28.

137. J.C. Beaglehole, ed., *The Endeavour Journal of Joseph Banks, 1768–1771*, 2 vols. (Sydney: Angus & Robertson, 1962) 2: 54; Sydney Parkinson, *Journal of a Voyage to the South Seas, in HMS The Endeavour* (London, 1773), 134. On the interactions between British passengers arriving with the First Fleet (1788) and their aboriginal neighbors, see Inga Clendinnen, *Dancing with Strangers* (New York: Cambridge University Press, 2005).

138. Anton Ploeg, "First Contact, in the Highlands of Irian Jaya," *Journal of Pacific History*, 30 (December 1995): 227–28, 234–35.

139. Michael Leahy, *Explorations into Highland New Guinea, 1930–35*, ed. Douglas E. Jones (Tuscaloosa: University of Alabama Press, 1991), 45–46.

140. Greg Dening, *The Death of William Gooch* (Honolulu: University of Hawai'i Press, 1995), 35–44.

141. "Notes on a Zoological Collecting Trip to Dutch New Guinea," *National Geographic Magazine*, 19 (July 1908): 469.

142. "The Stone Age Today," *Sydney Morning Herald* (17 July 1912); H.J.T. Bijlmer, *Anthropological Results* (Leiden, Netherlands: Brill, 1923), 356–57.

143. *Oxford English Dictionary* online (2013), s.v. "Stone Age"; J.F.C. Fuller, *Memoirs of an Unconventional Soldier* (London: Ivor Nicholson & Watson, 1936), 341, 354.

144. *P.I.M.* (October 1940), 17.

145. Territory of Papua, *Annual Report for 1927–28* (Melbourne, 1929), 1–2.

146. Ivan F. Champion, *Across New Guinea from the Fly to the Sepik* (London: Constable, 1932), 141; *Australian Dictionary of Biography*, 17: 1981–1990 (Carlton, Victoria: Melbourne University Press, 2007), s.v. "Champion, Ivan Francis."

147. C.H. Karius, "Report on the Crossing of New Guinea," Appendix D, Territory of Papua, *Annual Report for 1927–28*, 97.

148. Ibid., 88; Karius, "Exploration in the Interior of Papua and North-East New Guinea," *Geographical Journal*, 74 (October 1929): 306–07; Champion, *Across New Guinea*, 12, 41–42.

149. Champion, "Report of Sub-Patrol," Appendix B, Territory of Papua, *Annual Report for 1926–27*, 108–11.

150. Karius, "Report on the Crossing of New Guinea," Appendix D, Territory of Papua, *Annual Report for 1927–28*, passim; Champion, *Across New Guinea*, 186;

Frank Clune, *Prowling Through Papua* [1942] (Sydney: Angus & Robertson, 1948), 136–38.

151. Champion, *Across New Guinea*, 244.

152. [Murray], "Expedition of Mr. Karius and Mr. Champion, Across New Guinea," Territory of Papua, *Annual Report for 1927–28*, 2; Champion, *Across New Guinea*, 235.

153. Champion, *Across New Guinea*, 182.

154. G.H.L. Pitt-Rivers, *The Clash of Culture*.

155. Champion, *Across New Guinea*, 87.

156. Ibid., 200–01.

157. Karius, "Exploration in the Interior of Papua," 322. In 1929, King George V awarded Karius the Patron's Gold Medal of the R.G.S. Cancer would claim him eleven years later, at the age of 47. Ivan Champion enjoyed a much longer life, serving the united administration of Papua and New Guinea until 1964. Champion received the O.B.E. in 1953. He died in 1989.

158. Leahy and Crain, *Land That Time Forgot*, 1.

159. Connolly and Anderson, *First Contact*, 8–9.

160. Leahy and Crain, *Land That Time Forgot*, 31–32.

161. Leahy, *Explorations*, 27; Leahy and Crain, *Land That Time Forgot*, 131–33.

162. Unpublished diary of Michael Leahy for 20 November 1932, as quoted in Connolly and Anderson, *First Contact*, 69.

163. E.W.P. Chinnery, "The Central Ranges of the Mandated Territory of New Guinea," *Geographical Journal*, 84 (November 1934): 405–06; Michael Leahy, "The Central Highlands of New Guinea," *Geographical Journal*, 87 (March 1936): 229–30.

164. Despite not knowing for weeks that he and Dwyer had descended into the Purari River watershed, Michael Leahy later "forced" the Royal Geographical Society to certify his status as the discoverer of that river's source. Leahy, *Explorations*, editor's Afterword, 245.

165. Leahy and Crain, *Land That Time Forgot*, 110.

166. Ibid., 37–38; J.L. Taylor, "Mount Hagen Patrol," *Report to the . . . League of Nations on . . . New Guinea* (Canberra, 1935), 115.

167. Simpson, *Adam in Plumes*, 18–19; J.L. Taylor, "Mount Hagen Patrol," 115.

168. Leahy and Crain, *Land That Time Forgot*, 152–53; Leahy, *Explorations*, 82.

169. J.L. Taylor, "Undiscovered New Guinea," *Walkabout* (1 November 1934), 21.

170. Ibid.; J.L. Taylor, "Mount Hagen Patrol," 115.

171. Leahy and Crain, *Land That Time Forgot*, 157–58, 177–78; J.L. Taylor, "Undiscovered," 23; "Discoveries in New Guinea," *P.I.M.* (21 December 1933), 11.

172. Leahy and Crain, *Land That Time Forgot*, 165.

173. Leahy, *Explorations*, 104. Several years later Leahy would liken the cultural "gap" between Europeans and New Guinea highlanders to "the difference between a bow and arrow and the hydrogen bomb." (Ibid.)

174. "Get Busy or Get Out!" *P.I.M.* (22 October 1937), v–vi; "Discoveries in New Guinea," *P.I.M.* (21 December 1933), 11.

175. J.L. Taylor, "Undiscovered," 27–28.

176. Leahy and Crain, *Land That Time Forgot*, 125–26; J.L. Taylor, "Undiscovered," 27–28.

177. Leahy, "Tribal Wars in Unexplored New Guinea," *Walkabout* (1 November 1935), 11–12.

178. "Clashes with New Guinea Natives," *P.I.M.* (16 March 1934), 9–11. For Leahy's behavior as a source of concern for members of the League's Mandates Commission, see Susan Pedersen, *The Guardians: The League of Nations and the Crisis of Empire* (Oxford: Oxford University Press, 2015), 305–14.

179. Typescript copy of Sir Hubert Murray's diary for 24 June 1934, Mitchell Library, Murray Papers, ML A 3138; "Gold Prospecting in New Guinea," *Anti-Slavery Reporter and Aborigines' Friend*, series 5, 26 (January 1937): 200–02; "Shootings of Natives in New Guinea," *Anti-Slavery Reporter and Aborigines' Friend*, series 5, 27 (April 1937): 40–41; *Australian Dictionary of Biography*, 10: 1881–1939 (Carlton, Victoria, 1986), s.v. "Leahy, Michael"; Simpson, *Adam in Plumes*, 92–93.

180. J.P. Sinclair, *Kiap: Australia's Patrol Officers in Papua New Guinea* (Sydney: Pacific Publications, 1981), 68–69; Connolly and Anderson, *First Contact*, 34–36.

181. "Young Explorers Differ," *P.I.M.* (22 August 1935), 14; "Papua, Publicity and Patrols," *P.I.M.* (22 August 1933), 24; "Leahy Brothers in London," *P.I.M.* (20 December 1935), 9; Hubert Murray to Patrick Murray, 26 August 1935, in F. West, ed., *Selected Letters*, 184.

182. See Schieffelin and Crittenden, *Like People You See in a Dream*, passim.

183. J.G. Hides, *Savages in Serge* (Sydney: Angus & Robertson, 1938), 3–4.

184. Murray, "Introduction" to J.G. Hides, *Through Wildest Papua* (London: Blackie & Son, 1935), 5; J.P. Sinclair, *Outside Man* (Melbourne: Landsdowne Press, 1969), 10.

185. J.G. Hides, *Papuan Wonderland* (London: Blackie & Son, 1936), 123–24; Hides, *Through Wildest Papua*, 12.

186. *P.I.M.* (12 May 1934), 4.

187. Sinclair, *Outside Man*, 61–62.

188. "Midnight Pounce on Village," *P.I.M.* (16 March 1934), 5–6; Hides, *Through Wildest Papua*, 16–71.

189. "Papuan Patrol Officer," *P.I.M.* (17 May 1934), 4; Hubert Murray to Patrick Murray, 24 January 1935, in F. West, ed., *Selected Letters*, 179.

190. Sinclair, *Outside Man*, 260.

191. Hides, typescript copy of "Forenote" to his diary for 22 July 1935, Mitchell Library, ML A 3638.

192. E.W. Brandes, "Into Primeval Papua by Seaplane," *National Geographic Magazine*, 56 (September 1929): 253–332; R.W. Robson, ed., *Handbook of New Guinea* (Sydney: Pacific Publications, 1933), 18–23.

193. Schieffelin and Crittenden, *Like People You See in a Dream*, 52.

194. Sinclair, *Outside Man*, 150; Hubert Murray to Rosalind Toynbee, 26 July 1935, in F. West, ed., *Selected Letters*, 182.

195. Hides, *Papuan Wonderland*, 46, 69, 109–10, 201, 81–82.

196. Ibid., 55–56, 53–54.

197. Ibid., 174–75; Lisette Josephides and Marc Schiltz, "Through Kewa Country," in Schieffelin and Crittenden, eds., *Like People You See in a Dream*, 211–12.

198. Josephides and Schiltz, "Through Kewa Country," 213–15.

199. Bill Gammage, *Sky Travellers* (Carlton, Victoria: Melbourne University Press, 1998), 1–3, 211–12; Leigh Vial, "Exploring in New Guinea," *Walkabout* (1 October 1938), 14.

200. Richard Archbold and A.L. Rand, "With Plane and Radio in Stone Age New Guinea," *Natural History*, 40 (October 1937): 568; Vial, "Exploring," 15–16.

201. *Manchester Guardian* (15 August 1935 and 19 June 1936).

202. *P.I.M.* (22 August 1935), 7.

203. "Japanese Menace," *P.I.M.* (24 January 1936), 9; "Japanese Poachers in Pacific," *P.I.M.* (20 October 1936), 3–4; "Japan's Invasion of Pacific Shell Industry," *P.I.M.* (23 March 1937), 8.

204. Then just thirty-two, Hides succumbed to a lethal combination of beriberi and pneumonia in a Sydney hospital. Several months before his death, he and some companions had been found, malnourished and disease-ridden, floating in a raft on the Fly River.

205. Hides, *Papuan Wonderland*, 201.

206. Marshall, *Men and Birds of Paradise*, 55–56.

207. Napoleon A. Chagnon, *Yanomamö: The Fierce People*, 3rd ed. (Fort Worth, TX: Holt, Rinehart & Winston, 1983), 4–42; Chagnon, *Noble Savages* (New York, 2013), 7–9, 338, 26–28, 218–20, 437–39.

208. Survival International website: http://survivalinternational.org/info. This organization defines "uncontacted" peoples as those "who have no peaceful contact with anyone in the mainstream or dominant society." Such people need not be "unknown" to qualify as "uncontacted."

CONCLUSION

1. *Oxford English Dictionary* online (2015), s.v. "inversion." The notion of a "savage inversion" could include Europeans whose conduct, by Western standards, appeared barbaric. Arguably the best illustration of such conduct in modern Melanesian history involved an English missionary-trainee and his unprovoked slaughter of a Malaita boy in November 1955. For the case of Reginald Poole, see especially *Sunday Telegraph* [Sydney] (5 and 12 February 1956); *Daily Mirror* [Sydney] (1 and 3 February 1956); and *News of the World* [London] (5 February 1956).

2. Mitchell, "Foreword" to Martin Clemens, *Alone on Guadalcanal* (Annapolis, MD: Naval Institute Press, 1998), xi; "Islanders' Loyalty," *The Times* [London] (13 May 1943); Mitchell to Colonial Secretary, telegram of 17 May 1943, TNA, CO 875/14/6.

3. Marty Zelenietz, "Invisible Islanders," *Man and Culture in Oceania*, 7 (1991): 14–15.

4. A.J. Stockwell, "Imperialism and Nationalism," in Louis and Brown, eds., *Oxford History of the British Empire*, 4 (New York: Oxford University Press, 1999): 476; "Notes on the Evacuation of the Naga Hills District" [1942], H.J. Mitchell Papers, B.L., Oriental and India Office Library, MSS. Eur. D 858/2; *Manchester Guardian* (13 May 1942); Christopher Bayle and Tim Harper, *Forgotten Armies* (Cambridge, MA: Harvard University Press, 2005), 83–84, 388–90.

5. Judith M. Heimann, *The Airmen and the Headhunters* (Orlando, FL: Harcourt, 2007), 131–32; Philip Harkins, *Blackburn's Headhunters* (New York: W.W. Norton, 1955), 311–12, 321.

6. Asesela Ravuvu, *Fijians at War* (Suva, Fiji: Institute of Pacific Studies, 1988), 14–16; Brij V. Lal, "For King and Country," in Geoffrey M. White, ed., *Remembering the Pacific War* (Honolulu: Center for Pacific Island Studies, 1991), 18–20.

7. While white New Zealand officers helped prepare Fijians for tropical combat, New Zealand's own "natives," the Maori, distinguished themselves in such Western theaters as Greece, Crete, North Africa, and Italy.

8. Judith Bennett, *Natives and Exotics* (Honolulu: University of Hawai'i Press, 2009), 134–35; Mark Durley, as quoted in Eric Bergerud, *Touched with Fire* (New York: Viking Penguin, 1996), 113–14.

9. "How the Doughty Fijians Got Their 200th Man," *Fiji Times and Herald* [Suva] (21 February 1956).

10. Deborah B. Gewertz, *Sepik River Societies* (New Haven, CT: Yale University Press, 1983), 137–38.

11. Geoffrey M. White and Lamont Lindstrom, "Introduction" in White and Lindstrom, eds., *The Pacific Theater* (Honolulu: University of Hawai'i Press, 1989), 24.

12. Sydney H. Chance, *Lau Hereva* (Brisbane, Australia: Simpson, Halligan, 1946), 67.

13. Kipling, "Fuzzy-Wuzzy," in Daniel Karlin, ed., *Rudyard Kipling* (Oxford: Oxford University Press, 1999), 436–37.

14. Victor Austin, ed., *To Kokoda and Beyond* (Carlton, Victoria, Australia: Melbourne University Press, 1988), 76–77; John Waiko, "Oral History and the War," in G. White, *Remembering the Pacific War*, 8–9.

15. Dudley McCarthy, *Australia in the War of 1939–45* (Canberra: Australian War Memorial, 1962), 334–35; Chris Coulthard-Clark, *Where Australians Fought* (St. Leonards, New South Wales, Australia: Allen & Unwin, 1998), 102–03.

16. Austin, *To Kokoda*, 170–71; Hank Nelson, "Kokoda," *Journal of Pacific History*, 42 (June 2007): 76–77.

17. *Papua New Guinea Post-Courier* [Port Moresby] (12 June 2010). See also *PNG Post-Courier* (26 July 2011) and *Sydney Morning Herald* (26 April 2013).

18. Nelson, "Kokoda," 87.

19. Chance, *Lau Hereva*, 12–13; "How and Why the New Guinea Natives Are Being Spoiled," *P.I.M.* (August 1960), 57–58.

20. H.C. Brookfield, *Colonialism, Development* (Cambridge: Cambridge University Press, 1972), 87–88.

21. C.H. Grattan, *Southwest Pacific Since 1900* (Ann Arbor: University of Michigan Press, 1963), 517. In 1939, Fiji set up its own coastwatching service on a coconut plantation near the southern tip of Taveuni island. See coastwatching correspondence, F8/120, Fiji National Archives, Suva.

22. A.A. Vandegrift, *Once a Marine* (New York: W.W. Norton, 1964), 115, 118; Halsey as quoted in D.C. Horton, *Fire over the Islands* (London: Leo Cooper, 1975), 247; MacArthur in "Foreword" to Eric A. Feldt, *The Coast Watchers* (Garden City, NY: Doubleday, 1979), vii–ix.

23. *Annual Report . . . on the British Solomon Islands Protectorate, 1938* (London, 1939), 6; Walter Lord, *Lonely Vigil* (New York: Viking Press 1977), 4.

24. Martin Clemens, "District Officer's Diary, Guadalcanal," 10 and 11 April, 1942, typescript draft, MSS. Pac. s. 61, Rhodes House Library, Oxford University; Lord, *Lonely Vigil,* 17.

25. Robert J. Donovan, *PT-109* (New York: McGraw-Hill, 1961), 141–145, 174, 183–89; obituary of Eroni Kumana, *Los Angeles Times* (16 August 2014).

26. Lord, *Lonely Vigil,* 108–09, 204–08; Bergerud, *Touched with Fire*, 116–17.

27. *Among Those Present* (London: H.M.S.O., 1946), 28. Perversely, the Guadalcanal men who hauled American supplies up slopes too steep for jeeps found themselves stigmatized as the "Cannibal Battalion." John Miller, *Guadalcanal* (Washington, DC: Department of the Army, 1949), 237–38.

28. Vandegrift, *Once a Marine*, 136–37. Most other descriptions of Vouza noted his deep chest and exceptional strength.

29. Clemens's "Foreword" in Don Richter, *Where the Sun Stood Still* (Calabasas, CA: Toucan, 1992), 9; Allan Bevilacqua, "Coastwatcher Jacob Vouza," *Leatherneck*, 98 (August 2015): 24–28.

30. Richter, *Where the Sun*, 48–49.

31. Roger M. Keesing and Peter Corris, *Lightning Meets the West Wind* (Melbourne, Australia: Oxford University Press, 1980), 165–66, 169.

32. Hector Macquarrie, *Vouza and the Solomon Islands* (New York: Macmillan, 1948), 26–27.

33. Richard B. Frank, *Guadalcanal* (New York: Random House, 1990), 150–54; Clemens, *Alone on Guadalcanal,* 111–12, 12–13.

34. Clemens, *Alone,* 209–10.

35. Richter, *Where the Sun*, 390, 398–99; Masey to Gardner, 30 July 1968, Jacob Vouza Collection 3328, Box 2, Marine Corps Archives, Quantico, VA.

36. J. Bennett, *Wealth of the Solomons* (Honolulu: University of Hawai'i Press, 1987), 291–93.

37. Charles E. Fox, *Kakamora* (London: Hodder & Stoughton, 1962), 143–45. In very similar fashion, the champions of colonial rule in Northern Rhodesia had earlier taken credit for ending "the old fighting days"—when villagers huddled behind stockades and spent much of their time sharpening spears. See Mabel Shaw,

"Sanctuary," *Chronicle of the London Missionary Society* (January 1920), 5–6. I thank Rebecca Hughes for this reference.

38. David W. Gegeo, "World War II in the Solomons," in G. White, ed., *Remembering the Pacific War*, 31–32; Hugh Laracy, ed., *Pacific Protest* (Suva, Fiji: Institute of Pacific Studies, 1983), 19–20.

39. Laracy, *Pacific Protest*, 22–23. David Akin has noted that an "overbearing" Vouza was not universally popular among the Malaita headmen who supported Maasina Rule. See Akin, *Colonialism, Maasina Rule* (Honolulu: University of Hawai'i Press, 2013), 314–15.

40. W. Roger Louis, "Introduction," in Louis and J. Brown, eds., *Oxford History of the British Empire*, 4: 44; typescript interview with Sir Alexander Grantham, 21 August 1968, 38, MSS. Brit. Emp. s. 288, Rhodes House Library, Oxford University.

Index

Page numbers followed by f indicate material in figures. Ship names are in **bold**.

"Aboriginal Museum and Library" (proposed), 10

Aborigines' Protection Society (APS), 125–26, 139, 157, 237, 290n66, 293n137

"A Cannibal Feast in Fiji, 1869" (Reeves), 65, 65f

"accidental cannibalism," 39

Account of the Voyages Undertaken . . . for Making Discoveries in the Southern Hemisphere (Hawkesworth), 11

Across New Guinea (Champion), 231

Acts and Monuments of these latter and perilous days (Foxe), 74

Adler, Tony, 63

Adventure, 25, 34

Adventures (Coulter), 47

Adventures Among Cannibals (movie), 207–8

aerial surveys, 234, 240

Africa: big-game hunting in, 15; Edward Long on, 24; reports of cannibalism in, 43–45; romance of space in, 20; Stanley in, 6; "tribe"/"tribal" terminology, 19

agency of Islanders, 12–13, 128–140

agriculture in New Guinea, 233–35

Akin, David, 322n39

Albatross, 182

alcohol, introduction of, 12, 39, 82, 154–55, 190, 268n101

All the Year Round, 35

Amelia, 177

American Exploring Expedition, 50, 165

Among Cannibals (Lumholtz), 46

Among the Cannibal Isles of the South Pacific (Johnson, Martin and Osa), 205–6

Anatomy Bill (Britain), 38

Andaman archipelago/Andamanese, 8, 14–15, 194, 201

Andrew, Thomas, 64–65

Angas, George, 46

Anglicanism, 77, 80, 107–8, 112, 136, 162–63. *See also* Codrington, Robert Henry; Patteson, John Coleridge "Coley"

"Anna"/"Belangana" (Marovo Island), 187–88

anthropology/anthropologists: amateur, 39–40, 205–12 (209f), 220; "cannibal studies," 26–29; on European head market, 167; on evangelical colonialism, 110; exoticization by, 28; Fore practices and "kuru," 69; as guardians of primitivism, 243; on head-hunting, 159, 188; Hubert Murray's interest in, 220–21, 224; on Melanesian population decline, 154, 191; missionaries and, 111, 221; 279n87; P. T. Barnum and, 63; on racial stereotyping, 26; on regional differences, 18–19, 24; "salvage anthropology," 201–2; on unreliability of "sailors' yarns," 23, 29–30; as weapon of colonialism, 221; on will to live, 15. *See also* Codrington, Robert Henry; Rivers, W. H. R.

"anthropophagite," 23

"Anti-Slavery party" (Queensland), 151

Aoba, New Hebrides, 139

Aore (island), 133–34

APS (Aborigines' Protection Society), 125–26, 139, 157, 237, 290n66, 293n137

"Aratuga," 139

Arawak people, 23

Ardagh, Sir John, 16

Arens, Walter, 28

Arens, William, 69